Escaping the Trap

TEXAS A&M UNIVERSITY

☆ **14** ☆

MILITARY HISTORY SERIES

Escaping the Trap

THE US ARMY X CORPS IN NORTHEAST KOREA, 1950

By Lt.Col. Roy E. Appleman, AUS (Ret.)

Texas A&M University Press
College Station

The paper used in this book meets the minimum
requirements of the American National Standard
for Permanence of Paper for Printed Library Materials, Z39.48-1984. Binding materials have been
chosen for durability.

LIBRARY OF CONGRESS CATALOGING-IN-PUBLICATION DATA
Appleman, Roy Edgar.
    Escaping the trap : the US Army X Corps in
Northeast Korea, 1950 / by Roy E Appleman. —
1st ed.
        p. cm. — (Texas A&M University military
history series ; 14)
    Includes index.
    ISBN 0-89096-395-9 (alk. paper)
    1. Korean War, 1950–1953—Campaigns—Korea
(North)—Changjin Reservoir. 2. Korean War,
1950–1953—Regimental histories—United States.
3. United States. Army. Corps, 10th. I. Title.
II. Series.
DS918.2.C35A67 1989
951.904'2—dc20   89-4987
                                             CIP

Contents

Illustrations

TABLES

MAPS

Introduction

The question has often been asked: Why was the X Corps not joined to Eighth Army after the successful Inchon landing and the capture of Seoul in September 1950 and the simultaneous breakout of Eighth Army from the Naktong perimeter? At about 8:30 on the morning of 27 September, a platoon of L Company, 7th Cavalry Regiment, of the 1st Cavalry Division, Eighth Army, met elements of H Company, 31st Infantry, 7th Division, X Corps, north of Osan, for the linkup between Eighth Army and the X Corps. By the end of the month Eighth Army had arrived in the Seoul area. Elements of the X Corps never advanced beyond Uijongbu, 12 miles north of the city. On 7 October MacArthur made Eighth Army responsible for the Seoul-Inchon area, indicating a new mission for the X Corps.

Lt. Gen. Walton H. Walker and his staff felt that X Corps should have been made a part of Eighth Army in a unified command after the two forces joined in the Seoul area. It is not known whether General Walker ever discussed this subject with General MacArthur, but he did not submit his views in writing. On 26 September Walker wrote a discreetly worded letter to MacArthur saying that he would like to be informed of X Corps's progress. The next day General MacArthur informed Walker that X Corps would remain in GHQ Reserve at Inchon-Seoul, ready to undertake a GHQ operation, "of which you will be apprised at an early date." On the twenty-sixth, Gen. Doyle Hickey, MacArthur's acting chief of staff, informed Gen. Edwin K. Wright, the G-3 operations officer, that MacArthur wanted plans for a X Corps landing at Wonsan. It is plain that MacArthur himself decided to have a split command, with Eighth Army and X Corps reporting to him separately.

MacArthur had also decided by 26 September that X Corps would be moved by sea from Inchon around the peninsula to Wonsan on the east coast. Admiral Joy and his staff thought the sealift of X Corps to Wonsan unnecessary. X Corps from its present position could move overland to Wonsan more quickly than it could be embarked, moved by sea, and unloaded there. The Wonsan harbor was heavily mined, and clearing it would be a time-consuming task.

General MacArthur apparently contemplated an extensive operation in northeast Korea to reach the border at all places, and he felt that the force operating there could be supplied better from the east-coast ports of Wonsan and Hungnam than to have all of Eighth Army and the X Corps supplied from Pusan and Inchon. As one moved northward in the Korean peninsula, the Northern Taebaek Range grew ever higher, and roads across were fewer and poorer in quality. Ground contact between Eighth Army and X Corps in the northern extremities of Korea near the border would be extremely difficult, if not impossible. This factor made it seem likely that the two forces operating on the west and east sides of the Northern Taebaeks would have to operate as separate forces.

X Corps loaded out at Inchon between 8 and 16 October. The next day the 1st Marine Division started on its 830-mile sea voyage around the peninsula for Wonsan. It arrived there on 19 October. Meanwhile, Lt. Col. McCaffrey by air had established a X Corps Advance CP at Wonsan. But the Marines were not ashore until 28 October, after the harbor had been swept of mines. Beginning on 5 October the 7th Infantry Division moved overland from the vicinity of Ichon to Pusan, except for some tank units that loaded on LSTs at Inchon. At Pusan the 7th Division outloaded on ships 17 October but delayed sailing for many days because of the mined condition of Wonsan harbor. The division finally left Pusan when it was diverted to unload over the beaches at Iwon, 178 miles north of Wonsan, and take a road from there that led to Hyesanjin on the Yalu. The 17th Regiment of the division unloaded at the Iwon beaches on 29 October and took the road inland.

At the time that X Corps left Inchon MacArthur's plan had been that, from Wonsan, it would move west laterally across the waist of Korea to Pyongyang, while Eighth Army at the same time crossed the 38th Parallel and advanced north against Pyongyang. The two forces would act as a pincer in closing on the North Korean capital. As late as 16 October General Almond received orders to attack west from Wonsan toward Pyongyang. The next day his orders changed. He was then instructed to attack north from Wonsan. The reasons for the change were obvious. While the X Corps was moving by sea to Wonsan, Eighth Army had by itself captured Pyongyang, entering the city on 19 October. At the same time, the ROK Capital and 3rd divisions had advanced up the east coastal road on foot at a rapid pace. The ROK 3rd Division fought its way through Wonsan on 11 October, and the ROK Capital Division occupied Hungnam and Hamhung, 50 miles north of Wonsan, on 17 October. On 19 October Almond received final orders to attack north to the border. The next day he flew by helicopter from the deck of the battleship

Missouri to his Advance CP in Wonsan and assumed command of all UN troops in the X Corps area north of the 39th Parallel and east of the Taebaek Range, a boundary General MacArthur had established on 17 October.

On 14 November a cold front descended over all of North Korea, with temperatures reaching 35 degrees below zero in the X Corps area. The next day, the fifteenth, General MacArthur sent a directive to Almond that changed his mission from driving north to the border to one of turning west to the Manpojin-Kanggye-Huichon road, which ran south from the Yalu border at Chian to cross a low divide to the Chongchon River drainage. Now X Corps could help Eighth Army, which would be attacking north up the valley of the Chongchon on this road toward the border. The X Corps was to move west from Yudam-ni on the Chosin Reservoir to intercept this enemy MSR at Mupyong-ni. The 1st Marine Division was to carry out the main attack to cut the CCF main supply route. MacArthur's plan called for one Marine regiment to go up the east side of the reservoir to protect that flank of the division in its attack toward Mupyong-ni.

General Almond had some reservations about MacArthur's plan. He thought the 5th Marine Regiment should be united with the rest of the Marine division on the west side of the reservoir at Yudam-ni for the attack to the west. To replace it on the east side of the reservoir, he recommended a regimental-sized force from the 7th Division. He sent Lt. Col. Chiles, his G-3, to Tokyo on 24 November with the proposed change for review. The Far East Command approved the altered plan. The 7th Division now quickly had to scrape together an RCT to replace the 5th Marines on the east side of the reservoir before the X Corps attack date of 27 November. General Barr, the 7th Division commander, took elements of the 7th Division closest to the reservoir and hurried them to Chosin to relieve the 5th Marines by 26 November. It was purely an ad hoc group that resulted. His full force never arrived at Chosin. Before Almond could launch the X Corps planned attack on 27 November, bad news arrived from the west, where Eighth Army had started its part of the general attack on the morning of 24 November.

By evening of the next day the Eighth Army advance without opposition had reached the places on all avenues of approach where Chinese forces had been in hiding. The Chinese now launched simultaneous frontal attacks on all the advancing columns and that first night penetrated and virtually destroyed the three divisions of the ROK II Corps on the army's right flank in the vicinity of Tokchon. This crushing blow began a crisis for Eighth Army, which was at the same time suffering defeats almost everywhere else along its lines of advance. Thus started what the Chinese called their Second Phase Offensive. This operation is covered in a preceding book, *Disaster in Korea: The Chinese Confront MacArthur* (College Station: Texas A&M University Press, 1989).

The X Corps part of this campaign centered on the battles around the Chosin Reservoir and the subsequent retreat to the coast and evacuation of the corps from Hungnam harbor at the end of December. This volume tells that story. The 31st RCT of the 7th Division on the east side of the reservoir was destroyed. The 1st Marine Division on the west side and in positions along the MSR south of the reservoir withdrew only after two weeks of continuous battle, in an epic struggle. The full account is told in *East of Chosin: Entrapment and Breakout in Korea, 1950* (College Station: Texas A&M University Press, 1987).

At only two places did the X Corps reach the border: the 17th Regiment of the 7th Division reached Hyesanjin on the Yalu on 21 November; a week later, on 28 November, a platoon of K Company, 32nd Infantry, under 2nd Lt. Robert C. Kingston, reached Singalpajin, downstream on the Yalu from Hyesanjin. But Kingston barely had time to see the Yalu before receiving an order to turn around and start back at full speed for the coast. In the west, Eighth Army did not come close to reaching the Yalu at any point. These were the only times any parts of the UN forces reached the border and saw the Yalu. So much for General MacArthur's vaunted enterprise to secure the North Korean border and unify all of Korea.

Even if the Chinese forces had not crossed into Korea unobserved and unreported in their full strength, it is doubtful whether MacArthur's forces, with the ROK Army placed at the border as a garrison, could have held the 500-mile plus border, which extended along the northern reaches of Korea. North Korean survivors from the summer's fighting in South Korea, who withdrew north after the Inchon landing, were already reconstituting their units north of the border, and some were about ready to reenter the contest. The ROK Army almost certainly could not by itself have held the entire northern border, and the war would not have been ended with the country reunited.

In the circumstances that existed, MacArthur's goal of reuniting Korea was unobtainable. It would have been the better part of wisdom to consolidate the lateral communications route across the waist of Korea from Wonsan to Pyongyang, a distance of 105 miles, and to gain control of the Iron Triangle area, 50 miles south of it, which the Joint Chiefs of Staff had several times advocated. These areas might have been held with the forces then available, and their strategic control of communications from the border into Korea might have precluded the disastrous continuing years of the war.

The evacuation of X Corps from Hungnam was a model of its kind. It was mostly a naval operation, but the land forces had to provide a defensible perimeter, constantly shrinking, as the forces loaded out. All was handled in a most professional manner without panic developing and free from any danger of the loading out being hampered by enemy action or of the defensive perimeter being overrun, as was rumored in the United States, where it was reported that the evacuation was turning into another Dunkirk.

X Corps was moved to the southern tip of the peninsula, and most of it unloaded at Pusan and from there moved by rail and truck to assembly areas away from the port city. The corps was made a part of Eighth Army, and thereafter during the Korean War it fought as a part of it under the unified command of Gen. Matthew B. Ridgway and Gen. James A. Van Fleet.

Abbreviations

Throughout the narrative, numerous abbreviations appear that are commonly encountered in discussions of the Korean War and in US military usage generally. The most common are the following:

A&P	Ammunition and Pioneer
AAA AW	Antiaircraft Artillery, Automatic Weapons
AKA	Assault Cargo Ship
AMS	Army Map Service
APA	Assault Transport
APD	High Speed Transport
ATIS	Allied Translation and Interrogation Service
BAR	Browning Automatic Rifle
CCF	Chinese Communist Forces
CG	Commanding General
CO	Commanding Officer
CP	Command Post
CVE	Escort Aircraft Carrier
DA	Department of the Army
FA	Field Artillery
FAC	Forward Air Controller
FEAF	Far East Air Force
FEC	Far East Command
GHQ	General Headquarters
HQ	Headquarters
I&R	Intelligence and Reconnaissance
KATUSA	South Koreans attached to United States Army
KIA	Killed in Action
KMC	Korean Marine Corps
LST	Landing Ship, Tank
LSU	Landing Ship, Utility
LVT	Landing Vehicle, Tracked
MIA	Missing in Action
MLR	Main Line of Resistance

MP	Military Police
MSR	Main Supply Road
NK	North Korea
OPLR	Outpost Line of Resistance
PIR	Periodic Intelligence Report (Army)
POR	Periodic Operations Report (Army)
RAAF	Royal Australian Air Force
RCT	Regimental Combat Team
ROK	Republic of Korea (South Korea)
SAR	Special Action Report (Marines)
SP	Self-propelled
TAC(P)	Tactical Air Control (Party)
UN	United Nations
WD	War Diary
WIA	Wounded in Action
Comd. Rep.	Command Report (Army)

Escaping the Trap

1

X CORPS DEPLOYMENT IN NORTHEAST KOREA

This chapter sketches briefly the operations and events relating to the US X Corps in northeast Korea prior to 24 November 1950. The story to that date is told in some detail in my *South to the Naktong, North to the Yalu*. For the 1st Marine Division, it is told in great detail by Lynn Montross and Nicholas Canzona in *The Chosin Reservoir Campaign*, which is the third volume in the Marine Corps official history of the Korean War. For those who have not read these volumes and do not have ready access to them, a brief background of events in the last week of October and the first three weeks of November 1950 will be helpful as a frame of reference for what followed.

The initial concept for the X Corps when it outloaded at Inchon, 8–16 October 1950, for landings on the northeast coast of Korea at Wonsan, was to drive inland and westward from that city on the principal lateral road in this part of the country via Majon-ni, Yangdok, Onjong, Song-chon, and Kangdong to Pyongyang, the North Korean capital. In the meantime, the Eighth Army would be moving north from the Kaesong area near the 38th Parallel on the west side of the peninsula. These two operations would constitute a pincer movement that was intended to help Eighth Army capture the North Korean capital. As late as 16 October, Gen. Edward M. Almond of X Corps received orders from General MacArthur to attack west from Wonsan toward Pyongyang after landing his troops. But the next day MacArthur changed these instructions. Almond was ordered to attack north instead of west if Eighth Army captured Pyongyang in the meantime, which now seemed increasingly likely. On 19 October General Almond received the final order for X Corps to attack north in the eastern part of Korea, parallel to Eighth Army's advance in the west, with the watershed of the Taebaek Range as the boundary between them. The reason for this change was that, by then, the planned X Corps attack westward would have been useless. Eighth Army entered Pyongyang on 19 October. Also significant for X Corps's plans was the fact that the ROK Capital Division had occupied Hungnam and Ham-

The US invasion fleet in Wonsan harbor, northeast Korea, November 1950 (National Archives, USN 80-G 422091)

hung two days earlier, on 17 October. The ROK I Corps on the east coast had marched northward faster than anyone had anticipated.[1]

At noon on 20 October General Almond flew by helicopter from the USS *Missouri* to the Wonsan airfield and assumed command of all UN troops in the X Corps area north of the 39th Parallel and east of the Taebaek Range. These troops consisted of a small X Corps Advance CP group, established by Lt. Col. William J. McCaffrey, deputy chief of staff, X Corps, numbering about 40 officers and men; the ROK I Corps, which included the ROK 3rd and Capital infantry divisions, numbering more than 23,000 troops; and a few hundred men of the 1st Marine Air Wing already at the Wonsan airfield.[2] The tactical units of X Corps's American troops were still on board ship. When brought ashore, Almond's command would number about 84,000 men. Of these units, the 1st Marine Division was the largest, comprising about 25,000 men. Second in size was the Army's

7th Infantry Division, with about 18,000 men, of whom about one-third were attached South Koreans (KATUSA) being used as temporary replacements. Almond established his CP in Wonsan, where Lieutenant Colonel McCaffrey had already established a skeleton X Corps Advance CP.

Compelled to adjust quickly to a new situation and new orders, General Almond had to scatter his command over all of northeast Korea if he was to carry out his instructions to advance rapidly to the North Korean border and complete the conquest of North Korea in conjunction with Eighth Army's expected advance to the border in the west. He split the 1st Marine Division and the 7th Infantry Division into three regimental combat teams each. The 1st Marine Regiment was to relieve the ROK I Corps troops south and west of Hungnam; the 5th Marine Regiment was to secure and guard Yonpo airfield, south of Hungnam; and the 7th Marine Regiment was to relieve the ROK 3rd Division, which was advancing toward the Chosin Reservoir along the main Hamhung–Hagaru-ri road, and to secure the power installations of the Chosin and Fusen reservoirs. Meanwhile, the ROK Capital Division continued driving northward along the coastal road from Hamhung.

Initially, the ROK 26th Regiment of the 3rd Division led the advance northward toward the Chosin Reservoir. Thus far, X Corps had encountered only scattered North Korean soldiers and guerrillas trying to escape northward. But on the evening of 25 October, the ROK 26th Regiment reported it had captured a Chinese soldier about 30 miles inland from Hamhung, near the first of four power plants located along the road. The ROKs moved slowly ahead during the next two days after their prisoner told them there were about 5,000 Chinese troops in the vicinity. On 28 October the ROKs found themselves in a heavy battle in the vicinity of Sudong and suffered heavy casualties. Patrols that went forward to Chinhung-ni, and beyond toward Koto-ri, reported they had seen many enemy troops they believed to be Chinese. Two more Chinese were captured west of Sudong. The next day, 29 October, small-arms close combat swirled around the second power plant, and there was some 120-mm mortar fire. The ROK troops showed signs of demoralization in the afternoon as their supply of grenades ran low.

The most significant event of 29 October was the ROK capture of 16 Chinese soldiers from the 370th Regiment of the 124th Division, 42nd Army, XIII Army Group, Fourth Field Army. These prisoners said that the rest of the 42nd Army—three divisions, the 124th, 125th, and 126th—supported by a few North Korean tanks, blocked the way north. General Kim, the ROK I Corps commander, telephoned the news to General Almond. The next day General Almond went to the ROK I Corps prisoner compound and interviewed the captured Chinese through an interpreter. Almond learned much in this 30 October interview, including the fact

Maj. Gen. Edward M. Almond, commanding general of the US X Corps, northeast Korea, 1950 (National Archives, 111-SC 349458)

that these 16 Chinese soldiers had belonged to the ammunition platoon of the mortar company, 370th Regiment; that they were former Chinese Nationalist soldiers who had surrendered to the Communist forces near Peking the year before; that they were clothed with new cotton-quilted uniforms and warm headgear with ear flaps and were well dressed for winter, with the exception of the rubber-soled tennis-type sneakers they wore and their lack of gloves or mittens. The prisoners said that about three-fourths of the 124th Division were former Nationalist soldiers from Chiang Kai-shek's army. Almond now knew that he had in front of him more than a few Chinese "Volunteer" soldiers. They were, in fact, major units of the regular Chinese army. Almond reported his findings to his own command at once and to General MacArthur. The latter sent a detailed report on the subject to the Department of the Army in Washington on 31 October.[3]

At the end of October, the ROK 26th Regiment withdrew a short distance after a heavy battle with the Chinese. The 7th Marine Regiment moved up behind the ROK 26th Regiment and on 2 November relieved it in its positions.

During the ROK I Corps advance, the X Corps staff and the 1st Marine Division landed at Wonsan on 26 October. Three days later, on 29 October, the 17th Infantry Regiment of the 7th Infantry Division landed unopposed over the beaches at Iwon, 178 miles north of Wonsan.

The 7th Marine Regiment, after relieving the ROK 26th Regiment at Sudong, found itself in a series of heavy battles with the CCF 124th Division. These battles, starting on 3 November, began on the low ground below Funchilin Pass. They continued through 7 November, when the Marines reached the village of Pohu-jang and Power Plant No. 1, at the foot of the steep cableway incline that ran up the mountainside on the east to the Koto-ri plateau. Marine air strength and heavy mortar and artillery support helped the Marines decimate the Chinese 124th Division in these battles. The 7th Marines themselves suffered many casualties. After the continuous battles between 3 and 7 November, the Chinese faded away. Patrols for two days thereafter failed to establish contact with them. On 10 November the 7th Marines moved up over Funchilin Pass to the Koto-ri plateau without opposition and occupied the village of Koto-ri, about two and one-half miles north of the edge of the plateau.

That first day and night on the Koto-ri plateau was a harbinger of weather to come. It was an experience these Marines never forgot. The temperature dropped in the afternoon and during the night from 40 degrees above to 8 degrees below zero and was accompanied by a wind that blew at 30 to 35 miles an hour. Although the temperature at Chosin Reservoir later dropped as low as 35 degrees below zero, it did not produce the shock that did this sudden change in temperature with high winds the first night the Marines spent on the plateau. During the next four days more than 200 men became nonbattle casualties from cold and frostbite and had to be given special medical treatment. Candy was soon at a premium. Men who normally did not care for it now greedily ate all they could get in order to supply quick energy and combat the intense cold.[4]

On 14 November the 7th Marine Regiment continued on northward 11 miles from Koto-ri to Hagaru-ri, one and one-half miles south of the southern tip of the Chosin Reservoir. On 23 November the 1st Battalion, 7th Marines, moved out from Hagaru-ri along the western fork of the road, toward Yudam-ni, 14 miles to the northwest. They reached Yudam-ni two days later, on 25 November, after clearing the road of undefended enemy roadblocks and booby traps. The battalion encountered only a few small, scattered enemy groups on the way.

In the meantime, the 5th Marine Regiment, commanded by Lt. Col. Raymond L. Murray, had moved up behind the 7th Marines on the road to Hagaru-ri, where they took the eastern fork, along the eastern side of the reservoir. Eight miles north of Hagaru-ri, the leading 3rd Battalion passed through a once-populated village shown on the maps as Sinhung-ni, but now virtually nonexistent. It crossed an arm of the reservoir there and continued another four miles, where it stopped on 24 November. At this place on hilly ground, the 3rd Battalion established a defense position. The rest of the 5th Marine Regiment closed behind the 3rd Battalion on the east side of the reservoir. Only patrols from the 3rd Battalion went farther the next day. They encountered a few Chinese soldiers. Meanwhile, the 1st Marine Regiment was concentrating along the Hamhung–Hagaru-ri road. Its 3rd Battalion, less G Company, was at Hagaru-ri; another battalion, the 2nd, was atop the plateau at Koto-ri; and the 1st Battalion was at Chinhung-ni.

The X Corps now had a front of about 400 miles, held with widely scattered regimental and battalion teams. Nowhere except on the road to Hagaru-ri, in the zone of the 1st Marine Division, did any of these troops encounter Chinese soldiers, except for a Chinese regiment of the 126th Division, elements of which the 3rd Battalion, 7th Infantry Division, encountered on the east and north sides of Fusen Reservoir on 8 November. These Chinese withdrew from contact after losing about 50 men killed. Everywhere else enemy contacts were with remnants of North Korean Army units trying to escape north, or with North Korean guerrillas engaged in harassing and delaying tactics. The largest organized resistance east and north of the 1st Marine Division consisted of North Korean troops trying to stop or delay the ROK 3rd and Capital divisions of the ROK I Corps, particularly the Capital Division, which was advancing rapidly up the east coastal road toward the North Korean border.

The general disposition of X Corps in November had the 1st Marine Division concentrated on the Hamhung–Hagaru-ri road, after the US 3rd Infantry Division landed and relieved it on 6 November of responsibilities for controlling guerrilla activities west and southwest of Hamhung. The 7th Infantry Division began landing at the Iwon beaches on 29 October. Its 17th Regiment moved north over a dirt road through Pungsan

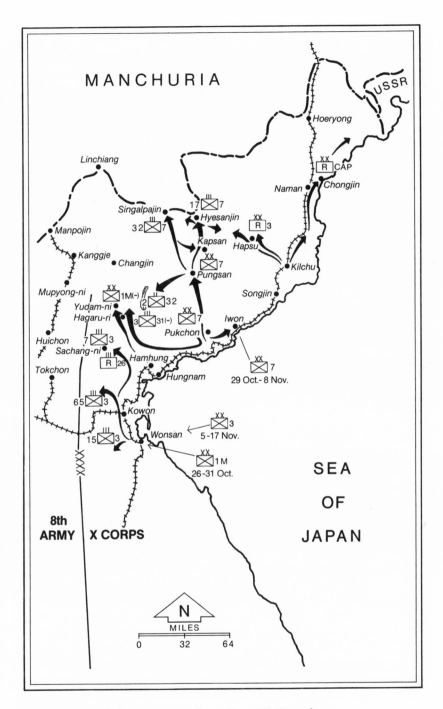

MAP 1. X Corps deployment in northeast Korea, 28 November.

and Kapsan toward Hyesanjin; the 3rd Battalion of the 32nd Infantry turned west through Samsu and toward Singalpajin on the Yalu, and the 31st Infantry veered west toward the Fusen Reservoir. The ROK 3rd and Capital divisions continued north together along the coastal road above Iwon as far as Songjin, a major North Korean town on the east coast. Farther up the coast at Kilchu, the ROK 3rd Division turned northwest toward Hapsu, and beyond that town it continued in two separate regimental combat teams to the north and northwest. Beyond Hapsu they were in an almost trackless mountainous waste in the distant northeast part of Korea. The Capital Division continued on up the coastal road and passed through Nanam and Chongjin before events elsewhere caused the X Corps to order it to withdraw southward. Chongjin was a major industrial center and only 65 air miles southwest of the Soviet border. The ROK I Corps in this impressive coastal advance had some major battles against stubbornly resisting North Koreans in front of it.

Of all the X Corps troops, only the 17th Infantry Regiment of the 7th Division at Hyesanjin reached the Yalu River and the North Korean border in any force, although a platoon of K Company, 32nd Infantry, reached Singalpajin on the Yalu and the border briefly on 28 November. The 17th Infantry Regiment on the way to Hyesanjin encountered difficult weather and terrain conditions. One tank company in going from Chori to Pungsan climbed 4,600 feet in 11 miles in going over a pass. The lead tank took two and one-half days to make the 11 miles. Another tank platoon had to shovel ice and snow off the road in order to cross one of the passes. There was great difficulty with steel tank tracks skidding and sliding on the ice, particularly on bends in the road.[5] Despite all difficulties of ice, snow, and subzero temperatures, the 17th Infantry pushed up the 120 road miles through mountains, crossed the Ungi River and more mountain passes, against North Korean resistance, to enter Hyesanjin on the morning of 21 November. General Almond had flown into Kapsan the previous day. Together with Maj. Gen. David G. Barr and Colonel Powell, who commanded the 17th Regiment, Almond and the others accompanied the 1st Battalion, 17th Infantry, that led the way into Hyesanjin on 21 November. The Yalu here had dwindled to a small, shallow stream, about 50 to 75 yards wide. It was frozen over except for a six-foot wide channel. Four days later, the river was completely frozen over. Upstream, 300 yards from Hyesanjin, on the Siberian side of the river, was an undamaged Chinese village. American troops at Hyesanjin could see Chinese sentries there walking their rounds.[6] The small force led by 2nd Lt. Robert C. Kingston, a platoon leader of the 32nd Infantry, which reached Singalpajin a week later, had scarcely entered the Yalu River village when it was ordered back to begin the long withdrawal to Hungnam.

When dawn broke on 7 November 1950, the Chinese troops had disappeared from in front of the 7th Marines below Chosin Reservoir, just as they had disappeared from in front of Eighth Army in the west along the Chongchon River. There must have been coordination at a high level of Chinese command for these simultaneous withdrawals from contact with the UN forces in both east and west. On 10 November the 1st Battalion, 7th Marine Regiment, climbed over Funchilin Pass, unopposed, to reach the Koto-ri plateau. Once on the plateau, the Marines frequently saw groups of Chinese in the distance but had no encounters with them until 11 November, when there was a short skirmish — and then the Chinese vanished.

The 3rd Battalion, 31st Infantry, 7th Division, was reconnoitering the approaches to the Fusen Reservoir when it encountered parts of a Chinese regiment in the mountain country east of the reservoir. The Fusen Reservoir was a smaller body of water than the Chosin Reservoir and lay about 20 air miles northeast of it. After a couple sharp fights, the Chinese forces withdrew, and the 3rd Battalion lost contact with them.

Cold weather struck like a bayonet into the bodies of the American soldiers on the Koto-ri plateau and those in the mountains east of Fusen Reservoir. On 14 November a cold front from Siberia descended over northern Korea, covering the entire X Corps advanced positions inland from the coast. In the Chosin and Fusen Reservoir areas, the temperatures dropped to 35 degrees below zero at night. In the west, in the Eighth Army sector, the weather was also cold, going down to 10 to 20 degrees below zero at night. The ensuing campaign of the 1st Marine Division and parts of the 7th Infantry Division in the Chosin Reservoir area was the coldest ever endured by American soldiers.

In mid-November only North Korean remnants fleeing north in delaying actions hampered the ROK I Corps and the 7th Infantry Division. The US Army's 3rd Infantry Division was in the X Corps rear in the Wonsan-Yonghung area.

On 14 November at 1 P.M. the 7th Marine Regiment, unopposed, occupied Hagaru-ri at the southern end of the Chosin Reservoir. The next day, General MacArthur issued a directive to X Corps that changed its direction of advance to set in motion the deployment of X Corps troops and soon brought them into fierce battle with Chinese forces.

The Far East Command in Tokyo, and Eighth Army in Korea, considered the Chinese MSR axis of advance and possible attack from Manchuria into North Korea to be along the Manpojin-Kanggye-Huichon road, which ran almost due south from the Yalu River to the Chongchon River valley, where Eighth Army was concentrated. At Chian in Manchuria, a highway bridge crossed the Yalu six miles west of Manpojin. The main rail line from central Manchuria ran south to the Yalu at Chian, where it turned east and ran upstream along the river bank, crossing to the south side of the Yalu at Manpojin in Korea. From there the main rail and highway net in north-central Korea ran south through Kanggye, an important road and rail junction point, and on south to Mupyong-ni, where, just below the town, the main road from the east and the Chosin Reservoir joined it. The rail line and highway then crossed a divide separating the Yalu and Chongchon drainages to reach Huichon, and from there they followed the Chongchon valley southwest through Kujang-dong, Won-ni, Kunu-ri, and Sinanju to the Yellow Sea. This communications MSR from Manchuria and China was of the greatest importance to the CCF throughout the Korean War. The Chian-Manpojin area was an essential troop and supply crossing point from Manchuria and China into Korea. Only the western crossing point from Antung in Manchuria to Sinuiju in Korea at the mouth of the Yalu rivaled it.[7]

The distance from Manpojin to Kanggye was about 30 road miles. At Kanggye the railroad forked, a branch line running into the mountains to the southeast; a secondary highway followed this branch rail line. A more important road forked off the main Kanggye-Huichon highway a few miles south of Mupyong-ni and ran generally a little south of east to Yudam-ni on the west side of the Chosin Reservoir. It traversed mountainous terrain the entire distance. MacArthur's order of 15 November to X Corps called for the 1st Marine Division to advance along this mountainous dirt road from Yudam-ni to Mupyong-ni and there cut the main Chinese supply road to the Eighth Army front below Kanggye. This change in the X Corps plan of advance was intended to help Eighth Army, since the latter was to put its main force of attack along the Huichon-Kanggye axis toward the border. If the American commands succeeded in their planned maneuvers, the Eighth Army and the X Corps would meet somewhere in the vicinity of Mupyong-ni or Kanggye. Should the CCF stop or delay the Eighth Army attack farther south, then the X Corps, if its maneuver succeeded, would be in the rear of the Chinese force opposing Eighth Army and could cut its MSR. Then, instead of driving north to the border from the Chosin area, the 1st Marine Division had a different primary mission—that of correlating its action with Eighth Army to help the latter achieve its military mission and to give it protection. The 1st Marine Division was to lead the attack westward from Yudam-ni on the road running west to the Kanggye-Huichon road, which it would enter a few miles south of Mupyong-ni.

In improving its communications to the front, the X Corps had to undertake heavy construction to make the road from Hungnam to Hagaru-ri usable to trucks and tanks, especially over Funchilin Pass, which carried the road from the low valley leading northward from the coast to the high Koto-ri plateau, in which lay Hagaru-ri and the Chosin Reservoir. The first tanks arrived at Hagaru-ri on 18 November, after consid-

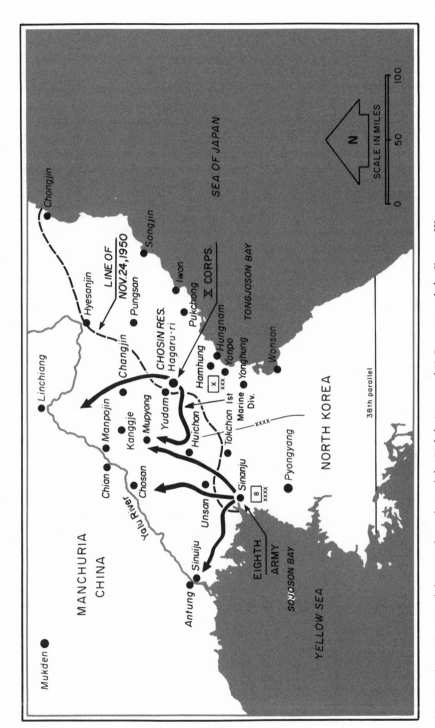

MAP 2. The main axis of the UN planned attack by Eighth Army and X Corps to end the Korean War.

erable engineering work had been accomplished on the steep, tortuous trail that climbed to the Koto-ri plateau. Another high pass, Toktong Pass, had to be crossed on the road from Hagaru-ri to Yudam-ni that left the shoreline of the jagged and very irregular west side of Chosin Reservoir to cut across mountainous terrain to the Yudam-ni road junction.

Chosin Reservoir, about 13 air miles long on a north-south axis and about eight miles wide at its widest, lay atop the Koto-ri plateau at an altitude of 3,400 feet. Its shoreline was exceedingly irregular, with fingers and arms of water pushing into mountain valleys that drained into and fed the reservoir. The shore was generally steep, and hills and mountains rose from its edge to reach in some cases to 3,000 feet above the reservoir's surface, peaking about 5 to 10 miles distant. A few miles east of the reservoir, one peak rose to an elevation of 6,700 feet; west of the reservoir, Toktong Peak reached 4,740 feet, and another peak about four miles north of Yudam-ni was 5,070. These hills and mountains had sparse foliage as well as fir, aspen, and miscellaneous brush. This was the terrain in which the battles of the Chosin campaign were fought, most of them on the lower hillls and ridges and in the valleys near the reservoir shoreline.

On 24 November, the day Eighth Army moved out in attack to the north from the Chongchon valley in the west, X Corps sent Lt. Col. John H. Chiles, its G-3, to Tokyo with a revised plan for final review. MacArthur approved the plan with only one change. In the 1st Marine Division sector, he moved the boundary between Eighth Army and X Corps in the southwestern section of the X Corps area. X Corps thereupon issued its operation order the next day, 25 November. It called for the X Corps attack to begin at 8 A.M. on 27 November.

The main features of the X Corps attack plan were the following:

1. The 1st Marine Division was to drive west from Yudam-ni and seize Mupyong-ni on the Manpojin Huichon road.
2. A regimental combat team from the Army's 7th Infantry Division, which had relieved the 5th Marine Regiment on the east side of Chosin Reservoir, was to attack up the east side of the reservoir, seize Changjin, and advance north to the Yalu.
3. The ROK I Corps was to advance up the east control road to Chongjin.
4. The 3rd Infantry Division was to protect Wonsan and the left flank of the 1st Marine Division, support the 1st Marine Division on order, and establish contact with the east (right) flank of Eighth Army.

The plan was optimistic, spreading troops over a vast expanse of the frozen northeast of Korea, with little possibility that any major unit could support another in any sudden crisis. Only if all went well could it work.

The most important part of the plan centered on the 1st Marine Divi-

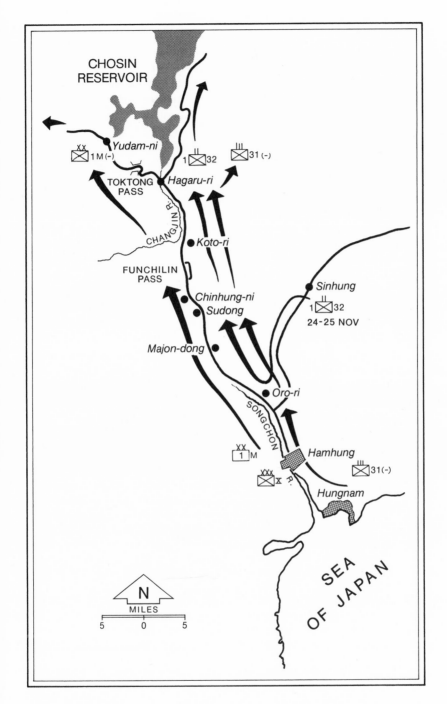

CHOSIN
RESERVOIR

Yudam-ni

XX
1M (-)

TOKTONG
PASS

Hagaru-ri

1 32

31 (-)

Koto-ri

FUNCHILIN
PASS

Chinhung-ni
Sudong

Sinhung

1 32

24-25 NOV

Majon-dong

Oro-ri

SONGCHON R.

XX
1 M

Hamhung

XXX
X R.

31 (-)

Hungnam

N

MILES

5   0   5

SEA
OF JAPAN

MAP 3. Main supply route of 1st Marine Division and 31st Infantry Regiment, November–December.

sion. Mupyong-ni lay 55 miles west of Yudam-ni, across mountainous terrain traversed by a poor road. From Mupyong-ni, it was another 40 miles north to Manpojin on the Yalu River and the border. After the 1st Marine Division advance got under way, the 3rd Infantry Division would have responsibility for the supply road and area south of Hagaru-ri to Ham-hung. But actually, that division was spread so thin and its units so far apart that, as events developed, it could hold only the MSR from Sudong southward. In this situation, the 1st Marine Division kept battalion-sized perimeters at Chinhung-ni and at Koto-ri, below and at the top of vital Funchilin Pass.

Before the X Corps started its attack, bad news came from the west. During the night of 25 November, the second day of the Eighth Army attack and two days before the X Corps was to launch its own, a surprise Chinese attack pushed back the ROK II Corps near Tokchon, on the Eighth Army's right flank, about 70 air miles southwest of Yudam-ni. That same day, 25 November, strong elements of the 7th Marine Regiment seized Yudam-ni, after fighting their way through Toktong Pass against some Chinese resistance. The full regiment proceeded to concentrate at Yudam-ni, in preparation for the attack west from there on 27 November.

Meanwhile, the 5th Marine Regiment, which had moved up the east side of Chosin Reservoir from Hagaru-ri with the mission of attacking north to Changjin, had its mission changed. It would hastily move west to join the 7th Marines at Yudam-ni. But in the meantime, its advanced 3rd Battalion encountered and skirmished with small groups of Chinese. One of its patrols reached nearly to the north end of Chosin Reservoir on 24 November. On 25 November the 1st Battalion, 32nd Infantry, 7th Division, relieved most of the 5th Marines on the east side of the reservoir. It was expected that two battalions of the 31st Infantry Regiment of the 7th Division would follow and complete relief of all elements of the 5th Marines east of Chosin the next morning, 26 November. The 5th Marines were to proceed to Yudam-ni as soon as relieved, pass through the 7th Marines there, and lead the attack westward on 27 November.

2

BACKGROUND TO CHOSIN RESERVOIR BATTLES

The CCF IX Army Group in Korea

The CCF IX Chinese Army Group moved to the Chosin Reservoir area in the last half of November 1950 and conducted the campaign there against the 1st Marine Division and elements of the 7th Infantry Division. The 30th Army supplied the 88th, 89th, and 90th divisions as reinforcements to the IX Army Group, one division to each of the three armies. Only nine of the 12 divisions were positively identified in combat during the Chosin Reservoir battles and the Hungnam evacuation of the X Corps. CCF divisions at full strength were supposed to number about 10,000 men. Information obtained from CCF prisoners during the Chosin operations indicated that their divisions were understrength and numbered about 6,500 to 7,000 men. The three CCF divisions not identified as being in contact in battle in the Chosin Reservoir operations were the 90th, 78th, and 88th (see table 1).

The Third Field Army was considered second in combat efficiency only to Lin Piao's Fourth Field Army in the Chinese People's Liberation Army, and the 20th and 27th armies were among the four most noted in the field army for their mobility. Most of their equipment was of Japanese origin, but a considerable part was American.

Gen. Sung Shih-lun commanded the IX Army Group, considered to be the best in the Third Field Army. Sung was about 40 years old when his troops in 1950 confronted the 1st Marine Division at Chosin. He had been a student of Chou En-lai at the Whampoa Military Academy and had commanded troops in battle since he was 17 years old. At first he led guerrilla groups in action west of Peking, and in the Long March of 1934–35 he commanded a regiment. About 1942, he returned to the Communist stronghold in Yenan and studied at the Central Party School. There he became familiar with the doctrines of Karl Marx, Lenin, and Mao Tse-tung. He was a Communist representative at the peace talks between Chiang Kai-shek's Nationalists and Mao's Communists in 1946 at Peking.

TABLE 1.
Chinese IX Army Group, Third Field Army,
Gen. Sung Shih-lun, CO

Army and CO	Divisions	Regiments
20th,	58th	172nd, 173rd, 174th
Gen. Liu Fei	59th	175th, 176th, 177th
	60th	178th, 179th, 180th
	89th (30th Army)	265th, 266th, 267th
26th,	76th	226th, 227th, 228th
Gen. Chang Jen Chu	77th	229th, 230th, 231st
	78th	232nd, 233rd, 234th
	88th (30th Army)	262nd, 263rd, 264th
27th,	79th	235th, 236th, 237th
Gen. Chen Yi-fu	80th	238th, 239th, 240th
	81st	241st, 242nd, 243rd
	90th (30th Army)	268th, 269th, 270th
Total:		
3 armies	12 divisions	36 regiments

SOURCE: FEC, Daily Intelligence Summary No. 3207, 21 Jun 51 (captured CCF document giving order of battle); X Corps, Special Report on Chosin Reservoir, Comd. Rpt., 27 Nov–10 Dec 50, Maps A and B and Maps 1–3; Montross and Canzona, *The Chosin Campaign*, App. G, Enemy Order of Battle; Riggs, *Red China's Fighting Hordes*, pp. 29, 86–87; FEC, Order of Battle Information, Chinese Third Field Army, Korean War, 1 Mar 1951, Box 413; HQ, FEC, *Intelligence Digest*, 1, no. 3 (16–31 Jan 1953): 30–37, Box 225.

After the final defeat of the Nationalist forces in the Chinese civil war in 1949, Sung became garrison commander of the Shanghai-Wusung area. Quick-tempered, he was nevertheless considered a good tactician and a master of guerrilla warfare. His bravery in battle was not questioned—he had been tested many times. On occasion he had served as commander of the entire Third Field Army.

The formal commander of the Third Field Army in 1950 was Gen. Chen Yi. Chen Yi commanded the forces that captured Shanghai, and, apparently, he remained in Shanghai as its mayor, holding command of the Third Field Army at the same time. There is no evidence that he exercised any command function of the IX Army Group in Korea. But the IX Army Group reflected some of the characteristics for which Chen Yi was noted. He had studied in a French school at Grenoble, France. After the school expelled him, Chen had gone back to China and become an instructor at the Whampoa Military Academy. He fought in many guerrilla operations, but he had not been on the Long March. He was careful in choosing subordinates and was considered a cautious, conservative commander. He favored night attacks and stressed infantry use of grenades and bayonets. His soldiers fought some of the hardest battles of the Chinese civil war. In the course of that struggle, Chen Yi bought off many Nationalist generals and took whole Nationalist divisions into his own ranks. Many of these former Nationalist divisions entered Korea as part of the IX Army Group with their American weapons. His Third Field Army was scheduled to make the amphibious attack on Formosa, until events in Korea in the summer and fall of 1950 brought about a change in plans, and some of his best troops were sent north to enter the fight there.

Under General Sung and the IX Army Group, Gen. Liu Fei commanded the 20th Army; Gen. Chang Jen Chu (or Len-chu) commanded the 26th Army; and Gen. Chen Yi-fu commanded the 27th Army. The IX Army Group entered Korea from Manchuria during November 1950. The 42nd Army of the Fourth Field Army had previously entered Korea during October and had proceeded to the Chosin Reservoir area as east-flank protection for the main force that had attacked American and ROK troops north of the Chongchon River in the west. But between 15 and 20 November, the 42nd Army left the Chosin area and moved southwest toward Tokchon to join its parent unit, the XIII Army Group of the Fourth Field Army, which had massed against the Eighth Army. At that time, the IX Army Group took over responsibility at Chosin in a double role. First, it acted as the east-flank protection of the larger Chinese force in the west, and second and more important, it had the mission of destroying the 1st Marine Division, which was then in the process of assembling in the Chosin area.[1]

In general it may be said that the 27th Army was the most effective in the Chosin campaign, attacking Yudam-ni and the 7th Division troops on the east side of the reservoir; the 20th Army was the next most effective, cutting the road at numerous places south of Yudam-ni and Hagaru-ri and fighting the battles at those places; and the 26th Army was the least effective, most of its action being in the vicinity of Koto-ri.

Upon arriving at the Yalu, the 20th Army crossed the river on a pontoon bridge at Chian and then moved six miles northeast to the Korean river town of Manpojin, where a road ran southward. The other two armies reached Linchiang, Manchuria, 65 air miles upstream and northeast of Manpojin. The 27th Army crossed there upon arrival; the other, the 26th, remained on the north side of the river in army-group reserve. Linchiang, the farthest upstream Yalu River crossing used by Chinese soldiers entering Korea, was also the farthest upstream and easternmost river-crossing site from Manchuria to Korea reached by a railroad. This railroad connected the crossing site to Mukden to the west and Harbin to the north. Linchiang lay about 100 air miles almost due north of the Chosin Reservoir.[2]

Nearly all the Chinese soldiers of the 20th, 26th, and 27th armies that

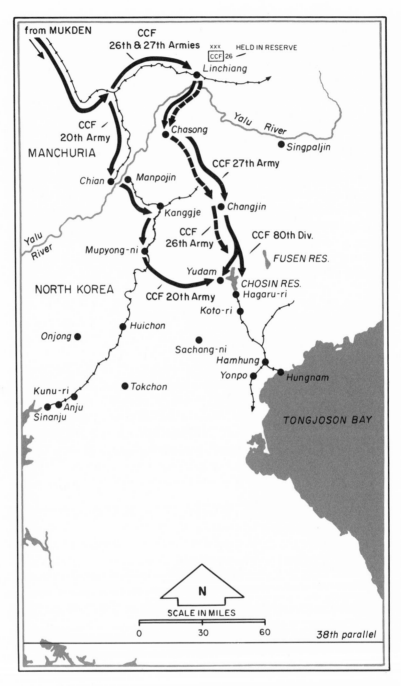

MAP 4. The Chinese Communist Forces' movement to Chosin Reservoir, November 1950.

made up the IX Army Group, but not the three divisions from the 30th Army that reinforced the IX Army Group, came from the Chinese province of Shantung. Most were farmers or sons of farmers. Shantung lay on the Chinese coast on the west side of the Yellow Sea, opposite the southern tip of Korea and Kyushu, and in the same latitude. The climate there was relatively mild, about like that of Illinois in the United States. These soldiers were not inured to the cold, harsh winters of Manchuria and northern Korea. This was an important factor in the outcome of the Chosin Reservoir campaign.

Actually, General Peng Te-huai, made commander of the Chinese volunteers on 8 October 1950, was in overall command of joint Chinese–North Korean operations in Korea after the Chinese intervened in the war. General Sung is thought to have established his IX Army Group headquarters in the mountains about ten miles north of Yudam-ni, from which he directed the Chosin Reservoir operations.

Three CCF Armies in Korea

General Liu Fei, commanding the CCF 20th Army, led the vanguard of the IX Army Group into Korea. This army had taken part as the 1st Column of the East China People's Liberation Army in the East China campaigns that ultimately destroyed the Chinese Nationalist armies north of the Yangtze River. In the spring of 1949, redesignated the 20th Army, it crossed the Yangtze River and helped in the capture of Shanghai in May 1949. It then remained in the Hangchow area, south of Shanghai, and underwent amphibious training, presumably for the projected attack on Formosa. But in the summer of 1950, after the outbreak of the war in Korea, it moved north to Shantung Province and there was reinforced by the 89th Division of the 30th Army.

The 20th Army began leaving Shantung province by rail on 6 November 1950 and closed into Chian, Manchuria by 10 November. It crossed the pontoon bridge at Chian, moved the six miles northeast to Manpojin, and there entrained for the next leg of its journey. The trains moved only at night, hidden during the daytime in tunnels along the mountainous route southward. The railroad ran 40 miles southeast of Manpojin to Kanggye, and from there another 28 miles southwest to Mupyongni. There the 20th Army left the rail line and marched along the narrow, twisting mountain road that led eastward 55 miles to Yudam-ni, on the western side of Chosin Reservoir, where it closed between 13 and 15 November, five days after crossing the Yalu. It relieved the 42nd Army, elements of which had been acting as a delaying force against the 1st Marine Division. The 42nd Army then moved southwest to join sister units of the Fourth Field Army that were massed against the US Eighth

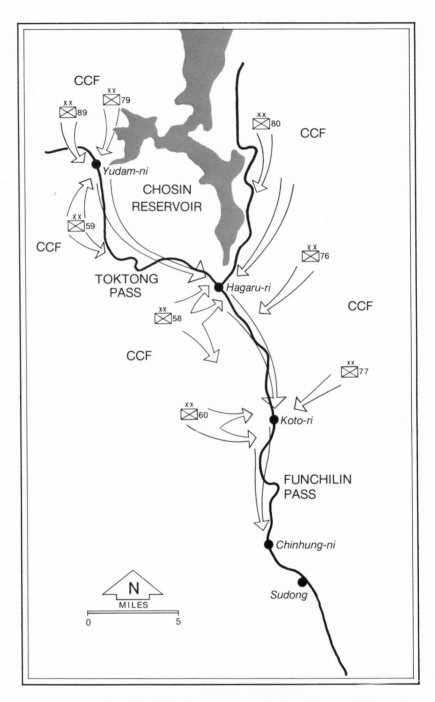

MAP 5. Deployment of the CCF IX Army Group, Third Field Army, 27 November–10 December.

Army. Except for a few small groups, the 20th Army remained effectively concealed until 27 November. The 20th Army's mission was to cut the road between Yudam-ni and Hagaru-ri and thus isolate the 1st Marine Division, which was concentrating at Yudam-ni.[3]

The 26th Army had also participated actively in the Chinese civil war and, like the 20th Army, had engaged in the battles south of the Yangtze and helped in the capture of Shanghai. It had earlier been the 8th Column of the East China People's Liberation Army, but in the army reorganization in 1948, it had been redesignated the 26th Army. This army left Tenghsien, Shantung Province, by train beginning on 1 November, and by 5 November it had closed on Linchiang, Manchuria. General Sung held the 26th Army at Linchiang in reserve until about the end of November and the first days of December, when it became apparent that the 20th and 27th armies were not going to defeat the X Corps troops and destroy them in the Chosin Reservoir area. He then started the 26th Army south, but only two divisions of it arrived in the Chosin area in time to join efforts to cut off the 1st Marine Division and 7th Infantry Division troops before they reached the Hungnam perimeter at the coast. It played the smallest role of the three Chinese armies in the Chosin campaign.[4]

The 27th Army had formerly been the 9th Column of the East China People's Liberation Army. In January 1949, it was redesignated the 27th Army. This army had a long series of battles in the Chinese civil war, including the battles for Shanghai. It was considered highly mobile, capable of long, sustained marches, and had distinguished itself in attacks against fortified places. It was regarded as one of the most effective units of the Third Field Army. It remained in the vicinity of Shanghai after the fall of that city in May 1949 as an occupational force until October. It then moved to Hangchow Bay and engaged in intensive amphibious training until the summer of 1950, when it, too, suddenly went to Shantung Province. Reinforced there by the 90th Division of the 30th Army, it began leaving that province by train on 25 October 1950. It traveled northward and closed into Linchiang, Manchuria, by 1 November 1950. It crossed at once into Korea and headed for the Chosin Reservoir.

Upon reaching the northern tip of the reservoir, the 27th Army split its forces. The 79th Division went down the west side of the reservoir to attack Yudam-ni; the 80th Division followed the east side of the reservoir with the mission of attacking Hagaru-ri, but ran into the Army 7th Division elements then arriving there. Two of its divisions, the 81st and 90th, may have been in the Fusen Reservoir area or in reserve in the Chosin area during the Chosin battles, as there was no recorded battle contact with them until after the X Corps troops at Chosin had withdrawn into the Hungnam perimeter. The two divisions of the 27th Army, the 79th and 80th, that engaged in the battles at Chosin Reservoir on the night of 27 November were perhaps the most effective of all the Chinese units in the campaign.

STRENGTH OF OPPOSING FORCES

While General Sung had 12 divisions in the IX Army Group available for the Chosin operations, the actual battle contacts and Chinese prisoner statements indicate that only eight of the 12 divisions, or two-thirds of the IX Army Group strength, were committed to battle. It must be remembered that these Chinese divisions were not at full strength. If eight divisions were involved in battle, as the best postbattle intelligence suggests, then the Chinese employed between 52,000 and 56,000 men in the Chosin Reservoir campaign against the 1st Marine Division, elements of the Army 7th and 3rd divisions, and the 41st Royal Marine Commandos (British, numbering 234 men). The 1st Marine Division had an effective strength of 25,473 men at the time.[5] But the division did not have all its support strength in the Chosin area. Altogether, the equivalent of about two army regiments from the 7th and 3rd infantry divisions and the 41st Royal Marine Commandos were engaged, together with the 1st Marine Division, in the Chosin combat operations, adding another 8,000 men, counting supporting units. The opposing ground forces, then, totaled about 55,000–60,000 Chinese light infantry against about 30,000 American and British infantry, who had powerful artillery, tank, and air support, with logistical support. The Chinese IX Army Group was essentially a light infantry force without motorized transport, artillery, air support, or tanks. Its largest weapons were mortars. It had no resupply of ammunition or food after it entered battle. When one considers the volume of firepower available to the American forces and their capability of resupply of ammunition and food, as contrasted to Chinese deficiencies in these areas, one must reject the popular notion that the Chinese had overwhelming force.

THE TERRAIN AND ROUTES OF COMMUNICATION

The battles X Corps fought in the Chosin Reservoir area were in the roughest terrain and during the coldest and harshest weather of any in the Korean War. And the routes of communication were among the poorest and most precarious of any used in the war by American motorized forces. Not until UN forces approached the high mountains of the Hwachon Reservoir, Kumsong, Heartbreak Ridge, and the Punchbowl area of east-central Korea in the summer and fall of 1951 did the terrain become anything like the high forbidding knife-edge ridges and high passes that surround the Chosin Reservoir, and then it was without the Siberian winter that characterized the Chosin Reservoir campaign. No American troops before or since have ever fought in as harsh and hostile an environment as did the Marine and Army troops of the US X Corps in Korea in November and December 1950. In order to understand the true measure of the military accomplishment — in which most Marine and Army units escaped from the trap they entered, with only one road of egress from the mountain fastnesses, in paralyzing cold, and with ever-present Chinese infantry on all sides — the nature of the country involved and of its roadnet must be comprehended.

In general, the elevation of the hills increases from the southern tip of the Korean peninsula to the country's northern border at the Yalu and Tumen rivers. In the Chosin Reservoir area the mountains reach 7,000- to 8,000-foot elevations in the Yangnim Range, which extends northward to the Yalu River. These mountains are drained by rapid streams flowing in sharp-sided valleys or in gorges. The valleys are forested, and the mountainsides sometimes covered by grass or trees. Rocky slopes predominate. The timberline goes up to 7,000–7,500 feet in places. This whole northern reach of Korea is almost unpopulated. Where there were people, they congregated in small villages in the valleys. There were few roads. Most of these ran generally north-south, following the stream drainages either northward to the Yalu or southward or southeastward to the Sea of Japan, and in the west to the Yellow Sea. When X Corps entered northeast Korea in the fall of 1950, even the best of these roads were one-way roads for most of their distances, with a dirt-gravel surface. There were no lateral roads worthy of the name in this northern fastness — only trails of different degrees of passability.

Across the breadth of northern Korea, beginning on the west coast at the Yellow Sea, a road followed the south bank of the Yalu upstream northeastward as far as Hyesanjin. South of it, from Sinanju and Anju at the mouth of the Chongchon River, a major road followed that river northeastward to Huichon and then continued over a pass and watershed to a north-flowing stream, following it to Mupyong-ni, Kanggye, and Manpojin, where it met the Yalu. Eastward, the next important road was that leading from Hungnam and Hamhung northward to the Chosin Reservoir. There, a left-hand fork turned west at Hagaru-ri, and after reaching Yudam-ni, it took a more direct western course, meeting the Huichon-Kanggye road, previously described, a few miles below Mupyong-ni. There it merged with it to continue northward to Manpojin and the Yalu River. Still farther east a fourth road, 30 air miles up the coast from Hungnam, passed northward from Iwon through Pukchon and Pungsan to reach the Yalu at Hyesanjin. Beyond this road eastward there were only tracks through the mountains until one reached the east coastal road that wound its way between the Sea of Japan and the base of nearby mountains northeastward through Kilchu, Songjin, and Najin to the Soviet border.

From the valley of the Chongchon River, the axis of US Eighth Army's advance, eastward to the Sea of Japan, there were no through lateral roads — only a jumble of tracks that ran for relatively short distances and then branched off into trails in different directions. In this area there was no physical contact between the Eighth Army in the west and X Corps in the northeast.

THE GAP BETWEEN EIGHTH ARMY AND X CORPS

In this area a so-called gap was said to exist between Eighth Army in the west and the X Corps in the east. It was a physical gap, to be sure, but it was not a gap that either side could use in a military way for effective action or maneuvering against the other. Neither side could supply large numbers of troops in this area, and thus neither side used it for military purposes.

There has been more nonsense spoken and written about MacArthur's presumed error in allowing this gap to develop between his two major forces in the Korean War than any other topic. It came at the time, and has come since then, from high military sources in the Pentagon and eminent military commentators in the United States and in Europe. Critics have simply not understood the terrain conditions in this part of Korea. MacArthur did. The plain fact is that there was no gap between the Eighth Army and the X Corps that could have been used militarily. If operations were to be carried on simultaneously in northwest Korea where Eighth Army was located and northeast Korea with the purpose of reaching the northern border and ending the war in all of Korea, they simply had to be executed independently of each other.

The idea that the war could end by December 1950 may validly receive criticism, but not the alleged existence of a dangerous gap between Eighth Army and the X Corps. MacArthur will have to stand charged with major errors in judgment in the Korean War, but the creation of a gap between the Eighth Army and the X Corps cannot be one of them if all of North Korea was to be occupied. Once MacArthur had decided to try to reach the border over most of Korea to end the war and secure a united Korea, he was justified in separating Eighth Army and the X Corps for the impending operations, for in no other way could he have reached the border over its whole distance and held the places needed to secure and unify the country. The wisdom of that decision and its probability of success is another matter, and judgment depends on a correct interpretation of enemy intelligence available to him and the intent and capability of the Chinese. But the gap did not contribute to the success or failure of the UN in Korea. It was irrelevant to the outcome.

The geography and climate of the northern part of Korea mandated that one force be based and supplied from Pusan at the southern tip of the peninsula and its internal communications system be supplemented by west-coast facilities, such as those at Inchon and Chinnampo. The second force, operating in northeast Korea, had to be based on the eastern ports of Wonsan and Hungnam, particularly the latter. This second force, X Corps, simply could not have been supplied from the bases and communications system that supplied Eighth Army.

That either Eighth Army in the west or the X Corps in the east was defeated or forced to retire by enemy forces operating against them through this gap is not true. One only has to follow the troop movements and battle operations of both sides from 24 November 1950 on to discount this view. Too many highly placed military men and journalists who pronounced on this subject merely looked at a map and saw that 50 or more miles separated the two forces and concluded that the space should have been closed. They were ignorant of the terrain and its limitations for military operations and of logistic factors involved in supporting the two forces.[6]

The most striking characteristics of Korean hills and mountains and their intervening valleys is the sudden rise of the ridge slope from relatively flat ground at their bases. The incline is sudden and steep, and the crest is knifelike in its narrow, sharp edge. Often it is only as wide as a footpath. Tanks cannot reach the crests; it would be impossible for them to operate on the steep slopes. Only the foot soldier can negotiate them, and to do so is extremely arduous. The knifelike edge of the topographic crests usually makes it possible for only a squad or a platoon to advance along them. In the small valleys the shallow streams are generally fordable, except when at flood. But their fordability for vehicles really depends more on the approaches. Steep banks prevent vehicular fording unless the banks are cut down. In the winter, with streams frozen over and the ground hard, vehicular crossing of the streams is easier than in spring and summer, when wet ground and flooded rice paddies make vehicular crossing of them all but impossible.[7]

From Manchuria and the rest of China, railroads reached the Yalu border for transport of large numbers of men and supply shipments across into Korea at only three places. On the west, a major rail and highway system crossed the border from Antung in Manchuria to Sinuiju in Korea, 20 miles upstream from the mouth of the Yalu River. The second major rail system reached the Yalu through Manchuria at Chian and Manpojin, crossing the river to the south side at the latter place. Generally, however, the troops unloaded at Chian and crossed the river on a pontoon bridge. The third rail line to reach the Yalu was really a branch of the second and came down to the river at Linchiang on the Manchurian side of the border about 65 air miles northeast of the Manpojin crossing. The Linchiang rail line did not cross to the south side of the river. Chinese troops who crossed at Manpojin were bound for both Eighth Army and the X Corps fronts.[8]

The axis of entry into the mountains and advance toward the border by the main force of X Corps, the 1st Marine Division, and elements of the US Army's 7th Infantry Division was from Hungnam on the east coast northward to the Chosin Reservoir. There the road split, one arm going to the right around the east side of the reservoir to Changjin and hence on northward with many twists and bends to the Yalu River opposite Linchiang. The other arm turned west at Hagaru-ri and crossed a high mountain range at Toktong Pass to reach Yudam-ni, about midway up the west side of the reservoir. Here two main forks of the road carried one arm northward along the west side of the reservoir; the other fork turned due west toward Mupyong-ni. It ran 55 miles to a junction below Mupyong-ni with the main Chongchon Valley road that ran northeastward from Anju through Kunu-ri to Huichon, Kanggye, and Manpojin on the Yalu River. There was a cross-country track, rather than a road, along a narrow-gauge railroad from Kanggye as far as the Changjin vicinity, north of Chosin Reservoir. From Yudam-ni there was another road that needs to be mentioned. It ran down a valley southwest toward the Taedong River divide. Otherwise, there were virtually no cross-country, lateral east-west roads in all this northern reach of Korea, except perhaps pack routes and trails.

It was along the Hungnam–Hagaru-ri–Yudam-ni road that the 1st Marine Division and elements of the Army's 7th Infantry Division advanced to the Chosin Reservoir. As it was their only route of advance, so also was it their only route of withdrawal. This road was all-important to the X Corps, which was isolated and cut off by the Chinese at the reservoir and at key points on the road south from Yudam-ni and the reservoir, beginning on 27 November.

THE ROAD FROM HUNGNAM TO YUDAM-NI

The east-coast port of Hungnam lies at the mouth of the Songchon River, where it empties into the Sea of Japan. A broad, flat coastal delta area extends southward from Hungnam for about 18 miles and inland narrows gradually to end just north of Hamhung, eight miles from Hungnam. Hamhung is the largest city in the Songchon delta and in all of northeast Korea. It had about 85,000 population in the 1940 census. The coastal railroad and highway that extend to the Soviet border pass through Hamhung from the south before bending to the coast at Hungnam and then continuing north to the border.

The Songchon River rises in the mountains east of the Chosin and Fusen reservoirs. A western tributary of the Songchon, the Hungnim, rises below the 4,000-foot plateau, wherein lies the Chosin Reservoir. The Hungnim River flows south to join the Songchon at Oro-ri, eight miles north of Hamhung and 16 miles inland from the port city of Hungnam. A narrow-gauge railroad, two and one-half feet wide, and a dirt-gravel road run inland along the east bank of the Songchon from Hungnam through Hamhung to Oro-ri, where they cross the stream to the west side and then follow the Hungnim River upstream to the northwest.

From Oro-ri the road continues on flat or semiflat ground with gentle curves through low hills, following closely the narrowing channel of the Hungnim River and a tributary, until it reaches the village of Chinhung-ni, 43 road miles from Hungnam. Thus far, the road is relatively flat, but with many turns and twists in a narrowing stream channel. But from Chinhung-ni the road climbs northward to the top of the Koto-ri plateau by a cliff-hanging, twisting narrow road that climbs 2,500 feet in elevation in eight miles. This stretch of road was called Funchilin Pass.

Two miles beyond the southern edge of the plateau is Koto-ri. There atop the plateau, the Siberian temperatures that gripped the Chosin area in late November and in December may be said to have begun. From Koto-ri to Hagaru-ri was another 11 miles, and beyond Hagaru-ri northwest to Yudam-ni, another 14 miles. Neither Hagaru-ri nor Yudam-ni lay immediately at the edge of the reservoir. Hagaru-ri was about one and one-half miles from the southern tip of the reservoir, with the Changjin River flowing through a flat marshland north of it into the open waters of the reservoir. Yudam-ni lay in a flat bowl about one mile west of a large arm of the reservoir that protruded westward into the Kuumni River valley about midway up the western side of the 14-mile-long reservoir. The total road distance from Hungnam, the port city, to Yudam-ni was 78 miles.

It was along this road, the only one available in this part of Korea for a major force to penetrate northward from the coast, that the 1st Marine Division and other X Corps forces engaged in the Chosin Reservoir campaign both entered and withdrew from that part of Korea. And it was along this route, particularly the 48 miles from Majon-dong northward to Yudam-ni, that the major battles were fought, excepting those of 7th Infantry Division elements on the east side of the reservoir north of Hagaru-ri, which were along a right (east) fork of the road that turned up the east side of the reservoir at Hagaru-ri.

The Hungnam–Yudam-ni road was two-way as far as Chinhung-ni. There it degenerated into a narrow one-way trail that climbed Funchilin Pass for eight miles to the Koto-ri plateau. From there on to the Chosin

Reservoir and Yudam-ni, the road was of varying width, but never more than a narrow two-way dirt-gravel track, and seldom straight and then only for short distances. Once on top the 4,000-foot plateau above Funchilin Pass, the road from just north of Koto-ri followed the shallow headwaters channel of the Changjin River, which flowed into the upper (south) end of Chosin Reservoir. Near there, at Hagaru-ri, the left (west) fork of the road turned abruptly west, crossed the river, and climbed over 5,372-foot-high Toktong Mountain on a southern shoulder by way of 4,700-foot-high Toktong Pass. The road then dropped steeply to the Muonni valley and followed it northward to Yudam-ni. This valley had high ridges close on the west side, and lower finger ridges extending from another mountain mass farther away on the east side, beyond which lay the Chosin Reservoir.

The narrow-gauge railroad became a cableway at Samgo Station, 500 yards north of Chinhung-ni, for the climb up to the Koto-ri plateau. The steep incline part of the cableway started at Pohu-jang about a mile farther north, and went straight up the mountain side of Funchilin Pass to the top of the plateau southeast of Koto-ri. Once on top the plateau, the cableway ended, and the narrow-gauge railroad track continued. It followed north down the valley of the Changjin River, parallel to the dirt-gravel road, to Hagaru-ri. There the narrow-gauge rail track turned to the east side of the reservoir and followed its shoreline north to the Pungnyuri River, where an eastern arm of the reservoir extended up the lower reaches of this stream. A small village named Sinhung-ni lay just north of this finger of the reservoir. The narrow-gauge railroad turned eastward up the Pungnyuri-gang, passed close to Sinhung-ni, and continued on toward the Fusen Reservoir. Actually, in 1950 there was no village of Sinhung-ni there—only a few huts scattered along the stream that emptied into the reservoir—just as there was then no town of Changjin, 30 air miles north of the reservoir. But these names appeared on all the maps the X Corps troops used at that time, based on 1916 data, and their names are in the records.[9]

The grade from Chinhung-ni, about 500 feet in altitude, up to the top of the Koto-ri plateau was steep. The narrow-gauge railroad could climb it as far as Pohu-jang and therefore was operational that far in 1950. But the railhead for transport of military supplies at different times was Sudong and at Majon-dong, seven miles farther south, because of the limited depot and storage space available at both Pohu-jang and Sudong. The cableway had been severed and was inoperable for the X Corps during the Chosin campaign. For practical purposes, therefore, the narrow-gauge railroad could be used for transport of supplies with certainty only as far as Majon-dong, 30 miles from Hungnam port, and sometimes eight miles farther to Pohu-jang. The seven miles between the two places was more or less a depot area where supplies were unloaded and stocked, depending on the space available at any given time. The 73rd Engineer Battalion had the responsibility of developing the MSR from Hamhung to Chinhung-ni; the 185th Engineer Battalion had the same responsibility from Chinhung-ni to Hagaru-ri.[10]

Most of the mileages given in this work for distances in extreme North Korea (for instance, from places in the Eighth Army zone to others in the X Corps zone) are given in air miles as measured on maps to provide some idea of the relative distances between places. Actual road-mile distances simply were not available then and are not available now. The trails often ran for distances that were only partly measured or completely unknown. These unknown distances that troops on foot would have to travel in the northern part of Korea where military operations of late 1950 took place were nearly always much greater than the air mileage. Sometimes the road distance was twice the air miles; on average it would probably be at least one-third greater. For example, from Chinhung-ni to Koto-ri is ten road miles but only six air miles; from Yudam-ni to Mupyong-ni, 55 miles by road but 40 by air; from Hagaru-ri to Yudam-ni, 14 by road and eight by air; and from Hunghung to Hagaru-ri, 60 road miles but 40 air miles.

The main supply road of the X Corps from the coast to the Chosin Reservoir had been measured carefully by the engineers who worked to improve and maintain it, and the distances between points along this road are known. It was along this MSR that the heavy battles took place, and the place-names along it will be mentioned frequently. It seems useful, therefore, to give in table 2 the names of places and the distances between them on this road.

UN commanders in 1950 often could not tell from their maps whether a road actually led from one point to another. The roads often degenerated into tracks and trails unusable by any vehicle. One example of such a situation was a relatively good dirt-gravel road branching off the MSR toward the Fusen Reservoir at Soyang-ni, about four miles south of Oro-ri. Actual road reconnaissance demonstrated that the road did not lead to the Fusen Reservoir, nor did any branch of it, although the Sinhung Line of the narrow-gauge railroad did go to the southern tip of the reservoir, where it ended.

MacArthur Changes the X Corps Mission

In mid-November 1950, Brig. Gen. Edwin K. Wright, General MacArthur's G-3, Far East Command, sent a personal letter, dated 10 November, to General Almond, stating that General MacArthur wanted the X Corps to do everything it could to help the Eighth Army in the west. Almond

TABLE 2.
Road Mileage from Hungnam to Yudam-ni

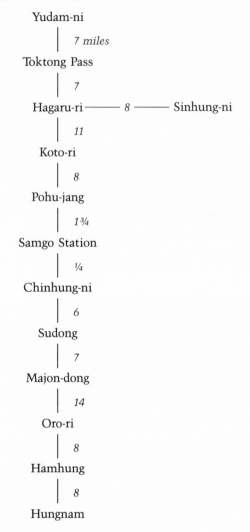

Yudam-ni

| 7 *miles*

Toktong Pass

| 7

Hagaru-ri ——— 8 ——— Sinhung-ni

| 11

Koto-ri

| 8

Pohu-jang

| 1¾

Samgo Station

| ¼

Chinhung-ni

| 6

Sudong

| 7

Majon-dong

| 14

Oro-ri

| 8

Hamhung

| 8

Hungnam

Summary: Hungnam to Chinhung-ni 43 miles
             Chinhung-ni to Hagaru-ri 21
             Hagaru-ri to Yudam-ni <u>14</u>
             TOTAL 78 miles

SOURCE: Compiled from Montross and Canzona, *The Chosin Campaign,* p. 96, and Maps 7–10; X Corps, Chosin Reservoir Special Report, pp. 84ff.; Geer, *The New Breed,* pp. 242–43; Map of Korea, scale 1:250,000, AMS 1, L552, 1950.

replied to this letter on 15 November, saying that he could do this best by continuing the attack north and then west after getting north of the Chosin Reservoir. The Far East Command replied the next day, 16 November, that X Corps should develop a plan to reorient the attack to the border by moving west from Changjin (35 air miles north of the Chosin Reservoir) to cut the Manpojin-Kanggye-Huichon enemy MSR leading south into the Eighth Army zone. This message requested that a plan to do this be sent to General MacArthur when it had been prepared. This message was the first official instruction from the Far East commander in chief since his order of 24 October that the X Corps mission was to attack north to the border.

General Almond's staff drafted an order along the lines indicated by MacArthur's message of 16 November and gave it to Almond for his review the next day. The main feature of the plan was to drive west from Changjin to Kanggye. Almond rejected it on the ground that it would too greatly extend the X Corps MSR. Instead, he directed his staff to modify the plan so that the corps would advance west from Hagaru-ri to Yudam-ni, turning west toward Kanggye from there instead of from Changjin. This advance west from the reservoir would be along the Hagaru-ri–Mupyong-ni axis, as Almond called it. He also directed that the plan include developing the Hamhung–Hagaru-ri road as the MSR, with maximum effort by X Corps troops and engineer units. The US 7th Infantry Division was to supply a force that would proceed north of the Chosin Reservoir to seize Changjin and protect the right flank of the 1st Marine Division, which he considered to be the main force to drive west from Hagaru-ri to Kanggye and Mupyong-ni. Almond thought the two main objectives, Changjin and Mupyong-ni, were too far apart to be under the control of one division (the 1st Marine Division), as the Far East Command initially proposed. He also said the plan should reflect the fact that the extreme minimum temperatures of 30 to 40 degrees below zero from December through March would restrict the operations of both his own troops as well as those of the enemy.

On 21 November a new draft of the plan incorporating the changes he had suggested was presented to Almond. This was known as OPN PLAN No. 8, Draft 2. Almond approved this draft with some modifications. On 23 November he sent his G-3, Lt. Col. John H. Chiles, to Tokyo to present the revised plan, now OPN PLAN No. 8, Draft 3, to the Far East Command. Chiles presented it to General MacArthur and his staff on 24 November. By message that same day to General Almond, General MacArthur directed him to implement the plan, with only one change — that the proposed boundary between Eighth Army and the X Corps be moved farther west and south in the 1st Marine Division zone.

Pursuant to General MacArthur's directive of 24 November, the X

Corps issued Operational Order No. 7 on 25 November. It assigned several missions to the subordinate units of the corps for the forthcoming attack. The X Corps would attack on 27 November with the objective of severing the enemy line of communications at Mupyong-ni and destroying the enemy in that zone north to the Yalu River border and to the mouth of the Tumen River on the east at the Soviet border. The 1st Marine Division was to begin its attack at 8 A.M. on 27 November from the west side of the Chosin Reservoir from Yudam-ni toward Kanggye and Mupyong-ni. The 7th Infantry Division force at the same time was to attack north from the east side of the Chosin Reservoir toward Changjin, and hence on to the Yalu. The ROK I Corps was to advance from the Hapsu and Chongjin areas to the border in the northeastern extremity of Korea. The 3rd Infantry Division was to gain and maintain contact with the Eighth Army along the army-corps boundary and protect the west flank of X Corps, be ready to support the 1st Marine Division on corps order, protect the harbor and airfield facilities in the Wonsan area, and destroy guerrilla forces operating in its zone. This plan for the first time ordered the 7th Infantry Division to provide a regimental combat team to relieve the 5th Marine Regiment on the east side of Chosin Reservoir so that it could join the main Marine force at Yudam-ni for the attack westward.[11]

X Corps in Position for Attack

The X Corps established its headquarters at Hamhung on 11 November, moving there from Wonsan. General Almond was characteristically active throughout November as preparations for major military operations accelerated. He traveled daily from unit to unit and flew over main supply routes to note their condition, the movement of his own troops, and the presence or absence of enemy.

On 24 November his intelligence officer indicated that there were five areas of enemy concentration and activity in the corps area. This estimate placed about 6,000 North Korean troops opposing the ROK Capital Division near Chongjin on the coastal road, major elements of two North Korean infantry regiments and one artillery regiment engaged in delaying actions against the 17th Infantry Regiment near Hyesanjin at the Manchurian border, an unknown number of Chinese troops of the CCF 126th Division near the Fusen Reservoir, remnants of North Korean divisions in the Huksu-ri and Sachang-ni areas west of Hamhung that had withdrawn northward after the collapse of the Naktong River and Seoul operations in the preceding months, and similar North Korean forces in the Yonghung area southwest of Hamhung. It was estimated that, altogether, 10,000 to 13,000 North Korean soldiers were west and southwest of Hamhung.

An estimate of the strength of Chinese forces in the Chosin Reservoir and Fusen Reservoir areas posed a special problem. Their strength was unknown. It was known that the CCF 124th Division had suffered very heavily in the fighting in the Sudong–Chinhung-ni area in the last days of October and the first week of November and had then withdrawn from contact. The 3rd Battalion of the 31st Infantry Regiment, 7th Division, had encountered part of a regiment of the CCF 126th Division east of Fusen Reservoir, and the 7th Marines had captured a few prisoners from the same division in the vicinity of Hagaru-ri. But this CCF division was still largely intact. There was strong indication that these two divisions and the 125th Division, not engaged, between 15 and 20 November were moving southwest out of the Chosin area to join their parent organizations, the XIII Army Group, Fourth Field Army, in front of Eighth Army and would probably appear in the Tokchon area on that army's eastern flank. These three Chinese divisions were in fact being replaced by new Chinese formations in the Chosin Reservoir area, but this movement was not known to American intelligence at the time. A few prisoners from the CCF 89th Division taken in the Chosin area indicated that some new enemy forces had arrived in the area, but American intelligence did not consider their strength to be significant.[12]

As late as 26 November the 1st Marine Division intelligence estimate of enemy strength did not give the Chinese an offensive capability in the Chosin area. This estimate said in part:

> The only reports supporting the probable presence of an unusually large number of enemy in the area originated with the local civilians. Their reports, based on past experience, were usually accurate as to position, but grossly exaggerated as to number. In addition, there was an absence, as of this time, of aggressive enemy patrolling, and a failure of both ground and aerial reconnaissance to reveal the presence of large enemy concentrations. Because the enemy had failed to defend the critical road junction and crucial terrain point of Yudam-ni with any great amount of determination, it was felt that a general weakness in his defensive capability was indicated to the immediate front.[13]

Adding to the confusion of American intelligence was the fact that three different enemy troop formations seemed to be in the X Corps zone, each with its own movements, apparently unrelated to the others. There were many North Korean soldiers moving north from the Huksu-ri area; Chinese from the 42nd Army were moving southwest from the Chosin Reservoir and Yudam-ni areas toward the Eighth Army front; and some new Chinese units were identified in the reservoir area, but of these prior to 27 November only the 89th CCF Division had been identified. In the afternoon of 27 November, units of the CCF 79th Division were identified north of Yudam-ni.[14]

On 24 November X Corps strength totaled 114,313 men, a force far greater numerically than known enemy strength in the X Corps zone. The principal elements of the X Corps strength were in the organizations listed in table 3.

In considering the figures, one must keep in mind that, excluding the attached ROK troops (KATUSA), the 1st Marine Division was equivalent in strength to about three Chinese divisions, and an American Army infantry division was equal to two Chinese divisions. Thus, in the Marine division and the two Army infantry divisions, there would be roughly the equivalent of about seven CCF divisions. But they did not possess the same proportion of frontline combat troops. The average of the Chinese division in the Chosin Reservoir operations was 6,500 to 7,000 men, nearly all of them frontline combat troops. In reckoning the relative combat strength of the two opposing forces, it must be remembered that the Chinese did not have artillery. Their principal supporting weapons were the 81-mm and 60-mm mortars, some 76-mm guns, and a few 122-mm mortars, their biggest caliber weapon. And they had no air support.[15]

FINAL PREPARATIONS FOR THE ATTACK

In the west, Eighth Army had already launched its attack, beginning on the morning of 24 November, intending to reach the Chinese border. The X Corps attack was to start three days later, on 27 November. X Corps staff officers scanned intelligence they received from the Eighth Army on 24–25 November with interest, but without any great apprehension. It was generally expected that Eighth Army would make a slow but steady advance northward. During 24 and 25 November, nothing came over radio communications or by liaison plane until late on the twenty-fifth to unsettle this expectation. Then the X Corps heard about ROK reverses near Tokchon on the army right flank. In the meantime, X Corps continued moving its attack formations to their lines of departure for its part in the general attack northward on the morning of 27 November. General Almond's X Corps issued its Operational Order No. 7 on 25 November for this attack two days later. This order defined major unit responsibility in the attack.

From 23 November on, the 1st Marine Division made hurried moves to concentrate at the reservoir for its part in the attack. By 25 November all three battalions of the 5th Marines were on the east side of the reservoir. But it was planned that they would move to the west side of the reservoir, at Yudam-ni, just as soon as elements of the 7th Infantry Division could relieve them east of the reservoir. On the twenty-fifth, a platoon-sized patrol of the 3rd Battalion, 5th Marines, made contact with Chinese soldiers on the east side of the reservoir near its northern end.

TABLE 3.
X Corps Strength, 24 November 1950

Unit	Strength	Attached ROKs	Total
1st Marine Div.	25,323	110	25,433
3rd Inf. Div.	16,082	6,096	22,178
7th Inf. Div.	16,001	6,794	22,795
1st KMC Regt.	2,378	0	2,378
41st Royal Marines (British)	234	0	234
ROK Capital Div.	11,495	0	11,495
ROK 3rd Div.	11,706	0	11,706
Engineer Special Brigade	1,324	0	1,324
1st Marine Air Wing	1,844	0	1,844
X Corps Combat Troops	3,904	229	4,133
Total	90,291	13,229	103,520[a]

SOURCE: X Corps, WD, 24 Nov 50, POR No. 59, p. 4.
[a]Personnel from X Corps and ROK I Corps headquarters and service troops added about 8,500 more men.

But no large groups were met or sighted. The story of what happened on the east side of the reservoir in the days that followed is covered in chapter 5.

Gen. Oliver Smith held the 7th Marine Regiment at Hagaru-ri until the 1st Marine Regiment had started its concentration on the Hamhung–Hagaru-ri MSR behind the other two Marine regiments. Then, on 23 November he ordered the 7th Marines to begin moving from Hagaru-ri to Yudam-ni. The 1st Battalion led out. A force of possibly 200 Chinese held positions overlooking Toktong Pass, halfway to Yudam-ni. They were scattered by combined infantry attack, air strikes, and artillery barrages. Lt. Col. Raymond G. Davis's reinforced 1st Battalion cleared undefended roadblocks and booby traps from the road and made it passable for other units to follow. On the twenty-fifth, his men captured six Chinese soldiers in the vicinity of Toktong Pass, seven miles west of Hagaru-ri. They said they were from the 267th Regiment of the 89th Division. The 1st Battalion continued on and seized Yudam-ni on 25 November against only minor enemy resistance. The town was deserted and had been almost completely destroyed by US air strikes.[16]

The Far East Command's intelligence estimate of enemy capabilities as of 25 November is of more than passing interest in view of what happened in the next week. Concerning the Eighth Army attack, already under way in the west, the estimate said in part, "Eighth Army is now properly deployed with reserves to contain any enemy attack. This course of action would probably hasten the enemy's destruction." In discussing further the Eighth Army plan of attack, the estimate continued, "Eighth Army has adopted a conservative plan to make a general advance with the main effort in the center generally parallel to the enemy's MSR (Huichon-Kanggye). This course of action is designed to meet any course of action which might be exercised by the enemy." The estimate concluded that "the X Corps plan of action to sever the enemy MSR at Mupyong-ni will greatly assist Eighth Army's planned advance by isolating enemy elements south of a potentially strong defensive position," adding that "a strong enemy reaction to the X Corps thrust toward Mupyong-ni should be expected, unless the enemy intended to withdraw from Korea."[17] This estimate on 25 November probably represents fairly enough the general feeling in Eighth Army, X Corps, and the Far East Command headquarters about prospects in Korea as the UN attack to end the war was getting under way. Apparently no one anticipated a calamity.

On 26 November the 31st Infantry Regiment's headquarters group and its 3rd Battalion, 7th Infantry Division, traveled nearly all day en route to the Chosin Reservoir area, where, on the east side of the reservoir, they expected to join the 1st Battalion, 32nd Infantry, which had arrived there the day before. On this same day the bomber command temporarily suspended attacks on the Manpojin bridges because of heavy antiaircraft fire from the Manchurian side of the Yalu River and concentrated instead on making multiple cuts in the railroad and highway leading southward from Manpojin. In the afternoon of this cold Sunday, the 2nd Battalion, 5th Marines, commanded by Lt. Col. Harold S. Roise, completed its move from the east to the west side of the reservoir, and in the evening it deployed south of Yudam-ni. The rest of the 5th Marines, commanded by Lt. Col. Raymond L. Murray, were moving to join the 2nd Battalion at Yudam-ni.[18]

By 26 November all of the 7th Marine Regiment had moved to Yudam-ni except for the 2nd Battalion headquarters and F Company, which were still at Hagaru-ri. The battalion headquarters was scheduled to reach Yudam-ni the next afternoon, after being relieved in Hagaru-ri by the 3rd Battalion, 1st Marine Regiment. The night of 25–26 November was quiet at Yudam-ni. Col. Homer L. Litzenberg, Jr., commanding the 7th Marines, opened his CP at Yudam-ni on 26 November. During that day the regiment took up positions on commanding ground around the little road-junction village about a mile west of Chosin Reservoir. The 1st Battalion, with D and E companies attached, occupied Hills 1260 and 1167 north of the village. When D Company occupied Hill 1167, it found five civilians who had been shot, their hands tied behind their backs. At dusk D and E companies were in their defensive positions a little more than half a mile north of Yudam-ni. Patrols had encountered enemy groups, and others were observed at a distance. The largest group sighted, about 50 men, was dispersed by an air strike. Other elements of the 7th Marine Regiment advanced about a mile on the road west from Yudam-ni and

Maj. Gen. Oliver P. Smith, commanding general of the 1st Marine Division in north-east Korea, 1950 (portrait made in 1952) (US Marine Corps photograph A88899)

received small-arms fire in the afternoon. This enemy opposition was silenced by an air strike. Aerial reconnaissance reported seven roadblocks, at one-mile intervals, on the road leading west-northwest out of Yudam-ni. This was the intended axis of the Marine attack to Mupyong-ni. The aerial reconnaissance saw no enemy but reported that all houses showed signs of occupancy.[19]

Perhaps the most significant development of the day was the capture of three Chinese prisoners at 4 P.M. about two miles southwest of Yudam-

Lt. Col. Raymond L. Murray, commanding officer of the 5th Marine Regiment in northeast Korea, 1950 (US Marine Corps photograph A-1523)

ni. These three CCF soldiers, carrying leaflets when they surrendered, said they had deserted from the 60th Division, 20th Army, Third Field Army, on 21 November. They said other divisions in the 20th Army were the 58th and 59th divisions. They stated they had crossed the Yalu River at Manpojin on 11 November and had reached Yudam-ni on 20–21 November. Their mission, they alleged, was to move southwest and then south from Yudam-ni and take positions to attack the Marines' MSR after two Marine regiments had passed beyond their positions; this attack was

Col. Homer L. Litzenberg, commanding officer of the 7th Marine Regiment in north-east Korea, 1950 (photographed when holding rank of lieutenant colonel) (US Marine Corps photograph 36033)

to be launched only at night. The march from Yudam-ni had been the 60th, 59th, and 58th divisions, in that order, they said. A civilian from the area where these three soldiers surrendered told a 7th Marine inter-rogator that same day (the twenty-sixth) that he had been forced to act as guide on the night of 23–24 November for an "immense" number of enemy moving southwest from Yudam-ni. This was momentous news. The Marine command did not accept it fully, wanting to make further confirmation. But it was an ominous warning, passed on to General Smith by radio at once.[20]

Col. Lewis B. Puller (*left*), commanding officer of the 1st Marine Regiment, northeast Korea, 1950 (photographed when holding rank of lieutenant colonel) (US Marine Corps photograph 77435)

On 26 November, at the same time the 7th and 5th Marine regiments were concentrating at Yudam-ni, with the bulk of the 11th Marine Artillery Regiment, Col. Lewis B. ("Chesty") Puller established his CP for the 1st Marine Regiment at Koto-ri. The 1st and 2nd battalions, based at Koto-ri and Chinhung-ni, continued to protect the MSR. Lt. Col. Thomas L. Ridge's 3rd Battalion, 1st Marines, less G Company, closed at Hagaru-ri and took up the task of protecting that vital place.

Meanwhile, work on a C-47 airstrip at Hagaru-ri continued. The site for the airstrip had been selected by Maj. Gen. Field Harris, commanding the 1st Marine Air Wing, and General Smith on 16 November. Work began on the strip on 19 November. General Almond insisted that the airfield be completed in the shortest possible time. One of his standard operating procedures was that a C-47 airstrip be built at all important major CPs in a zone of operations for which he was responsible.[21]

General Almond made a wide-ranging flight over X Corps's widely dispersed units on 26 November to get a firsthand impression of the situa-

Aerial view of the eastern side of Chosin Reservoir. The inlet perimeter is around the white, frozen inlet of the Pungnyuri-gang at right center. Hill 1221 is at the lower left. (US Army photograph SC 363267)

tion. He flew first up the coast to Chongjin and noted that the town had been largely destroyed by air strikes and that ROK troops were north of the city. He then turned inland and to the southwest to Kapsan and on to Hyesanjin, finding no evidence of enemy activity there. At Pungsan he saw a C-47 airstrip under construction, as he had also seen at Hyesanjin. Almond then continued on southwest to the Chosin Reservoir. There on the east side of the reservoir he saw the 1st Battalion, 32nd Infantry, deployed along the road and, he thought (mistakenly), engaged with an enemy force. On the west side of the reservoir, he saw some napalm bursts and assumed that the 7th Marines there had encountered enemy. At Hagaru-ri he noted bulldozers and trucks busily engaged in work at the airstrip. He continued his flight down the MSR to Hamhung, seeing several truck convoys on the way.[22]

That Sunday evening, 26 November, both Generals Smith and Almond had ominous news when they returned to their CPs at Hamhung after a busy day with forward units that were scheduled to begin the X Corps attack on the morrow. The news came from the Eighth Army front. At 3 P.M., radio word arrived at the X Corps headquarters, and was passed on to General Smith's 1st Marine Division headquarters, that Chinese forces were attacking all across the Eighth Army front in the west and had forced a ROK II Corps withdrawal in the Tokchon area on the army east, or right, flank. In effect, the Eighth Army appeared stalled in its attack; Chinese forces in front of it had brought it to a standstill before the X Corps in the Chosin Reservoir area could jump off in their attack the next day.[23]

3

JUMP-OFF FROM YUDAM-NI, 27 NOVEMBER

GENERAL ALMOND, US X CORPS COMMANDER

Maj. Gen. Edward Mallory Almond, commanding the US X Corps at the Inchon landing in September and now commanding the same corps and the ROK I Corps in northeast Korea, was a major figure in the Korean War. He was 58 years old when he faced the Chinese onslaught against his X Corps in northeast Korea in November and December 1950. He was promoted to lieutenant general in February 1951 and held that rank when he returned to the United States in July 1951 and became commandant of the Army War College the next month.

General Almond in 1950 and 1951 in Korea had several nicknames. Generally, he was known to his friends and close associates as Ned. Other names were "Ned, the Anointed," which meant he was a favorite of General MacArthur's, and "Ned, the Dread," which referred to his power, brusque manner, and sometimes arbitrary actions. He was nearly always decisive in his actions.

Almond gave unswerving loyalty and dedicated service to his superior, General MacArthur, thereby becoming controversial at times in the orders he issued as X Corps commander and in the relationship between the X Corps and the US Eighth Army in Korea. To most in the Eighth Army, Almond and his X Corps were thought unduly favored at the Far East Command during September–December 1950. Later, this feeling largely disappeared when the X Corps became a part of the Eighth Army—certainly it did among the more objective and observant. General Ridgway commented that he knew of no evidence that MacArthur favored Almond over other elements of the American command in Korea. Ridgway considered Almond a mainstay and a standout among his corps commanders of Eighth Army in 1951, and stated privately several times that Almond was his best corps commander.

The belief that General MacArthur showed favoritism to Almond and the X Corps at the expense of General Walker's Eighth Army was heightened when, after the Inchon landing and the capture of Seoul, MacArthur decided to keep the X Corps separate from Eighth Army. He did not subordinate it to General Walkter in a unified Korean command but sent it to northeast Korea to clear the region of scattered North Korean troops, maintaining it as a command reporting directly to him in Tokyo.

I first met General Almond on 13 December 1951 at the Army War College, Carlisle Barracks, Pennsylvania. That conversation with him lasted an hour and 15 minutes in his large comfortable office. Later that evening the interview extended for another two and one-half hours at his quarters, the large commandant's home at the old military post. Throughout the years since then, I have had numerous meetings with General Almond and have had a rather voluminous correspondence with him on questions relating to the Korean War and interviews on controversial questions relating to the war.

When I first met General Almond in December 1951, I wondered what kind of reception I would have, because I intended to ask questions that I thought he might find objectionable. I survived that danger. Over the years, Almond demonstrated a profound interest in military history. Even in my last meeting with him, when he was 85, I found him keen of mind, incisive, and able to concentrate without a break for five hours, though suffering from a malady that had stricken him—a picture of courage, firmness, and adherence to lifelong ideals of loyalty and patriotism.

His undeviating loyalty to Gen. Douglas MacArthur is a characteristic that one must know and accept to understand Almond's actions in the Korean War. When I brought up the charge that he had obtained supplies for the X Corps in its east-coast landing in October 1950 that should instead have gone to Eighth Army, Almond denied the allegation vehemently and paced the floor, disturbed and angry. He denied any special influence with MacArthur in the matter. To him, the issue was simply one of carrying out MacArthur's orders. The criticism, as he viewed it, I thought, was an attack on General MacArthur. Almond never failed to rise to MacArthur's defense in all matters. In this conversation he said to me at one point that he did "not give his loyalty to a crook—and I will say that to Bradley" (Gen. Omar Bradley, then chairman, Joint Chiefs of Staff). He stuck out his chin with those words and glared at me.

My impression of General Almond on this first meeting, in December 1951, may be worth recording here from notes written that evening: "Hair turning gray, bright blue eyes, ruddy complexion, fairly tight skin over face, several deep horizontal furrows across brow when he frowns, hands rather small—at least not large, nails picked off denoting his excess nervous energy and temperament, medium stature, slightly stooped across shoulders. Obviously positive, energetic, and I would say personally fearless—a fearless fighting man. No doubt impetuous and guilty of mistakes. But he will act."

Almost four decades after that meeting, and on the basis of considerable correspondence and several lengthy interviews with him and many years of study of the Korean War and his role in it, I believed General Almond to have been a man of integrity and courage, an old-fashioned patriot, one who was loyal to his friends, a brave soldier, and probably the best American corps commander in the Korean War. His greatest weakness as a commander in Korea was his conviction that MacArthur could do no wrong. This stance led him to think ill of MacArthur's critics and in turn brought into question his own ability to form independent judgments of enemy intentions and capabilities. This was a view also held even by some of the more devoted and discerning of his own staff in the X Corps operations in northeast Korea and the Chosin Reservoir campaign in late 1950.

Let us pass on from these subjective views to Almond's credentials as a soldier and commander at the time he led X Corps. His whole life and training had been for the Army. Born in Luray, Virginia, on 12 December 1892, he attended grade and high school there and in Culpeper and went on to the Virginia Military Institute, from which he graduated in 1915. The next year he entered the United States Army as a second lieutenant in the First Provisional Class at Fort Leavenworth, and after three months' training there, he was assigned as a second lieutenant with the US 4th Infantry on the Mexican border at Brownsville, Texas. Later he commanded a company in that regiment, and subsequently one in the 58th Infantry. When the 4th Infantry Division was formed at Gettysburg, Pennsylvania, he served in it as a company commander. When it went to Europe during World War I, Almond, now a major, was commander of its 12th Machine Gun Battalion. He served in all its major engagements in the Aisne-Marne and Meuse-Argonne offensives in France. He was wounded in action in August 1918. He held the rank of major, infantry, at the end of the war.

After nearly a year's duty in the army of occupation in Germany, Almond in the next 24 years held a number of varied assignments in the Army, including attendance at just about all the special military service schools in the United States. General Ridgway later described him as one of the best militarily educated soldiers in the US Army in all-around military theory and special military tactical and weapons practices. After World War I he served as professor of military science and tactics at Marion Institute, Alabama; was a student at the Infantry School at Fort Benning, Georgia, for a year, and then an instructor in tactics at the infantry school for four years; and afterward attended the Command and General Staff

School at Fort Leavenworth for two years. Upon completing that course in 1930, he was assigned to the 45th Infantry at Fort William McKinley, Philippine Islands, where he commanded a battalion of Philippine troops for three years. He came back to the United States after this duty and attended the Army War College in 1933–34; served in the military intelligence section of the War Department General Staff for four years; attended the Air Corps Tactical School at Maxwell Field, Alabama, as a ground officer learning the principles of combat aviation; was a student at the Naval War College; and in 1940 was G-3, VI Army Corps, at Providence, Rhode Island, and later became the corps's chief of staff. He held the rank of colonel at that time.

After the United States entered World War II, Almond became assistant division commander of the 93rd Division, and subsequently, in August 1942, the commanding general of the 92nd Infantry Division, a post he held during its training in the United States and in its combat operations in Italy from September 1944 to May 1945, when the war ended there. Almond's command in Italy covered the area of the Ligurian Alps and the coastal area from Pisa and Genoa westward to the French border. At one time he had under his command not only the 92nd Infantry Division but also the famous Japanese-American 442nd Regimental Combat Team from Hawaii and the 473rd Infantry Regiment, several tank and artillery battalions, for a strength of about 24,000 men. With this force he drove up the Ligurian coast to capture Genoa and on to the French border and to the headwaters of the Po River, near Turin. In this campaign, the 442nd Regimental Combat Team, as usual, performed as the principal assault force, with its customary distinction.

At the end of World War II in Europe, General Almond was given command of the 2nd Infantry Division, then assembling from Europe for the purpose of redeploying to the Pacific Theater to assist in ending the war there. But before the 2nd Division and others designated for the purpose could be redeployed, the war with Japan ended. Almond continued to command the 2nd Division in the United States until June 1946, when he and 11 other general officers were transferred to Tokyo. There Almond was assigned as MacArthur's G-1, the personnel officer, for Army matters. After six months in that role, near the end of 1946, he became deputy chief of staff, Far East Command, for Army functions, under MacArthur.

In February 1949, General MacArthur made Almond his chief of staff. He held that important and powerful post until MacArthur, on 12 September 1950, gave him command of X Corps for the Inchon landing. It seems that Almond actually held two posts—commanding general of X Corps and chief of staff, Far East Command. It appears that MacArthur intended to lend Almond temporarily from his permanent post as chief of staff, FEC, to lead the X Corps in what MacArthur apparently believed would be a relatively short campaign that would end the war. Almond would then return to his chief of staff post in Tokyo. Maj. Gen. Doyle O. Hickey, deputy chief of staff, would serve as acting chief of staff for Mac-Arthur during Almond's absence with the X Corps. Almond's dual status caused considerable talk in military circles in the Far East Command, but it was MacArthur's wish that Almond have this status. Almond remained in Korea as commanding general of X Corps until 15 July 1951, when he was rotated back to the United States as commandant of the Army War College. As X Corps commander under Ridgway, he performed outstandingly in command of the east-central front in South Korea.[1]

GENERAL ALMOND AND GENERAL SMITH

The beginning of the story of the tug and pull between Maj. Gen. Edward M. Almond, the X Corps commander, and Maj. Gen. Oliver P. Smith, 1st Marine Division commander, belongs chronologically before 24 November 1950. This aspect of developments is mentioned in *South to the Naktong, North to the Yalu*, and some background is included in chapter 1 above. The beginnings of the Smith-Almond disagreements on the conduct of the war in northeast Korea may be traced to similar differences that began with the Inchon landing and the 1st Marine Division drive on Seoul in September. General Smith wanted to follow Marine doctrine about holding a tight perimeter at Inchon until a strong base of supply had been built up on shore before undertaking a strong push on Seoul. General Almond wanted him to proceed rapidly against Seoul with his Marine division and get there before the North Koreans could strongly reinforce the city after the surprise Inchon landing. And there was also the question of Almond's bringing in the 7th Infantry Division to help in the attack on Seoul when Smith objected to it and thought there was no need for the Army infantry division to enter the city for that purpose.[2]

The major differences of opinion between the two generals in northeast Korea centered on the way the 1st Marine Division should be concentrated and used in the Chosin campaign. Essentially, General Smith resisted a rapid movement of the Marine division toward Chosin in battalion and regimental combat groups, separated from each other, and a subsequent attack northward, without first building up bases of supply along the MSR from Hamhung and Hungnam and concentrating his division units within supporting distances of each other. General Almond wished to carry out General MacArthur's orders for a northward advance as rapidly as possible. The two views necessarily came into conflict.

General Almond's own personal views on the details of these problems, as distinct from General MacArthur's orders, are not easy to discern. It is a matter of record that, when ROK troops of the 26th Regiment, ROK 3rd Division, captured 16 Chinese prisoners from the 370th Regiment, 124th Division, near Sudong, on the road from Hungnam to the Chosin Reservoir on 29 October, and they divulged to General Almond the next day in his personal interrogation of them that three Chinese divisions, the 124th, 125th, and 126th, of the Chinese 42nd Army were in the vicinity of the reservoir and that the 124th Division was approaching Hamhung on the road from the reservoir, Almond considered this news of paramount importance. When he immediately communicated this news to the Far East Command, it seems clear that the command did not take this intelligence of strong Chinese forces in northeast Korea as seriously during the next two weeks as did General Almond. After the 7th Marine Regiment relieved the ROK 26th Regiment in front of the Chinese 124th Division and, in a series of heavy battles, caused the remnants of the Chinese division to withdraw northward toward the reservoir out of contact with the 7th Marines, the Far East Command issued orders that minimized the possibility of strong Chinese opposition to its plan to advance to the border.

Major General Willoughby, MacArthur's G-2 intelligence chief, announced in a meeting at Wonsan early in November to assembled Far East Command and X Corps command staff officers that the Chinese encountered were volunteers and numbered no more than 10,000.[3] It is unknown how much influence Willoughby's views had on General MacArthur, but most officers close to both men at the time thought it was limited — that MacArthur formed his opinions independent of most of his staff officers. In any event, General Almond's initially cautious and apprehensive views on the possibility of massive Chinese intervention seemed to change in the next two weeks, and by the middle of November he adopted MacArthur's view that the advance to the border could probably be carried out without serious enemy interference. This led to frequent disagreements with General Smith, who had the main mission of advancing from the Chosin Reservoir.

On 7 November, after the 7th Marine Regiment had decisively defeated the CCF 124th Division in the vicinity of Sudong and Chinhung-ni, below the Koto-ri plateau, Smith conferred with Almond and repeated his desire to lessen the dispersion of his Marine forces and suggested that, with the Siberian winter approaching for that part of Korea farther north, the advance should be halted for the winter because of the difficulty of operating in extreme cold and of maintaining necessary supplies farther north in an almost roadless area. Almond listened to his proposal that only enough terrain be held for the winter to secure Wonsan, Hamhung, and Hungnam and that they not try to hold positions north of Chinhung-ni. Almond agreed to concentrate the 1st Marine Division, but he felt that it should hold Hagaru-ri on the Koto-ri plateau at the foot of the Chosin Reservoir. He also said he was considering stopping the advance of ROK I Corps on the northeast coast and giving the 7th Infantry Division a smaller zone of action. This conservative view may have surprised Smith. It did show that Almond had been made more cautious by the late October and early November Chinese defeat of Eighth Army units in the west and the X Corps contacts with major Chinese units in the advance from Hamhung to Chinhung-ni.[4]

But after Chinese withdrawal in the west from in front of Eighth Army in the second week of November, and from in front of the 7th Marines on the road to Hagaru-ri at the same time, General MacArthur issued new orders for the X Corps to continue its advance to the Yalu. General Almond was not one to drag his feet on an order from General MacArthur. In the third week of November, therefore, Almond increased his efforts to concentrate troops in the Chosin Reservoir area to carry out MacArthur's orders.

REDEPLOYMENT OF THE 1ST MARINE DIVISION

The 5th Marines completed its move from the east side of the reservoir on 26–27 November, joining the 7th Marines on the west side at Yudam-ni. Thus, General Smith, constantly prodded by General Almond and his X Corps staff, had the 1st Marine Division concentrated at the Chosin Reservoir and along the MSR leading south from it by evening of 27 November. Most of the concentration had been completed by the night of 26 November, as required by General Almond's order, as the Marines were to attack from there westward on the morning of 27 November. Elements of the 2nd Battalion, 7th Marines, remained at Hagaru-ri for security until they were relieved by most of the 3rd Battalion, 1st Marines, at noon the next day, 27 November. Nearly three-fourths of the artillery firepower of the 11th Marine Regiment, the artillery support for the 1st Marine Division, was at Yudam-ni. The 1st Battalion, the 4th Battalion, and Batteries G and I of the 3rd Battalion, 11th Marines, were at Yudam-ni by 27 November, with 48 105-mm howitzers and 18 155-mm howitzers. The 4.2-inch mortars of both the 5th and the 7th Marine regiments were also there, as well as the 75-mm recoilless rifles of the 5th Marine Regiment.

The 1st Marine Regiment was dispersed in three battalion-sized perimeters at Hagaru-ri, Koto-ri, and at Chinhung-ni along the MSR behind the rest of the division. A considerable amount of ammunition and rations had been stockpiled at Hagaru-ri.

The focal point on 26 and 27 November was Yudam-ni. There both Col. Homer L. Litzenberg, commander of the 7th Marines, and Lt. Col.

Raymond L. Murray, commander of the 5th Marines, had their CPs. Disposed in defensive positions on high ground around Yudam-ni were 12 rifle companies of the 5th and 7th Marines. Two battalions of the 5th Marines were in the valley near the village. Two rifle companies, C and F, of the 7th Marines were in isolated hill positions several miles back down the road near Toktong Pass, which lay about halfway between Yudam-ni and Hagaru-ri.[5]

THE MARINE PLAN OF ATTACK

The 1st Marine Division received a X Corps order on 24 November that oriented its axis of attack from Yudam-ni westward instead of northward. The same order directed that the C-47 airstrip being built at Hagaru-ri be completed by 1 December. The 1st Marine Division's plan for beginning its attack west from Yudam-ni on the morning of 27 November called for the 5th Marine Regiment to pass through the lines of the 7th Marines and lead the attack all the way to Mupyong-ni. There the 1st Marine Regiment would pass through the 5th Marines, take the road to the north and continue the advance to the Yalu River. The 7th Marine Regiment meanwhile would cover the rear of the 5th Regiment all the way back to the Chosin Reservoir. Other elements of the X Corps during this time would move up and take over security of the MSR from the reservoir back to Hungnam.[6]

MARINES ATTACK FROM YUDAM-NI

Upon arriving at Yudam-ni during the afternoon and evening of 26 November, Lt. Col. Harold S. Roise deployed his 2nd Battalion, 5th Marines, south of Yudam-ni, and then made a reconnaissance in preparation for beginning the attack the next morning. The next morning at 8:30 A.M., 27 November, the 2nd Battalion passed through the lines of the 7th Marines two and one-half miles west of Yudam-ni and started its attack westward. It met increasing enemy resistance, some of it heavy, and by evening had gained less than a mile. The battalion consolidated its position for the night on high ground astride the road, with two companies on the slopes of Northwest Ridge, and one company south of the road on Southwest Ridge. In the meantime, the 3rd Battalion, 5th Marines, arrived at Yudam-ni at 2 P.M. from the east side of the reservoir and went into an assembly area behind the 2nd Battalion. The 1st Battalion of the regiment also had arrived at Yudam-ni. All three battalions of the 5th Marines were now at Yudam-ni. During 27 November elements of the 7th Marines engaged an unknown number of enemy south and southwest of Yudam-ni.[7]

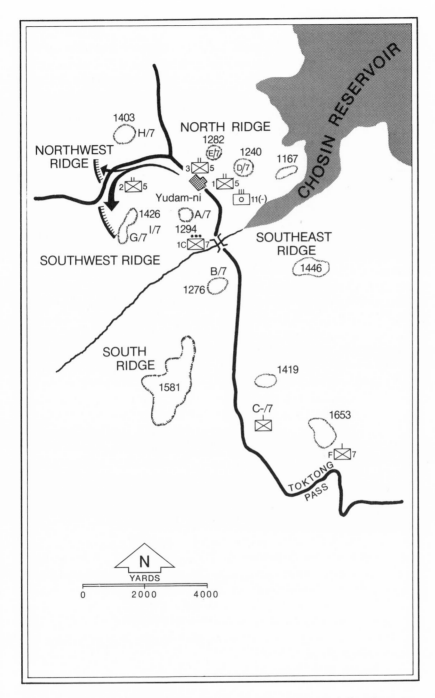

MAP 6. 2nd Battalion, 5th Marines, attack west from Yudam-ni, with the 7th Marines holding high ground, 27 November.

The badly battered village of Yudam-ni lay in flat ground near the water's edge at the west side of Chosin Reservoir. It was a road hub in this mountain country. Three dirt roads ran north, west, and south-southwest from it. A fourth road, little more than a track, branched off the southern road to the southeast in a valley about two miles south of Yudam-ni. Five high mountain ridges rose from the Yudam-ni plain and dominated it on all sides. The Marines named these ridges in relation to their direction from the valley and village. Counterclockwise they were North, Northwest, Southwest, South, and Southeast ridges. The finger of Chosin Reservoir that came nearly to Yudam-ni lay between North and Southeast ridges. On the crests and slopes of these five ridges, the heavy battles of the first and second nights, 27–28 November, were fought.

The road running west from Yudam-ni was the axis of the 5th Marines attack. After leaving Yudam-ni, this road passed between Northwest and Southwest ridges. The 7th Marines were disposed in a perimeter around Yudam-ni, occupying the terminal hills of four of the five ridges. Only Northwest Ridge was not held by the 7th Marines on 26 November. It was occupied on 27 November. The 2nd Battalion, 5th Marines, held defensive positions on its southern slope at the end of its first day's advance, and H Company, 7th Marines, had seized its crest, Hill 1403, during the day.

While the Marine attack was getting under way west of Yudam-ni, Colonel Litzenberg ordered Capt. William E. Barber, commanding F Company, 7th Marines, to take his company from Hagaru-ri to Toktong Pass and protect that vital spot on the MSR. Captain Barber left Hagaru-ri at 11:30 A.M. on 27 November, with F Company reinforced by a heavy machine-gun section and an 81-mm mortar section from the Weapons company. There were 240 men in his reinforced company. Barber had already reconnoitered the Toktong Pass area, and when he arrived there in the afternoon, he posted his company in a perimeter on an isolated hill just north of the road at the pass. Toktong Peak, Hill 1653, with an elevation of 5,370 feet, was to the northwest of Barber's position. F Company's perimeter was six miles from supporting artillery at the edge of Hagaru-ri, extreme range for 105-mm howitzers. Barber's company was dug in by 9 P.M. It had met no opposition. Already in position about two miles closer to Yudam-ni, about a mile north of a village called Chinhung-ni at the northern foot of Toktong Pass, C Company, 7th Marines, far weaker than F Company, was also isolated from the main Marine positions at Yudam-ni.[8]

General Smith wanted tanks at Yudam-ni to help the Marines in their attack to the west, and for that purpose he ordered the Provisional Tank Platoon to join the 7th and 5th Marines at Yudam-ni. Four Sherman tanks (M-4) made the first effort, but four miles west of Hagaru-ri all of them slid off the ice-coated road, one of them throwing a track. Three regained the road and returned to Hagaru-ri. First Lt. Richard Primrose in the meantime had arrived at Hagaru-ri with a platoon of heavier Pershing (M-26) tanks. He thought they might make it over the road, and to test the possibility he started out with one tank, dismounting all the crew except the driver, Sgt. Clyde Kidd. Primrose stood in the turret. Weaving its way slowly through heavy truck traffic, and moving carefully over the snow and ice in Toktong Pass, the big tank reached the top and began a careful descent. It made it into the Yudam-ni perimeter. Then Primrose and Kidd returned to Hagaru-ri in a helicopter to prepare for bringing the rest of the platoon to Yudam-ni the next morning.

That night Chinese soldiers cut the road between Yudam-ni and Hagaru-ri. No other tanks ever got to Yudam-ni. This one tank, No. D-23, eventually achieved a unique kind of fame. Colonel Litzenberg, informed of the stranded tank without a crew, radioed a request that a crew be brought in by helicopter to operate it. S. Sgt. Russell Munsell and a crew from C Company of the tank battalion volunteered for the job. They flew into Yudam-ni in the midst of the battle there and fought with the tank from then on until they led the advance in the fighting retreat from Yudam-ni.[9]

GENERAL ALMOND DRIVES TO YUDAM-NI

On 27 November General Almond left his CP at Hamhung and drove by jeep with Lieutenant Colonel Waters, Marine liaison officer, and his senior aide, Major Ladd, to Colonel Litzenberg's CP at Yudam-ni. Almond found the road jammed with truck convoys moving supplies into Hagaru-ri and Yudam-ni. The weather on the plateau around the Chosin Reservoir was bitterly cold, reaching 25 degrees below zero that night. Almond learned that the 7th Marines had made strong contact during the day with Chinese forces on almost all points of the compass around Yudam-ni and that the 5th Marines in their attack had made only small gains. Almond left Yudam-ni at 4:50 P.M. as dark was settling, and his party returned to Hamhung, arriving there at 9:30 P.M. He noted in his diary for the day that truck drivers were not practicing convoy discipline. If he had made a postdated entry, he could have noted that he got out of Yudam-ni and passed southward over the road just in time, as Chinese troops cut the Yudam-ni road southward as far as Chinhung-ni at half a dozen places soon after he passed over it.

The last group of vehicles to make it out of Yudam-ni southbound that night was a long train led by Lt. Col. Olin Beall, commanding officer of the Marine 1st Motor Transport Battalion. He had taken the truck convoy loaded with supplies into Yudam-ni during the day. Late in the evening he started the convoy back to Hagaru-ri, with many wounded in the trucks. His trucks were just ahead of the Chinese troops that cut the road between Yudam-ni and Hagaru-ri after dark.[10]

MARINE ATTACK STALLS

The results of the first day's attack west from Yudam-ni revealed certain definite facts as night settled over the forbidding landscape. While the 2nd Battalion, 5th Marines, had attacked west along the main attack axis, the 7th Marines had moved to higher ground on the hills around Yudam-ni, particularly the northwest and southwest, to protect the advance of the 5th Marines. In some cases they seized terminal peaks without opposition. In other cases they ran into a storm of enemy gunfire, mostly from heavy machine guns and mortars. Perhaps the greatest opposition during the day came from the high ground of Southwest Ridge, where by nightfall enemy soldiers had stopped three Marine battalions, two from the 7th Marines and elements of the 2nd Battalion, 5th Marines.

On Northwest Ridge, H Company of the 7th Marines seized terminal Hill 1403 unopposed. A patrol from D Company, 7th Marines, moved across North Ridge and ran into heavy machine-gun and mortar fire as it advanced north along the bank of the reservoir, about two and one-half miles from Yudam-ni. An air strike covered the patrol's withdrawal.

On 26 and 27 November, 7th Marine patrols in platoon and company strength responded to Korean civilian reports that large numbers of Chinese soldiers were in the vicinity of Hansang-ni, five miles southwest of Yudam-ni. Patrols moved into the hills bordering the valley of the Kuumni River and found the reports correct. In the vicinity of Hansang-ni strong Chinese forces met them and drove the patrols back with losses. It was apparent, therefore, as dusk settled over Yudam-ni on the evening of 27 November, that strong enemy forces completely surrounded the 5th and 7th Marine positions.[11] Fortunately, most of the artillery of the 11th Marines had arrived at Yudam-ni by evening of the twenty-seventh and had been emplaced in firing positions in the flat ground between the village and the reservoir, generally southeast of the village and east of the MSR leading back to Hagaru-ri.

Not known then by X Corps, but from information developed later from captured enemy documents and prisoner interrogations, the Chinese 20th Army and part of the 27th Army had clearly surrounded Yudam-ni in accordance with the CCF IX Army Group's plan to destroy the 1st Marine Division and possibly the bulk of the X Corps. The CCF 89th Division had led the advance of the 20th Army from the west and had the initial mission of relieving the Chinese 42nd Army at the reservoir and of blocking Marine advance beyond Yudam-ni. At least some elements

The 5th Marine Regimental area at Yudam-ni on 29 November 1950. The frozen bodies of Chinese killed in the previous night's battle are clad in white camouflage uniforms. (US Marine Corps photograph A-4839)

of the division were in the vicinity of Yudam-ni by 15 November. The entire division and the other three divisions of the Chinese 20th Army—the 58th, 59th, and 60th—were there by 22 November. The 89th Division had constructed many roadblocks between Hagaru-ri and Yudam-ni and on the road immediately west of Yudam-ni. The Marines had made minor contacts with small elements of this division between Hagaru-ri and Yudam-ni in their advance to the latter place.

On arrival the 59th Division had gone into hiding to the southwest of Yudam-ni, mostly in the villages and caves in the high ground bordering the Kuumni River. The 89th Division was west and northwest of Yudam-ni, also in hiding. The 58th Division on the night of 27 November was farther south, in the vicinity of Samdaepyong, about 15 miles southwest of Hagaru-ri. The CCF 60th Division was in the hills west of the road between Hagaru-ri and Koto-ri. On the night of the twenty-seventh, it moved eastward into positions and cut that road the next day, attacking any troops or convoys trying to reach Hagaru-ri from the south.

The Chinese 79th Division from the 27th Army attacked Yudam-ni from the north on the night of the twenty-seventh, carrying out the most persistent and vicious of all enemy attacks that night. Its sister division, the 80th, at the same time attacked the US Army's 7th Division elements on the east side of the reservoir.

Three CCF Divisions, therefore, made the attack on the 5th, 7th, and 11th Marines at Yudam-ni on the night of 27–28 November. While the Chinese resisted the efforts of the 5th Marines to advance during daytime on the twenty-seventh and opposed efforts of the 7th Marines to seize certain commanding ground southwest of Yudam-ni, it was not until later, about 10:30 P.M., that they launched their coordinated attack at the Yudam-ni perimeter.[12]

The Chinese achieved surprise in massing their divisions around Yudam-ni and in keeping them undiscovered, except for the few small parties that in themselves gave no indication of the enemy strength in the region. This surprise was as great to the X Corps and the 1st Marine Division as it had been to Eighth Army in the west when it encountered the Chinese formations that had massed in the hills along the valley of the Chongchon and the mountains surrounding Tokchon. The Chinese offensive of late November, now in full swing against both Eighth Army and X Corps, was an achievement of the first order in secret movement and tactical surprise. The Chinese seemed to have accomplished what Frederick the Great advocated when he said that, if his nightcap knew what was in his mind, he would throw it into the fire.

4

BATTLE OF YUDAM-NI, 27–28 NOVEMBER

Events at Yudam-ni on 27 November did not bode well for the Marines scattered about on the hilltops and valleys around the battered little village. What would the night bring? No one knew. But most feared it would be a frigid nightmare.

Late in the afternoon, a patrol of the 7th Marines ran into enemy on the far side of North Ridge. It killed a Chinese captain, on whose body the patrol found documents identifying him as being from the CCF 79th Division, a new and previously unidentified Chinese formation. He had instruments and maps with him that showed he had been surveying for artillery and mortar registrations. This was bad news.

Already, the 2nd Battalion, 5th Marines, had been stopped in its tracks only a mile beyond its jump-off point leading westward. Had the Chinese command been flexible and perceptive, it would have allowed the battalion to go on at least two or three miles farther. Then, after darkness, Chinese soldiers could have closed around and behind it. The 2nd Battalion would have been hopelessly cut off from effective help. Better still for General Sung's objective, had the Chinese along the western road allowed the remainder of the 5th Marine Regiment to move out in trace behind the 2nd Battalion and delayed their own prepared assault one more day, they could have isolated the entire regiment. Both the 5th and 7th Marines would then have been isolated from each other and probably beyond mutual effective help.

But the Chinese did not do this. They held to their previously conceived plan and their prepared positions just west of Yudam-ni. Their plan called for them to attack as soon as two Marine regiments reached or passed beyond Yudam-ni. In their adherence to this plan lay the salvation of the 1st Marine Division. The Chinese attack came when the two Marine regiments and most of the 1st Marine divisional artillery, the 11th Marines, were concentrated in a defensible perimeter at Yudam-ni.

The Marine Positions at Yudam-ni

When the relative quiet of dusk settled on 27 November over the mountains and valleys, the Marines held the following positions. The 5th Marines had one battalion in defensive positions west of Yudam-ni, and two battalions at the west and north edges of the village, basically in reserve. The 7th Marine Regiment was in defensive positions from northwest of Yudam-ni in an arc to the east and south of the village. The high ground around Yudam-ni was posted as follows:

> *North Ridge.* This massive formation of high mountains was the closest to Yudam-ni of the series of ridges that surround the crossroads village. Two companies of the 2nd Battalion, 7th Marines, were on the high ground north of the village — E Company on Hill 1282 and D Company on Hill 1240, nearly 1,000 yards southeast of Hill 1282.
>
> *Northwest Ridge.* H Company of the 7th Marines was on Hill 1403, about one and one-half miles northwest of Yudam-ni. E and F companies of the 2nd Battalion, 5th Marines, were north of the west road in positions they had taken for the night when their attack stalled in the afternoon. Across the road on the south side, and nearly opposite E and F companies, D Company had taken a defensive position for the night.
>
> *Southwest Ridge.* G and I companies, 7th Marines, were on Hill 1426, with I Company on the crest, 1,200 feet above the valley floor and one and one-half air miles from the village. A Company, 7th Marines, was on Hill 1294, an eastern knob of the same hill mass, but only one-half mile from the village and directly overlooking the Yudam-ni valley and the MSR that came north from Hagaru-ri and Toktong Pass.
>
> *South Ridge.* B Company, 1st Battalion, 7th Marines, held Hill 1276, one and one-half miles south of Hill 1294 and A Company, and it too was on the west side of the MSR, directly overlooking it.
>
> *Southeast Ridge.* This ridge, Hill 1446, was undefended close to the village; but four miles south on the east side of the MSR, C Company, 7th Marines, had that afternoon (27 November) taken a position on a spur ridge that came down close to the road. C Company was understrength, with only two rifle platoons and a section of 60-mm mortars. Higher ground to the east and Hill 1419 overlooked its position. Two miles southeast of C Company was another isolated rifle company, F Company of the 7th Marines. It had arrived there that afternoon, taking a defensive position on the east (or, more accurately, the north) side of the MSR near its highest point, where it twisted through Toktong Pass. The two companies were separated from each other by mountainous country. Both were vulnerable to enemy attack.

In the valley floor at Yudam-ni, Colonel Litzenberg had his 7th Marine CP near the center of the village. Lieutenant Colonel Murray's 5th Regimental CP was on the western edge of Yudam-ni. The 3rd and 1st battalions, 5th Marines, had arrived at Yudam-ni only that afternoon, the

1st Battalion after dark. Both battalions had gone into assembly areas on the northeast and northwest edges of Yudam-ni. In effect, they were at the base of North Ridge, behind D and E companies, 7th Marines, and a strong reserve against any attack from the north. The bulk of the 11th Marines' artillery had taken firing positions in the flat, frozen valley floor, southeast of Yudam-ni. Some of the guns were near the western arm of Chosin Reservoir, which jutted into the flat land at this point. Altogether, there were ten rifle companies of the 5th and 7th Marines on high ground around the village. Two companies of the 7th Marines were isolated four and six miles as the crow flies south of Yudam-ni, and the artillery and heavy mortars were concentrated in good firing positions at Yudam-ni.[1]

THE CCF NIGHT ATTACK

The winter sun sank early over the mountains in the west on 27 November at Yudam-ni. At 6:30 it was already night, and gradually the temperature sank to 20 degrees below zero on the hills. As the cold night settled down over North Ridge, men there who had scraped and tried to dig in through the frozen ground with their wholly inadequate entrenching tools had an omen of what was to come. Borne on a stiff northern wind came the faint sound of bugles and horns—Chinese signals and communications. Through enemy intelligence learned later, it appeared that General Sung, the Chinese commander, had established his headquarters for the impending battles on towering Paemyangangji-san, about ten miles northeast of Yudam-ni, on the road that ran northward and then eastward through the mountains on the west side of the reservoir. Down that track came the CCF 79th Division of the 27th Army in a direct attack on Yudam-ni. It brought them over North Ridge. The fiercest close-in fighting between Marines and Chinese on the entire Yudam-ni perimeter took place there.

The other CCF assault division that attacked Yudam-ni that night was the 89th, which attacked from the west and northwest. It was the reinforcement division from the 30th Army attached to the 20th Army for the Chosin operation. Thus, two CCF divisions made the frontal attack on the Marines at Yudam-ni on the night of 27–28 November. This attack was intended to begin the destruction of the 1st Marine Division.

The moon rose at 6:10, four days past full. A misty overcast obscured its light. The two rifle companies of the 7th Marines on North Ridge, E Company on Hill 1282 and D Company on Hill 1240, did not occupy the highest ground of the ridge, but the highest knobs of the ridge close to Yudam-ni. Hill 1384 rose still higher to the north half a mile back of Hill 1282. There were other high hills in this massive ridge, but Hills 1282 and 1240 were considered the two most important for the defense

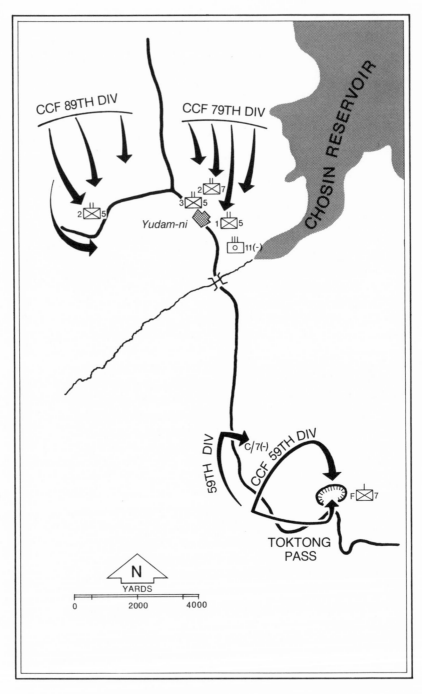

MAP 7. CCF 79th, 89th, and 59th divisions attack Yudam-ni, night of 27 November through 29 November.

of the Yudam-ni perimeter from that direction. Flares had been set out in front of the perimeter on North Ridge. In the valley below, the heavy mortars and artillery had registered to fire in front of the infantry positions on the hills, and in the gaps between units. The perimeter was too large to permit physical contact all around between units; it was in the shape of a large oval approximately ten miles in circumference, and about three miles in diameter north-south and four miles east-west.

The Chinese 79th Division plan to capture North Ridge had its three regiments attack three peaks it considered critical, a regiment to a peak. The Chinese seem to have expected all the peaks to be occupied. The 237th Regiment was to hit the towering peak of Hill 1384, the 235th Regiment was to attack Hill 1240, and the 236th Regiment was to take Hill 1167. These peaks formed an arc running southeast from Hill 1384, farthest north, to Hill 1167, which overlooked the reservoir, east of Yudam-ni. This series of hills lay northeast of Yudam-ni. Hill 1240, the middle hill, was closest to Yudam-ni. It was the only hill of the three that Marine troops occupied. This situation shows clearly that the Chinese had formed their plan on their own judgment of what the critical terrain of North Ridge was and that they had not reconnoitered the land carefully in the past day, because the Marines had occupied the two isolated hills 1282 and 1240 only that day. It is apparent, therefore, that the Chinese had not had time for their usual reconnaissance of the Marine positions before they attacked. Hill 1282 was not in the Chinese attack plan.

The 1st Battalion of the CCF 235th Regiment assigned its 1st and Special Duty companies to take Hill 1240. But in its approach march the battalion veered from its course and mistakenly reached Hill 1282, held by E Company, 7th Marines. The 3rd Battalion of the CCF 236th Regiment, assigned to attack Hill 1167, based its approach march on the course of the 1st Battalion, 235th Regiment, and accordingly missed its target also, ending up in front of Hill 1240, occupied by D Company, 7th Marines. Thus, when the Chinese attack began at 10 P.M. on Hill 1282, they thought they were on Hill 1240. The confusion of the Chinese 235th Regiment's approach march delayed the 236th Regiment, so that it was not ready to start its attack on Hill 1240 until nearly two hours later, all the time thinking it was on Hill 1167. This information comes from captured CCF prisoners and documents. The Marines were ignorant of the Chinese confusion at the time.[2]

The Chinese attack against Capt. W. D. Phillips's E Company on Hill 1240 began in typical Chinese manner—small fire teams probed for the positions and especially for boundaries between units. Once they had located these, the Chinese formed for assault. Captain Phillips cautioned his men to hold their fire and not to set off the flares in front of their positions until the Chinese were almost on them. As the enemy attack formations climbed the hill, bugles, horns, and whistles blared and a strange Chinese chant reached the ears of the fascinated but nearly frozen Marines. At first, Marine 81-mm mortar illuminating shells, requested to light up the scene, were denied. When flares set out in front of E Company were set off as the sound of shuffling feet grew louder, an awe-inspiring and chilling sight flashed into view. A line of Chinese skirmishers was caught full in the glow, 15 yards behind it was a second line, and behind the second, a third line. And beyond, still more shadowy forms could be seen advancing. When the trip flares were pulled, the previous silence, save for the feet shuffling or padding in the snow, gave way to a bedlam of bugles, shepherd horns, and whistles as these sent forth their orders and signals.

Marine 81-mm and 60-mm mortar shells rained down on the Chinese soldiers, and the heavy and light machine guns, Browning Automatic Rifles (BARs), rifles, and grenades all joined to form a curtain of steel fragments and lead bullets—a curtain of death. The Chinese loss in this sudden holocaust was very great. Chinese bugles called an end to the assault. The quilted uniformed figures that survived scurried back down the hill. The dead and wounded lay about on the snow, now illuminated by 81-mm mortar shells that burst overhead. Some dead lay within ten feet of Marine positions. Silence prevailed on the hill.

Losses were not all on the Chinese side. The enemy grenadiers and tommy gunners had worked much havoc among the Marine defenders in the sudden, sharp encounter. Soon the Chinese came back in another attack that was worse than the first, and this fight continued until 2 A.M. in the morning of 28 November. The Chinese came on, fire team after fire team, in squad or greater strength, and if one group was cut down, another was close behind to replace it.

A common trait of almost all Chinese attacks, not then fully understood by American troops, was to concentrate at a given point and to keep hitting that same spot until it was demolished and a penetration made. Then other troops would go through the penetration and, from flank or rear positions, place devastating small-arms fire and grenade attacks on nearby positions. The attack on E Company now was of this kind, and it was a fierce, classic demonstration of its kind. The Chinese achieved a penetration. Captain Phillips grabbed a rifle, stabbed the bayonet end into the snow, and shouted, "We hold here!" The words had hardly passed his lips when small-arms fire hit him, and he fell dead. Command passed to 1st Lt. Raymond O. Ball, already twice wounded. From a sitting position he gave orders and continued to fire his rifle, but he was soon hit several more times, collapsed, and died at an aid station. By 3 A.M. the Chinese 1st and Special Duty companies had been annihilated on Hill 1282.

The Chinese battalion commander on the scene then committed his 3rd Company to finish off E Company, which was now much reduced in strength. The Chinese fire teams approached in squad size, from eight to ten men at a time, and struck the top repeatedly. But the desperate situation of E Company was known in the valley below, and 2nd Lt. Nicholas M. Trapnell led the 1st Platoon of A Company, 5th Marines, up the hill. He found the remnants of E Company just below the crest. All the company officers had been killed or wounded. Few able-bodied men were left. First Lt. Robert E. Snyder now arrived with the 3rd Platoon of A Company, 5th Marines. These two reinforcements enabled the Marines to hold on the reverse slope below the crest. The night battle had by now reduced E Company to platoon strength. At 5 A.M., the Chinese 3rd Company held the crest. In the night battle for Hill 1282, the Chinese had lost about 250 men in casualties; the Marines had lost about 150.[3]

Capt. Jack R. Jones, commanding C Company, 5th Marines, led his company, less one platoon that had already gone as reinforcements to Hill 1240, up Hill 1282 to help E Company and the two platoons of A Company already there. It was a two-hour climb in the predawn darkness. On the way up they passed wounded and cold-numbed men coming down. At 4:30 A.M., Jones reached about 20 E Company survivors 100 yards below the crest of Hill 1282. They told him the situation. Jones arranged for a counterattack, but first he called on the 81-mm mortars in the valley below to place a barrage on the summit.

Just after daylight Jones led the two platoons with him in a counterattack against about 50 Chinese soldiers of the 3rd Company, who, armed with machine guns and grenades, held the crest. Jones's men surged forward through a hail of machine-gun fire and bursting grenades to clash hand-to-hand with the Chinese. The 2nd Platoon of A Company then arrived on the scene and filled a gap to shut off enemy reinforcements. Enemy reports obtained later said that only six or seven men of the 3rd Company survived that fight. The 2nd Company of the Chinese battalion was now committed to regain the crest, but it was decimated in its effort. The soldiers of this company fought almost to the last man, charging again and again, even though only three or four men were left in a squad. Finally, the 1st Battalion, 235th Regiment, committed its last reserve squad of its last platoon. The 2nd Company lost 94 of its 116 officers and men. This, together with the virtual annihilation of the 1st and 3rd companies and the Special Duty Company, brought the 1st Battalion's losses to about 400 men, including virtually all the company commanders, platoon leaders, and noncommissioned officers. Most of the wounded Chinese on Hill 1282 that night could not be evacuated and froze to death.

At midmorning, 28 November, remnants of E Company, 7th Marines, and A and C companies, 5th Marines, controlled Hill 1282. C and A companies, 5th Marines, had won and held the peak in the final battles. They lost 15 killed and 67 wounded. E Company, 7th Marines, originally defending the hill at the beginning of the night battle, had made an incredible stand. It lost about 120 men killed and wounded.[4] The Marines altogether lost nearly 200 casualties during the night of 27–28 November in holding Hill 1282 north of Yudam-ni. Members of Headquarters Company, 1st Battalion, 5th Marines, spent the entire morning bringing wounded down from the slopes and crest of the hill to battalion and regimental aid stations. Captain Jones directed the evacuation at the crest. Several times he ran down the forward slope of Hill 1282 to drag back wounded and immobilized and freezing Marines in the face of enemy fire. Enemy soldiers still held positions on the northern slope of the hill and fired at anyone seen on the crest and within their view. This fight continued throughout the day. At 4 P.M. in the afternoon of the 28th, Captain Phillips's E Company was relieved and left the hill.

NORTH RIDGE, HILL 1240

Things had not gone as well on neighboring Hill 1240, a little more than a half mile to the southeast. To begin with, Capt. Milton A. Hull had difficulty withdrawing D Company, 7th Marines, to the hill under heavy enemy pressure when he ventured northward to the reservoir in the afternoon. He had 16 casualties then from Chinese fire and escaped to Hill 1240 only under the cover of very heavy air attacks on the CCF.

The CCF attack on Hill 1240 that night started later than on Hill 1282. Just before midnight Chinese made their first probing infiltration against D Company on Hill 1240. The 3rd Battalion of the 236th Regiment made the initial attack on the hill. Some of the Chinese probing teams soon found the gap between D Company on Hill 1240 and E Company on Hill 1282. Soon many enemy soldiers passed over this saddle and were in a rear position to fire on the 5th and 7th Marine regimental headquarters areas in Yudam-ni. A few minutes after 1 A.M., 28 November, the Chinese assault formations of the 3rd Battalion hurled a furious attack against D Company on Hill 1240. They overran the platoon holding the northwest end of the position by 2:30 A.M., and half an hour later the Chinese overran the weapons platoon CP. Survivors of D Company withdrew about halfway down the hill, reduced to remnants in the unrelenting Chinese close attack. Hull nevertheless organized a counterattack, surprised the Chinese, and recaptured the crest. Hull by now had a grenade slash on his forehead and a rifle bullet in the shoulder. At dawn he and his 16 men still able to fight held only a precarious toehold on a spur of the crest.

At 4 A.M. on the twenty-eighth, 2nd Lt. Harold L. Dawe went to Hull's aid, starting from the valley with the 3rd Platoon of C Company, 5th Marines. He and his small force were heavily engaged, however, on the lower slopes of the hill by enemy, and he had a hard time fighting his way slowly up the hill. He eventually joined with Hull and his 16 survivors. Before noon a strong enemy counterattack drove them from their positions. Enemy fire then pinned them down until B Company, 5th Marines, came up the hill and relieved them at 5 P.M. Hull lost virtually all of D Company, 7th Marines, and Dawe lost about half his platoon in fighting for Hill 1240.[5]

NORTHWEST RIDGE, HILL 1403

Northwest Ridge was separated from North Ridge by the road that ran north from Yudam-ni through a saddle along the west side of Chosin Reservoir. Marines of H Company, 7th Marines, on top of Hill 1403, Northwest Ridge, and of E and F companies, 5th Marines, on the lower slopes of Hill 1403 near the road that ran west from Yudam-ni, grew colder and their weapons less servicable as the frigid night descended and the temperature reached 20 degrees below zero. While they waited in their shallow foxholes, some of them dug with Chinese picks and shovels captured earlier, since their own entrenching tools were all but useless in the frozen ground.

Chinese soldiers of the 266th and 267th regiments of the 89th Division were on the move. They had left their assembly areas several miles distant and were padding forward through the snow toward the Marine positions on Northwest Ridge. The bulk of the 89th Division coming from the west was to join the 79th Division coming from the north in making what General Sung thought would be the decisive assault on the Marine force at Yudam-ni. Already a third division, the CCF 59th Division, was in position farther south to cut the road from Yudam-ni to Hagaru-ri as soon as the frontal attack began.

The 89th Division assault troops were in position to attack Northwest Ridge earlier than were those of the 79th Division to attack North Ridge to the east. The night battle therefore began earliest on Northwest Ridge. There the Chinese troops had approached undetected to within a few hundred yards of Marine positions by 9 P.M. To divert attention, a Chinese patrol had struck at the Marine roadblock on the road at the foot of the ridge. A few Chinese probed F Company's lines on the lower spur close to the road. Others probed for the boundary between F and E companies, higher up the slope. They found it. Chinese grenadiers and submachine gunners crawled close to the Marine positions. Suddenly bugle-call signals blared into the night. The attack was on. Enemy machine guns opened up all along the ridge, it seemed, and mortar shells fell on the Marine positions. Grenades started falling among the men.

After some minutes of this opening din, all enemy weapons fell silent, except the mortars, which lifted their fire to fall back of the Marine front line. Whistles blew at the same time, and enemy assault teams rose out of the white, shadowy night to hit the boundary area between E and F companies, 5th Marines. It was 9:25 P.M. The Chinese fire teams attacked on a narrow front. They advanced in column until within grenade range and then quickly deployed as skirmishers, coming in close to heave their grenades, without regard to personnel loss. Marine machine gunners up and down the line covered the assault point and piled up Chinese dead. But soon Chinese soldiers penetrated between E and F companies, and many more enemy waiting behind hurried into and through the gap. Their next move was to try to roll up the flanks of the two companies from the gap and from the rear. The right-hand platoon of Capt. Uel D. Peters's F Company was overrun. Across a draw from the overrun platoon, Capt. Samuel Jaskilka's E Company was in its defense position northeast of the penetration. Jaskilka immediately sent a machine-gun section and a squad of riflemen to reinforce his 1st Platoon at the edge of the penetration. Second Lt. Jack L. Nolan commanded the 1st Platoon, and when the reinforcement arrived, he bent that flank back and turned back a line of men along it at the edge of the penetration. Marine mortar fire tried to close the gap. But Chinese were now in the rear of F Company and might soon be in position to attack the 2nd Battalion, 5th Marines, CP and the supporting weapons positions. Fortunately, mortar, machine-gun, and rifle fire cut down most of the Chinese who passed through the gap. Those who got through to positions in the rear were killed there.

Fifteen minutes after the battle had flared with such sudden violence, the 2nd Platoon of E Company turned its machine guns on a hut that stood about 200 yards away up the draw. Enemy might seek protection there. When the machine-gun fire hit the hut, the straw-thatched roof burst into flames. This illuminated the surrounding area brightly and revealed an amazing sight. The draw and its closed-in slopes were alive with enemy troops. Machine guns and every other weapon at hand that could fire were turned at once on these men. They turned out to be the main enemy force forming for attack to overrun E and F companies and to clear the way to reach the road below. In the next hour of battle this Chinese force was annihilated.[6]

Almost simultaneously with their attack against E and F companies, 5th Marines, other Chinese formations of the 89th Division attacked Capt. LeRoy M. Cooke's H Company, 7th Marines, on the summit. This company was isolated on the crest of Hill 1403, as the first Chinese probes soon discovered. About 10 P.M. the right-hand platoon collapsed under the attack. After Cooke radioed for all available supporting fire, artillery and mortars in the valley dropped a heavy volume of shells on his right front. When this fire lifted, Cooke led a counterattack in which he was killed at the head of his men. Second Lt. James M. Mitchell, H Company executive officer, climbed the hill in the midst of the fight to join the hard-hit company and took temporary command. A lone sniper in the rear of the company had been creating havoc with a burp gun whenever anyone in his vicinity moved. He let loose a burst at Mitchell as the latter neared the crest. He missed but was close enough to the mark to cause Mitchell to hit the dirt. Mitchell had seen the gun flashes. In a moment he rose and dashed headlong toward the flash spot. He killed the sniper, a Chinese captain. In the meantime, the 3rd Battalion commander, Lt. Col. William F. Harris, sent 1st Lt. H. H. Harris up the hill to take command of H Company. Harris reached the top safely, reorganized the depleted company, led a counterattack, and regained enough of the lost ground to hold the company position. After these first attacks on the two-mile front of Northwest Ridge, the Chinese remained quiet for a while. They were bringing up fresh units.

About 3 A.M. this second assault formation was ready. Several hundred Chinese with grenades, submachine guns, and rifles attacked simultaneously the several Marine positions on Northwest Ridge. Jaskilka's E Company directed a curtain of machine-gun fire into 300 Chinese moving down the draw in front of it. The first wave crumbled under this fire. Those behind took cover and thereafter were satisfied with a static position and exchange of fire. Against F Company farther down the spur, about 200 enemy soldiers maneuvered and finally overran two machine guns and inflicted heavy casualties. On top of Hill 1403, H Company held out against repeated attacks for about an hour, but at 4 A.M. Lt. Col. William F. Harris, 3rd Battalion commander, 7th Marines, ordered the company to withdraw to the rear of E Company, 5th Marines. H Company accomplished this in a two-hour fighting withdrawal led by 1st Lt. H. H. Harris. The Chinese were now in possession of Hill 1403, a key terrain feature for the defense of the Yudam-ni perimeter. But the 2nd Battalion, 5th Marines, still held the lower southwestern spur above the road. In all the night fighting they had lost only seven killed and 25 wounded, but they had 60 cold-weather casualties. In front of E and F companies lay roughly 500 CCF dead.[7]

This statistic does not fully reveal the intensity of the fighting. An example of the courage in the two companies of the 5th Marines that held the lower spur of Hill 1403 that night came in a counterattack E Company made right after daylight of the twenty-eighth. An enemy machine gunner, firing from the right side, pinned down the counterattacking force. Pfc. R. A. Jackson spotted the gun position and crawled through the snow toward it, finally getting within grenade range. He rose quickly to his feet and threw a grenade. As it left his hand, a burst from the enemy gunner hit and mortally wounded him. His grenade, however, was already on its way. It landed in the machine-gun position and killed the entire gun crew.[8] The counterattack resumed.

Lt. Col. R. D. Taplett, commanding the 3rd Battalion, 5th Marines, had moved his battalion from its assembly area into a defensive position around his CP in the Yudam-ni valley, below Hill 1403 of Northwest Ridge and Hill 1384 of North Ridge. He wanted to be prepared for any enemy breakthrough from either of those directions during the night. He placed a platoon of I Company as an outpost on a lower spur of Hill 1384 when he learned it was unoccupied by friendly troops, and 300 yards behind and below it he placed a platoon of South Korean police with two heavy machine guns. About 8:45 in the evening, before any units on the outer perimeter reported enemy attacks, the I Company platoon reported receiving fire from the higher ground of Hill 1384. It probably came from advance enemy elements of the 237th Regiment of the 79th Division, scheduled to attack the hill. Finding it undefended, some of the Chinese probably continued on down toward the Yudam-ni valley and stumbled into the I Company outpost. While this was happening, a few men of H Company, 7th Marines, on Hill 1403 came into the 3rd Battalion, 5th Marines, position barefooted and only partially clothed. They must have been surprised in their sleeping bags. Under questioning, they told Lieutenant Colonel Taplett that Chinese had overrun and seized their 60-mm mortar position on the hill.

Taplett listened to the increasing tempo of battle on the hills as the night wore on. Shortly after 1 A.M. he decided to place his 3rd Battalion in the valley on a full alert. Half an hour later, reports from his I Company outpost and from H Company on Hill 1403 said enemy were moving down in such a way that they would cut the road above and west of Yudam-ni. About 2:20 A.M., an estimated two companies of Chinese charged down the spur from Hill 1384, overran the I Company outpost, and then attacked the two heavy machine guns the South Korean police held. The Chinese drove off the South Koreans, but later examination of the ground when it was regained showed that the South Koreans had piled up an impressive number of CCF dead in front of their gun positions before they were driven from them. The Chinese soldiers that had penetrated to the lower slopes of Hill 1384 spread out and placed plunging fire into the lower ground around the 3rd Battalion CP. It was defended by Headquarters-Service and Weapons companies. The Headquarters and Service Company fell back across the road. Although the Weapons Company held its position north of the road, the battalion CP was now vulnerable. Lieutenant Colonel Taplett stayed in his blacked-out tent, continuing his command functions, while Maj. Thomas A.

Durham, his S-3 operations officer, stood by with drawn pistol, and Pfc. Louis W. Swinson, a radio operator, stood outside the tent with a rifle. The Chinese did not attack the tent or fire on it; they apparently thought it was unoccupied.[9]

THE MARINES ABANDON NORTHWEST RIDGE

Amazingly, in the midst of the night battle, Lieutenant Colonel Murray at 1:45 A.M., 28 November, ordered Roise's 2nd Battalion, 5th Marine Regiment, to resume the attack westward at daybreak. Even at that time, apparently, the full scale of the Chinese attack was not comprehended at regimental headquarters. Or perhaps it was just the fact that the attack had not been countermanded by higher headquarters. Murray intended to deploy the 3rd Battalion in attack westward after the 2nd Battalion had advanced far enough to give him room behind it. But at 5:45 A.M. Murray changed the orders, indicating that the 2nd Battalion would probably withdraw to Southwest Ridge instead of continuing the attack. Lieutenant Colonel Roise, on learning of the new order, thought it a mistake and checked with Murray. What had caused the change in orders?

Murray visited Colonel Litzenberg on the morning of 28 November, after the nightlong battle, and both agreed the Chinese had demonstrated such strength that a change in their plans, from offense to defense, was warranted. This was done on the old principle that the commander on the scene must make emergency decisions when he deems the situation warrants them. Neither Litzenberg nor Murray had official command over the other for joint action—so both regimental commanders conferred and agreed on the proper action to take. This conference led to Murray's canceling the attack west. Had the attack been resumed on 28 November, it almost certainly would have failed at the outset and have worsened the already bad situation.

At 11 A.M. on 28 November, Murray ordered the 2nd Battalion, 5th Marines, to withdraw to Southwest Ridge, and there to tie in with the 3rd Battalion, 7th Marines. To the east the battalion was to maintain contact with the 3rd Battalion, 5th Marines, whose line extended to North Ridge. In effect, this move abandoned Northwest Ridge. General Smith at Hagaru-ri was informed of these orders in the afternoon.

Less than half an hour before Smith received news of these changes at Yudam-ni, he had ordered the 7th Marines to attack south from Yudam-ni to open the MSR to Hagaru-ri. It is apparent that neither General Smith nor General Almond knew or comprehended the real situation at Yudam-ni on the afternoon of 28 November. Early in the afternoon, the 2nd Battalion started its withdrawal from Northwest Ridge, moving a company at a time. E Company was rear guard. The redeployment to

Southwest Ridge was completed by 8 P.M. Part of the 3rd Battalion, 5th Marines, deployed across the valley and the west road to protect Yudam-ni from the northwest.[10]

It was most unusual for a lieutenant colonel to command a Marine regiment. Yet, that was the case with the 5th Marine Regiment in Korea. Raymond L. Murray was 6 feet, 4 inches tall, an athletically built young officer. He had already distinguished himself by his command leadership abilities. Major General Almond, X Corps commander, had been favorably impressed by this stalwart, poised officer and feared that the US Marine Corps might replace him with a full colonel, which was the rank normally held by a regimental commander. General Almond asked General Smith if it was likely that Murray might be replaced on the issue of rank. Smith replied that Murray was considered one of the finest regimental commanders in the Marine Corps and that there were no plans to put a full colonel in command of the regiment.[11] The fighting of the 5th Marines in the Yudam-ni area, and in all of the Chosin Reservoir campaign, fully confirmed Smith's and Almond's judgment about Murray. Here was one thing the two commanders could agree upon.

THE CCF CUT THE ROAD

While the battles raged around Yudam-ni during the night of 27–28 November, the CCF 59th Division closed on the road between Yudam-ni and Hagaru-ri. At the same time, other Chinese troops cut the road from Hagaru-ri to Koto-ri. Chinese roadblocks appeared everywhere. Aerial reconnaissance planes reported 37 roadblocks, mostly constructed of bales of hay and logs, on the first six miles of road west of Yudam-ni. There were 11 known roadblocks on the ten miles between Hagaru-ri and Koto-ri, and the CCF during the night had blown all bridges between the two towns. Between Yudam-ni and Hagaru-ri there were innumerable roadblocks—no one seemed to know just how many. All X Corps northbound convoys on 28 November were held at Koto-ri. They could get no farther. Aerial reconnaissance also reported enemy troops were on the high ground above the roadblocks east of the road between Koto-ri and Hagaru-ri.[12]

The Marines at Yudam-ni were effectively cut off from all supporting troops south of them; and those at Hagaru-ri, including General Smith and the 1st Marine Division CP, were cut off from all other units of the division and X Corps troops to the north, northeast, and to the south. Troops of the 7th Infantry Division on the east side of Chosin Reservoir were similarly cut off unit from unit and from all other friendly forces south of them. The initial steps of the Chinese plan to fragment the 1st Marine Division and to destroy it piecemeal seem to have been executed on schedule, with the exception of a planned attack on Hagaru-ri on that first night by two divisions.

C AND F COMPANIES SURROUNDED

As a part of cutting the road between Yudam-ni and Hagaru-ri, Chinese troops attacked both C and F companies, 7th Marines, that had been left in isolated positions east of the MSR to guard Toktong Pass. Capt. John F. Morris's reduced C Company of two rifle platoons occupied a western spur of Hill 1419, four miles south of Yudam-ni and at the northern end of Toktong Pass, where the road descended to the valley. The company position faced toward the northeast and the crest of Hill 1419. During the night Chinese descended from that high ground and struck the company. They overran one platoon position, inflicting heavy damage, and a seesaw battle continued until dawn. Only heavy artillery barrages from guns emplaced at Yudam-ni on the enemy approach route to C Company saved it. Chinese forces also attacked F Company, two miles away, at the top of Toktong Pass. That story will be told later.

On the morning of 28 November, Colonel Litzenberg gave high priority to sending a relief force to rescue both C and F companies. He dispatched the 1st Battalion, 7th Marines, on this mission. But Lt. Col. Raymond G. Davis's battalion covered only three miles from Yudam-ni in five hours of fighting and climbing. At midafternoon the relief force was still a mile short of C Company's position. Heavy air attacks and 81-mm mortar fire finally enabled the 1st Battalion to reach high ground abreast of the surrounded company. From there Davis's battalion was able to hold open a route from C Company's perimeter to the road below. By this time it was dark. Litzenberg ordered Davis with his battalion and the rescued C Company with its 46 wounded to return posthaste to Yudam-ni before the entire force was cut off. Litzenberg meanwhile ordered F Company to fight its way to C Company's position and escape with it. But F Company could not move from its perimeter; it was in a fight for its life.[13]

During the day the Air Force, using C-47 planes flying from Yonpo airfield near Wonsan, had dropped ten tons of ammunition to the 5th and 7th Marines at Yudam-ni and 16 tons to the isolated elements of the 7th Division near Sinhung-ni on the eastern side of the reservoir. The drastic change in the battle scene at the reservoir, meanwhile, had set in motion at Ashiya airfield in Japan hectic activity in packaging all kinds of supplies for airdrop to the troops in the reservoir area.[14]

MARINE CASUALTIES AT YUDAM-NI

The number of battle casualties who had been collected and brought to the valley floor at Yudam-ni gave some indication of the cost of the night's battles. According to one account, there were 450 battle casualties and 175 nonbattle casualties, nearly all the latter being frostbite and cold-shock cases. Another count put the losses during the night as 95 killed and 543 wounded. Still another count on a somewhat different time span put the Marine losses for 27–28 November and the night between the two days at 1,226: 136 killed, 60 missing, 675 wounded, and 355 non-battle casualties. Compared to the losses on 27–28 November, the Marines in the 22-day-long Inchon-Seoul operation in September and early October had a total loss of 1,503 men, not counting the small number of nonbattle casualties. These casualties counts, although not altogether verifiable, are a measure of the ferocity of fighting during the night of 27–28 November at Yudam-ni.[15]

The official 1st Marine Division Casualty Reporting Section listed the following statistics for 27 and 28 November, with most (but not all) of the casualties occurring at Yudam-ni:

> 27 November. 37 killed, 1 died of wounds, 17 missing, 186 wounded, and 96 nonbattle casualties;
> 28 November. 95 killed, 3 died of wounds, 43 missing, 539 wounded, and 259 nonbattle casualties.

Most of the casualties given for 28 November were in the night battle of 27–28 November. The battle casualties for the two days and one night amount to 135 dead, 725 wounded, and 60 missing, for a total of 920.[16]

The battles of 27–28 November at the reservoir disclosed an interesting fact. The Chinese troops were armed for the most part with American weapons, most of them acquired, it seems, from the Nationalist troops that surrendered to or were captured by the Communists in the hundreds of thousands during the Chinese civil war that ended just the year before, in 1949. Among these weapons were 60-mm and 81-mm mortars, Thompson submachine guns, and heavy and light machine guns. One prisoner from the 60th Division said that 40 percent of the CCF 20th Army at Yudam-ni was equipped with the American M1903 rifle. Some hand grenades were of American manufacture.[17]

While the CCF 79th and 89th divisions spread havoc among the Marines around Yudam-ni on the night of 27–28 November, a sister division of the IX Army Group, the 80th Division, attacked elements of the Army's 7th Infantry Division on the east side of Chosin Reservoir at the same time.

5

CCF ATTACK EAST OF CHOSIN RESERVOIR

On 29 October the US 7th Division began landing over the Iwon beaches, 150 miles up the coast north of Wonsan. The 17th Regiment was the first ashore and headed north to Hyesanjin by the road that ran through Puk-chong and Pungsan. The 31st Regiment was the second to land, and on 4 November the 32nd Regiment, the third and last of the three regiments, came ashore and moved to a bivouac area northeast of Hamhung. General Barr, commanding the 7th Infantry Division, was in the process of moving the entire division north to the border in the vicinity of Hyesan-jin and Singalpajin on the Yalu when General Almond and his X Corps staff were working on the plan to implement General MacArthur's last order on 24 November for the attack north to the Chinese border. When the order was issued, it included a new feature that required the 7th In-fantry Division to provide a regimental combat team to be committed on the east side of Chosin Reservoir to relieve the 5th Marines there so that it could join the rest of the 1st Marine Division on the west side of the reservoir at Yudam-ni. Most of the 7th Division at the time was more than 100 miles away to the northeast, near the border.

Only the 1st Battalion, 32nd Infantry, had not yet moved to that area, but it was in the process of doing so. For General Barr it was nothing less than a chaotic scramble to assemble a force the size of a regimental com-bat team at Chosin Reservoir to be ready to take part in the general at-tack north, set for the morning of 27 November. The closest unit of the division was the 1st Battalion, 32nd Infantry, still in its bivouac area north-east of Hamhung, and it was the first to move to the reservoir area. The bulk of the RCT was to be from the 31st Infantry Regiment, which was scattered in the area east of the Fusen Reservoir and in the Pukchong area.

General Barr had to select the units nearest to the reservoir. The corps order stipulated that the 7th Division be on the east side of the reservoir by noon of 26 November. General Barr's effort to assemble an RCT force was entirely ad hoc. This force, later referred to generally as the 31st RCT, commanded by Col. Allan D. MacLean, commander of the 31st Infantry, was to include the 31st Infantry Regimental Headquarters and Head-quarters Company; the regiment's 2nd and 3rd battalions; the 1st Battalion, 32nd Infantry; the 31st Tank Company; the 57th Field Artillery Battalion, normally in support of the 31st Infantry, and D Battery, 15th Antiaircraft Artillery Automatic Weapons Battalion (AAA AW) SP attached, as the main combat elements. The 1st Battalion, 32nd Infantry, was chosen as the third infantry battalion of the RCT because it happened to be closest to the Chosin Reservoir at the time, in bivouac near the village of Kujang-ni, approximately 25 road miles northeast from the Hamhung–Hagaru-ri road to Chosin.

On 23 November a relief force from the 3rd Division arrived at the bivouac area of the 1st Battalion, 32nd Infantry, and the 1st Battalion by dawn of the twenty-fourth, with more than 1,000 men (715 Americans and 300 KATUSA), left Kujang-ni for their daylong trip of 160 road miles to Pukchong, where they were to go into an assembly area. Pukchong was the 7th Division's Rear CP. Earlier that morning Lt. Col. Don C. Faith, Jr., commander of the 1st Battalion, had started on ahead of his battalion to receive his orders from the regimental commander at Pukchong. Faith instructed his executive officer, Maj. Crosby P. Miller, to bring the battalion along behind him.

About 9 A.M. the 1st Battalion approached the northern outskirts of Hamhung, where a 7th Division liaison officer from X Corps met it and told Major Miller to halt the battalion and report to the G-3, X Corps Headquarters, for instructions. Lieutenant Colonel Faith had already passed through Hamhung, so he did not learn of the change in plans until he reached Pukchong. Miller reported to the X Corps headquarters, where he met Generals Almond and Barr. General Barr informed him that he was to take the battalion north to the area of the 1st Marine Division and then proceed on down the east side of the reservoir as far as possible. He told Miller that the 1st Battalion was now attached to the 1st Marine Division. Maj. Wesley J. Curtis, the battalion S-3, had held the battalion in a schoolyard close to the road while Miller was at X Corps.

When Miller rejoined the battalion Curtis learned that they were to go to Chosin Reservoir and there relieve the 5th Marines on the east side of the reservoir. At 11:30 A.M. Curtis started north with guides to locate a battalion assembly area for the night. Miller planned to leave with the battalion within half an hour. Curtis found an assembly area for the battalion that night at the village of Chinhung-ni, at the foot of Funchilin Pass.

In the meantime, Lieutenant Colonel Faith had driven all the way to Pukchong, and only on arrival there did he learn that his battalion had been ordered to the Chosin Reservoir. He started back immediately. He arrived at Chinhung-ni half an hour after midnight and rejoined his bat-

Col. Allan D. MacLean (*left*) and Lt. Col. Don C. Faith, Jr. (photograph courtesy Lt. Col. Erwin B. Bigger)

talion. Faith was 32 years old and had commanded the battalion for more than a year, ever since the 7th Division had been reorganized in Japan. During World War II he had served as aide to General Ridgway for more than three years, advancing during that time to the rank of lieutenant colonel. After World War II ended, Faith had several assignments in the Pacific Theater, including serving on General Barr's joint military advisory group in China. Except for the limited experience in the Inchon landing in September, he had never commanded any kind of military organization in combat. Faith was of athletic build, 6 feet tall, and he wore his black hair in a crew cut. His eyes and complexion were dark, reflecting his partial Spanish heritage. He was friendly, forceful, and charismatic to his enlisted men and officers alike.[1]

On the morning of 25 November, the traffic officer at the regulating point would not allow the 1st Battalion to proceed at once up Funchilin Pass because traffic in some places was one way. He did agree, however, to let Faith and a small party start at once, so Faith, Curtis, the operations sergeant, and the sergeant major left Chinhung-ni at 6 A.M. in two vehicles. Miller was to bring the battalion up the pass as soon as traffic conditions would permit. He started half an hour later.

On top of the plateau at Koto-ri, Faith and his party found the road covered with snow and ice. Upon reaching Hagaru-ri, the party took the right-hand road and entered the 5th Marine Regiment's zone of responsibility. A mile north of Hagaru-ri, at about 9 A.M., Faith met Lt. Col. Raymond L. Murray coming south. Murray told him that his Marine CP was with one of his battalions on the south side of the Pungnyuri-gang, a sizable inlet stream emptying into the reservoir, eight miles north of Hagaru-ri, and that his lead 3rd Battalion was in a perimeter defense position about four miles beyond his CP. Murray assigned an assembly area for Faith's battalion two miles south of his own CP. It was on Hill 1221 and the low ground around the village of Twiggae. Part of Murray's regiment had occupied this ground at Hill 1221 and had established defensive positions on the hill, facing north, consisting of bunkers and foxholes. These positions commanded the road below to the north, east, and southeast. Murray instructed Faith to occupy this position, with at least defensive outposts. He then continued on his way for a reconnaissance of the position he expected to occupy at Yudam-ni.

The 1st Battalion, 32nd Infantry, closed into its assembly area at Hill 1221 about 3 P.M. From there it had a clear view westward to the Chosin Reservoir, a mile away. The battalion occupied the high ground on both sides of the road, establishing a partially closed perimeter. Major Curtis and others described this position as the strongest they saw on the east side of the reservoir.

That evening, Faith, Curtis, Powell (the S-2) and Capt. Erwin B. Bigger (commanding D Company, heavy weapons) met Murray at the latter's CP. He told them that, during the day, Lieutenant Colonel Taplett, commanding the 3rd Battalion, 5th Marines, had sent a platoon-sized reconnaissance patrol, including tanks, from his forward perimeter, down the road toward Kalchon-ni, a village near the dam at the lower end of the reservoir. It had encountered and scattered a few small groups of Chinese soldiers, killing five, capturing one, and had destroyed an abandoned 75-mm gun. The patrol had found no evidence of large-scale enemy activity, so it turned back just short of the northern tip of the reservoir. Taplett had made a helicopter reconnaissance over the same area and farther north, but had observed no sign of significant enemy activity. Following this meeting with Murray, Faith and his staff drove north four miles to Taplett's 3rd Battalion at its hill perimeter astride the road. There they made a partial inspection of the Marine position. The night of 25–26 November passed quietly on the east side of the reservoir, and Sunday dawned cold and clear.

The 1st Battalion was in poor shape for a winter campaign in a cold climate. Most of the men, however, had received shoepacs, long underwear, pile liners, and parka shells. But the battalion was short of winter gloves and many other items needed for cold weather. Vehicles lacked tire chains and tarpaulin covers. Each company had only a kitchen fly for tentage.

Brig. Gen. Henry I. Hodes, assistant 7th Division commander, arrived at the 1st Battalion CP at Hill 1221 about half an hour before noon, 26 November. In World War II, Hodes had commanded the 112th Infantry Regiment in Europe. General Barr had sent Hodes to the reservoir as his agent in directing the operations of Colonel MacLean's 31st RCT after it had assembled.

Hodes brought much news to Faith. He said the 3rd Battalion, 31st Infantry, and the 57th Field Artillery Battalion, less its C Battery (attached to the 2nd Battalion, 31st Infantry), were on their way to join his battalion. He also said that Col. Allan D. MacLean and his staff, the 31st Intelligence and Reconnaissance (I&R) Platoon, a medical detachment, and a communications detachment would soon arrive. Upon his arrival, MacLean would assume command of the composite force. In effect, therefore, the 1st Battalion, 32nd Infantry, would no longer be attached to the 1st Marine Division. Hodes added that the 31st Tank Company had started on its way from Hungnam, but because of road conditions and traffic congestion, the time of its arrival was uncertain.

In this conversation, Faith told Hodes that, if the Marine division could give him a tank platoon and some artillery support, he could attack north before the arrival of other 7th Division support elements. Hodes disapproved this suggestion, left the 1st Battalion about 1 P.M., and went back south on the road to Hudong-ni.[2]

Faith, Curtis, Powell, and all company commanders and platoon leaders drove north the six miles to Taplett's 3rd Marine Battalion perimeter, where they made a detailed reconnaissance of the forward position. They returned to their own CP by dark.

A few hours after Faith returned from his reconnaissance of the forward Marine position, Lieutenant Colonel Murray sent a jeep messenger to him with a copy of his 5th Marine Regimental order issued that day, 26 November. It directed the 5th Marines to move from the east to the west side of the reservoir early the next morning. During this changeover, Faith had no orders as to what his mission would be. He telephoned Murray and asked for instructions, but the latter told him he had no information or instructions and suggested that Faith proceed no farther north without orders from the 7th Division.

About an hour later, Col. Allan D. MacLean arrived at Faith's CP. With him were Lt. Col. Berry K. Anderson, his S-3, and two or three other staff officers. Colonel MacLean told Faith he intended to attack north just as soon as his task force had closed on the area. He said the 3rd Battalion, 31st Infantry, would arrive the next day. He also told Faith that his battalion was now attached to the 31st Infantry Regiment. Faith asked permission to move the next morning to the forward Marine position, after Taplett's men had vacated it. MacLean approved this request.

The tempo of events began to pick up. An hour and a half later, Lt. Col. Ray O. Embree, commanding officer of the 57th Field Artillery Battalion, arrived. He confirmed that his battalion was on the way and should arrive before dark the next day.

MacLean went to establish a CP in the Hudong-ni schoolhouse, about a mile south of Hill 1221. This schoolhouse was in good condition and stood on the site of a former village, Hudong-ni. There was no village there now—only a number of old foundations outlining former structures.

COL. ALLAN MACLEAN

The Chosin mission had come to MacLean as a surprise. He first learned of it in a telephone conversation with General Barr in the evening of 24 November. MacLean had been in command of the 31st Regiment only about two months, succeeding to the command during the fight for Seoul, after the Inchon landing. During the summer he had been a senior staff officer in the G-3 section of Eighth Army. Before that he had been commander of the 32nd Infantry Regiment for about a year during its organization in Japan. Accordingly, he was well acquainted with Faith and all the officers of the 1st Battalion, 32nd Infantry, who were with it at that time. MacLean was aggressive by nature. He liked to be up front when action threatened or was in progress. This big, robust man was 43 years old when he arrived at Chosin Reservoir for what proved to be a fatal assignment.

On the twenty-fourth, when MacLean first learned of the Chosin Reservoir mission, most of his regiment was assembled near the east side of Fusen Reservoir, out of contact with enemy forces. He informed the regiment that it was to prepare for immediate movement and ordered a quartering party to be assembled at once and sent on in advance. Maj. Hugh W. Robbins, the 31st adjutant, assembled the party on the morning of 25 November and started over snow-covered trails for Pukchong, the 7th Division Rear CP, where he met MacLean. Robbins and his party stayed at Pukchong overnight. MacLean, Lieutenant Colonel Anderson, and Maj. Carl G. Witte (his S-2) went on ahead toward Hagaru-ri. Lt. Col. George E. Deshon, the 31st Infantry executive officer, stayed behind with the regimental rear at the Iwon beaches and never had a chance to join the 31st RCT at Chosin. MacLean told Robbins by telephone on the evening of the twenty-sixth, when Robbins called him from Chinhung-ni, that his CP was in a schoolhouse at Hudong-ni. Robbins arrived there about midnight.

The next morning, MacLean told Robbins to select a site for a small forward 31st RCT CP south of Faith's forward battalion position. He also said that, when the 3rd Battalion, 31st Infantry, arrived, it should take up a position about two miles south of his forward CP on the south side of the Pungnyuri-gang inlet of the reservoir. Lieutenant McNally, the 31st Infantry communications officer, returned to Hudong-ni to bring up the quartering party of about 35 men and returned with them about 2 P.M. By dark of the twenty-seventh, tents had been erected, and the 31st Advance CP was ready to operate. MacLean had told Robbins that he intended to stay overnight at the Hudong-ni schoolhouse Rear CP, but he changed his mind later and returned north after dark, stopped briefly at the new Advance CP, and then went on to Faith's forward position, where he spent the night.

On his way south to Hudong-ni, MacLean received a report alleging that a Chinese force of several hundred soldiers was in a village east of the inlet. He ordered 1st Lt. Richard B. Coke, Jr., commanding the 31st I&R Platoon, to patrol up the valley of the Pungnyuri-gang northeastward toward the Fusen Reservoir to check on this report. Coke and his platoon left in jeeps mounting machine guns, going along the narrow dirt road that followed the stream. No I&R report ever reached MacLean. Coke's platoon seemed simply to vanish.[3]

All day of the twenty-seventh, Lt. Col. William R. Reilly's 3rd Battalion, 31st Infantry, climbed from the vicinity of Hamhung northward toward the Chosin Reservoir. Behind it came Lt. Col. Ray O. Embree's 57th Field Artillery Battalion (minus C Battery). The 3rd Battalion arrived on the east side of the reservoir in the afternoon, closing there before dark. Reilly and MacLean stopped the battalion on the south side of the Pungnyuri-gang inlet, in a limited bivouac area, where it was to spend the night. A Battery, 57th Field Artillery Battalion, began arriving at the inlet about 11 A.M., and the remainder of the artillery closed there during the afternoon. When MacLean and Embree reconnoitered the area to locate the artillery, they decided to place the A and B firing batteries at the inlet with the 3rd Battalion, 31st Infantry. The Artillery Headquarters with Headquarters Battery would not go to the inlet but were to stop in a cove on the eastern side of the MSR about one road mile south of the inlet bivouac area, on the south side of Hill 1456, which intervened between the two positions.

On 26 November, D Battery, 15th Antiaircraft Battalion, Automatic Weapons, Self Propelled (minus the 2nd Platoon), was attached to the 57th FA Battalion; Capt. James R. McClymont commanded the battery. When he came to the 57th Headquarters in the cove half a mile south of the inlet, he pulled his battery off the road to join it at dusk. A Marine major, one of the last of the 5th Marines to depart the area east of the reservoir, was packing his things to leave. In a brief exchange with McClymont he said he had sent Marine patrols out for a distance of ten miles and none had seen signs of an enemy.

McClymont's platoon of antiaircraft weapons was of the utmost importance to Colonel MacLean's forces east of Chosin. The platoon had eight weapon carriers—four M19 (dual-40) full-tracked gun carriages, each mounting two 40-mm Bofors antiaircraft guns, and four M16 (quad-50) half-tracks, each mounting four .50-caliber machine guns, heavy barrels, M-2. On both the M19s and M16s the guns were mounted on revolving turrets. The M19 fired a bursting shell and, on automatic, resembled in killing and maiming power 240 fragmentation grenades dropping every minute among an enemy. The M19 40-mm shells were also good for hard-hitting flat trajectory fire at specific enemy emplacements or weapons up to a distance of two or three miles. An M16 (quad-50) could fire its four machine guns on automatic at the rate of 1,800 rounds a minute. It could sweep a front like a scythe cutting grain.

When McClymont arrived at Chosin, each vehicle pulled a fully loaded trailer packed with ammunition, C rations, gasoline, and bedrolls. The trailers carried two basic loads of ammunition that he had the foresight to obtain, instead of the usual one. McClymont set up his own CP a short distance from that of Embree and placed his weapons around the cove for protection of the CPs and the area.

Accompanying the 3rd Battalion, 31st Infantry, to Chosin on the twenty-seventh was Capt. George Cody's 31st Heavy Mortar (4.2-inch) Company, less one platoon that was attached to the 2nd Battalion, which MacLean expected to arrive at any time. Cody emplaced his heavy mortars in the flat marshland about halfway between the inlet and the 3rd Battalion on the south of it and Faith's 1st Battalion forward position to the north. From there the heavy mortars could deliver supporting fires to both infantry battalions. Faith had with him one platoon of the 32nd Infantry's Heavy Mortar Company. When Cody arrived, Faith had Lt. Robert Reynolds take this platoon to join him. Cody then had the equivalent of a full company of 12 heavy mortars, four to a platoon.

During the afternoon, A and B batteries (each had four 105-mm howitzers) of the 57th FA Battalion emplaced on the south side of the inlet, where the ground flared into a widening of semiflat land just short of the bridge and causeway that crossed the Pungnyuri-gang. A Battery emplaced farther east and closer to the bridge than B Battery, which was behind or west of it. Capt. Harold L. Hodge commanded A Battery; Capt. Theodore C. Goss commanded B Battery.

Reilly placed two rifle companies of his 3rd Battalion on a ridge about 900 yards east of his CP, which was in a small house south of the bridge and causeway. This spur ridge ran northward from Hill 1456, south of the bivouac area, descending to the south bank of the Pungnyuri-gang about half a mile east of the bridge. This long finger ridge controlled all the low ground that lay westward along the southern side of the inlet, where the artillery and the 3rd Battalion had bivouacked for the night. Reilly placed Capt. Robert J. Kitz's K Company on the lower part of the ridge and Capt. Albert Marr's I Company above K Company on the upper extension of the ridge. M Company, with Capt. Earle H. Jordan, Jr., commanding, was westward behind I Company. Capt. William Etchemendy's L Company seems to have been bivouacked in the vicinity of the artillery, but its initial location on 27 November has not been determined. Jordan says that it was dark before he had his 81-mm mortars emplaced in a dry wash just east of his CP and between him and I Company on the evening of 27 November.

The 31st Tank Company, commanded by Capt. Robert E. Drake, had loaded on an LST at Inchon, had a long three weeks' sea trip around the tip of Korea and northward up the east coast to Hungnam, and was greatly delayed in joining the regiment. It was at full strength when it arrived at Hungnam, having four platoons of five M-4A4 tanks each, all armed with 76-mm guns. There were two additional tanks in the command section armed with 105-mm howitzers, making a total of 22 tanks. He had been ashore only a few days when he received orders to join the 31st RCT at Chosin Reservoir. On the morning of 27 November he

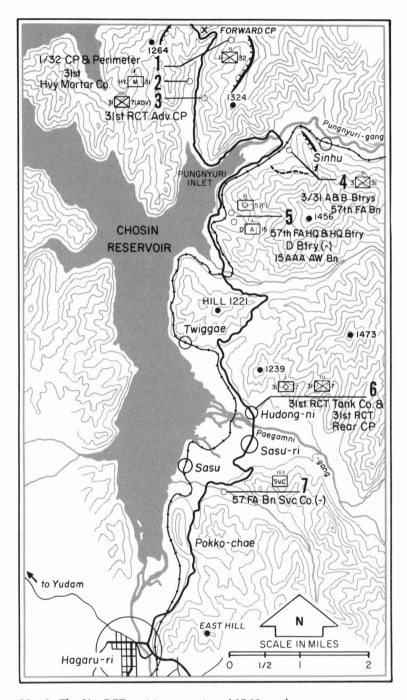

MAP 8. The 31st RCT positions, evening of 27 November.

Text within map:

X FORWARD CP
● 1264
1 1/32 CP & Perimeter
31st
Hvy Mortar Co.
HY M 3I
2
3I 7(ADV)
3
31st RCT Adv CP

1324 ●

Pungnyuri-gang
Sinhu

PUNGNYURI
INLET

4 3I 3I

3/31 A & B Btrys
57th FA Bn

57(-)
5
D A I5
1456 ●

57th FA HQ & HQ Btry
D Btry (-)
I5 AAA AW Bn

CHOSIN
RESERVOIR

HILL 1221

1473 ●

Twiggae

1239 ●

3I 7 3I 7

6

31st RCT Tank Co. &
31st RCT
Rear CP

Hudong-ni

Paegamni
Sasu-ri

-gang

Sasu

I(-)
SVC
7
57 FA Bn Svc Co.(-)

Pokko-chae

to Yudam

N

EAST HILL ●

SCALE IN MILES

0   1/2   1   2

Hagaru-ri

started with his tank company for Chosin. He arrived there in the afternoon and stopped at Hudong-ni for a rest and refueling. Colonel MacLean had already established his Rear CP and had an ammunition and petroleum dump there. Drake's tank company was the last combat unit of MacLean's RCT to reach the reservoir. The 2nd Battalion, 31st Infantry, which MacLean expected to arrive at any minute, never made it. It had numerous misadventures on its way north and never got beyond Koto-ri.

Drake instructed his men to make a full maintenance check of the tanks and then, with his Korean interpreter, started north by jeep to find Colonel MacLean. He went all the way to Faith's forward position but did not see MacLean. Faith told him of plans to attack north on the twenty-eighth but advised him not to try to bring the tank company up until the next morning. Drake returned to Hudong-ni without seeing MacLean. It is a curious irony that Drake never saw MacLean at the reservoir. MacLean had been at the schoolhouse at Hudong-ni but had left it to return to his own CP before Drake returned. They had passed each other somewhere on the road, probably at one of the 31st unit positions along the road where MacLean had stopped briefly on his way back north. Had Drake met MacLean, one may speculate what MacLean's orders might have been and whether he would have moved the tank company north to join one of the infantry battalions that evening. It is probable that neither MacLean nor Hodes, who conferred at Hudong-ni schoolhouse after the tank company arrived there and knew of its presence, had any definite plan for it and did not feel any urgency for its moving farther north that night. So Drake decided to stay overnight at Hudong-ni and go forward in the morning.

That evening, 27 November, Maj. William R. Lynch, Jr., of the 7th Infantry Division G-3 section, arrived at Hudong-ni. Lynch had been with the 17th Infantry Regiment in its advance to Hyesanjin but was recalled to the division CP at Pungsan. There, Colonel Paddock, the G-3, told Lynch that General Hodes was going to fly to Hamhung to X Corps to check on the rumor that the 31st Infantry was going to be sent to Chosin to join the 1st Marine Division. He instructed Lynch to take Sergeants Cox and Hammer of the G-3 Section and drive at once for Hamhung to join Hodes as his G-3 assistants. Lynch and the two sergeants left Pukchong by jeep on the morning of 26 November and arrived at Hamhung late in the evening. They stayed there overnight, learning at X Corps that General Hodes had already gone on to the reservoir. The next morning they continued on their way to join Hodes, traveling all day behind the tank company. Lynch reached Hudong-ni about 5:30 P.M. that afternoon and at once entered the schoolhouse CP, where he found Colonel MacLean and General Hodes in conversation. Subsequently he heard Mac-

Lean instruct Lt. Col. Berry Anderson, his S-3, to bring the rest of the regimental headquarters staff at the schoolhouse forward in the morning. MacLean left the schoolhouse about half an hour later, stating that he was going back north to his forward units. Thus, it appears that Mac-Lean left Hudong-ni about 6 P.M. after dark. Hodes and Lynch remained at the schoolhouse overnight. When Drake returned later to join his tanks at Hudong-ni, he did not see General Hodes and did not know that he was there until the next morning.

The Hudong-ni schoolhouse and the 31st Rear CP there stood at the southwestern base of a large hill mass, Hill 1472 (or Ko-bong, as some early maps had it). Drake was there three nights and three days and knew the area well. He said that below the schoolhouse the ground sloped south toward the low marsh area at the Paegamni-gang, a major tributary that flowed into Chosin Reservoir. Here there was an expanse of about 25 to 30 acres that could be used for an assembly area, ammunition and petroleum products dump, a tentage area, and a tank park. The road ran on the west side of the schoolhouse area. Beyond the road the Chosin Reservoir, about a mile away to the west, was visible.

The Service Battery of the 57th FA Battalion stopped for the night about a mile south of Hudong-ni. It came into Hudong-ni the next morning, the last unit of the 31st Infantry to reach Hudong-ni.[4]

FAITH'S FORWARD POSITION, 27 NOVEMBER

All morning of 27 November, Marine columns raised a haze of dust on the road past Hill 1221, where the 1st Battalion, 32nd Infantry, waited as they cleared going south on their move to the west side of the reservoir. By evening all the Marines on the east side of the reservoir had left except A Company, 1st Marine Engineer Combat Battalion, at Hill 1203 and the sawmill town of Sasu just north of the hill, about two miles north of Hagaru-ri, where the company was getting out timbers to rebuild the blown bridge across the Paegamni-gang.

In the early afternoon Taplett's 3rd Battalion, 5th Marines, had all left their forward position, and Lieutenant Colonel Faith was able to start his 1st Battalion, mounted in vehicles, north to occupy the positions the 3rd Battalion of Marines had just vacated. Taplett's Marine defense line had been well located, with several bunkers constructed and holes dug. Being fewer in numbers than the Marine battalion, Faith's 1st Battalion did not occupy all the Marine positions, especially on the right, or southern, flank. This did not concern the battalion, as it expected to be there only one night.

Major Miller, the 1st Battalion executive officer, described the position as being on high ground that stretched around in a

huge horseshoe, the open end of which was generally southwest of
the BN CP . . . the battalion was extended beyond its capabilities, but
the one road leading north was adequately covered. Able Company
on the north and west (left) end of the horseshoe was well disposed to
block the road. Charley Company extended east from the right flank
of Able Company, along the northern side of the horseshoe to its bend.
Baker Company closed off the bend and back along the southern leg
to the road [B Company did not extend to the road]. Dog Company, HQ
Company, and the Battalion HQ were in a deep ravine immediately
behind Able and Charley Companies.[5]

Neither A nor C company held a roadblock on the road where it passed
over a saddle between their positions. Lt. James O. Mortrude's 3rd Platoon of C Company held the left flank of C Company across the road
from A Company. The battalion front line was about two miles long, with
C Company holding the longest company sector from east of the road
along the ridgeline that ran uphill from northwest to southeast toward
the summit of Hill 1475, the boundary with B Company. The weakest
place on the forward perimeter was at its highest ground at the boundary
of C and B companies, where a spur ridge from a still higher peak eastward provided a good approach downhill to it.

In the evening of the twenty-seventh, Maj. Robert E. Jones, the battalion S-1 and adjutant, rejoined the battalion in its forward position. He
had driven all day from Pukchon, the 7th Division's Rear CP, in a 2½-ton
truck loaded with a two-weeks' accumulation of mail and some early
Christmas packages. He had stopped briefly at Hudong-ni, where he found
General Hodes and Colonel MacLean conferring in the schoolhouse, and
asked for the location of the 1st Battalion. He then continued on his way.
Jones was an old-timer in the battalion. He had been with it since the
early days of the 32nd Regiment's reorganization, coming to it from the
11th Airborne Division when the latter had returned to the United States
from Japan in 1949. Most of the time Jones had commanded C Company.
He had been on active duty in the Army since August 1940, and in World
War II in Europe he had jumped as a member of the 502nd Parachute Regiment of the 101st Airborne Division at Arnhem, Holland, in that ill-fated
operation. Jones was very popular in the 1st Battalion and considered by
everyone to be an outstanding soldier. He was a close personal friend of
Lieutenant Colonel Faith.

At about 8:30 P.M., soon after Jones's arrival at the CP, a liaison officer
from Colonel MacLean's forward CP brought an operations order directing the battalion to attack at dawn toward Kalchon-ni. Faith gave orders
to his company commanders at 9:30 for the advance at dawn the next
morning.

In preparation for the attack north the next morning, Lieutenant Colonel Faith late in the afternoon had ordered Capt. Edward P. Stamford, USMC, the forward air controller with the battalion, to move his Tactical Air Control Party to A Company's position so that he would be in a position to run air support, if needed, during the attack. Stamford's stay overnight with A Company on the evening of the twenty-seventh imposed on him duties no one expected. He had been attached to the 1st Battalion, together with his Marine TACP of four enlisted men, just as the battalion was loading out in Japan for the Inchon landing. At that time the Navy had lent him to the Army battalion as an FAC for the landing operation. He served with the battalion during the battle for Seoul and remained attached to it when the division moved to northeast Korea. Stamford was one of the many Marine enlisted pilots who received commissions in World War II. Stamford received his in September 1943, and the next month he went to the South Pacific, serving first as a second lieutenant in antisubmarine search. Later he served as a dive-bomber pilot in the Solomon Islands and other South Pacific combat areas.

In 1944, Stamford returned to the United States, where he attended the 13-week course at the Marine Air-Infantry School at Quantico, Virginia. This training course was important for Stamford in his later duties as a forward controller. It greatly increased his competence in that role because it gave him an understanding of infantry tactics and problems and he was better able to act as liaison between fighter and bomber pilots overhead and infantry on the ground. He was the communications link between the two. This training also qualified him for performance personally as an infantryman. Stamford was a powerfully built man, about 5 feet, 10 inches tall, compact with a barrel-shaped chest, heavily muscled legs and arms, and big hands. He was an experienced, cool operator at all times. There was never any doubt that he would do his duty as a soldier.

Two months after the Chosin action, Stamford wrote of the situation in A Company when he joined it on the evening of 27 November:

> Able Company's CP was protected by company headquarters personnel and the platoons were from the left in the order of 1st, 3rd, and 2nd. The 2nd was bent back to the rear on a spur. I was given two bunkers for myself and my 4 men. Captain Ed Scullion, Able Company commander, ordered me to use the bunker between the CP and the right flank of the 1st Platoon. I was given an SCR 300 to be in contact with him. I moved into the bunker with 2 of my men and put the other 2 in the bunker about 50 yards to the rear and bedded down for the night, keeping a radio watch.[6]

Before the fighting began, Colonel MacLean arrived at Faith's CP with his driver.

THE FIRST NIGHT IN THE FORWARD POSITION

Shortly before 11 P.M. persons at the battalion CP heard scattered rifle fire in the A Company position. At first this shooting did not cause any great concern, as it was common practice for ROK soldiers attached to the battalion to fire at imagined enemies after dark, and sometimes their ruckus developed into what sounded like a firefight before it could be stopped. Actually, however, Chinese soldiers had appeared. The first group seen in front of the A Company perimeter carried shovels. One Chinese soldier was captured, and the others scattered. Enemy patrols probed the company front for the next hour. Then, just after midnight, the Chinese struck.

They came from the north, marching straight up the road against A Company. At the saddle or just south of it, they veered right, west of the road, and immediately penetrated, or moved around the right flank of the 2nd Platoon, on the spur ridge that paralleled the road. This action put the Chinese behind the company CP, in the vicinity of the draw where 60-mm mortars were located. Part of this enemy force turned back toward the company CP area, and others went straight for the 60-mm mortars in the draw. The mortarmen, surprised, gave way and abandoned their weapons.

Stamford awoke sometime after midnight to the sound of shots and heard Scullion shouting. Before he could get up, he heard voices outside his bunker. The poncho at the back end was pulled aside, and Stamford saw a fur-rimmed face in the moonlight. He fired at it from a sitting position, but the Chinese soldier had already dropped a grenade inside the bunker, which blew up on the sleeping bag between Stamford's feet. Fragments wounded one of the two men with him, but he was unhurt. Stamford fired more rounds through the poncho. Enemy rifle fire then hit the bunker, some shots coming down from the top through cracks in the log roof. He and his two men moved from the bunker into the escape slit trench at the back end and remained hidden there for a few minutes. One of A Company's machine guns now opened up and swept a spray of bullets across the top of the bunker. This cleared it of Chinese soldiers. Stamford climbed out of his slit trench. He at once began to assemble the scattered men in his vicinity into a defense.

Scullion, whose shouts had helped to awaken him, lay dead nearby, shot down only a few yards from his CP bunker when he hurried out to learn what was happening. Stamford gathered enough men to hold the ground immediately around the command bunker. He then moved off to the 1st Platoon on the left to learn the situation there. He found that Lt. Raymond C. Dentchfield, the platoon leader, had been wounded.

First Lt. Carlos J. Ortenzi, A Company mortar officer, came up to Stam-

ford and informed him that, as the next senior man, Stamford would have
to take the company. Stamford sent one of his Marine TAC helpers to
obtain reports on the situation of the other platoons and placed 1st Lt.
Cecil Smith, A Company executive officer, in charge of the 1st Platoon.
Stamford received reports that the enemy had thus far hit A Company
only in the vicinity of the 3rd Platoon, the company CP, and had overrun the mortars. He moved two squads of the 1st Platoon from the left
to the right flank to strengthen the 2nd Platoon there. He left Corporal
Smith of his TACP with the one remaining squad of the 1st Platoon to
act as a getaway man to warn him in case of an enemy attack there. Then
he began searching out and destroying enemy in the CP area. He accomplished this without much trouble, and with his defense now organized,
he repulsed other attempts to overrun the company position.

Meanwhile, Lieutenant Ortenzi had rallied his mortarmen behind the
line and counterattacked the Chinese at their overrun mortar position.
In protracted fighting behind the line, Ortenzi and his men inflicted heavy
casualties on them and halted further penetration.

Both telephone lines and radio communications were out between A
Company and the battalion. Stamford learned later that two wire teams
had been lost when Captain Bigger tried to reestablish communications.
With the company position reestablished, Stamford gave orders that the
company was to hold precisely where it was, because, if the Chinese
broke through, they could enlarge the penetration south up the road to
the battalion CP and reach the 81-mm mortars. He had to reduce the rate
of fire, as the men were wasting ammunition (a common fault), and he
feared they would run out of ammunition before daylight. Stamford
strengthened his line by setting up two machine guns to cover a shallow draw enemy were using to gain a new entrance to his perimeter and
a 57-mm recoilless rifle fired on an enemy assembly area, which did
much to prevent the Chinese from mounting a successful attack from
that point.

In discussions with the author, Stamford expressed strong views as
to how the Chinese accomplished their initial surprise penetration of A
Company. He believed that they infiltrated through the line because the
men were not alert. He believed that Chinese caught the soldiers dozing
in their foxholes and simply bypassed or overran some positions before
they were discovered.

In his overnight impromptu command of A Company, Stamford had
performed like a veteran infantry officer. After daylight, Major Miller,
the battalion executive officer, came up to A Company and relieved Stamford, placing Lieutenant Smith in command. Stamford was needed as the
FAC at battalion headquarters.

At the battalion CP the Chinese surprise attack had started off on an incongruous note. When the first scattered shots in A Company area were heard, Faith called for Captain Bigger of D Company to come to his CP at once. Faith said to him, "Do you suppose those ROKs are firing at each other again?" Faith had had no word as yet of a CCF attack, but he added that he had received a garbled report that something had happened to Ed Scullion—that maybe he had been killed. Faith then turned to Capt. Robert F. Haynes, the battalion assistant S-3, and said to him, "You had better go up there to A Company and see what the situation is." Bigger quickly offered to go with Haynes, saying, "I know the troop situation up there and I want to check on my heavy weapons with the company."[7]

Bigger and Haynes started up the road toward A Company. Neither they nor those back at the battalion CP were yet thinking of a CCF attack. As they climbed the hill and approached the vicinity of A Company, they were suddenly challenged by a dark figure dressed in a parka, lying on the road and facing away from them. They did not understand the challenge, but this would not be surprising if it came from a South Korean. Thinking the prone figure was a South Korean, they replied with the countersign. The figure began to turn and started to raise a rifle. Bigger alerted Haynes, and they dived for the ditch as the unknown person fired. Bigger heard the wind go out of Haynes and heard him groan as he fell into the ditch. As Bigger moved to his side to learn how badly Haynes had been wounded, he saw the man who had fired the shot coming toward him. Bigger tried to work the bolt of his carbine, but it was frozen. He got to his feet to escape, but before he could move, two grenades exploded near him, one partially deafening him. They were the weak Chinese concussion grenades and did no further damage. Bigger now saw three other Chinese on the road embankment, coming toward him. He dashed into the roadside brush and escaped to the battalion CP, where he reported the incident. This encounter on the road occurred near the 60-mm mortar position that the Chinese had just overrun. After Bigger's report to Faith, there could no longer be any doubt that Chinese were behind the A Company line.

Although some tried, no one was able to reach Haynes until after daylight, when he was brought barely alive to the battalion CP. He had been shot through the stomach and also had bayonet wounds. Capt. Raymond Vaudreaux, battalion S-4, who had formerly been studying for the priesthood in the Catholic church, performed last rites for Haynes in the CP just before he died.

When enemy action started in A Company's position, 1st Lt. Hugh R. May, the battalion transportation officer in Headquarters Company, was in the ravine below the road, about 100 yards from the battalion CP. He reported to Faith, who asked him to stand by. A little later Faith instructed him to check CP security. He and 1st Lt. Henry Moore, the Ammunition and Pioneer (A&P) Platoon leader, Headquarters Company, established internal security and placed machine guns on both sides of the road, one controlling the road north, and the other south. After doing this, they and their men helped drive out the Chinese who had penetrated down the road from behind A Company. May remained in command of internal security until late in the afternoon of 28 November.

Enemy attacks spread to the rest of the battalion line. One of the first of these tried to penetrate between A and C companies by driving straight up the road between them with a tank and a self-propelled gun. Both were of North Korean origin, having come northward from the coast, and were now pressed into use by the Chinese.

These two formidable weapons clanked up the road from the north about 2 A.M. on 28 November. C Company, on the east side of the pass, had the best view of the road, since it was cut into the ridge slope on the west side of the drainage it followed. Cpl. James H. Godfrey of D Company had a 75-mm recoilless rifle, and his squad was on a high point east of the pass and had a commanding view of the road from the north. From this vantage point, when he judged the distance right, Godfrey opened fire on the enemy vehicles, destroying both of them.

Immediately, a force of about 100 Chinese soldiers, who had crawled unseen to within 50 yards of the 75-mm recoilless rifle, rushed from cover and tried to overrun the American squad. Godfrey at once turned the gun on them, killing and wounding many and scattering the rest. The survivors fell back in disorder. Later in the night, Godfrey destroyed an enemy mortar with the recoilless rifle, and with its firepower helped repel five more enemy attacks on the left side of C Company's line.

Other parts of the C Company line east of the pass were not defended so successfully against the Chinese. A strong enemy assault hit the middle of C Company. Another 75-mm recoilless rifle and its crew fired one shot, disclosing its position, and an assault team of Chinese immediately overran it and dragged the weapon away.

On C Company's right flank, Chinese drove away the right-hand squad and seized the highest ground of the perimeter at the boundary with B Company. This key point was never recovered; the Chinese held it against every counterattack, mortar barrage, and several air strikes. But the Chinese were never able to exploit this success. Nearby, Cpl. Robert L. Armentrout, gunner of a heavy machine gun from D Company, attached to C Company for the night, held a position almost by himself. A group of Chinese started up a steep slope toward his gun. He could not depress it enough to bring its fire trajectory on them. But he was strong enough to pick up the gun, hold it in his arms, and fire it directly into the Chinese. He decimated them with this fire.

Captain Cody's 4.2-inch mortars, which at first had been reliable for C and B companies, had begun to miss the mark because their base plates were breaking through the marsh crust and shifting. Cody hurriedly moved the mortars to firmer ground and was able to resume good support.

A crisis in B Company, which held the perimeter southeast of the battalion CP, came late in the night, about 4:30 A.M. By then the high ground at the boundary with C Company had been lost, and the Chinese occupied it in strength. Lieutenant Kemper of B Company was killed in the fighting there, and the situation turned bad so quickly that Captain Turner ordered 1st Sgt. Richard S. Luna to rouse everyone in B Company, including headquarters personnel, and to send them forward to the line, holding only "a handful" of cooks and command-post personnel behind. Luna did as ordered. He sat at the company CP with his "handful" until noon.

Before dawn the weather turned colder, and it began to snow. The enemy attack tapered off with daylight. The night battle had been loud and bloody. Chinese horns and bugles sounded frequently. After sunrise on 28 November, relief came, as four Marine Corsairs roared in. This was just what Stamford wanted. He directed them in a napalm attack on a ridge 300 yards from A Company where a body of Chinese soldiers had taken cover and instructed the pilots to hit the reverse slope of the ridge, where the Chinese had set up mortars and were lobbing shells into the 1st Battalion positions. When the aircraft struck the ridge, many Chinese ran into the open to escape the napalm. American machine guns and small-arms fire cut them down. The Corsairs followed up their napalm drops with 5-inch rocket and 20-mm strafing fire. This early morning air strike eased the situation for the ground troops at that part of the perimeter.

In Mortrude's 3rd Platoon, C Company position, daylight revealed a gruesome sight. In his foxhole at the left end of the platoon position sat a headless ROK soldier. His weapon and ammunition were gone. A Chinese soldier had evidently crawled close to the hole while the ROK apparently slept or dozed at the beginning of the attack, shoved a pole charge against his head, and set it off.

A count after daylight and the conclusion of A Company's counterattacks revealed that the company had lost eight men killed, including Captain Scullion, the company commander, and 20 wounded. The number of killed and wounded in the rest of the battalion in the night battle is not recorded, but by afternoon, about 100 men had passed through the battalion aid station. About noon, Sergeant Luna went to the battalion CP from B Company and saw the casualties. Many dead had been carried in frozen stiff.[8]

THE FIRST NIGHT AT THE INLET

From the time the Chinese began their attack against the 3rd Battalion, 31st Infantry, and the 57th FA Battalion at the inlet, it is clear that it was coordinated with that against Faith's forward perimeter. The Chinese attack against the inlet came from the east. As it happened, this was the only direction where the inlet bivouac had any defense. But the Chinese had no trouble in penetrating the eastern defenses, such as they were, and very quickly they overran the infantry line. They reached the 3rd Battalion CP and overran it and then continued on into the artillery positions of A Battery and the truck parking area. The attack at the inlet was far more successful than that at Faith's position—it all but overran the entire inlet position the first night.

The Chinese attack first developed about 1 A.M. on 28 November against the K Company line, coming from the east. Captain Kitz in his company CP first heard small-arms fire at his front line. At first it was light, but gradually built up in volume. The K Company roadblock force farther east up the valley of the Pungnyuri-gang reported that it heard firing between it and the K Company line. Thus far it had not been disturbed—enemy forces apparently bypassed it purposely. Half an hour later, by 1:30 A.M., the Chinese attack had built up to one of heavy pressure against both K and I companies on their ridge line at the east end of the inlet perimeter. Within another half hour the Chinese were closing on the K Company CP. At this point the ROK troops assigned to K Company broke and ran for the rear. Kitz intercepted and stopped them. But already the Chinese had broken through one platoon of K Company, and the entire line quickly disintegrated. Kitz had to abandon his position.[9]

Kitz hurriedly led his CP personnel west about 1,000 yards to the rear, to the A Battery howitzer position. Some of his front-line troops followed him, closely pursued by Chinese. This withdrawal exposed the 3rd Battalion CP.

It is not clear just what happened in I Company, up the spur ridge above K Company. But the Chinese broke through there and overran one of its platoons and then penetrated to the 81-mm mortars of M Company in the dry wash between the ridge and the M Company CP. The artillerymen were not spared long. Everything in front of them except M Company had folded within an hour of the first enemy attack. First Lt. Thomas J. Patton of A Battery said that about 2:30 A.M., 28 November, he was awakened with the news that the battery was under Chinese attack. Fifteen minutes later news arrived that K Company was withdrawing to the battery's rear, and at this time machine-gun fire struck A Battery's CP. Chinese fire ignited gasoline cans near the CP and set it on fire. Chinese ran up to the blaze and started warming themselves. Cap-

Litter parties gathering American dead in the eastern part of the inlet perimeter, 28 November 1950. Two Chinese dead in white uniforms are in the foreground. (Photograph courtesy Col. Crosby P. Miller)

tain Hodge killed one of them, and members of the gun sections shot others. A Batterymen fell back and joined B Battery's position. Lieutenant Patton said, "When daylight came we found sections of L and K Companies were mixed in with Battery A and B personnel. Capt. Kitz organized a force to retake Battery A's guns with Capt. Hodge leading the remainder of A Battery. . . . When the battery was retaken our howitzers were turned on the fleeing CCF. We then discovered that approximately 30 men from Battery A had remained in their foxholes and continued fighting even though they were completely overrun."[10]

Enemy dead lay all about the howitzers. About 30 CCF prisoners were captured in the counterattack, which regained the guns of A Battery. Almost all the survivors at the inlet, except M Company, seem to have retreated to the B Battery position and found there a good defensive position in which they joined to fight off the Chinese in the hours before dawn. There were infantrymen from all three rifle companies, L, K, and I, as well as the A Battery artillerymen. Throughout the night battle, however, many men were cut off in different places and continued resistance isolated from the main center, which developed around B Battery.

In the rapid onslaught that carried the Chinese to B Battery, they over-ran the 3rd Battalion CP. What happened there was not known to the rest of the battalion until daylight. The enemy held it from about 3 A.M. until just after daybreak. It was generally assumed that Lieutenant Colonel Reilly and most of his battalion staff had been killed or captured. Shortly after daybreak, 1st Lt. Henry ("Hank") Traywick, the 3rd Battalion motor officer, organized a counterattack party to drive enemy away from the 3rd Battalion CP and communications area. Under heavy machine-gun and small-arms covering fire, Traywick reached the two Korean houses where the battalion CP and communications center had been located, drove away the last of the Chinese soldiers there, and entered the CP. To their surprise, Traywick and his men found Reilly alive but uncon-scious. Apparently the Chinese had thought him dead. They had stripped him and others there of all weapons and anything they considered of value. The bodies of several of his staff were strewn around the inside of the small structure. Traywick took Reilly to the battalion aid station, where he recovered consciousness.

Later, Mrs. Celeste Reilly learned of what happened at the CP from her husband. He told her that he sat facing a window with gun in hand when the Chinese suddenly appeared at the CP. Chinese soldiers tried to climb in through a window, and he shot several at that time. In the fight that followed in the CP, Captain Adams, the battalion S-4, received a chest wound from which he died during the day. Reilly noticed that Lieutenant Anderson, the battalion assistant S-3, appeared frustrated that he could not get his pistol out of its holster. Reilly went in the dim light to him to see what was wrong. He found that Anderson's right arm had been blown off by a grenade. Anderson seemed not to know that his arm was missing. Reilly took the pistol from its holster and placed it in Ander-son's remaining hand. Anderson died during the night. Reilly himself had four wounds—a .50-caliber bullet wound through the right leg, a bullet through the toes of one foot, a splattering of mortar fragments on his up-per legs and hands, and a hand grenade concussion over the right eye, which had knocked him unconscious.[11]

During the CCF attack on the 3rd Battalion CP, First Lieutenant John-son, the forward air controller in the adjoining hut, was killed and his equipment damaged. How many others in the CP escaped or were injured there is not known.

The only forward unit of the 3rd Battalion to hold its CP during the night attack was Capt. Earle Jordan's M Company. The weapons company's 81-mm mortars were emplaced in a dry wash just east of Jordan's CP, which was in a hut about 200 yards south of the battalion CP and behind I Com-pany. Jordan's first knowledge of trouble was when he was awakened by the sound of small-arms fire in his mortar position between 1:30 and 2 A.M. He hurriedly arose and alerted all personnel in the CP. He then went outside and saw that enemy soldiers were overrunning his mortar position and that small-arms fire, coming from the east and south, was hitting around his CP. Chinese soldiers were already in the draw around his mortars. Jordan shouted to his mortarmen to fall back to his CP hut and courtyard. There he organized his defense, which held all night against repeated close-in Chinese attacks. Most in Jordan's group were either killed or wounded in the night battle, but the less critically wounded continued to fight in the desperate encounter. Jordan said, "When it was light enough to see I went around to check the damage, and counted over 60 dead enemy soldiers within yards of our position, nearly all armed with American sub-machine guns, 45 cal. and American ammunition." Jordan was wounded during the night battle but did not relax his control of the defense. An enemy hand grenade exploded a few feet from him, fragments of it cutting several flesh wounds on both legs, and the blast of the explosion severely wrenched his back. In addition, he had frostbite on both feet.

Jordan described how the first night's fight seemed to him at his position. He wrote, "The first night it seemed to me to be just a continuing battle at very close range, sometimes hand to hand, grenades used in large numbers by the Chinese, until dawn, when the remaining enemy withdrew. There was little room where one might assemble a group for counterattack as such. It would seem to me to be more clearly stated as a close range fight for individual positions."[12] No doubt it was much the same elsewhere.

It is clear that the Chinese almost overran the 3rd Battalion, 31st Infantry, and the two firing batteries of the 57th Field Artillery Battalion at the inlet on the night of 27–28 November. No count of the American and ROK casualties at the inlet during the night's battle was ever recorded. Nor was there ever any knowledge of the total number of enemy casualties, but they were heavy on both sides.

OTHER ENEMY ACTION THAT NIGHT

The CCF 80th Division's plan for the night of 27–28 November did not include action against the Hudong-ni area, possibly because of the presence there of the 31st Tank Company. In any event, all was quiet there during the night, but there was action only a mile or two north of it, although those at Hudong-ni were unaware of it at the time.

An hour or two after Captain Drake returned to Hudong-ni after failing to find Colonel MacLean, the 31st Medical Company arrived at Hudong-ni. Drake talked with the Medical Company captain, informing him of the dispersed nature of the 31st Infantry. The Medical Company commander was anxious to continue at least as far as the inlet and join the 3rd Battalion there for the night. Drake tried to persuade him not to continue that night but to remain at Hudong-ni overnight and to go forward the next morning with the tank company. The medical commander decided, however, to continue on, and after a time he and his company pulled out after midnight and disappeared up the road.

Sometime later in the night, the first sergeant of the Medical Company reappeared at Drake's CP. Excited and disheveled, he said that a Chinese force had ambushed the company a mile or two up the road and that he had escaped by crawling back in the road ditches. He was the only member of the company Drake saw after the ambush, but three or four others got back to Hudong-ni, according to Maj. Carl Witte, the regimental S-2. None of them knew how many might have broken through the ambush and reached the 3rd Battalion at the inlet. It appeared that the Chinese had killed an unknown number and had destroyed an unknown number of vehicles on the first hill north of Hudong-ni, Hill 1221.

The ambush had indeed taken place there, as was verified after daylight. American dead and several destroyed medical company vehicles cluttered the road about 400 to 500 yards south of the hairpin turn in the saddle, where the road bent sharply toward the reservoir to the west.

This ambush and roadblock on Hill 1221 was typical of Chinese tactics. While the CCF 80th Division was attacking the 31st RCT at Faith's forward position and the 3rd Battalion at the inlet frontally, it was cutting the road behind them, cutting off their escape route. Later events showed that at least a battalion of Chinese held the Hill 1221 ambush and roadblock throughout the entire period of action east of Chosin.

By the early hours of 28 November, garbled messages were received at the Hudong-ni Rear CP that told of confused enemy action at both the forward perimeter and at the inlet. But there was never any clear understanding of what was taking place. Communications soon deteriorated to the point of being virtually nonexistent.

Shortly after the first messages of enemy action north of Hudong-ni came in, Major Lynch tried by the regimental SCR-193 radio at Hudong-ni to reach Colonel Paddock, the 7th Infantry Division G-3 at Pungsan headquarters, 60 air miles to the northeast. To Lynch's surprise, General Barr, the division commander, answered the call. Barr told Lynch that he wanted to talk with General Hodes, who proceeded to outline the situation as he knew it and asked Barr to arrange for air support the next day. He also said the 2nd Battalion, 31st Infantry, had not arrived and was badly needed. This radio communication was broken before the end of the conversation and could not be reestablished. This was the only time the 31st RCT on the east side of Chosin Reservoir had communication with its division CP.[13]

The Chinese made still one more major attack during the night of 27–28 November—their third—but it came late, just before dawn. It must have been an afterthought, and it probably grew out of their establishing the road and fireblock after midnight at Hill 1221 and the ambush of the Medical Company.

In their small, covelike valley immediately east of the MSR, half a mile from the mouth of the Pungnyuri-gang inlet, Lt. Col. Ray Embree and his 57th Field Artillery Headquarters and Captain McClymont with his 1st Platoon of D Battery, 15th AAA AW SP Battalion, spent the night quietly, not knowing that a mile north of them, beyond Hill 1436, a furious battle was being fought, involving their two artillery batteries.

The quiet night changed suddenly for them. Shortly before dawn, 28 November, enemy appeared. The first sign was mortar fire that dropped around the 57th Field Artillery Headquarters and McClymont's AAA AW CP. McClymont ran to Sfc. Robert D. Denham's M19, near his CP tent, and climbed on its back. Small-arms fire was now whistling about, and the mortar fire had increased in volume. McClymont relates what happened next:

I raised my field glasses. The M19 crew were at their posts. I looked through the field glasses and with their light gathering ability, I could see movement on the side of a hill alongside of the road leading back to Hagaru-ri. I focussed the glasses and I could see that there was a column of soldiers marching in formation along the road, heading directly towards our position—they were about 200 yards from my CP and were closing on us. They would soon be on top of my 1st Platoon CP. Just then some sort of illumination shell or mortar round went off and we could see the column clearly. Dressed in dark winter clothes, quilted coats, with flapped caps, they were moving toward us. I ordered the M19 commander to load his twin 40 mms and to open fire. The twin 40s crumped simultaneously, and the traces leaped out. Immediately, the high explosive shells burst in the column of men, and I ordered fire at full automatic. In only seconds there was no movement from the column.

I felt someone grab my ankle. One of my cooks was standing on the ground. I leaned over and he said I was wanted on the field telephone. I jumped down and went to the phone in the CP tent. "This is Major Tolly [S-3 of the 57th FA Bn.] of the 57th," I was told, "those are friendly troops out there, cease fire!"

My heart sank. I had just erased a whole column of men.[14]

McClymont had indeed erased a whole column of men—but they were Chinese, as he had thought, and not the vanguard of the expected 2nd Battalion, 31st Infantry, which Tolly had guessed they were.

The quiet that followed the end of this dramatic incident was soon broken by a large volume of noise and weapons fire at his 1st Platoon

CP in the center of the little valley. When McClymont phoned it, he got no answer. Daylight was beginning, and McClymont could see that the hut in which the platoon CP was located was afire. He took three men with him, stating that he was going to the platoon CP. He wanted to make sure the road was secure before he left, so he and his three men moved south on the edge of the road first. They were fired on from enemy in a large foxhole. After considerable maneuvering they killed the five Chinese soldiers in it. He then shouted back for more men to join him. About ten men came up, and he now led his reinforced group up the road to where his M19 had stopped the column of marching men. Scattered along about 150 feet of the road lay the Chinese bodies, about 80 of them. Most of these Chinese had been armed with the American Thompson submachine gun. Each soldier who carried a Thompson submachine gun wore as an accessory a canvas apron strapped to his chest. These aprons had slots to hold a 20-round straight clip for the weapon. There were different models of the submachine gun in the group. McClymont examined several and finally chose one that suited him, and he took it and one of the aprons. He carried this weapon and its ammunition apron from that time on throughout his time in Korea.

Finding the road secure as far as a bend in it, he turned off the road and headed for his burning platoon CP. On the way he and his group came under fire from scattered Chinese, and he killed two of them. He made a hazardous approach to the CP hut and found an M16 near it inoperable. All enemy action had halted by the time McClymont reached the CP hut. He found Maj. Max Morris, the 57th Field Artillery executive officer, dead in the yard of the hut. Inside the hut Warrant Officer Calcotte lay dead, sprawled face down. He found Lieutenant Chapman, the 1st Platoon leader, alive. The first sergeant of D Battery had left McClymont's CP to go directly to the 1st Platoon CP, after McClymont had started up the road, and was killed halfway to it. Altogether, at the 1st Platoon CP and its vicinity, McClymont found two officers and four enlisted men killed, and one officer and six enlisted men alive. The Chinese there had knocked out the M19 near the CP. The M16 there would not operate because of battery failure and the frigid cold. Enemy fire had shot up two 2½-ton trucks. The enemy force that had caused these casualties and damage had come into the valley by crossing the ridge at its south side. M19 fire from near McClymont's CP had killed many of them and chased the survivors back south over this ridge.

It is not known how many artillerymen were killed or wounded in this attack, except those in McClymont's force, but the 57th CP was under enemy fire and suffered some casualties. Among them was Lieutenant Colonel Embree, the commander, who was wounded in the upper legs by small-arms fire early in the engagement. It seems likely that, had not McClymont's AAA weapons been present, the Chinese attack about dawn might have overrun the position.

After assessing the damage in the bivouac area, McClymont pulled what was movable of his weapons and equipment to his CP and then went to the 57th Artillery CP for orders. He learned that they all were to prepare at once for movement to the 3rd Battalion, 31st Infantry, perimeter at the inlet.[15]

THE NEXT DAY, 28 NOVEMBER

Colonel MacLean had left Faith's forward position about dawn on 28 November and returned on the road to his own Advance CP. He told his staff there that he thought the 1st Battalion, 32nd Infantry, had come through the night in pretty good shape. He apparently knew little about the situation at the inlet, only that there had been heavy fighting there during the night. His view of the general situation at daylight was reasonably optimistic. He expected his 2nd Battalion, 31st Infantry, to arrive during the day, and with this reinforcement and the tank company at Hudong-ni, he felt he could get control of the situation.

At Faith's position the first part of the morning was devoted largely to reestablishing their original lines with the help of air strikes and to bringing in the dead and wounded. Enemy activity, although greatly reduced, did not entirely cease. Except at the boundary on high ground of C and B companies, however, it was not important. Ammunition was redistributed.

At the boundary of C and B companies, the fight continued after daybreak and throughout most of the day. Reinforcements from Headquarters Company went there to try to recapture a commanding knoll the Chinese had seized during the night. Lt. Henry Moore's A&P Platoon bore the brunt of this fight. Moore was wounded by shrapnel but refused evacuation. Repeated air strikes failed to drive the enemy away and clear the knoll. Master Sergeant Russavage, the battalion sergeant major, joined the fight, leading a charge with his pistol. He fell in enemy territory, and his body could not be recovered when his group was driven back.

On the right of this critical area in C Company, the Chinese also pressed B Company, which had a hard time holding its position. The right flank of B Company bent around to the rear of the battalion CP, and there the CCF attacked hard on the south side. Faith organized most of Headquarters Company as an infantry force and put it into the line there. Stamford gave the heaviest air support during the day to C and Headquarters companies. The situation at the boundary of B and C companies led to withdrawing Mortrude's 3rd Platoon from C Company's left flank and moving it to the right flank. In the afternoon Mortrude's platoon was stopped just short of the high knoll the Chinese continued to hold.[16]

During the afternoon personnel of the 1st Battalion observed long columns of Chinese troops on the eastern skyline marching south past them. Some of them were mounted on Mongolian ponies. They were out of range of the 1st Battalion's fire. The men of the 3rd Battalion at the inlet also saw these Chinese troops moving south. Major Miller at the 1st Battalion position wrote, "We watched Chinese troops by-pass us to the east the entire rest of the day." Captain Bigger learned later that air strikes killed "hundreds of these Mongolian ponies" and presumably many CCF soldiers as well, east of American forces east of Chosin on 28 November.

About sundown A Company's forward observer saw about 300 to 400 enemy troops approaching on the road from the north with a tank and two self-propelled guns. Stamford talked over radio with the observer and directed an air strike by four Corsairs and four RAAF F-51s on this column, with devastating results. South African pilots flew the F-51s. It took about 20 minutes, Stamford reported, for the air strikes to knock out this enemy column as a fighting force.

GENERAL ALMOND VISITS THE FORWARD POSITION

On 28 November Maj. Gen. Edward M. Almond visited the 7th Division's forward element, the 1st Battalion, 32nd Infantry. He flew from Hamhung to Hagaru-ri in an L-17 plane with his 26-year-old junior aide, 1st Lt. Alexander M. Haig, Jr. There he conferred with Maj. Gen. Oliver Smith, commander of the 1st Marine Division, who had just established his CP there. Then Almond arranged for a helicopter to fly him to the 7th Infantry Division's forward position for a meeting with Colonel MacLean and Lieutenant Colonel Faith.

In his conversations with these two officers, Almond learned that neither of them knew anything more about the situation than he. Almond thought the previous night's battle was fought against elements of the Chinese 124th, 125th, and 126th divisions, which had been known to have been in the Chosin area for more than a month. Almond thought Faith seemed on edge during the conversations and resentful of the situation. Almond told Faith he should try to regain before nightfall the high ground he had lost during the night. MacLean told Almond he was establishing his regimental CP just south of Faith's position and that he thought his RCT could hold on, and he seemed to agree with Almond that, when his 2nd Battalion, 31st Infantry, arrived, he could advance northward. It appears that neither Almond nor MacLean knew at this meeting of the serious delays the 2nd Battalion had encountered in its move to join MacLean. Nor does it appear that either of them knew much about the situation at the inlet.

Before he left to return to Hagaru-ri, Almond told Faith he wanted to award three Silver Stars, one to him and the other two to members of the 1st Battalion that he should select. Faith protested that there were others more deserving than he, but Almond insisted that he should receive one of them. Faith selected Lt. Everett F. Smalley, a C Company platoon leader who had been wounded during the night's battle and who was sitting nearby, and asked him to come over to receive one of the medals. Headquarters Company Mess Sgt. George A. Stanley, who had performed well during the night, chanced to be passing the group. Faith called him over to receive the third decoration. Almond had awarded three Silver Stars to the Marines at Yudam-ni the day before, and this ceremony was to be an evenhanded award to the 7th Division Army men. After Almond had left the meeting to return to his helicopter, Faith angrily ripped the decoration from his parka and threw it onto the ground in the snow. Curtis, Bigger, Jones, and May have all confirmed privately the fact that they witnessed the ceremony. May was standing closest to Almond and Faith and heard Almond say to Faith he should not worry about the Chinese force—that it was only stragglers fleeing north. There was considerable talk in the battalion about this incident afterward. General Almond was the only officer of the 7th Infantry Division, the 1st Marine Division, or the X Corps (other than Lieutenant Haig) to visit the forward infantry battalion on the east side of Chosin after the Chinese launched their attack.

DRAKE'S FIRST TANK ATTACK, 28 NOVEMBER

Unknown to either of the infantry battalions or to the artillery, Captain Drake's 31st Tank Company moved out of Hudong-ni's 31st Rear CP area on the morning of 28 November to break through the Chinese roadblock on Hill 1221, about two miles north of Hudong-ni. He knew from the Medical Company's first sergeant, who had escaped the ambush the night before, of the enemy's presence on Hill 1221, but he had no precise information about enemy strength there. During the night General Hodes had decided that he would have Drake's tanks attack north in the morning to join the infantry and that Hodes would accompany the tanks. Drake had not known of Hodes's presence at Hudong-ni, but when Hodes conferred with him the next morning, it changed nothing for either man.

After all had breakfasted, Drake assembled three platoons of five tanks each with one of his command tanks mounting a 105-mm howitzer and having communications netting with the regimental command. He thus had a total of 16 tanks at his line of departure, which he marked on his map as three-quarters of a mile north of Hudong-ni. Drake pulled his jeep second in line behind the command tank. Hodes and the first sergeant of the Medical Company rode with him. Drake left his 4th Platoon of tanks and the second command tank with Lieutenant Jensen at Hudong-ni to defend the 31st Infantry Rear CP and the regimental dumps there. Drake, 27 years old, had graduated from West Point, class of 1944.

From his line of departure, the command tank led off northward with Drake and his passengers next in line. The three tank platoons followed without any infantry. About half a mile north, the road seemed headed straight into Hill 1221, which rose about 400 feet above the low ground around Twiggae. At the edge of Twiggae the road turned sharply to the northeast, angling up the lower slope of Hill 1221 toward a saddle about a mile distant. At this point the stretch of road leading up to the saddle came into full view.

At the road turn, the Medical Company first sergeant asked Drake to stop the jeep so he could point out places where the Chinese had been the night before. While he was speaking and pointing, a single shot from a sniper hit the sergeant in the head. Blood spurted over the map the three men had been holding. The sergeant died immediately. Hodes took cover, and Drake ran to his command tank. It was about 10 A.M. on 28 November.

When Drake reached his command tank, he divided his force into three parts. One platoon started up the road along the south face of Hill 1221, a second platoon attacked the south face of the hill north and west of the road, and the third platoon Drake held as a reserve at first behind his command tank. After the engagement was joined, however, Drake sent this third platoon to the east of the road along the right-hand edge of the flat ground at the lower edge of Hill 1473 (Ko-bong) in an effort to give flank support to the tanks on the road.

When the lead tanks advancing on the road neared some knocked-out vehicles of the Medical Company, the precise site of that ambush was revealed—about 400 to 500 yards south of the saddle at the east end of Hill 1221. There, enemy bazooka teams and supporting riflemen attacked the two lead tanks, scored hits with American-built 3.5-inch rocket launchers, and knocked them out. One of them blocked the road; the other slid off toward one side. Under covering fire the crew members escaped, some of them wounded.

Meanwhile the tanks that tried to cross the low ground east of the road found the ground soft in spots. Chinese soldiers rushed down to them, scrambled up their sides, and tried to lift the heavy engine-compartment doors, intending to drop grenades inside. Drake's command tank from the lower part of the road swept the tops of these tanks with machine-gun fire and tried for tree bursts of 105-mm howitzer shells above the

Chinese. Other tanks of the platoon directed machine-gun fire across the tops of the forward tanks, and quickly swept the Chinese soldiers from them. Two of the tanks, however, became mired down for a while, and it was a struggle to free them.

The tanks on the slope of Hill 1221, west of the road, were having a difficult time. They could not negotiate the slippery, frozen slope. One went out of control over a steep incline, and another threw a track.

While the tank attack developed, General Hodes watched its progress and saw that it would not succeed. Drake and Hodes discussed the attack, both realizing that it was failing. Drake said he would try again the next day if he could get some infantry support to get to the top of Hill 1221 and dislodge the CCF. Drake also said he wanted air support. Hodes promised he would do what he could, got into Drake's jeep, and drove back to Hudong-ni. Drake called off the attack in the afternoon. He reported his casualties as two officers and ten enlisted men. He lost four tanks.

Hodes arrived back at Hudong-ni about noon. He seemed intent on going to Hagaru-ri, the only place where help might be sought. While he was considering the situation, he told Lieutenant Hensen to make a reconnaissance from Hudong-ni to the northeast of the road to find a route in that direction to take the tanks around the Chinese roadblock at Hill 1221.

Hodes then told Anderson, Witte, and Lynch that he was going to Hagaru-ri in his jeep to seek help. There was discussion as to whether the road would be open, but Hodes did not seem disturbed by the prospect that it might be closed. Someone suggested that it would be better to go in a tank, since it would provide better protection and it also had radio facilities. This argument changed Hodes's mind, and he said he would go in one of the tanks. He left Hudong-ni just after noon and arrived at Hagaru-ri, only five miles south, in a short time without incident. Hodes never returned to Hudong-ni.

In the afternoon, Lieutenant Hensen started with one tank and a few men to carry out General Hodes's order to reconnoiter a route to the northeast around the Chinese roadblock. He started up a vehicle-wide trail that led up the slope behind the CP. Some distance along the trail the party ran into a group of Chinese, and in the exchange of fire between them, Lieutenant Hensen was killed, and his body could not be retrieved. The tank crew got the tank turned around, and the rest of the party returned to the Hudong-ni CP.

Before he left Hudong-ni, Hodes realized that the area was under observation by Chinese on higher ground in the mountains to the northeast. He told Major Witte, the regimental S-2, to lay out a perimeter, and Witte walked over it with him. Witte had no regular infantry for the perimeter, so he used an Engineer Platoon and regimental service troops. In the afternoon of the twenty-eighth, therefore, Lt. Col. Berry K. Anderson, the regimental S-3, by reason of seniority became the acting commander of the regimental Rear CP at Hudong-ni, pending any change that Colonel MacLean, the regimental commander, might make. But MacLean was never again in communication with Anderson or the 31st Rear CP. There were 150 miscellaneous 31st regimental headquarters and service troops at Hudong-ni. Counting Drake's tank company of about 176 men, the total number of troops there was approximately 325.[17]

During the tank action at Hill 1221 on 28 November, Drake had no communication of any kind with either the 3rd Battalion, 31st Infantry, and the 57th Artillery at the inlet, only two miles northeast, or with the 1st Battalion, 32nd Infantry. Nor did anyone at the inlet hear any sound of the tank battle. The infantry and artillerymen, only a mile or two away, had no knowledge of the effort being made to send armor to them. Also, the 31st Rear CP had by this time lost all communication with the units north of them.

AT THE INLET, 28 NOVEMBER

After the last Chinese had been driven from the 3rd Battalion CP and the communication huts in Lieutenant Traywick's dawn counterattack, the 3rd Battalion reoccupied its original CP. During the day, the 3rd Battalion infantry, with the help of air strikes, occupied their original ridgeline positions on the east side of the area. Stragglers from the rifle companies continued to filter into the perimeter during the day from their places of refuge during the latter part of the night. M Company improved its position for an expected continuation of the fight after dark came.

Although the Chinese withdrew from close contact at the inlet at dawn, they did not cease hostilities during the day. They deployed out of range to take control of the high ground around the small inlet perimeter. From the northern slopes of Hill 1456, they continued a harassing fire from the ridges on the east and the slope south of the perimeter. Several officers and men were killed or wounded by this fire during the day.

The most important event at the inlet on the twenty-eighth was Lieutenant Colonel Embree's order for the 57th Field Artillery Headquarters and Headquarters Battery, together with Captain McClymont's AAA AW weapons, to move into the 3rd Battalion perimeter. In making the move, McClymont had to leave one knocked out M19 (dual-40) behind in the little valley. The rest of his antiaircraft weapons, three M19s and four M16s, were taken into the 3rd Battalion perimeter. The move was completed about 1 P.M. without enemy interference. Air cover and the lethal power of the M19s and M16s made the situation unappealing to the Chinese. The American dead were left behind, and the wounded were taken to the middle of the perimeter.

The M19s and M16s were the most effective weapons for defending the inlet perimeter. Without them, it is unlikely the troops there could have survived another night. McClymont describes how he positioned the AAA weapons. "When we arrived at the 3/31 perimeter, I placed my weapons around the edge, with fields of fire such that the northern, eastern, and southern solid ground areas were covered by overlap—one M19 and one M16 also could cover the arm of the reservoir."[18] In the late afternoon, C-47 aircraft tried to drop 16 tons of supplies to the 31st RCT at the inlet, but because of strong winds a lot of it went to the Chinese on the southern slope.

THE SECOND NIGHT AT THE INLET

The CCF resumed the battle at the inlet perimeter before dark on the night of 28–29 November, so eager were they to finish off what they had so nearly accomplished the night before. The attack began against the infantry line on the east side of the perimeter. There they captured a machine gun and, for a time, achieved a penetration of K Company. When the incident was reported to Captain Kitz, he went to get mortar fire to stop the enemy. Many of his men criticized him for this act, thinking he should have stayed with his company. There is no explanation why telephone line was not in to the 81-mm mortars. It probably was Kitz who ran up to Sfc. Robert M. Slater, who commanded an M19, and ordered him to move his weapon to stop a CCF attack. Slater thought a captain had abandoned his company. He did not move his M19.

The Chinese who had overrun the machine gun were subsequently killed inside the perimeter. Some of the enemy penetrated during the night as far as the artillery, but the artillerymen stayed with their pieces and, aided by the M19 fire near them, killed or drove off the Chinese. The battle lasted all night, and at times was furious. There were many temporary penetrations, but in all cases they were liquidated. At daybreak, the perimeter still held, but shakily.

A new and ominous feature in the hours before dawn was the enemy attacks coming from the west, on the approach along the inlet by the road and railroad. The attacks at the western part of the perimeter lasted longest. These enemy troops had come from the *south*. They occupied land between the inlet and the perimeter before they withdrew just after daylight.

The main enemy close-in attack against the antiaircraft weapons guarding the artillery came after midnight. Sgt. Grantford R. Brown's M19 came under close attack, and a number of Chinese infiltrated right up to it.

At daybreak McClymont walked over to Brown's dual-40. He saw a trail of Chinese bodies beginning at the very side of the M19 and leading up the southern hillside out of sight. Brown told McClymont he had something to show him. He pointed out the body of a Chinese soldier lying beside the full-track, killed by small-arms fire. He said, "That fellow came in with the second rush. I was up on the turret directing fire when he climbed up alongside me. I saw he was carrying something and he looked Chinese to me, so I hit him with my fist. Almost broke my wrist, I did, and he fell over the side. One of my ROK soldiers under the M19 shot the Chinese as he hit the ground." Sergeant Brown then reached down on the top deck of the M19 where spare barrels were kept and raised the end of a six-inch-diameter bamboo tube. There were two fuses running into this homemade five-foot bangalore torpedo. Had the Chinese been able to find his matches, or had Brown been less alert, that M19 would have been blown sky high.

McClymont had his men gather up the Chinese bodies and put them in a pile. Two were still alive, and they told a ROK soldier that 4,000 Chinese soldiers surrounded the Americans and that their leader had placed a high price on the antiaircraft full-tracks and half-tracks, promising a great prize to any soldier who knocked out one of them. One of the M19s had an unexploded 60-mm enemy mortar shell wedged between the barrel jackets.

How did the night battle look to the men in the foxholes? Each had his own experiences. Sfc. John C. Sweatman, an assistant mess sergeant of K Company, gives a vignette of his: "The second night we were there, just before sunset, we dug a foxhole, took our position there, and every now and then they banz[a]ied. These kept up all night about every half hour. During the course of the night there were 3 jeep drivers that got caught outside their foxholes. Two of them fell on top of us and died. Just about that time we were hit by white phosphorus. There was one Hawaiian boy there shot in the back and also burned with white phosphorus. Another was burned up by white phosphorus."[19]

As they did the morning before, when daylight came, the Chinese began to withdraw. But action was still heavy at the southwest corner, where there had been no enemy the first night. Also there were large numbers of Chinese between the perimeter and the arm of the reservoir (the inlet) on the north side of the perimeter. These enemy withdrew at daylight along the edge of the inlet on the road and railroad leading south. Here the AAA automatic weapons had killed many Chinese near and along the side of the inlet. The Chinese had surrounded the inlet perimeter on all sides by daybreak of 29 November but withdrew because they feared air strikes. There were Chinese bodies everywhere around and inside the perimeter. One officer said that he counted 750 bodies, but this total may have been an exaggerated estimate of the dead in places that he could not inspect closely. But there is no doubt that the Chinese casualties were very heavy during the night.

THE SECOND NIGHT AT THE FORWARD PERIMETER

The second night started off more quietly at the forward perimeter of the 1st Battalion, in contrast to the situation at the inlet. Several officers gathered at the battalion CP, where a gasoline stove gave some warmth. Captain Vaudreaux, the battalion S-4, came in to report that ammunition had run low and that an airdrop would be needed the next day. MacLean and Faith went into a small side room to try to get some sleep. But Faith apparently could not sleep, and about 8 P.M. he returned to the main room and began telephoning his company commanders. They reported the situation was quiet.

Late in the afternoon Faith had to replace men in the line after Mortrude's 3rd Platoon, C Company, had been moved to the company's right flank during the day. Faith asked Lt. Hugh May to gather about a platoon-sized force from Headquarters Company and take them up the hill. May assembled about 40 men and arrived at the gap in the line on the right of the road at the saddle just before dark.

May appears to have been the oldest man in the battalion; in addition, he had perhaps as much varied experience, much of it in combat, as any man in the battalion. He obtained a battlefield commission as a second lieutenant when he was a member of a tank battalion in the Italian campaign of World War II, and his years of experience in the Army included training as an artilleryman and tanker. But at Chosin he served largely as an infantry platoon leader. He had seen enough service and combat to perform that role with distinction.

The wait in the 1st Battalion for the enemy attack ended at midnight. First there were a few probes. Then quickly the Chinese attack developed all around the perimeter. By 1 A.M. it was in full force, and at once the battalion was in trouble. On the battalion left in A Company, enemy cut off the left-flank 1st Platoon and threatened the entire company rear, killing the 1st Platoon leader. A counterattack failed to restore the position. The Chinese were now in a position where they could infiltrate around the A Company's left flank and reach the battalion CP and Captain Bigger's 81-mm mortars less than a mile to the rear.

At the same time, other Chinese attacked up the road against Lieutenant May's improvised platoon, which now held the east side of the road in the battalion line. When he went into the line just before dark, May had arranged with Lt. Cecil Smith, commanding A Company, that he would assume responsibility for the road during the night. May said he made this arrangement because A Company informed him that they had every man on their front line for the night's expected attack. The road proved to be the point to defend during the night. May covered it by two .30-caliber machine guns, one light and one heavy, and a recoilless rifle. Using these weapons plus small-arms fire, May's men beat back two enemy attacks during the night on the road approach. After these failures, the enemy tried to mount an attack up the steep northern slope leading into May's position. May adjusted 81-mm and 4.2-inch mortar fire on their assembly areas and prevented them from reaching his line. From his position on higher ground, May was also able to direct observed mortar fire in front of A Company's position on his left, where A Company was hard pressed.

C Company was in trouble on its right flank, where the critical point was still the Chinese-held knob at the B Company boundary. There Lt. James G. Campbell from the weapons company had two machine guns emplaced downslope from the enemy-held knob. The expected enemy attack from the knob came during an enemy mortar barrage, and it pushed C Company's right-hand squad off its position. Campbell moved one of his guns to an alternate position and reoriented the field of fire of the other. These changes limited any further penetration and prevented the Chinese from exploiting the situation. A little farther east, Lieutenant Mortrude's platoon received fire from the knoll and ridge in front of it but was able to stop it with well-directed mortar fire. At this time Capt. Dale Seever, the company commander, had his CP only 15 yards behind his front-line riflemen.

At the same time the Chinese penetrated C Company's right flank at the knoll, they persistently attacked adjacent B Company. Lieutenant Mazzulla there on the line with B Company reported to the 1st Battalion that the enemy had broken through the company line and was headed down the draw that led directly to the battalion CP. Faith thereupon sent all remaining headquarters personnel into the draw east of the CP. But B Company quickly closed the gap in its line, and Chinese never reached the battalion CP.[20]

Tension built up at the battalion CP as Colonel MacLean and Faith listened to reports from the company commanders. Suddenly, Lieutenant McNally, the 31st Communications officer who was outside with men guarding the CP, was called inside. He soon came back and told Major Robbins that Colonel MacLean had ordered the 1st Battalion to prepare to withdraw and to attack if necessary to reach the 3rd Battalion at the inlet. The decision to withdraw was reached at about 2 A.M. on 29 November, but the order did not reach all the troops until about two hours later.

Meanwhile, in the action on C Company's front, Cpl. James H. Godfrey, gunner of a 75-mm recoilless rifle, distinguished himself again as he had the previous night. In the Chinese continuing effort to use the recoilless rifle they had captured the night before, they found themselves engaged in a duel with Godfrey. He and his crew demolished the captured recoilless rifle and killed its Chinese crew. In this encounter Godfrey expended all his ammunition, and the rifle platoon to which he was attached was reduced to three men.

About 3 A.M. Major Miller climbed the spur ridge to the C Company CP. There, at about 3:30 A.M., he received a call from Faith, who relayed to him details of the projected battalion withdrawal, saying that it would start at about 4:30 A.M. Faith ordered Miller to organize and conduct a rear-guard action with A Company. Miller walked westward toward A Company. On the way he passed through Lieutenant May's position. He told May to withdraw to the battalion CP. He then crossed the road into Lieutenant Smith's A Company CP. The company was still under attack. When Miller arrived, Smith was in the act of organizing another counterattack to reach the cut-off 1st Platoon. Miller told Smith to prepare to withdraw the company down the draw in the company's rear.

MacLean wanted to start the withdrawal at 4:30, completing it during the hours of darkness, and to enter the 3rd Battalion inlet perimeter at daybreak. There were four road miles to cover between the two positions. Flank infantry guards on high ground east of the road would cover the vehicles. No one knew whether there were enemy troops there.

In general terms the conditions governing the withdrawal were the following: it would be in blackout, thus precluding the burning of any abandoned equipment and supplies; all trucks would be emptied to carry wounded; part of Headquarters Company would be advance guard on the road with the battalion headquarters and the vehicles; Captain Turner's B Company would travel on the high ground east of the road, and C Company would be east of B Company on still higher ground; Major Curtis was to accompany C Company; and Major Miller with A Company would command the rear guard. Because of a leg wound, Captain Seever turned command of C Company over to Lieutenant Mortrude, 3rd Platoon leader, for the duration of the withdrawal.

THE 31ST RCT CONSOLIDATES AT THE INLET

Major Robbins, S-1 of the 31st Infantry, watched the convoy form at the 1st Battalion CP. He estimated there were about 60 vehicles in it. Columns of foot troops formed on the road on each side of the vehicles and moved out to the front. All preparations were completed by about 4:30 A.M., and the column began to move forward. Places had been found for all the wounded in the trucks. The troops at the front lines had successfully broken contact with the enemy, and with the exception of A Company for a while, there was no pursuit. When A Company moved out as rear guard, it had to leave behind its cut-off 1st Platoon. As the troops on the high ground to the east of the road proceeded south parallel to the road column, it was a great relief to them and all in the convoy that they did not encounter enemy troops on the way. The withdrawal was well under way by 5 A.M., 29 November.

The convoy stopped at the heavy mortar position, halfway to the inlet, and there Major Miller joined it with the A Company rear guard. Captain Cody's mortar company joined the convoy. The leading vehicles were not far from the inlet. Here Lieutenant Colonel Faith ordered some infantry with the convoy to leave the road and climb the adjacent high ground on the east and get in position to help destroy a rumored enemy roadblock near the 3rd Battalion position. He then ordered the convoy to remain in place near the inlet while he went ahead with a small group to locate the roadblock. The command group became separated in groups as it went down the road on the north side of the inlet toward the bridge.

Faith, with a small party apparently comprising Lt. Henry Moore and a group of his A&P Platoon men, joined near the bridge by a few men (including Sergeant Luna) from B Company who had descended the steep slope of Hill 1324, found a roadblock of logs at the southern end of the bridge. This small group under Faith, numbering no more than ten men, attacked the roadblock and, under enemy small-arms and automatic-weapons fire from the east, cleared the logs from the road.

Some distance behind Faith and the lead troops came Colonel Mac-Lean and another small party, which included Capt. Erwin Bigger, commander of D Company, the Heavy Weapons Company. Bigger, who entered on active duty in the Army in January 1942, was considered an expert in the use of mortars. He was a close friend of Faith, who used him to coordinate battalion mortar and artillery fire. In World War II he had been a paratrooper in the 504th Parachute Infantry Regiment of the 82nd Airborne Division. He had been with the regiment at Gela, Sicily, and Salerno and was at Anzio for 62 days. He had activated the Weapons Company of the 1st Battalion and was considered an old-timer in the battalion.

The scene in the 3rd Battalion perimeter across the inlet was one of chaos in the early predawn light. Major Curtis, who at this time broke over the crest of Hill 1324 and had the inlet and the 3rd Battalion perimeter area spread out below him in one great panorama, wrote in his manuscript:

The "perimeter" of the 3/31 and 57th F.A. when I first saw it from the ridge line was a scene of destruction. It had been effectively "reduced" and was offering no organized resistance. There was smoke, fog, and very limited visibility. There was a sizable column of troops moving down the road to the southeast [Curtis subsequently corrected this to *southwest*] along what had been part of the perimeter. I recognized them as Chinese troops—and assumed (correctly I think) that they were bypassing the perimeter and moving south since the perimeter had been reduced.

Lieutenant Campbell of D Company had been with those who climbed the hill from the vicinity of the mortar position. He viewed the same spectacle that Curtis described from near the same spot and agreed with his assessment. He wrote that the 3rd Battalion area "appeared a scene of total devastation."[21]

Captain Bigger with Colonel MacLean saw the same spectacle as it appeared from road level along the inlet. Bigger wrote:

> As our Bn Command Group arrived on the north side of the Inlet we could look across the ice and see that the 3rd Bn., 31 and 57 FA were heavily engaged. Chinese were pouring down the surrounding hill toward the perimeter of the units. The quad 50 machine guns and the dual 40 mm anti-aircraft weapons of the 57th FA were taking a heavy toll of the Chinese columns. It was like being a spectator at a large screen movie for a moment. It was about this time that we observed a column of troops approaching the perimeter of the 31st *from the south* along the road.[22]

COLONEL MACLEAN DISAPPEARS AT THE INLET

Bigger said that the column coming from the south had not yet reached the western edge of the 3rd Battalion perimeter but was approaching it. He said that Colonel MacLean was overjoyed at the sight of the column approaching from the south across the inlet. He thought it was the 2nd Battalion, 31st Infantry, that he had been anxiously expecting to arrive and join him at Chosin Reservoir. There was firing from this group toward the perimeter and return fire from the perimeter. MacLean thought there was imminent battle between the two battalions of his regiment and that there was lack of mutual identification. Bigger wrote that MacLean looked at the scene for a moment and then said, "Those are my boys!" His immediate impulse was to get across the inlet and stop this firing between his two battalions.

MacLean turned to Bigger and said, "Here, take this order and give it to Faith." He rapidly delivered an oral order to Bigger that generally followed the usual five-point field order. He then turned and strode out onto the ice of the inlet, headed for the other side. Bigger watched. After MacLean got some distance out on the ice, Bigger could see that men on the other side were firing at him, and he saw him fall several times, but each time MacLean got up and continued on. As MacLean neared the other bank, Bigger could see Chinese soldiers come out to the edge of the ice, where they took hold of MacLean and pulled him to brush-covered ground. They led him up the bank and onto the road and then out of view. Bigger said the incident took place about half a mile west of the bridge, about midway between the turn of the road eastward along the inlet and the bridge.[23] Others saw MacLean cross the inlet, including Lieutenant Colonel Faith, Major Jones, and Major Curtis. Their reports essentially matched Bigger's.

Later in the morning, after he had crossed the inlet, Faith ordered C Company, which was to establish its position in a new perimeter along the south bank of the inlet, to make a search in that area for MacLean. The company made the search, necessarily limiting it to the area of the perimeter, but found no trace of MacLean. Inquiry disclosed that no one in the 3rd Battalion or the 57th Field Artillery had seen MacLean or witnessed his capture. MacLean had reached the south bank of the inlet *west* of the 3rd Battalion perimeter, and the folded nature of the ground and brush had obscured their view of him. The Chinese soldiers who had captured MacLean quickly left that part of the inlet as daybreak was at hand.

MacLean's ultimate fate was unknown until an American prisoner released by the Chinese said that, in early December 1950, he and Mac-Lean and many other prisoners were moved north from the Chosin Reservoir to a prison camp. He said that the Americans cared for and helped the wounded colonel all they could but that he had died of his wounds on the fourth day of the journey. His comrades buried him in a grave alongside the road.[24] MacLean was the highest-ranking officer in the US Armed Forces in northeast Korea to lose his life to enemy action.

FAITH DEPLOYS HIS TASK FORCE

Most of the foot soldiers crossed the inlet on the ice to the 3rd Battalion perimeter by 9 A.M., but it was about 1 p.m. before all the vehicles had crossed the bridge and causeway. Because they were under enemy small-arms and automatic fire from the east, each vehicle was individually dispatched across, one at a time, as fast as it could go.

Faith crossed the inlet during the morning with Captain Bigger and selected one of the railroad cuts within the perimeter as a site for his CP. Both men started to dig in at the side of the cut in the initial work to establish the CP. The low railroad cut where it went through one of the folds of ground would offer some protection from enemy fire.

Faith then went to Lieutenant Colonel Reilly's 3rd Battalion CP and conferred with him about the command of the perimeter force. It was agreed that Faith should assume command of all the 31st Infantry troops in the perimeter. From this time on the name "Task Force Faith" by common usage was applied to the inlet force. There was never any official order confirming the designation. Lieutenant Colonel Faith, with the help of Majors Miller and Curtis, spent the rest of the morning trying to find out what was left of I and K companies of the 31st Infantry (there was no L Company left) and tying them in with the 1st Battalion, 32nd Infantry, to form a new perimeter at the inlet. In the process of forming a new perimeter, Faith tried to include some high ground on the south side of it, in the A and B companies' part of it. They failed in their efforts during the afternoon to wrest any of this ground from the Chinese. So in the end Faith had to settle for a very restricted, unsatisfactory perimeter, all of it dominated by higher terrain.

In addition to the high ridge rising to its crest at Hill 1456, south of the perimeter, there were long finger ridges from that peak that came down on both the east and the west sides to the railroad, road, and shore of the inlet. Roughly, this high ground formed a flat U around the restricted American perimeter, with the open side of the U pointed north at the shore of the inlet.

The eastern spur ridge from Hill 1456 came down abruptly to the inlet about 500 yards east of the causeway and bridge, ending in a knob called Hill 1210. Its crest was 390 feet above the Pungnyuri-gang, and it dominated all the eastern end of the perimeter.

At the other, western, end of the perimeter, a spur ridge from Hill 1456 dominated the low ground there. This ridge spread out just above the inlet in a wide knob, called Hill 1250. Its steep northern slope dropped sharply to the edge of the reservoir. The narrow-gauge railroad there had cut into its lower slope to make the turn south. Hill 1250 rose nearly 530 feet above the level of the inlet and the reservoir, dominating the western side of the perimeter.

Faith's perimeter placed the 3rd Battalion of the 31st Infantry on the east, and the 1st Battalion of the 32nd Infantry on the north, west, and south, with the heavy mortars, the 57th Artillery, and the 15th antiaircraft guns in the center. Faith's perimeter departed little in dimensions and physical features from that originally held by the 3rd Battalion. The ground on the south side of the inlet did not allow any great changes. The horizontal dimension of the perimeter could hardly have been more than 1,400 yards wide, with the deepest part at its eastern end no more than 800 yards. From there its depth gradually narrowed as it extended westward, until it was no more than 300 to 400 yards. An erosional drain-

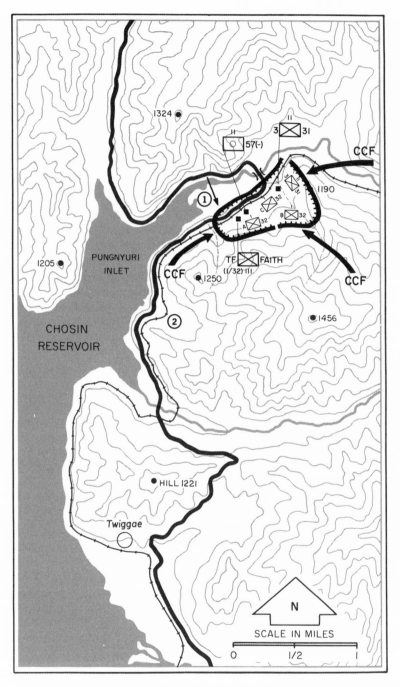

MAP 9. Task Force Faith perimeter, 29 November–1 December.

age ended this western low ground at the eastern base of Hill 1250. The draw there was the western border of the perimeter, the general outline of which resembled a bow with the bowstring taut. The road and railroad at the north along the inlet may be considered as the taut bowstring of the perimeter.

Faith's troop disposition along the perimeter was as follows: beginning at the northeast corner of the perimeter, the 3rd Battalion, 31st Infantry, held the line running from the river's edge up the spur ridge. A remnant of L Company under Capt. William W. Etchemendy, now part of a consolidated K Company, apparently had the lower part of this line where it met the boundary of C Company at the Pungnyuri-gang. Captain Kitz still commanded K Company, including the L Company remnants. Above K Company, Captain Marr's I Company carried the line to its upper and southern limit, where it met B Company, 32nd Infantry. From this point — the boundary of I and B companies (and of the 1st and 3rd battalions) — the 1st Battalion was responsible for the remainder of the perimeter. Captain Turner's B Company carried the line westward along the lower slope of Hill 1456, following the 1,160-meter contour line for perhaps 800 yards. A Company then picked up the line and carried it in a curve down to the railroad and road, where it met the C Company boundary. From there, just east of the drainage draw near Hill 1250, C Company had the line along the inlet, the north side, to a point about 500 yards east of the bridge. There it met the beginning of the 3rd Battalion line and closed the perimeter.

The C Company portion of the perimeter, less than a mile long, was the longest part for any of the rifle companies, but it was also the most easily defended, with the inlet at its front. The boundary between A and C companies at the road at the western end of the perimeter was perhaps the single most important defensive point of the perimeter. A Company was responsible for the road there, but throughout the battles C Company helped in its defense. In effect, it became a joint responsibility. Captain Jordan's M Company of the 31st Infantry remained in its original position behind I Company, which it had never lost. In a slight reorganization of his task force, Faith made Major Miller commander of the 1st Battalion, 32nd Infantry. Faith ordered that a platoon-sized force of D Company be uncommitted as a task-force reserve.

In his task-force reorganization at the inlet, Faith had his ad hoc CP and three battalion CPs. Major Miller commanded the 1st Battalion; Major Harvey H. Storms headed the 3rd Battalion; and Major Robert J. Tolly, S-3 of the 57th FA, took command of that battalion. Faith's old 1st Battalion staff continued to serve him as task-force commander.

In the afternoon of 29 November there were airdrops of supplies at the inlet, which Captain Stamford had requested. These emergency drops were prepackaged in Japan and did not contain sufficient ammunition in the needed variety. The most noted shortage was the lack of 40-mm ammunition for McClymont's M19s.

An hour after the airdrops, a helicopter landed at the inlet, sent by Brigadier General Hodes, then at Hagaru-ri. It took out two men, Lieutenant Colonel Reilly, 3rd Battalion commander, and Lieutenant Colonel Embree, 57th Field Artillery Battalion commander. This evacuation helicopter returned a second time, taking out two more unidentified critically wounded. But that was all—four men—before dark. Hodes tried to get the helicopter the next day, but the Marines denied his request because there was a higher priority for its use, presumably the evacuation of critically wounded Marines from Yudam-ni.

The failure to get the right airdrops of ammunition and supplies to the inlet had serious results. Captain McClymont's M19s did not get a single 40-mm shell during the entire time they were at Chosin. But one large drop of 40-mm ammunition was mistakenly made at Hudong-ni, four miles south of the inlet, where there was no use for that type of ammunition. And Captain Drake with the tanks there did not receive the 105-mm shells and tank machine-gun ammunition he had requested. Drake blew up the big stack of 40-mm shells the next day before his armor withdrew to Hagaru-ri.[25]

DRAKE'S SECOND TANK ATTACK, 29 NOVEMBER

After his return to Hudong-ni on 28 November, Drake spent the evening and part of the night preparing for a second try the next day with foot-troop support. He planned to leave the same number of tanks at Hudong-ni for their protection and to take the rest up the road to the Chinese position at Hill 1221. Because he had lost four tanks the day before, Drake now had only 11 with 76-mm guns and a command tank with a 105-mm howitzer. He counted on the foot troops to make a difference. Unless they could help control Hill 1221, Drake realized, his attack would go nowhere because one of his tanks now effectively blocked the road, and there was no alternative route to the inlet. He did not consider using the narrow-gauge rail track.

Lieutenant Colonel Anderson and Major Witte had few troops of any kind to send with Drake. They apparently did not draw on the approximately 100 troops of Service Battery, 57th Field Artillery, that had joined them the day before. This left only part of the 31st Headquarters and Headquarters and Service Company, an engineer platoon, a detachment of the Heavy Mortar Company, a detachment of the Medical Company, and some attached ROK troops. The exact number and makeup of the foot force is not known. Drake said there were "about 50 to 75 men who assaulted the ridge with tank fire support on 29 November." Nearly 30 years later Major Witte thought there were about three officers and 30 enlisted men from the service troops.

On 29 November, the tanks and the "infantry" force left Hudong-ni about 8 A.M. with good visibility and advanced the short distance to the turn of the road and Hill 1221. This time Drake directed his entire attack against the south face and crest of Hill 1221. The tanks again tried to climb the slope in support of the makeshift infantry force. But again they could not get traction and slipped. He had only one mortar with which to reach CCF positions just over the crest of Hill 1221, but he had no artillery support. The air support he had asked Hodes to arrange did arrive. But there was no FAC with Drake, so the necessary directions for effective air strikes could not be given to the Corsair pilots. As a result, when they made their strikes, their fire hit among the Americans as well as the Chinese.

The fight at Hill 1221 lasted about four hours, but in the end the tank attack failed. There were no tanks lost on the twenty-ninth, and no precise figure can be given for casualties in the composite body of foot troops, but Captain Drake said, "They were heavy—not many killed, but many wounded. They were not well trained—there were KATUSA along also. We lost track of the latter." A 7th Division document reported that 20 men were lost in this attack.

This was the last effort armor made to join the infantry battalions. Captain Drake's tanks remained at Hudong-ni one more day, until 30 November, when they were ordered to withdraw to Hagaru-ri. There never was any Marine effort from Hagaru-ri, either with infantry or armor, to assist the 31st RCT or Task Force Faith, although both the Marine Corps official history and the 7th Division Command Report say there was. The Marines at Hagaru-ri at the same time were fully occupied holding their own precarious perimeter.

MACARTHUR'S CONFERENCE IN TOKYO, 28 NOVEMBER

On the afternoon of 28 November, after he had left his meeting with MacLean and Faith at the forward CP east of Chosin Reservoir, General Almond returned to Hamhung, where he found awaiting him a message from MacArthur, requesting him to be present at Tokyo that evening for a conference. This conference was called because of the situation in General Walker's Eighth Army in the west. Walker had received a similar summons to go to Tokyo for the conference. When Almond arrived at the American Embassy in Tokyo after dark that evening, the others were awaiting his arrival. In addition to Walker and MacArthur, the commanders of the Far East Navy and the Far East Air Force were present, along

Maj. Gen. Edward M. Almond (*left*) awards Capt. Robert E. Drake (*right*) the Silver Star, as Maj. Gen. David G. Barr, commander of the 7th Infantry Division (*center*), looks on. (Photograph courtesy Col. Robert E. Drake)

with a few of MacArthur's top staff. The conference got under way about 9:50 P.M. and lasted about four hours, until 1:30 A.M. of 29 November.

MacArthur asked many questions of Walker and Almond. When Mac-Arthur asked Walker what he thought of the situation on his front and where the Eighth Army could make a successful stand, Walker replied that he expected to hold Pyongyang and to establish a defense line north and east of the city. When MacArthur asked a similar question of Almond, the latter euphorically answered that he expected the Marines and the 7th Division troops to continue their attacks west and north and carry out the plan to cut the enemy line of communications behind Eighth Army at or near Mupyong-ni and continue to the Yalu. Almond stated the same view he had held in his conversations with MacLean and Faith that afternoon.

MacArthur did not give any orders to his commanders during the conference, but his mind was made up about the X Corps. Before Almond left Tokyo on the twenty-ninth to return to his command in Korea, Mac-Arthur told him to end offensive action, withdraw, and concentrate the

corps in the Hamhung-Hungnam area. Almond left Tokyo at noon to return to Korea. Lieutenant Colonels McCaffrey and Glass and Major Ladd
were on the plane with him. Almond, acting on MacArthur's orders to
him, told McCaffrey and Glass to prepare a X Corps order to concentrate
the corps's troops at Hamhung. On arriving at Yonpo airfield in Korea,
Almond and his aides went immediately to the X Corps Headquarters,
where Almond held a meeting with the corps staff. Out of this meeting
X Corps Order 8 was formulated, which called for the X Corps to dis-
continue its attack and to withdraw its forces.[26]

THE THIRD NIGHT AT THE INLET

Contrary to expectations, the first part of the night of 29–30 November
proved to be relatively quiet at the inlet perimeter. From dark until near
midnight silence reigned, except for the distant sound of artillery fire from
the west, across the reservoir near the Marine positions at Yudam-ni, and
occasional bugle sounds to the north. A bright moon illuminated the landscape, but as the night progressed the sky clouded over and it began to
snow.

The first attack came shortly before midnight over the ridge and descending slope at the south side of the perimeter, where B and A companies of the 1st Battalion held the line. Lieutenant May of Headquarters
Company helped repel one enemy attack that came down a ravine at the
southeastern edge of the ridge. This clash lasted about an hour. If the
Chinese wanted to test the newly arrived troops, they did so to their re-
gret. Many were killed or wounded. They did not enter the perimeter and
finally withdrew from contact with a lot of bugle blowing.

We do not know what the enemy did at the forward position after Faith
led the 1st Battalion to the inlet. They probably spent the day pillaging
the vacated area. Although there was no coordinated assault on the inlet
perimeter during the night, there were infiltration attempts and probing
along the lines all night long, and two or three sharp attacks.

One of these was especially fierce, although it did not last long. It was
directed against both ends of the perimeter, where the road entered and
exited from it. The worst of this attack was at the southwestern end, where
A Company had established a roadblock to anchor its western boundary.
There an enemy assault party overran a heavy machine gun, and a mortar shell exploded on a 75-mm recoilless rifle, wiping out that position.
These two weapons had provided the bulk of the American firepower
there. The Chinese captured some of the crew members.

There was concern that enemy might attack over the flat, frozen area
of the inlet. Mortars walked a barrage up the inlet and then pulled their
rounds to within 100 yards of American foxholes. These shells did not

break the ice and expose running water, as hoped for to inhibit an enemy attack across the inlet. From time to time, mortars fired illuminating shells over the perimeter. A group of American stragglers from the 1st Battalion did successfully cross the inlet during the night—a risky undertaking.

McClymont remained in his foxhole underneath a quad-50 half-track. He had pulled his sleeping bag over him and was about to drop off to sleep. Suddenly, shooting started at a foxhole near the edge of the inlet. He grabbed his glasses and saw figures running on the ice, coming toward the perimeter. A star shell rose into the sky over the inlet. A quad-50 about 20 yards to his right opened up. The running figures had reached the south side of the inlet and the foxholes at the perimeter. The four machine guns of the quad-50 raked the edge of the inlet and ice. Each gun fires 450 rounds a minute on full automatic, and every fifth round is a tracer. The tracers showed the fire cutting into a bank and working over the edge of the ice at the inlet.

Closer to him, McClymont could make out movement, but he did not know if it was friend or foe. He and the two men with him withheld fire. But there was still fire from friendly foxholes in front of him, which led him to conclude that the movement represented enemy. At this point a soldier climbed into his foxhole from the rear. He told McClymont the edge of the inlet "was crawling with Chinese." McClymont and his men fired into the mass of moving shadows below them. The nearby quad-50 had by now reloaded, and it came to life with a swath of .50-caliber bullets along the edge of the inlet, only 40 to 50 yards away. After this moving scythe of fire passed along the edge of the inlet, things became quiet. This is the only recorded enemy attack across the ice of the inlet from the north to the south side. It came to a bloody end.

The nearby quad-50 had stopped firing. McClymont decided to check on its status. He went to it in the interlude of quiet and found that the gunner had been hit in the head as he sat in the turret, and the crew had not been able to remove him. He was a tall man. McClymont crouched down until he could feel the gunner's feet and slowly was able to turn them around. The crew then lifted the gunner from his place and laid him down alongside the quad-50. A new gunner slid into place in the turret.

The soldier from the inlet who had crawled into McClymont's foxhole had additional information. He said that a house near the inlet contained Chinese soldiers. McClymont went to one of the M19s and told the crew to direct fire on the house. The 40-mm shells soon made a wreck of it, killing a squad of Chinese inside it.

The Chinese picked out the M19 commanded by Sgt. Harold B. Haugland for repeated attacks just before midnight. The crew was able to kill most of the assault groups, but Haugland suffered a serious foot wound in this action and was taken to the aid station. Haugland returned to his M19 with his wrapped foot in an empty ration box. Enemy mortar fire succeeded in hitting the M19's ammunition trailer, causing the 40-mm shells in it to explode. Haugland went to the front of the M19 and succeeded in guiding it away from the exploding ammunition. The M19 continued in action during the night and was the dominant factor in preventing a penetration of the perimeter at that point. But during the battle the M19 suffered considerable damage, which rendered it immobile, though it was still able to fire its guns.

After the attacks on the antiaircraft weapons, enemy activity during the rest of the night was confined to machine-gun fire and to blowing bugles and whistles and setting off flares. These probably signified an enemy regrouping of forces.

That night an American soldier froze to death in a sitting position in his foxhole.

DAYLIGHT AT THE INLET, 30 NOVEMBER

Ground fog at daylight gradually gave way to clear skies at 10 A.M. Airdrops then came bringing supplies. Captain Stamford asked the pilots to bring in more ammunition, which was still critically short. Later there was a drop of .50-caliber machine-gun ammunition, but there was still no resupply of 40-mm shells for the M19s.

After dawn the men built fires to warm themselves and heat water for coffee. The Chinese on the high ground did not interfere and seemed to pay them no heed.

Early on 30 November Lieutenant Mortrude of C Company was ordered to clear the shoreline of the inlet in his 3rd Platoon area for a helicopter landing site; casualties were to be evacuated. The work was finished before noon, and the only helicopter ever to use it landed soon thereafter. The helicopter brought Major General Barr, commander of the 7th Division. Barr had flown to Hagaru-ri earlier in the day and had conferred with Gen. Oliver Smith. The status of both Barr and Smith had been changed by General Almond's X Corps order, effective at 8 A.M. that morning, 30 November, which placed all elements of the 7th Divison north of Koto-ri under the command of General Smith, the Marine division commander. Thus, Lieutenant Colonel Faith's task force as of that time was no longer under 7th Division command. This change may have been one of the reasons Barr wanted to confer with Faith and tell him of his new chain of command, since there was no other means of communicating it to him.

When General Barr stepped from the helicopter, Mortrude and some of his men were there to greet him. Mortrude said Barr responded with a brusque and unsympathetic comment and stalked off to locate Lieutenant Colonel Faith. Barr went into immediate private conversation with Faith, the meeting lasting about half an hour. What passed between them is not known. Faith did not disclose it to his staff, and no record of the conversation was ever made by either principal. But according to remarks that Barr made later in the day to Smith at Hagaru-ri, Faith evidently told him that in any breakout attempt he would have 500 wounded to bring out. He also told Barr about Colonel MacLean. This was the first information higher headquarters had of the loss of the regimental commander and of Faith's assumption of command. When he assembled his staff the next morning to announce a breakout attempt, Faith told them only that he was ordering it on his own initiative, that General Barr had given him no instructions as to what he was to do. After his conversation with Faith, Barr immediately returned to Hagaru-ri to attend a commanders' conference there that afternoon called by General Almond.

About noon, after the early Corsair strikes and supply planes' flights to the perimeter, Stamford's high-frequency radio ceased to operate. Stamford thought Lieutenant Johnson's equipment, damaged when Johnson was killed in the first night's attack on the 3rd Battalion, might be salvaged to repair his set. Johnson's equipment lay about 500 yards away from Stamford's position. Cpl. Myron J. Smith, the radio operator, and Pfc. Billy E. Johnson, another member of the TACP, volunteered to cross the area under fire to bring the equipment to Stamford. They succeeded in rescuing it and then worked four hours with bared hands in freezing weather to put together a radio set that worked. The repaired radio set enabled Stamford to continue as FAC, which was vital to Task Force Faith. It is sad that neither Corporal Smith nor Private First Class Johnson survived Chosin.[27]

In the afternoon, Lt. Hugh May was given one of the most difficult and dangerous jobs on the perimeter. He was to cover the road and narrow-gauge railroad leading south out of the perimeter. This was the boundary between A and B companies. The repeated enemy attacks there required that this critical point be reinforced. May recruited his force from drivers, cooks, and other headquarters personnel. His role here was almost identical to the one he had had in the forward perimeter. In addition to their individual weapons, his makeshift force was provided with a rocket launcher, two .50-caliber machine guns, and two .30-caliber machine guns. The Chinese continued their attack there during the afternoon, not waiting for nightfall. They kept up attacks from around an embankment about 100 to 200 yards southwest of the road outpost. May said the outpost had to withdraw to the perimeter boundary and set up their strongpoint there. Suicide attacks, he said, continued all that afternoon and night. At times the Chinese closed to within grenade range. In this continuing action the Chinese casualties were extremely heavy, but May's force suffered only a few killed and wounded.

As darkness settled over the perimeter, word was passed to those within it, "Hold out one more night and we've got it made!" Those words may have held out hope to some, but to others they seemed to mean that the situation was desperate.

COMMANDERS CONFERENCE AT HAGARU-RI

Sometime during the afternoon of 30 November at Hagaru-ri, after his return from Faith's CP at the inlet, General Barr told General Smith of the 500 wounded Faith had reported that he would have to bring out, which would be his biggest handicap in any breakout effort. In this discussion with Smith, Barr is said to have agreed that Faith could improve his situation and probably succeed in a breakout effort with strong Marine air support. That morning Almond had issued his X Corps Instruction 19, which gave Smith command of all X Corps troops north of Koto-ri in the Chosin area. It included ordering the 1st Marine Division to redeploy one regiment immediately from Yudam-ni to Hagaru-ri and gain contact with the 31st RCT.

Almond flew from Hamhung at 1:40 P.M. in an L-17 liaison plane for Hagaru-ri to lead a conference of commanders in the Chosin area. The conference began at 2:10. The group he had assembled included Generals Smith, Barr, and Hodes and Colonels Williams and Forney. Almond told the assembled group that the corps would abandon the Chosin Reservoir area and that all troops would be concentrated immediately in the Hagaru-ri area. Once concentrated there, they would be withdrawn to the coast. He was an entirely different man from the one who had visited his troops there two days earlier. He knew now that the survival of X Corps itself was at stake. He told Smith that he would resupply him by air if he felt the need to burn or destroy some supplies in order to hasten withdrawal. He stressed the need for speedy action. Smith replied that he would need everything he had to fight his way to the coast. He also added that the care and evacuation of wounded would be the biggest obstacle to a speedy withdrawal. Almond ordered Smith and Barr to prepare a plan and a time schedule for getting the Army units east of the reservoir withdrawn to Hagaru-ri.[28]

The conference lasted an hour and 20 minutes. At 3:30 P.M. Almond flew back to the X Corps CP at Hamhung. He then drafted a message to General MacArthur on the X Corps situation.

Back at Hagaru-ri, Generals Smith and Barr discussed how they could implement Almond's order to extricate the 7th Division elements east of Chosin. They agreed that not much could be done with the troops available at Hagaru-ri. Every man there was needed to hold that position. They agreed that, before anything could be done, the Marines would have to be withdrawn from Yudam-ni. Smith told Barr that Marine air support would be provided the next day on a preferential basis to help Faith fight out of the inlet perimeter to try to reach Hagaru-ri. Smith subsequently discussed the situation with General Hodes, directing him to prepare a message to Faith ordering him to fight his way out of the inlet perimeter to try to reach Hagaru-ri.[29]

Marine Withdrawal to Hagaru-ri

On the afternoon of 30 November the 31st Infantry Rear and Captain Drake's 31st Tank Company were ordered to withdraw from Hudong-ni to Hagaru-ri. Until then the presence of the tank company at Hudong-ni had kept the Chinese off the road south of the big roadblock and fireblock at the hairpin curve at the east side of Hill 1221, two miles south of the inlet perimeter.

On 30 November, the need for troops to bolster the Marine perimeter defense at Hagaru-ri was so great that General Smith ordered Captain King's A Company, 1st Engineer Marine Battalion, stationed about two miles north of Hagaru-ri at a sawmill near Sasu, to get out timbers to repair the blown concrete bridge over the Paegamni-gang, to move to Hagaru-ri. The Marine company had an outpost on Hill 1203, just south of Sasu, from which it could see Hagaru-ri. First Lt. Nicholas A. Canzona's 1st Platoon led the way back without incident and was committed that night to the fighting on East Hill. The recall of the Marine engineers together with the withdrawal of approximately 325 Army troops and the tanks from Hudong-ni left no American units between Hagaru-ri and the cut-off troops of Task Force Faith at the inlet.

One particular feature of the terrain at Hudong-ni was especially important. Directly north of Hudong-ni a long ridgelike spur descended from Ko-bong, 1473 meters high, in a southwesterly direction to end in a high knob, Hill 1239, about one-third of a mile north of Hudong-ni. From it a sharp finger ridge descended, ending directly above the road about 300 yards west of the 31st Rear CP, just north of the turnoff from the road into it. That finger of ground was to be the final critical point in deciding the fate of Task Force Faith the next day.

Because the removal of the 31st Rear CP and the 31st Tank Company from Hudong-ni occurred late in the afternoon of the day before Task Force Faith undertook its breakout from the inlet perimeter, and because the final end of that effort came virtually at the position those troops had held, the question presses: if they had still been there on 1 December, could they have saved Task Force Faith from destruction? Given the urgency of this question, it would be useful to know who ordered the withdrawal of those forces from Hudong-ni, just when their presence there became most important militarily. These remain questions for which only uncertain answers are available, but some rather direct evidence and much circumstantial evidence exist to warrant speculative conclusions.

The communications situation that then existed would indicate that the order would have had to come from Hagaru-ri, and from there it could have come only via the 31st Tank Company radio, which could communicate with Hudong-ni, and then only with other tanks of the 31st Tank Company under Drake's command. The 7th Infantry Division Command Report for the period says that the 1st Marine Division ordered Anderson and Drake at 11 A.M., 30 November, to withdraw to Hagaru-ri. In a memorandum to the commanding officer of the 31st Infantry Regiment on 12 December 1950, Captain Drake stated that he received the order to withdraw at 4 P.M. on 30 November, but he does not say who gave him the order. It would seem that it necessarily would have had to come directly or indirectly from Lt. Col. Berry K. Anderson.

All troops in the Chosin Reservoir area north of Koto-ri after 8 A.M. that morning were under the command of Maj. Gen. Oliver P. Smith, commanding the 1st Marine Division, by virtue of X Corps order. The order to the 31st Rear at Hudong-ni would have had to come from the 1st Marine Division command. And it could be transmitted only over the radio in the tank that Hodes had at Hagaru-ri. It is important to remember that Major General Barr, commander of the 7th Division, was in Hagaru-ri that morning and most of the afternoon and was in communication with both General Hodes and General Smith. Barr or Smith could have had Hodes transmit the order verbally to Lieutenant Colonel Anderson at Hudong-ni over his tank radio. If General Barr gave instructions to Hodes to give Anderson the order, he could have done so only with General Smith's tacit or oral approval. The Marine division operations journal for the day shows no order of that kind. In the situation that then existed it would not have been unnatural for General Smith to defer to General Barr's views on what should be done about the 7th Division troops at Hudong-ni, although he would have to bear responsibility for the decision.

General (then Major) Lynch states that he did not relay the withdrawal order to Anderson on behalf of Hodes or anyone else. He thinks all the circumstances in the situation indicate that General Hodes transmitted the order. I agree with that judgment, but it is impossible now to determine on whose instructions he acted, or precisely when the order was received at Hudong-ni. The order was probably issued in General Smith's name, verbally by General Hodes, who acted either as Smith's or Barr's agent, via tank radio to Anderson at Hudong-ni.

Lt. Gen. (then Lt. Col.) William J. McCaffrey, at the time deputy chief of staff, X Corps, has said privately that the order for the 31st Rear to withdraw to Hagaru-ri originated with General Barr. He said that, when General Almond heard about the withdrawal, he asked General Barr for an explanation and that the latter replied that he could not see any good coming from losing more men in behalf of those already lost.[30]

One further development occurred on 30 November at Hagaru-ri that does not appear in the official records. General Barr told General Smith that, to avoid possible embarrassment for all concerned and to avoid the semblance of conflict in command, he would recall Brigadier General Hodes from Hagaru-ri to 7th Division headquarters. Hodes apparently returned to the coast that day.[31]

The 31st Rear troops and the 31st Tank Company began their withdrawal from Hudong-ni about 4 P.M. on 30 November, with some tanks in the lead and others covering the rear. The march order included foot soldiers moving on either flank as the motor convoy and tanks followed the point up the road. Most of the troops rode in trucks, with Lieutenant Colonel Anderson commanding the movement. About a mile south of Hudong-ni, at a sharp bend in the road at the saddle of the first ridge south of the Paegamni-gang, and east of Hill 1167, Anderson ordered Drake to abandon two disabled tanks he was towing. He thought they retarded the movement of the convoy. Drake thus lost or had to leave behind six tanks east of Chosin. He continued the movement with 15 tanks.[32]

The 7th Infantry Division After Action Report for the period states that the convoy had a running fight with the enemy on their way to Hagaru-ri, but this account is inaccurate. Captain Drake reported that there was no significant enemy action directed at the movement. There was occasional small-arms and automatic-weapons fire, but at such a distance that it did no damage. No tanks or trucks were lost to enemy action, and there were no personnel casualties in the movement. Major Lynch and General Hodes met the tanks when they reached the Marine perimeter at Hagaru-ri. Lynch stated that, at the time, he understood that there was no enemy action.[33]

Drake and his tanks reached the Marine perimeter about 5 P.M., just before darkness fell. But Drake had time to get a reload of machine-gun ammunition and place his tanks in the perimeter in its northeastern arc before daylight entirely faded. He deployed the 16 tanks along the base of East Hill at a sector of the Marine perimeter that had been poorly defended. Drake said, "We were in a tight formation—50 to 110 yards apart—

thus we covered about 1,000 yards of the line. Our tents were within running distance from our tank line."[34]

Drake's tanks that night played an important role in turning back a
massive Chinese attack from East Hill. The Chinese at one point broke
through Drake's tank line and reached the tents in his rear, but they were
killed there or escaped back to East Hill. A body count the next morning
in front of two of his tanks showed 200 dead Chinese.

By dark of 30 November, then, Task Force Faith at the inlet perimeter
was isolated and alone. There were no friendly forces between it and
Hagaru-ri.

THE FOURTH NIGHT AT THE INLET

On the night of 30 November enemy mortar fire began about 8 P.M. and
built up to barrage level. It was taken as a prelude to an infantry assault.
Many heard the sound of steel on steel as mortar fragments repeatedly
struck nearby vehicles or other metal objects. Under the barrage, enemy
assault teams crept close to the perimeter, and those inside finally heard
the sound of rifle and submachine-gun fire. The enemy had begun to clash
with infantry in the outposts.

One of the early attacks came from the southwest along the road. It
headed toward Mortrude's 3rd Platoon of C Company where that unit held
a position near the boundary of A and C companies. His men there heard
voices and observed enemy crawling to their immediate front. Mortrude
requested and received mortar fire 100 yards to his front. He reduced the
range to 50 yards and called for "Fire for Effect," and after the impact he
heard much crying and shouting to his immediate front. This barrage
ended the pressure there for the present. Later, enemy mortar fire increased
near his platoon CP. First his acting Korean Platoon leader was slightly
wounded in the legs and back, and next, his platoon sergeant, Sergeant
First Class Campbell, was killed.

A little after midnight the Chinese attack built up to an intensity not
known on previous nights. Major Curtis thought the enemy was determined to overrun the perimeter at any cost. He thought that only the
determined holding of their positions by A and C companies prevented
the perimeter from being overrun. At one point, an enemy penetration
swept the infantry in front of and past one of the quad-50s, but crew
members stayed with their weapon and kept on firing. The penetration
was sealed off largely because of the heavy quad-50 fire, and the enemy
soldiers who had penetrated were killed inside the perimeter. During this
period Lieutenant Mortrude injured his knee while launching a rifle
grenade flare from a kneeling position. In the hectic action of the mo-

ment, he may have placed the butt of his carbine against his knee before firing. Thereafter it was difficult for him to walk. Heavy snowfall began after dark and made visibility difficult.

In his manuscript about the fighting during the night of 30 November, Major Miller said that the AAA weapons inflicted terrible destruction on the Chinese and that the enemy made repeated attempts to knock out these weapons. Major Curtis commented about one of the Chinese attacks against the A Company roadblock at the western end of the perimeter. He wrote,

> A body of enemy troops charged down the open road in such a manner that our men at first identified them as other friendly troops. This attack, however, was repulsed with great casualties to the enemy. Fighting became very close, and in some instances hand-to-hand in other parts of the perimeter. . . . Occasionally a Chinese soldier would infiltrate inside the perimeter and run about like a madman spraying with his burp-gun until he was killed. . . . Between 0400 and 0600 every man in the perimeter was in a defensive position operating a weapon. The question was whether the perimeter could hold out until dawn.[35]

From the very first night of their attacks, the Chinese had struck at the northeast corner from the valley of the Pungnyuri-gang above the bridge. There L and K companies of the 3rd Battalion, 31st Infantry, had suffered heavy casualties. In the predawn hours of 1 December, the renewed Chinese attacks hit this part of the perimeter hard. Pfc. Stanley E. Anderson of L Company distinguished himself in his use of a 3.5-inch rocket launcher in turning back one of the enemy assaults. But the CCF kept hitting this part of the perimeter, seeking a breakthrough.

About 3 A.M. on 1 December, the Chinese penetrated this northeast corner of the perimeter. Previous breakthroughs into the perimeter during the night had been eventually eliminated when Faith sent his preplanned counterattack force to the penetrated areas. This last breakthrough at the northeast corner, however, was not closed, and it gave the enemy control of a high knob overlooking the perimeter below it to the west. This position was just east of where the road crossed the inlet on the bridge and causeway.

Faith called D Company, ordering a counterattack force to recapture the knoll. First Lt. Robert D. Wilson, company reconnaissance officer, volunteered for the job and got together about 20 men. Just after daybreak he set off from the D Company area for his objective. His force was pitifully armed for the attack, but its condition was no worse than that of anyone still able to fight within the perimeter. His group had three hand grenades altogether, only small-arms ammunition, and no rifle grenades. Wilson carried a chrome-plated Thompson submachine gun captured earlier from the Chinese. Each man had an individual rifle or carbine.

Lieutenant Campbell saw Wilson pass his position, but Wilson soon passed from sight, dropping below one of the hummocks of ground near the inlet. Campbell moved to his northeast machine-gun position at Bigger's request so that he could report back on Wilson's counterattack. From this gun position he could see the enemy-held knob. When Campbell got to the observation point, he could see no movement on the objective. His gun crew there told him they had seen Wilson's attack, which did not get very far. Their comments and evidence from the survivors later indicated that Wilson reached the base of the knob and started up the slope with his men. Enemy fire soon hit him in the arm, knocking him down. He rose and continued on. Another bullet hit him, but he kept advancing. Almost immediately a third bullet struck him in the head and killed him. Sfc. Fred Sugua assumed command and climbed on with a small remnant, but enemy fire killed him within a minute or two. The leaderless men continued the fight and reached a part of the knob but were unable to gain control of it. The Chinese continued to hold the crest.[36]

The Chinese did not pull back from the perimeter everywhere at daybreak as they had on previous days. Many of them stayed in the low ground within the perimeter. From these positions they delivered small-arms grazing fire and some machine-gun fire. Also, enemy mortar fire resumed, with increasing accuracy. All this caused more casualties.

The Chinese made some desperate efforts at a final breakthrough after daylight. An assault force of 40 to 50 soldiers tried again to rush the recoilless rifle at the A and C companies' boundary on the road. The attack again came up the road from the west, this time along the ditch on the south side of the road. Cpl. Robert L. Armentrout used a heavy machine gun, damaged during the night by an enemy mortar round, to hold off the assault for a few minutes. Then the gun jammed. He sent his assistant gunner back for the only other heavy machine gun available. Armentrout killed approximately 20 of the enemy with this gun, repulsing the attack.

During the night the 1st Battalion aid station had received a direct mortar hit that wounded all the aid station medical personnel, including Captain Navarre, the battalion surgeon. Medical supplies were completely exhausted by dawn. Daylight revealed low clouds and fog. The prospect for receiving air support during the day was not good.

Curtis described well the situation at the perimeter after daybreak.

An attempt to describe accurately the scene inside the perimeter of Task Force Faith on the morning of 1 December 1950 runs the risk of appearing macabre. Very probably, however, even Hollywood will not be able to duplicate it in stark tragedy and horror. . . . By dawn on 1 December members of the Task Force had been under attack for 80 hours in subzero weather. None had slept much. None had washed or shaved; none had eaten more than a bare minimum. Due to the season of the year, darkness covered about 16 hours of each 24-hour period—and during the hours of darkness the enemy exploited his terror weapons such as bugles, whistles, flares, burp-guns, and infiltration tactics. The ground was frozen so solidly as to hamper digging, so riflemen and weapons crews occupied very shallow trenches.

The dead, concentrated in central collecting points had to be used as a source for all supplies including clothing, weapons, and ammunition. Everyone seemed wounded in one fashion or another and to varying degrees of severity. Frozen feet and hands were common. The wounded who were unable to move about froze to death. Trucks and jeeps and trailers were ransacked for ammunition and any kind of fabric that would serve for bandages or clothing.

But the factors that discouraged and disheartened most were these: Everyone could see that the weather was growing worse, which meant the loss of air support and aerial resupply; that relief from Hagaru-ri in any force less than regimental size could never reach us; that another night of determined attacks would surely overrun the position.[37]

As the bodies accumulated at the inlet, there was at first some effort to dig graves and bury them just below the bridge and causeway in the low ground along the inlet. But the frozen ground made digging difficult, and other pressing matters and the near-exhausted state of the troops led them to abandon it. Instead, most were carried to a sheltered place under a low embankment along the inlet not far from the causeway. There, frozen stiff, the bodies were laid in rows and stacked about four high. Only the recent dead were in the aid station at the end.[38]

BREAKOUT FROM THE INLET PERIMETER

A little after 9 A.M. on 1 December, in heavy clouds, a lone Marine fighter bomber appeared over the inlet. The pilot came from the carrier USS *Leyte* and must have made many previous trips to the inlet. However he managed it, his performance was of utmost value to the task force. The pilot established radio communication with Captain Stamford and told him that, if weather permitted, he would guide a flight of Corsairs into the perimeter about noon. Stamford gave this information to Faith and then told the pilot to relay to the 1st Marine Air Wing dispatcher at Hagaru-ri Faith's request for heavy air support during the day and to notify General

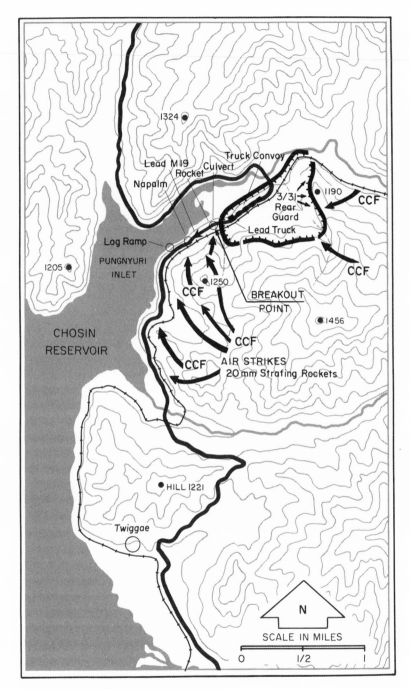

MAP 10. Task Force Faith breakout from the inlet perimeter, 1 December.

Barr of Faith's intention to try for a breakout. Faith's decision this early was probably influenced by the pilot's remark to Stamford that the weather report received that morning on the *Leyte* was that sunshine and broken clouds would most likely prevail shortly after noon.

In the meantime, Majors Curtis and Miller had been conferring with Faith, and they urged him to try for a breakout during the day, as they did not think the task force could hold the perimeter another night. Faith seemed to agree.

Faith called a conference with his battalion commanders and some staff officers at his CP for 10 A.M. There is no record of all the men present, but some who attended recalled that the group included Majors Miller, Storms, Tolly, Curtis, and Jones, Captains McClymont and Stamford, and Lieutenant May. Captain Bigger most likely also was present.

When his officers had assembled, Faith told them that, on his own initiative, he had decided to order a breakout from the perimeter. He said there was a chance the weather might improve by noon, and aircraft might arrive to aid them in an effort to reach the Marine perimeter at Hagaru-ri. They were to make preparations for the breakout if support aircraft appeared. He said no help from the Marines could be expected; he also said that he had no communication with higher headquarters. The task force would be on its own, except for the close air support he expected it to receive. Captain McClymont explained that he had very little ammunition for the antiaircraft weapons.

Faith then issued his verbal orders:

1. The 1st Battalion, 32nd Infantry, would lead off and open the way through the enemy position known to be just west and south of the perimeter along the road and would clear the road and sides for passage of the truck column.
2. The 57th Field Artillery Battalion and the 31st Heavy Mortar Company would expend their remaining ammunition just before the breakout in support of it, then destroy their pieces and mortar tubes and the personnel fight as riflemen in the center of the vehicular column.
3. The 3rd Battalion, 31st Infantry, would follow the vehicular column and protect its rear.
4. Jeeps and their trailers would be destroyed, except certain radio and machine-gun jeeps.
5. All 2½-ton trucks would be unloaded of whatever cargo they might have, and the wounded placed in them. All inoperable trucks would be destroyed.
6. All operable antiaircraft weapons would be in the column.
7. All supplies and clothing and unused equipment were to be burned or destroyed.

Faith told Stamford to ask that at least ten aircraft be over the breakout column at all times.

Major Miller asked Faith for an M19 full-track (dual-40) to lead the point of the breakout. He wanted it not only for its firepower but also because, with its full-track, it would be the best thing in the convoy to push obstacles off the road and to extricate vehicles that might get stuck. Faith approved this request.

Faith said the breakout would start on his order after the aircraft arrived. He gave specific orders to a few officers in the meeting. He told McClymont to put one M19 at the point, as Major Miller had requested, and another at the rear of the column and to intersperse the M16s (quad-50s) in the column. Lieutenant May said that Faith instructed him to prepare cargo vehicles, plus machine-gun vehicles, and to move only the wounded. These vehicles were to be put on the road, and he was told to remain in the rear of the column and to see that all vehicles fell into the column.[39]

Major Miller informed his 1st Battalion that C Company would lead off down the road as point, followed by B, D, and A companies. He ordered that all ammunition be picked up from dead or wounded for able-bodied men.

It is assumed that Major Tolly relayed Faith's instructions to the 57th Field Artillery Battalion and that Major Storms did the same to the 3rd Battalion, 31st Infantry. Captain Jordan, commanding M Company of the 3rd Battalion, however, said that only by watching the 3rd Battalion move out was he able to get his company into the column, although he had heard earlier that there was to be a breakout attempt.

Apparently there were not enough operable 2½-ton trucks to carry all the wounded, and some 3/4-ton trucks were used. Generally the trucks were loaded with 15 to 20 wounded. But in the case of Jordan's M Company, he had only one truck for about 50 wounded who could not walk. He built two decks in the truck and placed the wounded in the truck in three layers. It is not known precisely how many vehicles made up the convoy. Major Curtis estimates 25 or more 2½-ton trucks, but about 30 vehicles is closer to the mark, as it turned out. There was only one M19 dual-40 in the column, since the other one that was still mobile and operable could not be started when the column departed from the perimeter. There were only two M16 quad-50s interspersed in the column. McClymont stated that two of the M16s would not start when they were forming the column, and they had to be left behind.

When the enemy watching from the high ground around the perimeter saw the vehicles forming on the road and the wounded being loaded, they could readily surmise that the men in the perimeter were getting ready for an attempted breakout. At 11 A.M. 1st Sgt. Luna of B Company, in a temporary position along the railroad track, could see Chinese soldiers half a mile to his front coming off the hills to go into position along the road and the breakout route.

Stamford thought the troops were ready to move at 11 A.M., with the truck column on the road and the artillerymen, mortarmen, and the walking wounded headquarters men lined up as foot soldiers on either side of the trucks. It was now a matter of waiting the arrival of air cover. Very few machine guns were mounted on vehicles, Stamford said, because .50-caliber ammunition for them was almost nonexistent.

Seeing the preparations being made for a breakout attempt, the Chinese increased their mortar fire, which caused many late casualties. Major Robbins was wounded by mortar fire in the arm and legs and placed in one of the trucks. Another mortar shell made a direct hit on the 1st Battalion aid station. Two more mortar shells hit at the 1st Battalion CP, just after Faith's meeting ended and the officers were dispersing. A group, consisting of Lieutenant May, Captain Bigger, Capt. Jack Thompson, Captain Vaudreaux, Lieutenant Campbell, and an unidentified truck driver from B Company were standing outside the CP when one of the shells hit in the center of their circle. May was the only one of the group not hurt by the mortar shell explosion. The B Company driver was the most seriously injured. Captain Thompson had both legs broken. Lieutenant Campbell had mortar fragments in his left leg, left shoulder, and left side of his face. Bigger had mortar fragments in his face, one eye was blown from its socket, and he had bad leg and back wounds. A medic put the eye back in its socket and placed a patch over it. All these wounded were placed in the trucks.

Still another mortar shell landed about ten feet from where Major Curtis and Captain Seever were sitting on the edge of a hole, but it injured neither. Only two weeks earlier Seever had learned that his wife had given him their first son. Already wounded in the leg at the forward perimeter, Seever had remained in command of C Company in the days that followed. Now, escaping further injury from this mortar shell, Seever said to Curtis, "I feel like I am a thousand years old." Perhaps he felt that his luck had run out. By 3 P.M. that afternoon he was dead.

As the morning wore on, the Chinese began pressing on the perimeter. Faith began to fear that they might break in and wreak havoc before the expected air support arrival. He went to the 1st Battalion aid station and appealed for all wounded who were able to get a weapon and go back on the defense line. A few made the effort.

As preparations for the breakout ended, drivers of vehicles on the road began draining gasoline from inoperable vehicles to fill their own tanks. Not all the vehicles on the road could get full tanks. Small-arms ammunition was distributed to the men, but there was not much of it, and some men had only one clip.

Visibility was improving, just as forecast. Everything now depended on the Corsairs getting into the air from the USS *Leyte.* They arrived over the inlet a little before 1 P.M. Stamford moved up the road to take his place near the point to direct the air strikes. Mortrude took his 3rd Platoon forward past the truck column to the M19 waiting at the point. He got on the M19 because of his injured leg. His platoon formed on either side of it. The time was about 1 P.M. The Corsairs came on station.

When the planes first appeared, Stamford instructed the Corsair pilots to make a dummy run or two on the enemy positions just ahead of the panels marking the American perimeter. They did so, diving with guns silent. Their presence kept the Chinese down in their holes.

On Faith's order, Mortrude's 3rd Platoon started forward with the M19 and passed through A Company's roadblock. About 20 yards beyond the roadblock, Chinese machine-gun and small-arms fire hit the point. Men began dropping from this fire. Captain Seever had started the main body of C Company to move up behind the point platoon. As C Company reached the A Company roadblock, some A Company men close to the road on its east side joined it in an enthusiastic rush. The Chinese on their side did not hesitate but came right out on the road and moved in. The Americans were not more than 50 yards out of the perimeter when they were in the midst of a violent firefight at close quarters, closing with the Chinese. Faith called on Stamford for an air strike on the Chinese.

A flight of four Corsairs came roaring down the valley of the Pungnyuri-gang to the head of the inlet and on down above the road to where the breakout fight had been joined; their flight was from east to west. Stamford was about 20 yards behind the point and called for a napalm drop, which "landed short causing some casualties among our own personnel on the left side of the road." The main part of the napalm burst, however, splashed onto the target of intention. When it hit the Chinese, it caused terrific casualties. Stamford then called on the Corsairs to strafe with their 20-mm guns the Chinese vacating their positions to the left front. Captain Seever turned to him and asked him to get the Chinese in a culvert about 20 yards to the front in the drainage that crossed the road at that point. Stamford directed an F7F (a twin-engine fighter) to place a rocket when he told him to fire. The pilot followed instructions to the letter and destroyed the enemy in the culvert who were throwing grenades into the Americans on the road.[40]

Many men saw the horrible effects of the short napalm drop on Americans at the point and the chaos it caused momentarily. Lt. Cecil Smith, A Company commander, said five Americans burned to death. First Sergeant Luna of B Company wrote, "You could see them running all around just ripping their clothes off, just keep on running." Major Miller saw the whole thing. He wrote subsequently, "Eight or ten men in C Company were set on fire by the flaming gobs of jellied gasoline. Most of these men were seriously burned before they could be rolled in the snow and their burning clothing extinguished." None who saw the napalm drop would ever forget it. When panic started among the American troops at the lead during the napalm drop, Faith at once moved out among them and, with pistol drawn, rallied them to turn around and start back into the enemy, averting a disaster.

Miller appraised the overall effect of the air strike as follows: "I was in command of the battalion at this time and feel that Capt. Stamford's cool control of our aircraft, in which he directed the dropping of napalm not more than forty yards to our front, started the Chinese on the run and allowed the First Battalion to inflict tremendous casualties on the enemy in our immediate follow-up." The task force breakout apparently received the closest air support in a moving column that was engaged with an enemy in the Korean War. A Marine report later said that Stamford's radio code name was "Boyhood 14." A Marine pilot was quoted as saying that "Boyhood 14 kept calling for closer and closer support to less than 50 feet. The pilots could observe people practically clubbing the Reds off the trucks."

General Smith kept his promise to Barr. Faith did get air priority on 1 December. He allotted 20 planes to the breakout. They came in flights of four or six usually, and in relays. Beginning with the initial strike, the Corsairs and a few other types were over the task-force convoy all afternoon until dark prevented further support at Hill 1221. They swept the road ahead of the task force, strafed, rocketed, and bombed the high ground on the left of the road column, and one or more planes covered the rear. The survivors generally agreed that, without this close support, the task force may never have been able to clear the perimeter. Had the task force been willing to leave its wounded and abandon all vehicles, its men could have walked out over the hills and the ice and most of them would have escaped. But the mission was to escort the truck convoy with its wounded.

The tendency of the men on foot to rush ahead of the trucks was apparent early after the breakout. The officers and noncommissioned officers did not have much success in keeping the infantry on the high ground east of the road, where they could protect the truck column. They kept drifting down to the road and to the right of the road, where they were more protected. Major Miller noticed that the infantrymen were leaving the trucks behind. By this time his two radiomen were missing, and he could not communicate with the forward platoons. He wanted to slow them, because they were getting out of control. He sent runners ahead to B and C companies to keep the men on the left of the road. They were unable to accomplish their mission, however, and troops of the two companies were becoming intermixed. Miller felt that control was slipping away. He started trotting forward to catch the leading company. Curtis also thought the troops were getting out of control. He said that, after the initial success of the breakout, the troops "flooded down the road like a great mob and tactical control broke down almost immediately."[41]

Sergeant Luna of B Company was on the road with the trucks. Two or three days later he wrote about what he saw there. He said that 500 to 600 yards outside the perimeter, after passing the scene of the napalm drop and the dead of both sides in the initial clash, there were many enemy dead in the road—so many, he said, that one had to step over them, and in some places they had to be removed so that the trucks could pass. As the trucks moved forward, he and others put many newly wounded Americans on the trucks. He wrote, "We got what wounded we could out. I mean just kept loading them on and on the trucks. It was impossible to get all of them out. I do not recall just now how many were left behind. You couldn't possibly back up and take them with you."

At the rear of the column, Lieutenant May reported that the situation was also deteriorating. He said, "I saw no vehicles knocked out from the Inlet south to Hill 1221. . . . But many of our drivers were badly hit and had to be replaced." The drivers were on the left side of the trucks, the side from which enemy fire came. One driver replacement said one of his wounded was hit three times more in the truck. He said it was hard to find driver replacements, as nearly all the soldiers on foot looked upon driving as a form of suicide. Enemy fire was intense in the running fight, nearly all of it coming from the high ground on the left of the road.

The 3rd Battalion riflemen of I, K, and L companies had been combined into one company, K, still under the command of Captain Kitz before they left the perimeter. The company must have moved soon to the right of the road and out onto the ice of the reservoir. It is hard to see how the rear guard there could do much in protecting the convoy. Some of the men, including Captain Kitz, broke through the ice at the edge of the reservoir. Some of them drowned.[42]

About 3 P.M., after the column had traveled about two miles from the perimeter and neared the valley north of Hill 1221, Major Curtis said that the artillery observer's jeep-mounted radio picked up the following message in the clear: "To Colonel Faith: Secure your own exit to Hagaru-ri. Unable to assist you. Signed Smith, CG 1st Marine Division." The message had been prepared that morning by General Hodes at Hagaru-ri and signed by Smith. Curtis learned of this message firsthand, at the time it was received, from the operator of the jeep radio.

A part of the 3rd Platoon, led by Lieutenant Mortrude, was the first group in the breakout to reach the valley and stream just north of Hill

1221. He found the short single-span concrete bridge there broken in the middle and collapsed into the small stream that ran to the reservoir through the valley. The ends of the collapsed bridge were tilted skyward on their abutments. A short time later Lt. Herbert E. Marshburn, Jr., a platoon leader of A Company, with his men joined Mortrude at a hut near the stream. It was another hour before the head of the convoy arrived there. On the way across the valley toward Hill 1221, Mortrude and Marshburn could see many Chinese advancing toward them from the upper end of valley. At this time a bullet grazed Mortrude's left temple, rendering him unconscious. When he regained consciousness, Marshburn went on across to the road slanting up Hill 1221. Troops with the convoy had already arrived there.

The Convoy Is Halted

At about 3 P.M. Mortrude regained consciousness and found that the head of the convoy had arrived at the blown bridge and was piling up north of it. Most of the foot troops had moved around the blown bridge and were on the road slanting up Hill 1221 south of the bridge. Now began a critical period for the task force. A pressing need was to get the convoy of trucks around the blown bridge and across the frozen stream and marshland east and south of it. Darkness and the end of air cover was only an hour or two away.

The M19 in front of the convoy had crossed over the steep banks of the small stream and the partially frozen clumps of marsh grass and frozen earth and had climbed to the road again on the other side without difficulty. But behind it the first truck trying to cross became stuck at the stream when its wheels broke through the crust of ice.

Miller was among the first officers in the convoy to arrive at the blown bridge. He took in the scene and immediately turned the M19 back to throw a cable to the truck that was stuck at the stream. He had to do the same thing with almost every vehicle in the convoy and ended up towing them through. After he had started the process, Miller crossed the stream and went to a small house on the road at the far side of the valley. Enemy fire was coming from Hill 1221 on the men on the road. Miller found Major Curtis with a small group of men preparing to move directly up the road.

Captain Swenty arrived at the blown bridge after Miller had left it. He said, "As the trucks were running the by-pass you could hear the screams of wounded men in the trucks. Many had broken bones and I am sure several died from the shock of crossing the swamp. When a truck did get through, the driver would take it up the road 250 yards and wait."

Lt. Hugh May arrived at the blown bridge with the rear of the column.

He took charge of the bypass operation and fearlessly exposed himself in directing the crossing of each vehicle. He was at this task for about two hours.

Meanwhile, most of the foot soldiers had crossed the valley to the road up Hill 1221. There they bunched up. Nearly all the officers were there also, preparing to attack the hill. Major Miller started up the road ahead of Curtis and his group. In Curtis's group there were casualties almost at once. Curtis received a rifle slug in the right leg near the knee. Maj. Bob Jones was with Curtis at the time. He put a pressure bandage on the wound and found a broken tree limb that Curtis used for a crutch. With this he hobbled painfully on up the road. Jones soon outdistanced him as he hurried on ahead to help with the fight up ahead. Faith, in his jeep with sirens blaring, passed Curtis on the road. Curtis could look back and see May in the middle of the road at the blown bridge, ignoring the small-arms fire that had now started to hit there, directing the movement of the trucks across the stream.

May was in the best position to describe the situation at the bridge site. He wrote:

The rear guard passed us and left the rear of the column exposed. I collected a few men and put them in the RR cut to fire on the Chinese on the hill to our rear. I then returned to trying to get the last two trucks across the stream. After getting them across, one was knocked out by small arms fire and the driver of the other truck was killed. I unloaded the wounded who could walk, and sent them ahead. With some help from half-track crew, we transferred the remaining members to another 2½ ton nearby. One of the crew members from the half-track [full-track M19?] drove the truck out.

In another personal communication, Lieutenant May had more to say:

There was so much happening at this time, and I was trying to do a little bit of everything at the rear of the column. Trying to maintain some control and to keep things from getting completely out of hand. . . .

The 3rd Bn., 31st Inf. was assigned as the rear guard unit. At the time we were attempting to cross the last few vehicles at the blown bridge we started to get an awful lot of enemy small arms fire, from our rear and the high ground to our northeast.

At this time I found the 3rd Bn., 31st Inf. were deserting their mission and were streaming past our position. There were some junior officers strung out among the troops and completely ignoring my plea to stop and start firing on the CCF.

I did manage to get some troopers and a Sgt. stopped and into a railroad cut and to build up a base of fire on CCF to our rear and on hill to our east. However as soon as I returned to the job of getting the last vehicles over the bog and stream these troops pulled out, up and over Hill 1221.[43]

Major Jones called this crossing at the blown bridge "a very rough and difficult by-pass." He confirms May's and Curtis's report that it took until dark to get all the trucks across.[44]

Meanwhile, enemy forces coming from the east down the valley north of Hill 1221 had built up in sizable force on the ridge and hills across the valley from the road and were firing directly across the little valley into the trucks now on the road opposite them on the northern slope of Hill 1221 and into the mass of soldiers huddled around the trucks for protection. This fire took a terrific toll of killed and wounded. And at the same time, enemy holding Hill 1221 directed fire down on them.

From a position he had taken on the road at the foot of Hill 1221, Stamford was running air strikes on the Chinese on the surrounding hills and ridges. He had nearly a panoramic view of all the action. He gives his version of the initial attack of the 1st Battalion, 32nd Infantry, on the enemy roadblock at the saddle of Hill 1221 and the movement of the rear guard up the valley to help in this effort to reach the enemy's flank at the roadblock. He said he saw at least 300 enemy to the northeast of the rear-guard 3rd Battalion, 31st Infantry. "1/32 succeeded in forcing the roadblock and it seemed they would go on but they evidently ran into resistance and fell back. It looked as if they had lost their leaders. The retirement looked like a rout. The enemy again occupied the roadblock and inflicted heavy casualties on 1/32 with rifle and machine gun fire and was then able to do the same to 3/31 on the slopes below the road, causing them to withdraw."[45]

From the road ascending Hill 1221, Miller saw the same troop movements Stamford described, but with certain differences. He had to make some inferences as to why the 3rd Battalion troops abandoned their positions, without knowing the facts. He said,

> I noticed . . . that friendly troops (3rd Bn., 31st Inf.) on the high ground across the valley (north side) were leaving the hill and moving down to the road. I assumed that Colonel Faith, whom I had last seen at the blown bridge, . . . had ordered them forward to assist in clearing the hill from the right flank. These troops, however, were promptly replaced by Chinese who opened up with long range fire across the valley into the exposed left flank of the truck column. Captain Stamford, FAC, was able to get an air strike in on the Chinese across the valley that helped.[46]

With the high ground northeast of the road and the valley below the road unprotected and left to the Chinese, they moved across the valley and started to climb the slope to the road where the convoy of wounded, fully exposed, was stalled. Captain Stamford saw this threat and was able to bring in an air strike on them before they got to the road. The strike was successful. It scattered the Chinese, who fled back to the valley and were thereafter ineffective. Major Miller, now lying badly wounded in the roadside ditch, saw this strike. He wrote, "Chinese troops tried to close on the column along the hillside by moving up from the valley toward the road. Just before they overran us an A-26 aircraft [an F4U, Stamford says] came out of nowhere and strafed twice just below the road effectively driving back the enemy."[47] By now there was enemy mortar fire as well as machine-gun and small-arms fire on the stalled motor column. There was no effective response. Casualties mounted by the minute.

The Chinese positions on Hill 1221 and the high ground immediately west of the hairpin turn in the saddle of the hill were, for the most part, the same positions that elements of Lt. Col. Raymond Murray's 5th Marines had originally dug and occupied some ten days earlier when that regiment first arrived east of the reservoir. They subsequently were occupied by Faith's 1st Battalion when it first arrived at the reservoir. Major Curtis called Hill 1221 the best defensive position on the road east of the reservoir. The orientation of the old Marine positions fitted perfectly the needs of the Chinese when they made it the centerpiece of their defensive positions of fireblocks and roadblocks behind the cut-off 31st RCT.

After the first attack up the road, which Faith probably led, it was hard to get the troops to move from the partially protected area of the ditch on the right-hand side of the uphill road, where it had been cut into the hillside. The situation on the other side of the road, where it dropped off to the hillside, was dreadful. There was no protection there, and the trucks took the full force of the enemy fire. This wounded or killed many of those riding in the trucks, who were unable to get out. This disastrous condition was caused by the rear guard's failing to keep the enemy from taking positions across the little valley.

The words of two members who were in the rear guard are revealing. Pfc. James R. Owens served as a rifleman in the rear guard. When his unit reached the blown bridge, he said, "An officer told us to take a hill on the left side of the road. We took the hill and by the time we got to the top of the hill the Chinese were coming and they told us to retreat from the hill. After we retreated off the hill we crossed an open field and were told to try to take another hill. I witnessed the overrun of the rearguard."[48]

Intelligence Sgt. Ivan Long, 31st Infantry, at the inlet perimeter at the breakout, attached himself to the "flank company and moved forward with them." He was with the troops that went up the valley from the blown bridge to defend the task-force rear. In the late afternoon there, the Chinese launched what he termed a company-sized counterattack. He wrote,

"The outfit I was with took to their heels leaving me with only two men I could persuade to stay and face the attack. . . . We were exhausted from fighting but we fixed bayonets and took cover behind a wood pile in a farmyard. We got in a few good licks before my carbine jammed from snow and mud. We were all wounded and just overwhelmed by the onrushing Chinese."[49] Sergeant Long escaped that night and made his way to Hagaru-ri over the ice of the reservoir.

In the late afternoon of 1 December, many officers were killed or wounded on the road near the truck column. One of them was Major Miller of the 1st Battalion. After leaving Curtis and his group at the foot of Hill 1221, he moved up the road to find out if the high ground had been cleared. He spotted a heavy machine gun trained on him from just above the road and dived for the ditch. But he was hit in the leg by three bullets, and at the same time the last three fingers of his left hand were neatly removed by a bullet from across the valley. He lay in the ditch taking stock of a sorry situation. He sent a lieutenant lying in the ditch near him to tell Faith he had been hit and that the only way to clear up a desperate situation was to get troops to clear the high ground above the road.[50] Later at dusk, when the air cover departed, Stamford left his position at the foot of the hill and walked up the road beside the jeep. He spotted Miller lying in the ditch, stopped, and loaded him across the hood of his jeep.

During the afternoon numerous officers and some noncommissioned officers tried valiantly to form parties from the soldiers in the ditch to attack the slope and high ground of Hill 1221, and some succeeded in launching such attacks. One or two large groups got to the top of the hill but then went on down the other side to the reservoir and kept on going south until they reached Hagaru-ri. The earliest of these groups reached the Marine line before it was completely dark. Other groups of different sizes came into the Marine perimeter throughout the night. Most of them were wounded, but the first groups to arrive had fewer wounded. Faith went up and down the road trying to organize groups to climb the hill and knock out enemy positions so that he could organize an attack from the other (south) side of the hill to hit the enemy roadblock and fireblock in the saddle from the rear. He had indifferent results, encountering mostly dogged resistance to his exhortations. But those groups that did make the effort killed many Chinese, and the defenses of the hill gradually grew feebler. But the trucks still could not move and kept on taking casualties as they sat exposed to enemy fire from the left.

About dusk Faith and Jones decided to go up the hill and round up all the men they could find and to meet on the road south of the roadblock and attack it jointly from the south. Jones came down to the road south of the enemy fireblock at the point where the Medical Company and Drake's two tanks cluttered the road. This seemed to be the place where most of those who passed over the spur of Hill 1221 hit the road south of the enemy block, and from which they continued on south. Jones soon met Faith here. It was now dark. They formed two groups of the men from those they were able to stop. Jones had collected about 200 men; Faith had about 100. Jones took the right-hand side of the road; Faith took the left-hand side. He had the hardest going, over rough hillside terrain. Their attack was not coordinated; they had no communication with each other. Starting at the same time, both groups fired small arms and threw grenades as they advanced. Jones's group shrank in numbers fast as men dropped out. He reached the roadblock site first. It seemed they had knocked out the fireblock, as there was no enemy reaction when they reached it. He did not stop to remove the logs of the roadblock. Jones did not know where Faith was. He continued on down the road below the saddle to where the truck column stood silent.

About the time Faith and Jones were organizing their attack south of the saddle, Capt. Earle Jordan was preparing to attack the roadblock from the spur ridge above it. Of all who had crossed the ridge during the afternoon, his group was the only one to turn and hit the roadblock below. Jordan arrived at the stalled column late. He had been near the end of the convoy column. If the enemy had earlier been driven from the hill slope, they had reoccupied positions there by the time Jordan arrived. He made preparations at once to attack them. In his group Lt. Robert Schmitt, leader of M Company's Heavy Machine Gun Platoon, had one arm in a sling from a wound received at the perimeter and a weapon in the other hand. Lieutenant Gray, leader of the 81-mm mortar platoon, already wounded earlier at the inlet, got out of the truck and joined Jordan's force. These officers assembled about 25 to 30 men from the ditch and attacked the north nose of Hill 1221. They took it and arrived at the top with 10 men and no ammunition. Lieutenant Schmitt was killed in the action, and Lieutenant Gray was wounded a second time. Jordan said,

We assaulted the RB by yelling, shouting, and making as much noise as possible. We received a few rounds of small arms fire and then we were on the RB which consisted of many logs piled across the roadway. We started to remove the logs. . . . It was at about this point that we heard a voice demand who was making all the noise. I responded and it was Col. Faith. He made a comment and along with the small party with him moved along toward the truck column. Just a few minutes later we heard an explosion like a grenade. There was loud talking so I asked what was going on. One of the party stated that Col. Faith had been hit and they didn't know if he was dead or not. This took place just yards from the RB. There were enough people there to care for Col. Faith so we continued to clear the RB.[51]

Apparently a sole Chinese soldier hidden in a hole in the brush threw the grenade at Faith or his group. Heavy grenade fragments struck Faith above the heart. Jones, now with the head of the truck column, did not know what had happened to Faith.

Lieutenant May had by now got the last of the trucks around the blown bridge and reported to Jones at the head of the truck column. Jones put him and others to work unloading wounded from three inoperable trucks and reloading them into other trucks, piling the men higher and higher. These three empty trucks were pushed over the side of the road, which opened the road for movement of those behind them.

In the meantime, Captain Stamford had come up the road from the south with a few men, met no opposition at the fireblock in the saddle, and continued on down the road to the stalled truck column. He met Jones there and moved on down the road to the rear of the column. There he found two inoperable trucks loaded with wounded, blocking passage of the rear part of the column. He persuaded walking wounded there to help him unload these trucks and reload the wounded in others and then try to push the two inoperable trucks off the road and over the hillside. They failed time and again in this effort. The men who helped in this task reopened wounds and bled and were all exhausted. Stamford said he never in his life had to call on his last reserve of strength as he did at this time. Finally, they succeeded in getting the two trucks off the road. The way was now clear for the convoy to move up and over the saddle of Hill 1221. In the course of this work the convoy had become split into front and rear parts.

When the front part was ready to move, Major Jones told May to take about 20 to 30 riflemen and proceed up the road and through the pass and continue on and make sure the road was open for the trucks. May split his party into two parts, one to move on either side of the road to the saddle. They were fired on before they had gone more than 100 yards, but they were ready for this, and in the dark they were heard but could not be seen by the enemy machine-gun crew at the saddle. They immediately returned fire with rifles and knocked out the enemy machine-gun crew of three men, exploding what must have been a grenade in the position (judging from the loud noise it made). May's men then went through the saddle and started down the south slope of the hill.

Stamford led the second part of the convoy over the hill without incident and caught up with the front part before it reached the bottom of the hill at Twiggae. Stamford found Faith sitting in the cab of the lead truck.[52] Only about 25 vehicles were left in the convoy when it reached Twiggae at the south base of Hill 1221. The convoy was halted there while Stamford went forward to make a reconnaissance of the condition of the bridge over a small stream that ran down to the reservoir south of Hill 1221.

In the meantime, before Stamford's rear part of the convoy had caught up with the front part, Jones had stopped the front at the place where one of Drake's knocked-out tanks still blocked the road. He decided to leave a guard there with the trucks and to make a bypass for the column, while he took the rest of the able-bodied men and tried to reach Hagaru-ri to seek help. Lieutenant May led off with the point of Jones's party. He realized that they were approaching the river (the Paegamni-gang) near Sasu. Just short of the river, May halted the point and went back to check with Jones. He knew that Jones had not been over this ground in daylight, and he wanted to brief him on the terrain, particularly the high ground on their left, a logical place for another ambush. This was the nose of the ridge that came down to the road just north of Hudong-ni. May recommended that the party cut across to the railroad at this point; Jones concurred. The road was about 200 to 300 yards to the left of the railroad.

May heard troops to his front and halted the point until he could determine who they were. He found these troops to belong to the 57th Field Artillery. He warned them of the danger of an ambush to their left. May went back to bring up Jones and the main party. When he returned, he found that the artillerymen had gone on, and he could see them out on the railroad trestle. Flares appeared over the trestle, and Chinese opened fire on the artillerymen. May said, "We could hear a large group of Chinese talking and calling back and forth on the high ground to our left front." Jones and May conferred in the cut where they had stopped and decided they had better make a run for the darkness in the low ground along the river. The Chinese fired on them while they made a run for it, but fortunately there were no casualties. They then moved out to the edge of the reservoir and bypassed Sasu. They continued on south along the railroad bed until they entered the Marine perimeter north of Hagaru-ri.[53]

The convoy reached Twiggae perhaps an hour after Jones and May had passed it. When Stamford made his reconnaissance of the road bridge just ahead, he found it partially damaged—vehicles could not cross, but men on foot could. He found a trail that led from the road at Twiggae across to the narrow-gauge railroad, which approached the road at this point and ran south, parallel to it, for perhaps half a mile. He thought the convoy vehicles could get on the railroad and cross the stream on the short railroad trestle, which was still intact. That solution was attempted and found to be practical. After seeing the first vehicles across and back in the rice paddy approach to the road close by, Stamford took a few men and started down the road to see if it was clear for the truck convoy after it had crossed the trestle and regained the road. He had spoken to Faith in the cab of the lead truck and asked him if he wanted to try to continue on to Hagaru-ri. Faith replied with a weak yes. Stamford said that Faith could barely talk and seemed to be in extreme pain and on the verge of losing consciousness.[54]

Stamford and the three or four men with him moved down the road about half a mile. He came abreast of the high ground on the left of the road near Hudong-ni when suddenly shadows emerged from the roadside. Stamford and his men were taken prisoner before they could react. They were disarmed and made to lie down at the side of the road. Someone from the head of the convoy that had now reached the road fired several bursts down the road toward the enemy group that had captured Stamford, and their shots went over his head where he lay prone on the ground. Stamford could hear enemy on the high ground on the left of the road. Soon the lead truck ran the blockade and seemed to draw little fire.

A second truck in the convoy tried to run the fireblock where he lay captive. It passed him, but about 75 yards beyond, a Chinese rocket fired from the south, near the entrance to the Hudong-ni schoolhouse, hit the truck head on and stopped it. The other trucks waited on the road as word of another enemy roadblock passed down the line. During this period there was an exchange of fire from the trucks on the road and the enemy, near whom Stamford lay a prisoner.

In the confusion caused by this episode, Stamford rose to his feet and escaped across to the railroad and ran west of it until he entered a patch of scrub growth. He continued south to Sasu-ri and found it "dead." South of the town on a path, he encountered someone coming toward him. He changed course to evade him and was pursued. During this evasive scramble Stamford injured his ankle, but he continued to move toward Hagaru-ri, reaching the Marine perimeter at 2:25 A.M. on 2 December. Stamford always assumed that Faith was still in the lead truck, which had run past the enemy fireblock. As he moved south toward Sasu-ri, he saw it stop there and wait a while, but eventually it continued on up the road and he saw it last when it passed around a saddle in the first high ground south of the Paegamni-gang.[55]

Curtis was with the column at Twiggae, and after the convoy started over the trestle, he stayed there a long time watching the procedure. He said that there was little trouble getting the vehicles onto the rail track but that the process of crossing the trestle was slow and tedious. Only one vehicle was put on the trestle at a time. Short but narrow, the trestle was about 25 feet long, with about 15 to 20 rail ties in it, and the entire passage of the vehicles from entrance onto the rail track to the point where they left it, only about 100 feet long. But each vehicle had to be hand guided across the trestle. There was no enemy action at the time of the crossing, but the crossing of the trestle was very painful for the wounded in the trucks. Curtis said he would never forget their screams and moans as the

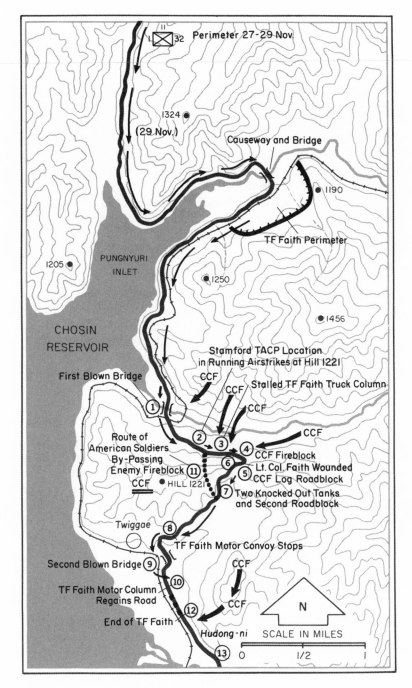

Perimeter 27-29 Nov.

1324

(29 Nov.)

Causeway and Bridge

1190

TF Faith Perimeter

1205

PUNGNYURI
INLET

1250

1456

CHOSIN
RESERVOIR

Stamford TACP Location
in Running Airstrikes at Hill 1221

First Blown Bridge

CCF

Stalled TF Faith Truck Column

CCF

CCF

1

Route of
American Soldiers
By-Passing
Enemy Fireblock

CCF

2

3

11

4

6

5

CCF

CCF Fireblock

Lt. Col. Faith Wounded

CCF Log Roadblock

HILL 1221

7

Two Knocked Out Tanks
and Second Roadblock

Twiggae

8

TF Faith Motor Convoy Stops

CCF

Second Blown Bridge

9

10

TF Faith Motor Column
Regains Road

12

CCF

N

End of TF Faith

Hudong-ni

SCALE IN MILES

13

0   1/2   1

MAP 11. Task Force Faith convoy demise, 1 December.

trucks jolted across the trestle. Seeing that the trucks on the road were not moving, Curtis decided to go there and investigate the trouble.[56]

Curtis estimated that the time was about 10 P.M. Moving along the line of trucks, he said he saw both Colonel Faith and Major Miller. Faith merely said to him, "Let's get going." Short of the head of the column, Curtis decided to leave it, go on to the ice, and try to reach Hagaru-ri. By this time enemy had caught up with the rear of the column on the road. Curtis heard firing there and saw white phosphorus grenades exploding among the rear trucks. He eventually made it to the Marine lines shortly after Stamford arrived there.

Miller, still lying across the hood of Stamford's jeep, thought it was near midnight when the long wait on the road was interrupted by enemy mortar rounds that gradually bracketed the truck convoy. He authorized a sergeant who came to him from the head of the convoy to move out in an effort to run the gauntlet. The convoy had moved only about 200 yards down the road to a bend when a terrific blast of rifle and machine-gun fire hit the column from a hill to the left of the road, Hill 1239. The lead truck driver apparently was hit as the truck piled into the ditch and blocked the road. The column was stopped cold and was being punished unmercifully by a hail of lead. Miller wrote, "I rolled off the hood of the jeep into the road and into the ditch away from the hill."[57] The convoy had reached its final point of advance, a short distance north of the nose of Hill 1239, a high mountain just north of Hudong-ni. Its western slope came down to the road just south of where the motor column was stopped.

Lieutenant Campbell was still in the convoy when it reached the end. Perhaps he has the best description of anyone of the final moments. He had left the truck he was riding and was in a gully alongside the road when the enemy fireblast came. He saw the third truck move forward and begin pushing a 3/4-ton truck just ahead of it, with no one apparently at the steering wheel. The 3/4-ton truck slowly began veering to the right and then toppled into the gully. Someone yelled and alerted Campbell, who started to scramble forward; the left front wheel passed over his boot, giving him a badly bruised foot and ankle. After it tumbled into the gully, the 3/4-ton truck turned over and landed upside down, the wounded in it screaming in pain. He heard someone inside kicking on the floor, now its roof. Almost immediately, Campbell said, the enemy began closing on the rear of the convoy. He could see hand grenades going off at the end of the line of trucks, which were in a straight section of the road. He estimated the number of vehicles at this time as being 15 plus.[58]

The Chinese pillaged the convoy and stayed around it most of the night, killing some and taking prisoners of others who could walk. At the end, each man had his own adventure, and some lived to tell it. Most of those who were not too badly wounded got out of the trucks during the night if the Chinese did not take them away. Those with severe body wounds or multiple leg wounds froze to death if the final Chinese assault did not kill them.

The Death of Lt. Col. Don C. Faith, Jr.

After darkness closed on 1 December 1950, Lt. Col. Don C. Faith, Jr., grievously wounded, blue with cold, slumped in the cab of a 2½-ton truck. A piece of metal from an enemy fragmentation hand grenade had pierced his chest just above the heart. Was Faith in the only truck to run through the last enemy roadblock, which ended the advance of the convoy and which, when last seen by Captain Stamford, rounded the saddle at the first high ground south of the Paegamni-gang just south of Sasu-ri? It would seem that he was.

Late in December Major Jones commanded the remnant of the 1st Battalion, 32nd Infantry, in a rehabilitation center near Taegu, in South Korea. Including Jones, there were three officers and 73 enlisted men there. Col. Charles E. Beauchamp, the regimental commander, ordered WO (jg) Edwin E. Anderson, assistant regimental personnel officer, to interview all of the men in order to reconstruct their personnel records, which had been lost at Chosin. Before the interrogations began, General Barr, the 7th Division commander, ordered Anderson to go further in his interrogations and to ask each man what he knew of Lieutenant Colonel Faith's death. He wanted all possible information when he wrote to Faith's widow again.

In the course of these interviews, one of the enlisted men, Pfc. Russell L. Barney, told Anderson that he had driven the truck in whose cab Faith had ridden during the breakout effort from Hill 1221 onward. Barney said Faith was wounded a second time by enemy small-arms fire while in the cab and that, when he left the truck, Faith was dead in the cab. Anderson's memorandum, 9 January 1951, to Maj. Gen. David Barr, reported on his interview with Barney. In it Anderson said Barney told him he drove the truck to map coordinate CV 5373, where he left it with Faith dead inside the cab. Unfortunately, Barney did not give, or Anderson did not report, the reason Barney abandoned the truck. It probably ran out of gasoline. The map coordinate puts the location of the abandoned truck about two and one-half road miles south of the place the task force convoy came to its final end near Hudong-ni, north of Mulgam-ni and south of Pokko-chae, in hill terrain, within a mile and a half of the Marine perimeter at Hagaru-ri.[59] I give the weight of evidence to Stamford's and

Barney's accounts of Faith's final hours and assume that his remains lie in the earth about two miles north of Hagaru-ri, a little distance north of Mulgam-ni.

Eventually, President Truman awarded the Congressional Medal of Honor, Posthumously, to Lieutenant Colonel Faith. The award was presented to (Mrs.) Barbara Faith in Washington, D.C., by Gen. Omar N. Bradley, chairman of the Joint Chiefs of Staff, in a ceremony on 21 June 1951. The official Department of the Army award and citation were published in its General Order No. 59, 2 August 1951.[60]

LIEUTENANT COLONEL BEALL RESCUES CONVOY SURVIVORS

Lt. Col. Olin L. Beall, USMC, commanded the Marine 1st Motor Transport Battalion, which held a segment of the Hagaru-ri defense perimeter on its northwest arc. In front of the perimeter there was an expanse of frozen marshland where the Changjin River emptied into the reservoir. During the late afternoon of 1 December, his CP received word that pilots had spotted friendly troops making their way south over the ice of the reservoir toward his perimeter. Just before dark a messenger told Beall a body of men was approaching his sector. He sent a squad through the minefield at his front to meet and identify the oncoming group and to guide them through the minefield. They were from the Army's 31st RCT at Hill 1221. Another group came through his perimeter at 10 P.M., consisting of about 50 Americans and 50 ROK soldiers. On 2 and 3 December Beall organized and carried out a rescue operation of men who had been able to walk or crawl away from the destroyed convoy near Hudong-ni and of some men the Chinese had captured and released. Lieutenant Colonel Beall was 52 years old at Chosin and had more than 30 years of active duty as a Marine enlisted man and officer.

After the night of 1–2 December, with large numbers of wounded men coming through his perimeter, on the morning of 2 December Beall thought there probably were other wounded men along the reservoir. He went out to scout the area and brought in six men. He then went back in his jeep. At Hudong-ni he spotted a cluster of wounded men on the ice. He and his men eliminated nine snipers on the shore on the way up. Upon trying to enter the marshland at the edge of the reservoir opposite Hudong-ni, they came under heavy sniper and automatic-weapons fire. They left their jeep out on the ice about 300 to 400 yards and walked in. He later wrote: "When coming under fire we would drop to the ice and they would not fire on us, so this we did and during the day we got out over three hundred (300) of the wounded men from the convoy. . . . There were many brave men here this day, men shot through the body helping a buddy, men with hands frozen helping a buddy with a broken leg, men with both legs broken dragging themselves along with their hands and elbows." Beall was at first accompanied by only two men. He obtained a sled and attached it to his jeep. With it he could evacuate 12 to 14 men at a time. He had trucks brought to the shore to carry the wounded men as he brought them in to an aid station, and he built warming fires on the edge of the reservoir. Two more jeeps joined him on the ice in the rescue work later in the day.

It seems that the Chinese did not search the marsh and brushland at the mouth of the Paegamni-gang west of Hudong-ni after daylight on 2 December, so all the men who could get away from the convoy had been able to hide there undisturbed. Beall had six men, including himself, working on the ice of the reservoir and in the land along its edges near Hudong-ni for 12 hours on 2 December in temperatures that reached 24 degrees below zero. They brought into their perimeter a total of 319 American and ROK soldiers during the day.

On the morning of 3 December aerial observers told Beall more wounded were on the ice. He took two men and went out again and found four men huddled under blankets in a fishing boat that was frozen tight in the reservoir. This time Beall and his men came under heavy fire. The observation plane called in air fighter planes to cover Beall. They came in at times within ten feet of the reservoir surface. Beall sent the four badly wounded men in his jeep to the Marine lines, and still under the fighter planes' cover he left his gun on the ice and walked ashore opposite Hudong-ni, where he could see the abandoned line of trucks on the road. Of this trip he wrote, "I went through that convoy and saw dead in each vehicle, stretchers piled up with men frozen to death trying to pull themselves out from under another stretcher. Yes, I saw this and I shall never forget it . . . (this statement later proven by the undersigned actually finding seventeen [17] stretcher cases in one 6 × 6 truck)."[61]

Beall went down the line of trucks from the first to the last but found no one alive. He returned to the ice, and Private First Class Milton was waiting for him in his jeep. The Marine Corps official history gave an estimate of 300 men dead in the trucks of the convoy, an estimate apparently given by Beall, because he was the only American to visit the silent convoy after the Chinese had stopped and overrun and plundered it. Altogether, on 2 and 3 December Beall and his helpers brought in over the ice from the vicinity of Hudong-ni a total of 323 men. These together with the estimated 300 dead in the trucks indicate that there were approximately 600 men in the trucks of the convoy when it came to its end. The 1st Motor Transport Battalion reported that all of the rescued men were wounded, "with more than 50% with very severe wounds." Most of these men were evacuated by air from the Hagaru-ri airstrip in the period 2–5 December. Some individuals who hobbled on their own into the Marine perimeter, such as Major Miller, had sagas of courage, willpower, and luck to relate.

6

FIRST BATTLE OF HAGARU-RI, 28–29 NOVEMBER

The first two series of battles of the Chosin Reservoir campaign were fought at Yudam-ni, on the west side of the reservoir, and at a series of perimeters on the east side. Yet the critical strategic spot was at neither of these places, but at Hagaru-ri. Its early loss to the Chinese might have spelled complete disaster for all X Corps troops in the Chosin Reservoir area. And lost it probably would have been, early in the Chosin battles, if the Chinese plans for attack on the first night, 27–28 November, had been executed as planned. The plan miscarried for the Chinese because the rank-and-file of the Chinese 58th Division showed lack of individual discipline and officer control at the moment of their breakthrough into the Marine Hagaru-ri perimeter and because the Chinese 80th Division never arrived on the night of 28 November to help in the attack. This division did not arrive from its approach march along the east side of the reservoir because it ran into the Army's 31st RCT of the 7th Infantry Division and allowed itself to become engaged with it at two perimeters rather than to bypass them and go for Hagaru-ri, its mission in the CCF higher-command plan.

It can perhaps also be argued that the critical battles of the Chosin campaign were fought the first night at Yudam-ni by the 5th and 7th Marine regiments. Had the Chinese been able to inflict on them what the 80th Division did to the 31st RCT at the same time on the east side of the reservoir, it is doubtful if these regiments would ever have been able to fight their way to Hagaru-ri later. And without these two regiments intact and battle worthy, present to lead the breakout attack toward the coast, perhaps the only Marines to escape would have been those of the 1st Regiment under Colonel Puller at Koto-ri. The 5th and 7th Marines, however, won their battles at Yudam-ni on the first night in very heavy fighting. They lost heavily in these battles, but the Chinese lost more heavily. Afterward, the Chinese were never able to muster the same attack capability against the Marines at Yudam-ni or in their fighting withdrawal to Hagaru-ri.

The CCF Plan for Capturing Hagaru-ri

Both the 58th and the 80th CCF divisions were to attack Hagaru-ri on the night of 27 November, simultaneously with the Chinese two-division attack on Yudam-ni. The 58th Division had previously moved southeast from the Yudam-ni area to be in position for its assault on Hagaru-ri from the southwest. The 80th Division approached Hagaru-ri from the north along the east side of the reservoir. Neither of these divisions attacked Hagaru-ri on the night of 27 November. The 58th Division apparently was not quite ready, and the 80th Division was held up by its encounter with the 31st RCT of the 7th Infantry Division. The latter Army troops had just moved into the 80th Division's path along the east side of the reservoir, but they were unaware of the Chinese approach or presence. It is unlikely that any part of the 80th Division reached Hagaru-ri on the night of the twenty-seventh. Its advance units were fully engaged with the 31st RCT troops that it encountered both above and below Sinhung-ni. But by the night of 28 November, part of the 80th Division apparently had arrived at East Hill, overlooking, and on the east side of, Hagaru-ri. By that time the 58th Division was ready to launch its attack from the southwest. Thus, the thinly defended American perimeter there was subject to attack from opposite sides. Had these attacks during the night of 28–29 November been coordinated, the place could hardly have been held. The failure of the CCF to attack Hagaru-ri on the night of 27 November and the subsequent failure or inability to coordinate their two separate attacks the next night gave the small defending force its only opportunity to hold on until reinforcements arrived.

The Marine and X Corps Situation at Hagaru-ri

Hagaru-ri was first occupied by the 2nd Battalion, 7th Marines, at 1 P.M. on 14 November. As the 2nd Battalion advanced on the town from Koto-ri, Chinese patrols and skirmishing parties withdrew from in front of the battalion, and it occupied Hagaru-ri without opposition. The town had been devastated by American aerial bombardment, and scarcely a building stood intact. The next day, 15 November, the temperature fell to 15 degrees below zero. The Marines had no battle casualties that day, but they had 200 men ineffective from frostbite, cold shock, and digestive disorders caused by eating frozen food. In the days that followed there was no enemy activity at or in the immediate vicinity of Hagaru-ri, and the Marines spent the time in establishing supply dumps, improving the road up the mountain over Funchilin Pass to Koto-ri, and working on an airstrip at Hagaru-ri.

Hagaru-ri lay in a flat bowl through which the Changjin River flowed

The village of Hagaru-ri, where the 1st Marine Division assembled to fight its way to the coast. The road in the foreground leads back 12 miles to Yudam-ni. Chosin Reservoir is to the left, off the edge of this picture. (US Marine Corps photograph A-5679)

to the south end of the Chosin Reservoir, about one and one-half miles northward. Some old maps name a small village on the east side of the Changjin River just north of the road fork as Hagaru-ri and the larger village or town on the west side of the river as Changjin. At the time Marines occupied the settlement and in subsequent military reports, both places were known as one place under the name "Hagaru-ri." The Changjin River was not a large stream at Hagaru-ri, rising not many miles to the southwest in the mountains west of Koto-ri. At the latter place the stream turned almost 90 degrees from an easterly flow to a northerly one and continued on this course to Hagaru-ri and the reservoir beyond. A long concrete bridge spanned the Changjin River near the northern edge of Hagaru-ri, and the road that forked westward crossed it and continued on to Yudam-ni. The road from Koto-ri followed the east bank of the Changjin River to Hagaru-ri and then continued on northward along the east side of the reservoir. The western fork to Yudam-ni did not follow the west bank of the reservoir but crossed a high mountain range by Toktong Pass in a more direct line. Hagaru-ri was dominated by high ground only on the east and northeast. This mountain mass came to be known as East Hill. On the southwest there was a draw south of the western end of the airstrip being built that offered an enemy a covered route of approach to the Marine positions. The terrain therefore indicated that Hagaru-ri was most vulnerable to attack from East Hill or the draw that reached the flat basin from the southwest.

LT. COL. RIDGE ASSUMES DEFENSE OF HAGARU-RI

Four days after the 2nd Battalion, 7th Marines, occupied Hagaru-ri on 14 November, five large bulldozers arrived and the next morning, 19 November, began work on an airstrip. The airstrip lay about 500 yards south of the village and lay on an east-west axis. The first tanks arrived at Hagaru-ri the same day as the bulldozers. D Company, 1st Engineer Battalion, 1st Marine Division, had the task of blasting and hewing from the frozen ground the planned 3,200-foot runway. The 7th Marine Regiment that had assembled at Hagaru-ri moved on to Yudam-ni by 26 November, except for F Company, reinforced, which had remained behind at Hagaru-ri as the only combat infantry unit there for its defense.

This airstrip at Hagaru-ri, and another one that was begun a little later at Koto-ri, ultimately helped save the 1st Marine Division. From them thousands of wounded and frostbite victims of the Chosin Reservoir campaign were evacuated to the coast and Japan. They could not have been evacuated from the reservoir area in any other way, except for a very few by liaison planes. And it was to these airstrips that various kinds of supplies were sent for the resupply that would ultimately make a breakout possible. That these airstrips were built as soon as possible after troops arrived at both places was due primarily to the standard operating procedure that General Almond insisted on in X Corps. He wanted some kind of an airstrip available for landing of L-5 or L-19 liaison planes at battalion, regimental, and divisional headquarters, for several reasons. One of them was to enable him to fly in to see what was going on. In such a vast mountainous country as northeast Korea, with his units scattered far and wide, with only a skeleton of a road system (and that a very poor one of narrow dirt and gravel roads), there was no other way he could go from place to place quickly and safely. In the case of Hagaru-ri, the airstrip was designed to permit the landing and take-off of C-46 and C-47 cargo planes.[1]

After dark on 26 November, Lt. Col. Thomas L. Ridge and his 3rd Battalion, 1st Marine Regiment, arrived at Hagaru-ri from Majon-ni to re-

lieve F Company, 7th Marines, which the next day moved on west to occupy a defensive position at the top of Toktong Pass, midway between
Hagaru-ri and Yudam-ni. Lieutenant Colonel Ridge had only about two-
thirds of his battalion with him. Capt. Carl L. Sitter's G Company and
a platoon of the Weapons Company had not been able to move north from
Chigyong for lack of transportation. Ridge had two batteries of artillery
with him at Hagaru-ri on 26 November. Thus, when F Company, 7th Marines, moved out for Toktong Pass the next day, Ridge in effect had only
two-thirds of a battalion of combat troops to defend Hagaru-ri—two infantry companies, two platoons of the Heavy Weapons Company, and two
batteries of 105-mm howitzers.[2]

Someone in the Marine defenders likened Hagaru-ri at this time to
a partly demolished Klondike gold-rush camp, lying in a frozen bowl-
shaped plain, mountains on the east and others farther away several miles
to the west, and a frozen, tundralike marshland extending northward along
the Changjin River to the southern tip of the Chosin Reservoir. East Hill
had ice- and snow-covered slopes that came down almost to the edge of
the town. The narrow-gauge railroad and the road up the east side of the
reservoir ran close to the edge of the steep slopes; only 200 to 300 yards
separated the eastern edge of Hagaru-ri from the slopes of East Hill at
their closest approach. The spur ridges running down from the crest toward Hagaru-ri, and the crest itself, dominated the town and its immediate vicinity.

In his reconnaissance of the ground, Ridge and his staff thought that
two regiments would be needed for a proper defense of Hagaru-ri, but with
the troops available, Ridge settled on a four-mile-long perimeter, with a
thin defense in most places and none in others, except for mortar and
artillery fire that could be directed into unmanned sections of the defense line. Ridge planned to place his two infantry companies with their
supporting weapons and the artillery and tanks at the most critical places
on the perimeter, which he intended to determine on the basis of the
best intelligence he could obtain of enemy strength and attack plans. No
such enemy plan was known to him on 26 November when he arrived
at Hagaru-ri. Ridge knew he would have to fill out most of the perimeter
line he chose to defend with miscellaneous service and headquarters
troops, as well as some X Corps Headquarters and Army construction
and service units that arrived at Hagaru-ri on 27 and 28 November.

On this basis he placed 1st Lt. Joseph R. Fisher's I Company in the
position that F Company, 7th Marines, had vacated on the twenty-seventh,
at the southwest angle of the perimeter and facing the draw that approached it from the southwest. Capt. Clarence E. Corley's H Company
went into line adjacent to I Company on the east-northeast of it and carried the line to a road running south out of Hagaru-ri on the west side

of the Changjin River. Both the infantry companies were reinforced by supporting units of the Weapons Company. In addition, the Weapons Company established a strong roadblock on the Hagaru-ri–Koto-ri road at the base of a spur of East Hill that came down abruptly to the road east of H Company. A few tanks and various engineer troops then ran the line north and northwest along the base of East Hill and across the marshland south of the reservoir. Initially, East Hill was virtually abandoned, but during 28 November, Ridge was able to place some X Corps and 3rd Infantry Division service and engineer troops on parts of the hill. Ridge placed his CP just inside the western edge of the perimeter, and west of Hagaru-ri, on the road leading to Yudam-ni. A narrow road ran south from it past the western tip of the airstrip into I Company's position. The airstrip was within the perimeter and behind I and H companies' lines, about midway between them and Hagaru-ri.[3] The airstrip was about one-fourth completed on 27 November. Work continued at night under floodlights and tractor headlights.

Word reached Hagaru-ri about midnight, 27 November, of the massive CCF attacks under way at Yudam-ni. Word also came during the night of CCF attacks against 7th Infantry Division troops to the north, only a few miles away on the east side of the reservoir. Everyone at Hagaru-ri was apprehensive the rest of the night, anticipating an enemy attack there. But there was no enemy attack at Hagaru-ri during the night of 27–28 November. Why? No one would be better qualified to answer that question than Lieutenant Colonel Ridge. During the entire Chosin operation Ridge was the defense commander at Hagaru-ri, although Major General Smith, commander of the 1st Marine Division, was there from about noon of 28 November on, until the breakout to the coast started. Ridge's views should be included here. He wrote:

> I can only speculate on this question. I suspect that the planned (?) attacks (CCF) at Yudam-ni and Fox Hill on the one side and delays, as you commented on, incident to actions against elements of the 7th Inf. Div. on the other side contributed to delays in whatever plans they may have had. In addition to these, you should also note the recon. and minor actions south of Hagaru-ri. In the 1950's I had a better than average knowledge of CCF tactics over the prior decade, and recall *then* thinking of the CCF tendency to be rather certain of the exact situation prior to deciding on a major attack. Recall that the CCF had only patrol reporting or local civilian reports at the time. Also consider the probable confusion existing at CCF HQ at the time.[4]

CCF Cut the Road South of Hagaru-ri

During the night of 27–28 November, while the CCF attacks were in progress against the Marines at Yudam-ni and the 7th Infantry Division troops east of the reservoir, the CCF 60th Division carried out its mission of cutting the American MSR south of Hagaru-ri. Before midnight this road was closed to traffic completely. Intelligence gained later from prisoners and captured documents showed that the CCF 60th Division had taken positions on the road from Hagaru-ri all the way south past Koto-ri to and beyond Chinhung-ni. They built numerous physical roadblocks of logs and hay and destroyed all the bridges. An effort was made to open the road during the morning of 28 November, and in the late afternoon it was reported open. But in fact it was closed again almost at once, just as soon as darkness fell. Ground help to all Americans caught in the reservoir area between Yudam-ni and Chinhung-ni was virtually fore-closed. Below Hagaru-ri, Col. Lewis B. Puller, commanding the 1st Marine Regiment, held Koto-ri with his 2nd Battalion as the principal defense force, together with the regimental CP personnel. Lt. Col. Donald M. Schmuck's 1st Battalion, 1st Marines, held Chinhung-ni, at the foot of the pass. The 1st Marine Division at the time of the Chinese attack was thus concentrated in four main perimeters—Yudam-ni, Hagaru-ri, Koto-ri, and Chinhung-ni.[5]

RIDGE GAINS INTELLIGENCE OF CCF PLANS

All day on 27 November Korean refugees came into Hagaru-ri from the north and northwest with stories that Chinese troops in great numbers had evicted them from their homes. Ridge placed great importance on gathering intelligence of enemy dispositions and plans and then basing his own plan on it. In the Marine operations from the Inchon landing to the capture of Seoul in September, he had added a "lost" ROK lieutenant to his staff who spoke English and was adept at intelligence gathering behind the enemy's lines. In this work he had received some coaching from the battalion intelligence section. Ridge used him often to great advantage. Second Lt. Richard L. Carey, the 3rd Battalion's S-2, or intelligence officer, on 27 November decided on a dangerous plan. He sent the ROK lieutenant and another trusted Korean agent on a circuit of the Marine perimeter to the north, west, and south, at some miles distant from it, to make direct contact in the hills with CCF forces Korean refugees said were there. Before leaving on this mission the two agents talked extensively with those refugees who seemed to have the most reliable information.

That night the two Korean agents returned to Hagaru-ri. They reported they had met well-equipped Chinese forces to the south and west of Hagaru-ri. On the next day, 28 November, Carey sent the same men out again. Surprisingly, they returned successfully and said they had talked freely with Chinese troops, including some officers, who said they would attack and occupy Hagaru-ri that night. The agents reported strong enemy forces concentrated to the southwest within five miles of the town.

It was standard practice for Chinese combat forces to remain outside medium artillery range of American perimeters during the day to escape the artillery shelling in their assembly areas and to hide from air strikes, which usually were directed at the houses in which the CCF hid. Then after dark they would begin an approach march, usually five to six miles, to their line of departure for the assault. The 58th Chinese Division followed this operating procedure. Darkness came about 5:30 P.M. at Chosin in late November. Putting together the information Ridge now had available, it seemed likely that the Chinese from the 58th Division would be at their line of departure and ready for their attack on Hagaru-ri about 9:30 P.M. Lieutenant Colonel Ridge accepted Lieutenant Carey's report and based his defense plans for the night of 28 November on it.[6] Ridge appears to have had no special information about the situation on East Hill.

Ridge's intelligence confirmed his initial disposition of troops. He kept Captain Corley's H Company at the southeast section of the perimeter, and First Lieutenant Fisher's I Company at the southwest corner. Together, H and I companies held about a third of the perimeter, a distance of about one and one-fourth miles, or 380 yards to a platoon. During the morning of 28 November, Ridge asked that his G Company and the 41st Royal British Commandos be hurried up to Hagaru-ri. Ridge expected Captain Sitter's G Company to take over the defense of East Hill. He was disappointed; G Company and the 41st Royal British Commandos got no farther during the day than Koto-ri. Enemy turned them back about a mile north of that town. The Chinese ultimately turned back every effort on the twenty-eighth to open the road to Hagaru-ri from Koto-ri and south of there.

At 3 P.M. on 28 November, General Smith, who had arrived at Hagaru-ri to establish his CP, appointed Lieutenant Colonel Ridge as Hagaru-ri defense commander. Ridge in turn made Lt. Col. Charles L. Banks, commander of the Regulating Detachment, 1st Service Battalion, commander of the northern sector. He had been in charge of establishing the large supply dumps in this area and was considered a logical choice for subcommand there. The only combat troops in this sector were detachments of the 2nd Battalion, 7th Marines, that had not been able to join their regiment at Yudam-ni. The main units assigned to defense of East Hill were D Company, Army 10th Engineer Combat Battalion, 3rd Infantry Division; a X Corps Signal Battalion detachment; and some other miscellaneous units. Most of the latter were not on East Hill but on an arc west from the north end of the East Hill.[7]

A few minutes after General Smith appointed Ridge the Hagaru-ri defense commander, a solitary Chinese 76-mm shell struck in Ridge's battalion CP and fatally wounded Capt. Paul E. Storaski, the battalion supply officer. Had the Chinese then or later shelled the central part of the perimeter, they could have done tremendous damage. But they could not do this with impunity during daylight hours because air strikes and counterbattery fire would certainly be directed at their guns. After dark, for some reason, enemy guns fired only at the front line of the perimeter.

H and I companies of the 3rd Battalion, 1st Marines, were well dug in at what was considered the most critical part of the perimeter, despite the six to eight inches of frozen ground they had to cut through at the surface. They did this by the ingenious device of exploding charges in ration cans to break through the frozen ground where a foxhole or a gun position had to be prepared. The dirt below the frozen crust was easily scooped out, and it, together with sandbags, was heaped in front of the holes as a protective parapet. The entire perimeter force was on alert and ready for an enemy attack by 9:30 P.M. Snow began to fall soon after dark, and three hours later two inches of new snow lay atop the crust of earlier falls.

CCF Assault from the Southwest, 28 November

There were two major assaults on Hagaru-ri during the night of 28–29 November. The first came from the CCF 58th Division from the southwest. The second came from East Hill after midnight from an unidentified CCF formation that was probably the 80th Division. The first attack was one that Lieutenant Colonel Ridge expected.

Ridge's intelligence led him to believe that the Chinese would begin their attack on his defenses about 9:30 P.M., approaching from the southwest. The Chinese were a bit behind Carey's and Ridge's estimated time of attack, but not by much. At 10:30 P.M. the 172nd Regiment, 58th Division, set off three red flares near the Marine perimeter. They were followed by three blasts of a Chinese police whistle, which signaled the attack. In a few minutes, Chinese probing patrols set off Marine trip flares and antipersonnel explosives in front of H and I companies. Enemy mortar fire came in accurately on the Marine front-line positions. Then came the main assault with skirmish lines of grenadiers and tommy gunners, one after the other, coming up to grenade-throwing range. In some instances it seemed that enemy appeared out of the snowy mist right in front of the 1st Platoon of H Company. They accomplished this penetration by rolling down the slight slope to the Marine foxholes. The full force of the Chinese assault hit H and I companies on the southern part of the perimeter. Even though Marine supporting arms covered charted fields of fire in front of these two companies and cut down succeeding

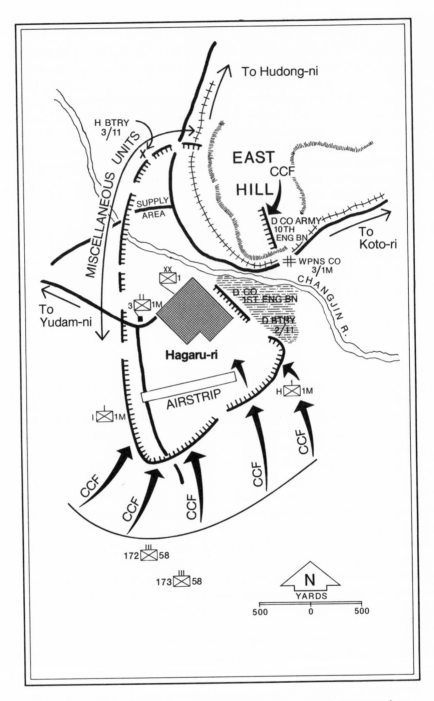

MAP 12. First battle of Hagaru-ri, night of 28 November through 29 November.

attack groups, others behind immediately took their places. Many Chinese reached the Marine perimeter foxholes, despite their staggering losses.

Almost every survivor from the two Marine companies could have told gripping stories of his part in the night battle. One or two examples must suffice. Second Lt. Wayne L. Hall commanded the 3rd Platoon of I Company. He was in the center of the company position when three Chinese came at his foxhole. His carbine jammed. He pulled his pistol and killed all three of them, the last one pitching forward into his foxhole as the bullet struck him. The enemy attack throughout was at close quarters, with grenades and burp guns or submachine guns the principal weapons. The enemy concentrated its attack on an 800-yard stretch in the center of H and I companies' positions. There, two platoons and parts of two others received the heaviest blows.

This assualt was typical of Chinese infantry frontal assault tactics. They chose a particular area and then repeatedly sent assault teams into the same path of attack. The Chinese broke through the 3rd Platoon, H Company, and a sizable number of them reached the company's rear area, some even firing on the bulldozers still working on the airstrip. By about midnight, they had surrounded the H Company CP. The Chinese did not exploit their penetration and go for a decisive victory, however. Many of the Chinese pulled their knives and slashed at tents, looting the galley and provision area, especially for clothing. One wounded Marine saved his life by pretending to be dead while Chinese soldiers stripped his parka off him. While the Chinese scrambled for food and clothing, the Marines hurried up reinforcements, reorganized their scattered front-line men, and then turned a killing firepower on the foraging Chinese.

In 1st Lt. Robert C. Needham's 2nd Platoon of I Company, which was adjacent to H Company's right flank, Needham had to rely on his runner to carry messages after he lost wire communications with the tanks in his rear that were supporting him. Twice his runner, Pfc. Ronald Lavasseur, who had volunteered for the hazardous task, dashed across the fire-swept open area to the tanks and returned, taking his place again in the defense line. A third time he volunteered to take a message to the tanks. He carried the bucket to the well once too often, for this time Chinese fire killed him as he raced toward the tanks.[8]

The crisis mounted in the H Company area, but by 4 A.M. the attacks slackened, and it was apparent the enemy had done his worst for that night. When daylight came the new snow that had fallen through the night had softened the crumpled bodies of fallen men into white-shrouded mounds—Chinese soldiers who would never see the paddy fields of South China again. H Company lost 16 killed and 39 wounded during the night.[9]

I Company successfully beat off the attacks on it. Gradually the Chinese attack on the southern part of the perimeter decreased in intensity, and at daybreak the enemy there broke off the fight. In front of H and I companies the Marines counted 750 dead Chinese. Red streaks in the snow left trails where wounded had crawled or limped to the rear. Chinese prisoners said the 172nd Regiment lost 90 percent casualties in this night battle. It appears that the 58th Division used only the one regiment in this battle. Why it did not commit troops from its other two regiments is not known.

Lt. Col. J. L. Winecoff, in describing the scene that daylight disclosed on the morning of 29 November in front of H and I companies, said that few of the Chinese in the attack there ever got back—that they were under orders to take the Marine position at all costs. "You could note the dead lying in windrows in front of the MG's as if successively they had come as far as they could before being shot down. One POW said that the mission given his unit was to destroy the 1st Marine Division. All of these CCF were wearing thin-soled tennis type shoes except for a very few that we saw wearing the rough field shoes, resembling ours."[10]

CHINESE THREATEN FROM EAST HILL

While the first direct threat to Hagaru-ri came from the southern part of its perimeter in the attacks of the CCF 172nd Regiment, 58th Division, during the first part of the night of 28 November, a serious situation was simultaneously shaping up on East Hill, the rough, irregular mass of high ground rising 600 feet above Hagaru-ri on the east-northeast. A little before 2 A.M. on 29 November, word came to Ridge's CP that things were going badly on East Hill. With the situation then tense inside the Hagaru-ri perimeter because of the enemy assaults from the south and southwest, the thinly held and exposed positions to the northeast of the town could become critical factors in the outcome.

It chanced that a number of X Corps miscellaneous and service troops arrived at Hagaru-ri on 26–27 November to build a X Corps Advance CP for the projected X Corps westward attack from Yudam-ni and northward from Hagaru-ri through Changjin. These troops formed an important part of the force that Lieutenant Colonel Ridge pressed into combat service on the night of 28–29 November on East Hill. Lt. Col. William J. McCaffrey, X Corps deputy chief of staff, took an advance party to Hagaru-ri. A platoon of the 4th Signal Battalion had already arrived to install communications for the X Corps Advance CP.

McCaffrey located the CP west of the Koto-ri–Hagaru-ri road and about 200 to 300 yards south of the sector of the perimeter controlled by H Company, 1st Marines. Thus, it was outside the perimeter, a location unthinkable if an enemy attack was expected in the near future. But on 26–27 November no such thing was expected; the X Corps still accepted FEC's concept that the forthcoming X Corps attack would be little more than a march to the border. The Signal Platoon put in communications for the X Corps Advance CP, and McCaffrey set up an operations tent. The advance staff, however, was approximately only 50 men altogether, and Advance CP operations were not yet established.

McCaffrey received orders from X Corps to return to Hamhung for what was called an important conference. He left Hagaru-ri by jeep late in the afternoon of 27 November, passed through Koto-ri at dusk, and reached a Marine strongpoint at the edge of the escarpment about two miles distant, where the descent of Funchilin Pass began. He stopped there to talk briefly with the Marine sergeant in charge. There he and the sergeant received sniper fire from a hill to the west. The sergeant told him that the road was clear toward the coast, that trucks had come up earlier in the afternoon, but that he had received intermittent sniper fire at his position all afternoon. McCaffrey continued on without trouble and arrived at Hamhung about 9 P.M.[11] He was one of the last persons to drive down Funchilin Pass and reach the X Corps headquarters before Chinese closed that part of the road.

D Company, 10th Engineer Combat Battalion, an Army unit, also found itself at Hagaru-ri on the night of 27–28 November, arriving there just ahead of the Chinese closing of the road southward. It arrived just in time to find itself in a hard battle for which it was not prepared. Its story illustrates the hectic situation at the time and shows why the unexpected happened to many miscellaneous construction and service units that arrived at Hagaru-ri from the south on 27 November.

D Company, 10th Engineer Combat Battalion, 3rd Infantry Division, arrived in Korea on 20 November, landing at Wonsan. After about a week there in road-maintenance work, Capt. Philip A. Kulbes, commanding D Company Engineers, received orders to report to X Corps headquarters at Hamhung. Lt. Norman R. Rosen, commanding the 3rd Platoon of the company, went ahead with an advance party, arriving at X Corps in the afternoon. There he learned that the engineer company was to proceed at once to the Chosin Reservoir, where it was to build a X Corps Advance CP at Hagaru-ri. About midafternoon Captain Kulbes arrived with the company. Rosen told him their mission and added that, when he asked the briefing officer about the tactical situation, he was told that everything was secure, that "the marines drive up and down the road with their lights on." After refueling their vehicles, the engineer company started for Hagaru-ri. At Chinhung-ni (Santong-ni in Rosen's narrative) the column was delayed for six hours by traffic control on a one-way mountain road—Funchilin Pass. It arrived at its bivouac area south of Hagaru-ri at 2 A.M. on 28 November. In a drive of 150 miles on the twenty-seventh, it experienced a weather change from 20 degrees above zero to 15 degrees below. Despite their heavy winter clothing, the men suffered from the sudden cold.[12]

That morning at 9 A.M. the officers roused the tired and still sleepy men and started to prepare breakfast. While the cooks were at work on this task, a civilian came in and told them that enemy soldiers were on the road south of them. Just after this incident, a Marine officer and his driver walked into the engineers' camp and told them that they had driven into an enemy roadblock in a defile only a mile south and had to abandon their vehicle to escape. The driver was wounded. Kulbes and Rosen organized a platoon-sized patrol and started down the road to investigate. They soon met heavy fire from dug-in enemy. Word came to Kulbes that a Marine force was on its way from Hagaru-ri to deal with the enemy roadblock and that they could return to their bivouac area. There, the engineer company began to dig foxholes, and breakfast was served to them in small groups. After breakfast D Company, 10th Engineers, started to haul materials for the construction of the X Corps Advance CP.

At 2 P.M. a major of the G-2 section, 1st Marine Division, arrived at D Company's CP to tell them that Hagaru-ri was surrounded, that enemy attacks were expected that night, that the perimeter defense lines were thinly held, and that D Company would have to occupy a portion of it. He pointed out the position the engineers were to occupy. It was only 300 yards away, up the road and on a ridge to the right. He instructed them to go into prepared positions on the steep ridge, tie in with a platoon of the 4th Signal Battalion on their left, and anchor their right on the steep slope that overlooked the Marine Weapons Company's roadblock on the Koto-ri–Hagaru-ri road, about a mile east of Hagaru-ri. D Company moved all its vehicles and equipment inside the Marine perimeter; it left its tents and stoves in its bivouac area for future use and prepared to go into the assigned perimeter position—the steep spur of East Hill that rose abruptly 300 feet from the narrow-gauge railroad track at the base of the spur ridge. It was the critical high ground that most closely approached Hagaru-ri, immediately below which the Marines Weapons Company had its all-important roadblock.

D Company had four officers, 77 American enlisted men, and 90 South Korean (KATUSA) soldiers who had been integrated into its units down to squad level—a total company strength of 171 men. The South Koreans had joined the company in Japan two months earlier. The company was heavily armed. Each man was given three units of fire (a total of 288 rounds) for his M-1 rifle, two grenades, and all the machine-gun ammunition he could carry. In addition to individual weapons, the company had four heavy .50-caliber machine guns, five light .30-caliber machine guns and six 3.5-inch rocket launchers. But it had no mortars or recoilless rifles.

The D Company engineers were late in starting the steep climb and did not get to their position until dark. Many holes were already dug there, but not in an organized defensive position. Captain Kulbes placed the 1st Platoon on the right of his line just above the road, the 2nd Platoon in the center, and the 3rd Platoon on the left. The company front faced south and southeast. In effect, the company position did two things: it helped the Marine Weapons Company roadblock on the road immediately below the end of the spur ridge protect the approach to Hagaru-ri from Koto-ri, and it guarded the spur ridge approach from the crest of East Hill to the road at the base of the hill and the Hagaru-ri defenses. It was a critical position, and had the troops been available, it certainly would have been held by a strong infantry unit.

Lieutenant Rosen commanded the 3rd Platoon on the high ground at the left of the company position. He started out to his left flank to tie it in with the Signal Battalion platoon the engineer company had been told was there. He found instead a platoon of South Korean labor troops and three or four American soldiers with an American captain in command.[13]

When D Company engineers started up the East Hill spur to take their position on the defense perimeter, Marine Capt. John C. Shelnut and his radio operator, Pfc. Bruno Podolak, accompanied the engineers to maintain radio communication with Lieutenant Colonel Ridge's CP and to act as Ridge's liaison men with the engineer company.

About 10 P.M. Lieutenant Rosen and his 3rd Platoon heard firing on their left. A Chinese force had slipped up on the South Korean labor platoon and almost immediately penetrated it and came on down the spur toward Rosen's 3rd Platoon. This enemy force attacked Rosen's platoon from both the left (east) and the rear (north). Rosen tried to turn his men around to meet the unexpected attacks from these directions. His men, not trained for such a maneuver under fire, executed it poorly. In this fighting and attempted maneuver he lost most of his left-hand squad and suffered casualties in the rest of his platoon. The 2nd and 1st platoons were soon partially demoralized, and most of the company withdrew on the 1st Platoon position. In this withdrawal and confused fighting, Captain Shelnut was killed, but Private First Class Podolak with his radio stayed on the ridge above, hidden in a hole, and was unseen by the Chinese. From this position he was able to report once or twice to Ridge's CP as to what was happening on this part of East Hill.

By 3 A.M. all platoons of D Company engineers were in a tight perimeter at the south end of the spur ridge. They held out there during the rest of the night, suffering many casualties to CCF white phosphorus shells directed at them. The Chinese above assaulted the engineers' perimeter several times but were cut down by heavy concentrated machine-gun and small-arms fire. One of the few messages recorded in the Marine Division G-3 Journal file relating to this action came in a telephone call from Lieutenant Colonel Ridge's 3rd Marine Battalion headquarters to Colonel Bowser, 1st Marine Division G-3, at 2:30 A.M., 29 November. It was transcribed in the message book as follows: "About an hour ago, enemy appeared on East Hill. A group of enemy sneaked up to a bunch of Banks's men and hand-grenaded hell out of them and took position." Podolak may have sent this message. In any event, the message apparently referred to the overrun South Korean labor troops above and on the left of Rosen's 3rd Platoon of D Company, 10th Engineers.[14]

Before he was killed, Captain Shelnut communicated with Ridge's headquarters once about the serious situation developing on East Hill. He was told that the engineer company must hold at all costs. The engineers did just that, but not all of its original position. It did hold the lower part of it and turned back every effort of the Chinese to reach the road below and the edge of Hagaru-ri. It was almost dawn before a composite group of about 100 Marine service and headquarters personnel reached their position. After daylight an air strike hit the Chinese above them on the ridge and gave immediate relief. About noon on 29 November, D Company was relieved on the spur ridge and moved to another part of the perimeter.

Under the circumstances, the engineers of D Company, 10th Engineer Combat Battalion, did well in this night battle. The South Koreans attached to the engineers, however, did poorly. They soon became demoralized, and there was the usual problem with the language barrier. When the Americans ran low on ammunition and asked their South Korean buddies if they had any, the latter replied no. Later it was learned that they had just about all that had been issued to them—they had done little fighting and simply had not used it. The engineers found that their own weapons performed poorly at times—they had not been recently cleaned of dried oil and dirt and tended to respond stiffly, and sometimes not at all. In this situation they frequently picked up American weapons Chinese dead had dropped near their foxholes, mostly Thompson submachine guns and carbines, which worked better than their own weapons. D Company, 10th Engineers, lost about half its men that night. Of the 81 Americans in the company, ten were killed, 25 were wounded, including two officers, and nine men were missing. Of the South Koreans attached to them, 50 were killed, wounded, or missing (the larger number were missing). The enemy lost much more heavily. After daylight on the twenty-ninth, when the Chinese had been driven back up the hill some distance by air strikes and a counterattack, more than 400 enemy dead were counted in front of D Company, 10th Engineers. Many of these dead were probably killed by artillery fire from Hagaru-ri during the night and from air strikes after daylight. But there can be little doubt that most were killed by D Company itself in repelling repeated enemy assaults on its tight and heavily gunned perimeter during the night.

The Marine command and many of its rank-and-file tended to be critical of D Company rather than appreciative of its help in the battle the night of 28–29 November on East Hill. They took little account of the company's inexperience in combat and its sudden commitment to the fight for Hagaru-ri with little orientation and no ground support. As Lieutenant Rosen commented, "Months passed before the marines gave us recognition for even having been in their perimeter."[15] In fact, the engineer company did hold the lower part of the most important and critical terrain feature of East Hill.

The small group that Lieutenant Colonel McCaffrey had left behind at Hagaru-ri on the afternoon of 27 November fared badly in the CCF attack. About midnight, McCaffrey, now at Hamhung, received a call from the officer he had left in charge. He said there was small-arms fire in their vicinity and asked permission to move the group inside the Marine perimeter. McCaffrey immediately authorized it. The next night when the attack came, most of those people were put on the Marine defense line, including the platoon from the 4th Signal Battalion, X Corps. They suffered heavy casualties. When the Marine and Army troops evacuated Hagaru-ri and the Chosin area a week later, McCaffrey said fewer than a dozen of the X Corps Advance CP group could be accounted for.[16]

MARINE COUNTERATTACK, 29 NOVEMBER

As the battle on East Hill above D Company, 10th Engineers, worsened during the night, Maj. Reginald R. Myers, executive officer of the 3rd Battalion, 1st Marines, offered to lead a counterattack up the hill if Ridge thought it necessary. If the Chinese continued their drive down the spur ridge, the Hagaru-ri defenders might easily lose the road at the base of the hill and the bridge over the Changjin River by which the road entered the main part of Hagaru-ri and went on west to Yudam-ni. If this happened and the Chinese destroyed the bridge, the Marines westward at Yudam-ni would be cut off from the escape route southward, and all the artillery of the 11th Marines and the transportation of nearly three regiments of Marines would be in jeopardy. Ridge felt that East Hill, or some parts of it now in the hands of Chinese, would have to be retaken at all costs to prevent the enemy from obtaining control of the road below the southwestern spur and the nearby supply dumps. When things started going bad on East Hill, he had immediately ordered part of his artillery to shift trails so they could fire into the threatened area above the engineers and prevent enemy reinforcements from reaching the victorious Chinese in their advance positions. Ridge at the same time was able to assemble about 100 miscellaneous Marine rear-echelon troops and send them to Captain Kulbes as reinforcements for his engineers. These men came into the D Company perimeter on the spur ridge just before dawn.

At 5:30 A.M. on 29 November, Lieutenant Colonel Ridge decided on a counterattack up this spur ridge toward the East Hill crest and assigned Major Myers to lead it. Ridge assembled all the reserves he could find — clerks, typists, truck drivers, stragglers — anyone who could be found from the 55 different units that had reached Hagaru-ri by this time — to form a Marine, Army, and ROK counterattack force of 315 men. Most of this motley force were strangers to each other. After full daylight, Major Myers led this composite force up the hill, passed through the engineer perimeter, and climbed toward the crest.[17]

Fog enshrouded East Hill. As soon as the fog lifted enough for aircraft to operate, about 9 A.M., Marine fighters and bombers came over the area. They struck first with napalm and bombs in front of the engineers' perimeter. Marine air squadron VMF-312 flew 31 sorties over the Hagaru-ri perimeter during the day, most of them against East Hill. The Chinese still held the commanding ground on the crest of the hill. The *Badoeng Strait*, off the coast, had one fighter squadron on call; the 5th Air Force had the 35th Fighter-Bomber Group at Yonpo airfield; at Yonpo airfield MAG-33 had one fighter squadron and one night-fighter squadron; and MAG-12 at Wonsan had two fighter squadrons and one night-fighter squadron. The Marine command used all these air forces on 28 and 29 November to help Marine and Army troops surrounded and beleaguered in the Chosin area.[18]

Pfc. Bruno Podolak had been lucky enough to establish radio contact from his hole near the mountain crest with Cpl. J. D. Mitchell, a radio operator with Myers at the foot of the hill as his force prepared to attack, and informed him that he estimated enemy in battalion strength held the crest. At first as he led his counterattack force up the spur ridge, Myers found the terrain more an obstacle than anything else. The mountain slope was deeply eroded with gullies and exposed rough, rocky ledges. Men seemed to drop out and disappear as the force struggled upward. As the constantly thinning force neared the crest, Myers came upon Podolak, who joined him with his radio. Shortly thereafter, a bullet hit Podolak in the back, going through his radio before it entered his body. The radio had saved his life. Although wounded, he kept going with Myers's group.[19] About 75 of Myers's original force, only one-fourth of it, neared the military crest. The dug-in Chinese there, and others just beyond on the reverse slope, stopped Myers's men with machine-gun and small-arms fire and grenades. Myers had to order his survivors to find cover short of the crest in a defensive position and to hold there until help arrived. This was to be Capt. George W. King's A Company of the Marine 1st Engineer Battalion, which had been ordered to East Hill. The engineer company had been working at a sawmill preparing timbers for reconstructing a blown bridge at Sasu-ri, about two miles north of Hagaru-ri on the east side of the reservoir. With his improvised force of miscellaneous troops, not trained for infantry fighting of the ferocity it encountered, Myers had held an estimated enemy regiment to the crest of East Hill and had prevented them from capturing the southwest spur and entry to Hagaru-ri and the road south to Koto-ri. In accomplishing this, his improvised force had lost 170 in killed, wounded, and missing in action during 14 hours of action. Major Myers received the Congressional Medal of Honor for his role in this successful defense of terrain vital to holding Hagaru-ri.[20]

A Company, 1st Engineer Battalion, reached East Hill at noon on the twenty-ninth. First Lt. Nicholas A. Canzona's 1st Platoon led the advance. His platoon made an exhausting climb to Myers's position up the southwestern spur of East Hill but then received orders to come back down and make another approach to the crest from the northwest. This second approach was just about opposite that made on his arrival and would put Canzona's platoon at the military crest of the northern edge of the enemy-held hill. The idea seems to have been that from there Canzona could attack the Chinese from the rear. If he reached his assigned objective on East Hill, Canzona would be at the northern end of the heights, while Myers was just beneath the crest at its southwestern end.[21]

In his second approach to the East Hill crest, Canzona had only 20 men of his 1st Platoon; he had neither radios nor supporting arms and had only one light machine gun. The men had their small arms and grenades. When the platoon reached the military crest at the north end of East Hill, CCF machine-gun fire pinned it to the ground—an enemy machine gun swept the trail, which was only a few feet wide along the knife-edge ridge, from which nearly vertical slopes dropped off at either side. There was no room for maneuver. The one machine gun in the platoon proved inoperative after it was brought up from the rear of the column. Only three men, Canzona, S. Sgt. Stanley B. McPherson, and Pfc. Eugene B. Schlegel, could deploy for attack. Schlegel was wounded, became unconscious, and rolled like a log down the slope. The platoon hugged the ground while a crew brought another machine gun up from the foot of the hill. But even with it in position and firing, Canzona's engineers could not advance. A request for mortar fire brought only two rounds of 81-mm, and that only after a long delay. It was now late in the afternoon.

Canzona walked back down the hill to consult with Captain King. The latter had just received orders to withdraw A Company to a defensible reverse slope position. Canzona returned to his men and withdrew halfway down the hill. Sergeant McPherson covered their withdrawal with the machine gun. The sun sank as Canzona's men set up their night defense. Artillery below them at Hagaru-ri now took the Chinese position to their front under heavy barrage. Canzona estimated the enemy force in front of him as only a platoon; Myers thought that possibly a company held him up at the other end of the hill. Myers, with the equivalent of about two platoons remaining in his force, stayed in position that night of 29–30 November below the crest at the south end of East Hill.

At dusk on 29 November the situation was tense at Hagaru-ri. The defenders there had lost more than 500 casualties. The CCF had had it within their power to overrun the town during the preceding night and day. Why they had not used the full 58th Division to attack Hagaru-ri from the southwest in coordination with the attack from East Hill during the night of 28–29 November and the day of the twenty-ninth is unexplained. The small Marine garrison and a sizable number of noncombat troops pressed into the perimeter defense had barely held on. General Smith had remained calm throughout the battle; Lieutenant Colonel Ridge had used his resources ably and deserves admiration for the way in which he directed the defense of Hagaru-ri on 28–29 November.

Smith and Ridge had expected strong reinforcements to arrive at Hagaru-ri from the south during the day. Sitter's G Company, 3rd Marine Battalion, the 41st Royal British Commandos, four platoons of Marine tanks, an Army infantry company, and a large convoy of trucks had left Koto-ri that morning, only 11 miles away, under orders to fight their way into Hagaru-ri. Sitter's company was scheduled on arrival to take over the fight for East Hill. But on the way this column ran into great trouble —a continuous gauntlet of Chinese soldiers on the eastern ridges flanking the road. This story of Task Force Drysdale will be told later. The column did not reach Hagaru-ri as scheduled.

CCF Capture and Hold East Hill

Who were the Chinese that captured East Hill on the night of 28–29 November and then stubbornly held it through the rest of the Hagaru-ri battles? Intelligence of their unit identity is obscure because few if any of them were captured or their dead searched, because their positions were never captured. It seems that there was no effort to learn from the dead in front of D Company, 10th Engineers, on the southwestern spur ridge of East Hill their formation and unit identity—or if it was done, it was not recorded. It seems unlikely that any of them were from the 58th CCF Division, which was on the opposite side of Hagaru-ri, whose assembly areas were miles away to the southwest.

It could be surmised that they were elements of the CCF 80th Division, which had by now roughly treated the 7th Infantry Division troops on the east side of the reservoir. At least a regiment of that division would have been free on 28 November to continue on south and take up positions on East Hill that night. Two of its regiments, or possibly even fewer, would have been adequate to remain behind and finish off the 7th Division troops in their scattered perimeters, and then in Task Force Faith after the 31st and 32nd Infantry troops had united at the inlet perimeter. We know that Maj. William R. Lynch, when General Hodes ordered him to come to Hagaru-ri from Hudong-ni on the afternoon of 28 November, saw Chinese on the hills to the east in solid columns marching south toward East Hill, and that Capt. Robert E. Drake, during his tank attack that morning against the enemy roadblock below the 31st Infantry perimeter, saw long columns of Chinese, including horse-mounted soldiers, proceeding south on the hills to the east of the road. These Chinese soldiers could hardly have been from other than the 80th Division, perhaps the tail-end regiment of the division in the march order. It is also possible that some of the enemy troops that appeared on East Hill during the night of 28–29 November came from the CCF 60th Division that controlled the road south of Hagaru-ri all the way to Chinhung-ni. It appears from the action on East Hill and from estimates by several American commanders of enemy strength in front of them during the fighting that night that there were perhaps no more than two battalions of enemy engaged there that night. Considering all the known facts and the general deployment of the Chinese forces at this time, it seems plausible to speculate that the enemy force that seized East Hill on the night of 28–29 November and threatened Hagaru-ri from there comprised units of the CCF 80th Division.

Only artillery fire from Hagaru-ri, covering the approaches to the lower ground of East Hill and the thin American defense line there, seemed to offer hope of holding off the Chinese threat from the northeast in the early hours of 29 November. By 4 A.M. there appeared to be little chance of stopping an enemy breakthrough from East Hill if the Chinese made the effort. The 1st Marine Division CP and the supply dumps lay at the foot of the hill just below them. Only a hastily formed line of service and rear-echelon troops, clerks, and odds and ends of detachments, together with a few tanks and machine-gun positions strung along the base of the hill, stood in the way. Any strong effort could have broken through here. But the attack did not come.

Why the attack did not come can only be surmised. First, one might wonder why the CCF 58th Division to the southwest remained quiescent —it had committed only one of its three regiments in the initial attack. Why did it not bring up at least another regiment and continue the assault? The Chinese troops on East Hill, after turning back the Myers and

Canzona counterattacks by dark of 29 November, seemed content merely to stay on the crest and hold the high ground. They may have been relatively few in number by this time and perhaps did not feel strong enough to launch an attack downhill on the perimeter. Such an assumption would go along with the thought that they were mostly elements of the CCF 80th Division that had pressed on ahead while the bulk of the division was still engaged behind them with the surrounded elements of the Army 31st RCT and Task Force Faith. It seems clear that the CCF 58th Division attack from the southwest of Hagaru-ri was not coordinated with the later attack from East Hill on the other side of the town. It is known that the Chinese forces had very poor communications between their scattered major forces, almost no telephone or radio communication, and that it would have been very difficult for a higher command to have coordinated the actions of the 58th Division with the East Hill enemy force. No doubt the first Chinese on East Hill could see a good bit of what was taking place below them in the earlier action of the 172nd Regiment, 58th Division, but it is unlikely that they knew anything of its details. They may have thought after that action tapered off and failed that the best thing they could do with their numbers would be to hold the strategic heights above the town, after their own effort to capture the southwestern spur of the hill failed.

7

YUDAM-NI, 28–30 NOVEMBER

The night of 28–29 November was relatively quiet at Yudam-ni, a great relief from the incessant battles the previous night. It seemed the Chinese were as worn out as were the Marines. They, too, were human, and the numbing cold was as hard, if not harder, on them than on the Marines. The Chinese troops were not as well clothed. And they had suffered far more casualties, crippling in some of their assault units. Then, too, the air attacks during the daylight hours kept them pretty well out of sight, except on parts of North Ridge, and to the south, where they vigorously opposed the Marine relief force sent to rescue C Company, 7th Marines. After dark on 28 November the CCF had to regroup.

During the night the Marine aid stations moved south of Yudam-ni, where they were safer from enemy attacks. On 29 November some Marine wounded had to be taken care of on straw in the open and covered with heavy tarpaulin. By 30 November there were aid tents at Yudam-ni to shelter about 500 wounded. It was so cold at night during this time at the reservoir that dressings of wounds sometimes could not be changed. And in some places a wounded man's clothing could not be cut off of him, for he would then have frozen to death. Often it was best just to leave the wounded untreated for the time being.[1]

29 NOVEMBER AT YUDAM-NI

Most of the 1st Marine Division headquarters reached Hagaru-ri on or before 27 November, and General Smith notified his staff there that he expected to move his CP to Hagaru-ri the next day, when he planned to arrive there himself. General Smith's CP was in the northeast section of Hagaru-ri, near the concrete bridge over the Changjin River. Hagaru-ri was at this time virtually a tent city, as only a few houses or buildings of any type remained undestroyed by numerous earlier air attacks. A small Japanese-type wood house that was one of the few structures remaining in Hagaru-ri was repaired and covered with heavy tent canvas for General

Smith's use. He arrived at Hagaru-ri by helicopter from Hungnam at 11 A.M. on 28 November and immediately opened his CP. A Marine Rear CP in charge of Col. Francis A. McAlister, the division G-4, remained at Hungnam to oversee supply problems for the division.[2] Thus, General Smith was in personal command at Hagaru-ri before the Chinese made their first attack there.

During the night of 28–29 November, Colonels Litzenberg and Murray decided that all troops of the 5th and 7th Marines at Yudam-ni were needed for defense and that none could be spared for the relief column General Smith had ordered to open the road to Hagaru-ri. Yet, the order from Smith could not be wholly ignored, and as an expedient, a composite battalion was formed from some units on the morning of 29 November. Maj. Warren Morris, executive officer, 3rd Battalion, 7th Marines, was given command.

Morris's composite battalion moved out southward from Yudam-ni at 8 A.M. on 29 November in an effort to reach and rescue F Company, 7th Marines, above Toktong Pass, and continue on toward Hagaru-ri. The leading troops of the battalion had hardly left the perimeter when they came under heavy machine-gun fire from both sides of the road. Repeated air strikes on enemy positions allowed it to make slow progress. The battalion was only two and one-half miles from Yudam-ni when planes dropped two messages saying that enemy forces in great strength were just ahead on both sides of the road. The planes gave the same message to Litzenberg in Yudam-ni. On receiving this warning, Litzenberg modified his order to Morris to rescue F Company, ordering him instead to return to the Yudam-ni perimeter before dark. Meanwhile, Morris with every passing minute was increasingly in danger of being surrounded. At 3:15 in the afternoon, Litzenberg sent an urgent message to Morris to return to Yudam-ni. Air strikes and artillery concentrations fired from Yudam-ni covered his disengagement and successful return to the perimeter.[3]

It was abundantly clear by now that the Chinese not only had constructed innumerable roadblocks between Yudam-ni and Hagaru-ri, but they also had heavy forces in position along the 14 miles of road and meant to deny any movement along it toward Hagaru-ri. In two days now they had turned back three efforts from Yudam-ni and Hagaru-ri to open the road. Yudam-ni was effectively cut off from Hagaru-ri, and relief forces from both Yudam-ni and Hagaru-ri had been unable to get close to F Company, 7th Marines. It was cut off, surrounded, and fighting for its life in its isolated position above Toktong Pass.

Not only were the two companies from the 7th Marines cut off in their isolated positions on the MSR between Yudam-ni and Hagaru-ri, but an event taking place at the same time many miles southwest of them at

Sachang-ni was baffling, and of possible ominous import to the Marines cut off at Yudam-ni. Sachang-ni was an important intermountain village about 30 air miles south of Yudam-ni on the dirt road that slanted southwest from it to the headwaters of the Taedong River. Sachang-ni was connected by a poor track running eastward from it through Huksu-ri to Chinhung-ni on the main road north from Hamhung to Hagaru-ri and the Chosin Reservoir. Sachang-ni was about the same air distance, 30 miles, from Chinhung-ni as it was from Yudam-ni. It would be necessary to capture this road crossing if the CCF meant to make a deep enveloping move south of Yudam-ni and then east to reach the X Corps MSR at Chinhung-ni, at the south end of Funchilin Pass. The route from Yudam-ni south through Sachang-ni and from there east to Chinhung-ni was the only one possible for an enveloping force to use—there was no other in all that mountainous region. If Sachang-ni was found undefended, the CCF had many options open to them in the future course of the Chosin Reservoir campaign. It was not surprising, therefore, that a strong CCF reconnaissance in force arrived at Sachang-ni at the same time the heavy opening battles took place on both sides of the Chosin Reservoir.

Although this event is somewhat obscure, because we lack information as to the enemy's purpose, a brief digression from the main events taking place at the reservoir must be made to relate what happened there and the possible threat to the entire X Corps position that hung in the balance on the outcome. Elements of the US 3rd Infantry Division had occupied the town, on the left flank of the X Corps position, after its arrival in northeast Korea as one of its key points for the protection of the 1st Marine Division's advance to the reservoir.

THE FIGHT AT SACHANG-NI, 28–29 NOVEMBER

Anxiety developed when a strong enemy force, identified as part of the CCF 89th Division, attacked the 1st Battalion, 7th Infantry Regiment of the US 3rd Division, in defensive positions at Sachang-ni on the night of 28–29 November. Capt. Robert F. Peterson, commanding C Company, 7th Infantry, estimated the enemy force as at least a battalion. C and B companies held defensive positions around the town, C Company on the hills north and northeast of the town. B Company was east of C Company. Both companies had their CPs on the road west of Sachang-ni. East of B Company's CP was the ammunition dump and the 1st Battalion headquarters.

A few rounds of 120-mm mortar shells fell in the C Company area after dark, about 7:30 P.M. on 28 November. Three hours later, just before midnight, a Chinese force attacked down a ridge that led into C Company's position from the north. This first enemy force apparently had used ladders to get to the top of the ridge, where it was lightly defended because of an almost vertical cliff, at places 60 to 70 feet high. C Company comprised about 65 to 70 American soldiers together with approximately 140 attached South Koreans. The enemy attack on top the ridge struck the 3rd Platoon and almost immediately penetrated it at a point where an American sergeant and a ROK assistant manned a machine gun. The sergeant was wounded, and the ROK ran off. A platoon sergeant was also killed here. The Chinese immediately fired a green flare, a signal for about 300 waiting Chinese soldiers to pour through the penetration point and enter the C Company position. They reached the east-west lateral road west of Sachang-ni and turned east on it. Another force had meanwhile climbed a connecting ridge to the area of the first penetration, and it also entered the perimeter. The Chinese that first reached the road and turned east on it approached the C Company CP.

Captain Peterson had by now called in mortar and artillery fire on the enemy penetration point and enemy approach routes to it. This fire seemed to have pretty well closed off further enemy troops getting into the perimeter from that quarter. The lead Chinese force on the road reached the C Company CP and attacked it. The fight there was at close range, and sometimes hand to hand, in the form of Americans swinging clubbed rifles. In the dark Captain Peterson grabbed a man he thought was one of his own men, only to find he was a Chinese soldier, who cut loose with a tommy gun. A company clerk shot the Chinese soldier. Within the company CP, the Chinese ran about, setting several buildings on fire; they were in the kitchen and around most of the vehicles but took nothing. Peterson's CP personnel finally cleared the area; 28 enemy bodies lay within it.

Another part of the Chinese breakthrough force silently approached and attacked the 60-mm mortar section and killed or wounded most of the mortarmen. There was no blowing of bugles in this attack. It was a silent approach and a quick and deadly assault. For reasons unknown, this enemy force withdrew but stayed in the vicinity until about 5 A.M. of the twenty-ninth. The Chinese had a large number of submachine guns; C Company collected 21 of them the next day. Some were American made, others were of Soviet manufacture.

American weapons malfunctioned frequently in this cold night battle. Some M-1 rifles froze up, and a 60-mm mortar froze in one of its working parts, but the carbines functioned well, which was a bit unusual for them.

The enemy force did not go beyond the C Company CP in any force. Good targets for them lay just beyond—the B Company CP, the ammunition dump, and then battalion headquarters. According to Captain Peterson, most of the B Company personnel vacated their positions and nearly all the ROK troops attached to his own company did so. He did not get them back until the next day. C Company lost five killed, 17 wounded, and one man captured in this fight. Most of the casualties were from the mortar section and company headquarters.

American artillery and the 4.2-inch mortar fire on Chinese approach areas must have been an important factor in causing the Chinese to withdraw. On 29 November, more than 150 Chinese bodies were found in a draw leading to the road, a Chinese approach route where 4.2-inch mortars had concentrated their fire. Some of the bodies or parts of them had been blown into trees.

After daylight of the twenty-ninth, and when the enemy force had withdrawn from contact, a patrol found a ROK sergeant who had been in the Japanese Army in China during World War II, a good soldier, tied to a tree and still alive, with the flesh stripped from one arm down to the bone. He died about half an hour after he was found.[4]

The significance of the fight at Sachang-ni lies in the fact that at least one battalion of the Chinese 89th Division went south from Yudam-ni on a reconnaissance-in-force mission, while the rest of the division stayed at Yudam-ni to participate in the battles of 27–28 November and later. This reconnaissance would accomplish two purposes: it would protect the Chinese fighting at Yudam-ni against a surprise American attack from the south, and it would reveal whether X Corps was protecting the left flank of the 1st Marine Division and the western approaches to Hamhung and Hungnam. It apparently accomplished its mission.

29 November along the Chosin Reservoir MSR

By 29 November CCF troops were on the Chosin Reservoir MSR as far south as Chinhung-ni. A platoon of CCF exchanged fire on the twenty-ninth with a Marine patrol there near the railhead. And at Koto-ri Colonel Puller's staff watched Chinese all that day on the surrounding high ground. They obviously were observing and studying the defenses of the place. All up and down the MSR, and particularly in the reservoir area, Marine aircraft flew sortie after sortie during the twenty-ninth—125 sorties in all—in support of the ground forces, striking 61 different enemy troop concentrations. Five Marine helicopters lifted Marine and Army wounded from forward combat areas to Hagaru-ri, where X Corps L-5 planes evacuated them to the Hamhung airstrip. From there, ambulances took them to further evacuation points. But these were relatively few of the hundreds of wounded that could not be evacuated. All day long artillery from Hagaru-ri and Yudam-ni fired on known enemy positions within range, and aircraft roamed the sky to locate and report on enemy targets and enemy movements. These aerial reports indicated large groups of enemy on the hills south of Yudam-ni, northeast of Hagaru-ri, and both north and south of Koto-ri. All available aircraft were sent to napalm and strafe these groups. Cargo planes dropped ammunition and supplies to the ground forces at Hagaru-ri, Yudam-ni, and to the 7th Infantry Division elements cut off on the east side of the reservoir.[5]

The air resupply drops by the United States Air Force, Far East Combat Cargo Command, to the cut-off troops of the 1st Marine Division and the Army 31st RCT at Chosin Reservoir were vital to their survival, and it would be wrong not to mention their importance and the outstanding performance of this command. The commanding officer of the command was Maj. Gen. William H. Tunner. General Vandenberg wanted the best man available for the job and picked him for it. Tunner had previously commanded the India–China Hump air-cargo operations and the Berlin airlift. Tunner began organizing the Far East Combat Cargo Command for the Korean War in early September 1950 at Tokyo. Tunner was considered by his subordinates a hard man to work for, but as one officer said, "He was a great guy if you were a cold infantryman on the main battle position." In November 1950, the FEAF Combat Cargo Command airdrop system was geared to handle about 70 tons a day. The limiting factor was the Army's capability to package and load airborne supplies, including rations, ammunition, petroleum products, clothing, and weapons. At Ashiya airfield in Japan, the 2348th Quartermaster Airborne Air Supply and Packaging Company augmented its strength with Japanese employees, and during the Chosin operations it worked around the clock to get airdrops ready and loaded. General Tunner sent a C-119 detachment and quartermaster packers to Yonpo airfield in Korea for quick preparation and delivery of specially needed ammunition and equipment to X Corps front-line units. A C-47 detachment flew from Wonsan on similar missions. On 28 November this latter detachment dropped ten tons of ammunition to the 5th and 7th Marines at Yudam-ni and 16 tons to the 31st RCT troops at the inlet perimeter on the east side of the reservoir. The next day, 29 November, General Almond, X Corps commander, requested airdrop of more than 400 tons of air supply to these cut-off troops at the reservoir. This demand was too great to be met in full. On 4 December General Stratemeyer ordered General Tunner to use all his C-46s, C-47s, and C-119s in support of the X Corps. The Combat Cargo Command reached a capacity of 250 tons of airdropped supplies by the first days of December.[6]

At 1:30 in the afternoon of 29 November, General Smith asked Litzenberg for a report on the progress being made to open the MSR from Yudam-ni to Hagaru-ri. Litzenberg informed Smith that he was unable to form a relief force strong enough to rescue F Company without endangering the safety of Yudam-ni and the troops there. He asked that a relief force including tanks be sent from Hagaru-ri to reach F Company. He indicated that, if that was not feasible, he intended to order F Company to break out overland to reach the MSR between Hagaru-ri and Koto-ri on the night of 30 November.[7] This was certainly a desperate scheme and probably would not have worked.

At Yudam-ni on 28–29 November 1950, one has an excellent example of the old military rule that the local commander on the ground has to be the final authority in deciding what the military situation requires and is justified in departing from existing orders if that seems necessary to save his force or to avoid overwhelming losses and defeat. Colonels Litzenberg and Murray acted jointly in issuing commands to their regiments because neither had command authority over the other, although Litzenberg was the senior officer. They found it necessary to issue orders contrary to existing orders from their commander, General Smith. And the latter, himself, at his level, issued orders on the twenty-ninth to Colonel Litzenberg for a movement of the 7th Marines that was not in accord with existing orders from his commander, General Almond. In all these instances the local commanders acted correctly, as events proved.

Chapter 5 above covered the conference that General MacArthur called at Tokyo on the night of 28–29 November as a result of the critical situation in Eighth Army and the issuance of oral orders on the morning of 29 November to General Almond to cease offensive action in the X Corps zone and to concentrate his troops at Hagaru-ri, preparatory to withdrawing them to the coast. Thus, only two days after the X Corps had started its attack to the north to reach the border and end the war, everything was put in reverse.

General Almond's Orders, 29 November

A little more than an hour before midnight, 29 November, General Smith at Hagaru-ri received X Corps's order to redeploy one regiment immediately from Yudam-ni to Hagaru-ri, and from there to gain contact with the stranded elements of the 7th Infantry Division east of the reservoir. The same order placed all Army elements in the Koto-ri and reservoir area under General Smith's command.[8] It was impossible for Smith to redeploy a regiment from Yudam-ni to Hagaru-ri immediately, as Almond ordered. They had to fight their way to Hagaru-ri. And long before these troops arrived from Yudam-ni in a three-day-and-night fight along the 14-mile MSR, the Chinese 80th Division had destroyed the 7th Division elements east of the reservoir. This is an example of an order easily given with a correct desired result in mind, but impossible to implement in the prevailing circumstances. There was no way it could have been successfully executed.

The night of 29–30 November was generally quiet at the Yudam-ni perimeter. But the cold was intense. The troops were on 50 percent alert. Half of them tried to get some rest while the others stood to their arms, but few could sleep. This was the third virtually sleepless night in a row for them, and there had been no hot meals since Thanksgiving dinner on 23 November. At its perimeter position above Toktong Pass, F Company had no 50 percent rest, as did those at Yudam-ni, but went through another night of CCF attacks. Fortunately, the company position was within extreme 105-mm howitzer range of the artillery at the edge of Hagaru-ri, and they gave important assistance.

After dawn broke on the morning of 30 November without any serious CCF attack against the Yudam-ni perimeter, the Marines there began to feel that the CCF had shot their bolt, and confidence began to return that they would survive. Also, a helicopter brought news that cheered them — Hagaru-ri had had a quiet night after the big battle there the previous night, 28–29 November.

In retrospect, one can see that the CCF were following their traditional and successful tactics of the Chinese civil war. They had assaulted frontally with some success, but not completely so at Yudam-ni, Hagaru-ri, and on the east side of the reservoir. They had been entirely successful in cutting the MSR behind all these positions. The CCF had cut off the only supply and escape route for the beleaguered Americans at and near the reservoir to a depth of 30 miles back from Yudam-ni. They held positions of great strength and in large numbers all along this road, and they had turned back all efforts to open the road in the past two days. Perhaps the Chinese felt confident that they were now in a position of power and that they had only to wait and hold the noose tight to gather in the entire 1st Marine Division and elements of the 7th Infantry Division in the reservoir area. In addition to being cut off, all the American units there had suffered heavy casualties in the fighting thus far.

The same tactics worked, with much less cutting of roads to the rear, against Eighth Army in the west, where there was no real isolation of its units comparable to what had taken place in the X Corps. Another explanation for diminished Chinese assaults at Yudam-ni at this time could be the huge number of casualties they suffered on the night of 27–28 November. It seems likely that about this time General Sung called up at least two of the four CCF divisions of the 26th Army he had left behind in reserve north of the Yalu at Linchiang. Two of these divisions were identified as being in contact with the Marines for the first time on 5 December near Hagaru-ri. It would have taken them four to five days to move up to the front, probably traveling only at night.

8

TASK FORCE DRYSDALE, 27–29 NOVEMBER

Lt. Col. Allan Sutter brought the 2nd Battalion, 1st Marine Regiment, into Koto-ri on 24 November and it remained there as the principal infantry defense during the Chosin operation. The 1st Marine Regimental commander, Col. Lewis B. Puller, established his regimental headquarters there. Sutter placed his principal defense units on the west, north, and east of the perimeter, his three infantry companies on the north and west sides. A 4.2-inch mortar platoon and a battery of the 11th Marines artillery added heavy-weapons support. Subsequently, many miscellaneous Army and Marine units arrived at Koto-ri and, unable to go farther, added to its defense strength, with some given definite assignments on the perimeter, chiefly on the east and south sides. By 28 November ten tanks were placed at several places on the perimeter.

To the south of Koto-ri, at the foot of Funchilin Pass, Lt. Col. Donald M. Schmuck put his 1st Battalion, 1st Marine Regiment, in a defensive perimeter around Chinhung-ni, and as early as the night of 26 November had an exchange of fire with several enemy patrols, but they did not then know the enemy's identity. Schmuck sent out patrols to the west during the next two days and from them learned that the enemy was Chinese in about battalion strength, staying in civilian houses in a mountain valley during the day. On 30 November Schmuck led parts of A and B companies in a sortie on the mountain valley to the west. A battery of artillery laid down supporting fires, and 81-mm and 4.2-inch mortars with the infantry helped Schmuck burn and destroy the houses and run the Chinese out of the valley. The Marines brought the local civilians back to their perimeter with them. This sortie got rid of the major Chinese force near Chinhung-ni as the heavy battles were being fought to the north on top the plateau. At Koto-ri, perched on top the plateau, the CCF then placed more troops, who closely watched the town. They allowed no traffic north from the town.

KOTO-RI, 27–29 NOVEMBER

The first encounter with Chinese at Koto-ri occurred on 27 November, when a patrol from E Company, 1st Marines, had a fight with some enemy troops, a little west of Koto-ri. This group withdrew, leaving behind two wounded. The Marine patrol followed the withdrawing enemy on foot until a much stronger force that was dug in on a ridge line turned the patrol back. It returned to the Koto-ri perimeter in the late afternoon, bringing the two wounded Chinese with it. These prisoners said they were members of a Chinese division assembling to the west, with its headquarters in a mine shaft.

Koto-ri lay in the valley of the Changjin River, where the stream made an abrupt turn north from its easterly flow, which originated in the high ground to the west. Sharply rising hills were just west of Koto-ri. Another row of hills dominated Koto-ri on the northeast, where a small airstrip was being built. This high ground rising above the narrow valley of the Changjin River to the west and northeast gave Chinese observers an excellent opportunity to study the defenses and the troop dispositions of the Koto-ri perimeter, and all day of 28 November, Colonel Puller and his staff saw Chinese doing just that. It was apparent to Puller and most of the troops at Koto-ri that there were many Chinese now in their vicinity. Shortly before 9 A.M. one of the Marine outposts northeast of Koto-ri received heavy small-arms fire. It was reinforced by a platoon of E Company, but this was not enough, and the men at the outpost were withdrawn and an air strike called on the enemy-held hill.

Just after this incident, General Smith at Hagaru-ri ordered Colonel Puller to send a force north on the road from Koto-ri to meet a tank patrol he intended to send south from Hagaru-ri, hoping the two groups could reopen the road. Reconnaissance planes that landed at the Koto-ri airstrip reported enemy roadblocks on the road to Hagaru-ri. Pursuant to General Smith's order, however, Puller sent D Company, mounted in vehicles, out at 1:30 P.M. to open the road north. The last part of the 1st Marine Division Headquarters troops followed D Company, hoping to reach Hagaru-ri. About a mile north of the perimeter, Chinese held the high ground on both sides of the road in dug-in positions. When it came under fire, D Company infantry detrucked and deployed to clear the enemy from these positions. But even though the company was supported by 81-mm mortar fire from Koto-ri, it got no farther. At 5:35 P.M. it was ordered to withdraw to Koto-ri. Under cover of an air strike on the Chinese, with four killed and 34 wounded, D Company and Headquarters Company elements returned to the perimeter. They brought with them three Chinese prisoners, who said they were from the 179th Regiment of the CCF 60th Division.[1]

While this effort to open the road to Hagaru-ri on 28 November failed and showed that the CCF 60th Division held the dominating ground on both sides of the road in strength, various Army and other units streamed into Koto-ri from the south on their way to Hagaru-ri, only to find they could go no farther. The Koto-ri perimeter was packed with these people the night of 28 November. Colonel Puller placed some of these troops on his perimeter to strengthen it. The Army 185th Engineer Battalion, for instance, took over the southeast side of the perimeter; G Company, 31st Infantry, 7th Division, held the southern arc; and the Headquarters and Service Company of the 2nd Battalion, 31st Infantry, held the southwestern sections of the perimeter. Colonel Puller had his CP in about the center of the enclosed perimeter area, east of the village, the road, and the narrow-gauge railroad.

TASK FORCE DRYSDALE MOVES OUT

Among the troops that poured into Koto-ri during the day and night of 28 November from the south were two infantry-trained combat organizations — G Company, 41st Commando, British Royal Marines; and B Company, 31st Infantry, US Army. The commando unit arrived in the evening, and B Company about 9 P.M. that night. Both had left Hamhung that day for Hagaru-ri. The British commando unit was attached to Colonel Litzenberg's 7th Marine Regiment and was to join it at Yudam-ni. The Army's B Company, 31st Infantry, was on its way to join Col. Allan MacLean's 31st Infantry, east of Chosin Reservoir. Colonel Puller and his staff that night, 28–29 November, organized these two combat units and Capt. Carl L. Sitter's G Company, 1st Marines, together with many service and headquarters troops, into Task Force Drysdale, with orders to its commander, Lt. Col. Douglas B. Drysdale of the 41st Commando, British Royal Marines, to fight its way into Hagaru-ri the next day.

The 41st Commando, Royal Marines, numbered about 240 officers and men, all volunteers. The unit had been formed in England in August and flew to Japan on 1 September. There it underwent some training in the use of American-made weapons. Later it made three raids on North Korean rail lines behind the front lines, following the Inchon landing on the west coast of Korea. In mid-November a decision was made to transfer the commando unit to northeast Korea, where it would be attached to the 7th Marine Regiment and used as a second reconnaissance company. The commando arrived at Hungnam on 20 November and eight days later started north for the Chosin Reservoir. That evening it arrived at Koto-ri, where its commander, Lieutenant Colonel Drysdale, learned that it would continue its journey on the morrow and that he would be commander of a combat task force to open the road to Hagaru-ri.[2]

On 27 November Lt. Alfred J. Catania received orders to take his Army truck platoon, the 377th Truck Battalion, to X Corps HQ, Hamhung. There he learned he was to transport parts of two infantry regiments, 7th Division, to the Chosin Reservoir. On 28 November he loaded B Company, 31st Infantry, reinforced, comprising 325 men, and carried them north about 15 miles, where he had been told to unload them and return for a second shuttle. When he arrived back at Hamhung, Catania received instructions from a messenger to return north, reload the reinforced company he had just left, and take it to the 31st Infantry CP on the east side of the reservoir. There were some delays on the road after Catania had reloaded B Company. At about 9 P.M. that night a Marine outpost halted him near Koto-ri and said that Chinese held a roadblock north of the village and that he would have to stop within the Marine perimeter for the night.[3] During the night Capt. Charles Peckham, commander of B Company, 31st Infantry, learned that his company would be part of Task Force Drysdale on the morrow.

Lieutenant Colonel Drysdale's plan of attack was for an artillery barrage from Koto-ri on the hills on both sides of the road leading north, that to be followed by an air strike, and for the infantry to move out in attack at 9:30 A.M., 29 November. Three objectives were to be seized in the first part of the advance from Koto-ri. The 41st Royal Commando would lead off and attack the first hill east of the road; then Capt. Carl Sitter would lead his G Company, 1st Marines, against Hill 1236 farther north after passing through the commando; the third objective was Hill 1182, on the east side of the road and about three miles north of Koto-ri. Capt. Charles Peckham's B Company, 31st Infantry, was in reserve and would follow on the road until called for. These three infantry units, together with 12 tanks, Marine 1st Tank Battalion, equipped with 90-mm guns, and five tanks of a platoon of the Antitank Company, were the main combat troops in the task force. In addition to these major units there were detachments from the 1st Marine Division Headquarters Battalion; 1st Signal Battalion; 7th Motor Transport Battalion; Service Company, 1st Tank Battalion; an Army truck platoon, 377th Transportation Truck Battalion; Marine Military Police; and a few other minor groups.

The estimated total personnel strength of the task force was 922, with 29 tanks and 141 vehicles. But this total figure anticipated that 12 tanks of B Company, 1st Tank Battalion, and 15 or more vehicles would join the task force in the afternoon. They did leave Koto-ri in the late afternoon but were never able to join Task Force Drysdale.[4] Task Force Drysdale was Colonel Puller's response to General Smith's instructions to him on 28 November that he needed reinforcements at Hagaru-ri and that they should be sent to him the next day, even though they might suffer heavy losses in fighting through to Hagaru-ri.

The three infantry combat units that led out of Koto-ri on 29 November had a total count of about 630 men—235 from the 41st Royal Commando; 205 from G Company, 1st Marines; and 190 from B Company, 31st Infantry. The tank units added another 115 to 120 men. Thus, altogether there were about 750 combat troops in the task force. About another 100 men were service, headquarters, and miscellaneous troops. The long transport column was under the command of Maj. Henry J. Seeley, 1st Marine Motor Transport officer. It could progress only as the infantry and tanks cleared the way—driving the Chinese from the hills flanking the road and removing the physical roadblocks.

At 9:30 A.M. on 29 November the 41st Royal Commando moved out of the Koto-ri perimeter, following an artillery barrage and an air strike, against the first enemy-held hill east of the road north of Koto-ri. It took the hill against only slight resistance. Captain Sitter's G Company of Marines then moved against Hill 1236, about a mile and a half north of Koto-ri. Chinese were well entrenched on this hill, and they repulsed Sitter's attack until M. Sgt. Rocco A. Zullo got to within 200 yards of their main positions and fired his 3.5-inch rocket launcher into them. This brought the enemy troops out of their foxholes in a short time. The Marine company then seized the crest. G Company had 14 casualties in taking Hill 1236.[5]

The 41st Royal Commando and Sitter's G Company moved astride the road toward Hill 1182, the third objective, also on the east side of the road. There the attack stalled about two and one-half miles north of Koto-ri. The Chinese refused to be driven from their positions. They used mortar and machine-gun fire effectively. It was nearly noon. Drysdale had just received word from Colonel Puller at Koto-ri that two platoons of tanks from D Company, 1st Tank Battalion, would be up to join him at 1 P.M. Drysdale decided to call off further attack until these tanks arrived. During the morning, snow flurries had hampered air strikes, and this weather had sharpened Chinese resistance. At 1:30 P.M. Capt. Bruce Clarke arrived at Drysdale's position with two platoons of 12 tanks from D Company, 1st Tank Battalion, and five tanks from the Antitank Platoon, 5th Marine Regiment. This formidable strength of 17 tanks was badly needed.[6]

There followed a discussion of how the newly arrived tanks should be used in the column. Drysdale thought the tanks should be interspersed in the column. Clarke objected to this; he wanted them grouped together in the lead. Drysdale acceded to this view. Just before 2 P.M. Lt. Alfred Catania was ordered to take his platoon of trucks to Drysdale's position and there entruck B Company, 31st Infantry, in preparation for the attempt to go up the road in a motorized column, with the tanks clearing the way. Drysdale ordered Sitter's company off the hill and down to the road to be entrucked also. Drysdale's column march order at this point had the tanks in the lead; B Company, 31st Infantry, following; then G Company, 1st Marines; and the 41st Royal Commando and headquarters and service troops in the rear. Drysdale started his column north again at 2 P.M.[7]

Almost immediately, heavy enemy fire from the east side of the road stopped the lead tanks. They returned the enemy fire. But when the tanks stopped, the column behind them stopped. The troops of B Company, 31st Infantry, piled out and went into the roadside ditches. Chinese fire inflicted casualties. Captain Sitter left his unit and walked forward to learn the cause of the stop. This capable Marine commander had joined the Marines as a private in July 1941, as a 19-year-old only one year out of Central High School, Pueblo, Colorado. By now, 28 years old, he was a seasoned combat veteran who had come up from the ranks.

At the head of the column Sitter discovered that Chinese were defending a roadblock they had formed at a blown bridge. Most of the Chinese soldiers apparently were in houses on the east side of the road and opposite the bridge. Tank 90-mm fire was directed at these houses and destroyed them. When the Chinese inside broke into the open, machine-gun fire killed most of them. By the time this had taken place, Sitter's executive officer, 1st Lt. Charles Merrill, arrived with Sitter's G Company, having moved them from their place in the column up and around the stalled vehicles to the tanks' lead position. Sitter now had his company just behind the tanks.

A platoon of tanks made a trial run by themselves around the blown bridge, up past the destroyed huts, and some distance beyond. They soon returned. The tank commander, Captain Clarke, reported to Lieutenant Colonel Drysdale that he thought the tanks could make a run for it and reach Hagaru-ri but that the trucks and other vehicles in the column could not get through. The tanks pulled off in a dry streambed and refueled. Drysdale reflected on the situation briefly. After the tanks had refueled, he decided to push on with the entire column, but first he reorganized the march order. The 17 tanks of D Company and the Antitank Platoon were to lead, followed by G Company, 1st Marines, in 22 vehicles; then came the 41st Commando, Royal Marines, in 31 vehicles; B Company, 31st Infantry, was next in 22 vehicles; and headquarters and service detachments followed in 66 vehicles. It is not clear at what time in the afternoon this reorganized column started north again, but it must have been about 3 P.M. or shortly thereafter.[8]

The task-force column met immediate enemy fire. It stopped often, while the tanks in the lead cleared away a roadblock or checked enemy fire. At one point an enemy mortar round hit a truck carrying part of the 3rd Platoon of G Company, wounding every Marine in it. The three infantry companies behind the tanks alternately rode in the trucks short distances and scrambled out when they stopped. At these times they engaged in firefights with Chinese. In addition to these engagements along the road, craters and roadblocks in the road slowed the tanks and vehicles. About 4:15 P.M. the column came to another of its innumerable halts during the afternoon, but this stop was critical. At this juncture the column was less than halfway to Hagaru-ri, only about four miles north of Koto-ri. The tanks in the lead reported that further advance was inadvisable in view of the road conditions. In some places vehicles jammed the road; in others, stretching back nearly two miles, they were scattered out. This stop was about one-half mile south of the village of Pusong-ni. Some evidence indicates that it was just about this time that the 12 tanks of B Company, 1st Tank Battalion, were leaving Koto-ri in an effort to join the task force.[9] Most of the radio equipment in the column had been shot up and was inoperable by this time, and there was poor communication between units in Task Force Drysdale. The commander was beginning to lose control of the task force. One British writer later said that, at this point, "common sense suggested a withdrawal."

Lieutenant Colonel Drysdale decided that he should request a command decision from Colonel Puller at Koto-ri as to what he should do. Accordingly, he got into radio communication with Puller by the tank commander's tank radio. Puller in turn reached General Smith at Hagaru-ri and relayed the substance of the situation to him. Smith gave Puller the order to have Drysdale push through to Hagaru-ri. The need for reinforcements at Hagaru-ri was so great that Smith felt he would have to sacrifice part of the task force, if necessary, to get the reinforcements needed to hold Hagaru-ri.[10] In this interlude, while the column was at a standstill, a continuous series of air strikes kept the Chinese in their foxholes and relatively inactive. The tanks refueled during this time

General Smith's order left no alternative but for the task force to continue. The troops in the meantime had been in the roadside ditches and anywhere they could find cover. At this stop, just south of a massive roadblock at Pusong-ni, there were many casualties in the column, including Commando Royal Marine adjutant Lt. Dennis Goodchild, wounded; Sitter's machine-gun officer, 2nd Lt. James L. Crutchfield, wounded; his executive officer, Lieutenant Merrill, wounded; and Sitter's own jeep destroyed. It was here that Pfc. William B. Baugh, squad leader in the Antitank Platoon, was just starting to get out of the truck that carried his squad when an enemy soldier threw a grenade into it. Baugh saw the grenade and threw himself on it just before it exploded. He died of wounds in a few minutes, but no one else in his squad was injured. Baugh was later awarded the Medal of Honor.[11]

When General Smith's order had been relayed down the line, the order went out for the men to load up in their vehicles. They were all to make a run for it. There was already some confusion and intermingling of trucks and vehicles on the road, and when the men went hurriedly to get into a vehicle, they frequently did not get into the one from which they had dismounted. There was, as a result, a nearly complete breakdown of unit integrity. Many vehicles had British Royal Commando, Marine, Army, and service troops in them. The Army platoon leader of the trucks carrying B Company, 31st Infantry, later wrote, "As a result of loading under fire, the infantry got all mixed up and lost its tactical unity. Other convoys [in addition to his truck platoon] began moving at the same time, and we were soon mixed with Marine and Army trucks. The British Commandos were riding with our Marines."[12]

The column that started forward again did not travel far before it stopped. A short distance ahead there was a defile in the relatively broad valley here. This defile was just south of Pusong-ni, about halfway between Hagaru-ri and Koto-ri. A high bluff commanded the road through the defile, and Chinese soldiers with machine guns and mortars held it. In the defile below a roadblock of various kinds of debris closed the road. Behind this roadblock enemy fire stopped the column, with mortar fire causing an increasing number of casualties. Hills rose sharply immediately east of the road and the narrow-gauge railroad. West of the road a frozen stream meandered northwest through a broad valley to the Changjin River.

This was the scene, with the long column stopped at the defile just south of Pusong-ni, when an enemy mortar shell struck and set fire to a truck at the south end of the valley near the rear of the Royal Marine Commando section of the motor column. This created a temporary block that split the column. The Chinese at once concentrated heavy small-arms and mortar fire on the troops in the vicinity of the burning truck, preventing them from pushing it into the ditch or to the side of the road. These troops scurried for cover on the west side of other vehicles nearby or scrambled into the roadside ditches. It was now getting dark, and air cover ended. The potent air strikes that all day had helped the column out of its worst difficulties would cease until the following morning.

FORWARD ELEMENTS FIGHT INTO HAGARU-RI

The front part of the column, with tanks in the lead, poured fire into the enemy position on the bluff above the roadblock, succeeded in knocking out a machine-gun emplacement on the narrow railroad embankment, and then moved through the physical roadblock, the tanks pushing most of it aside. The two tank platoons of D Company; the five tanks of the Antitank Company; Sitter's G Company of the 1st Marines; about three-fourths of the 41st Commando, Royal Marines; and some of B Company,

31st Infantry, with Drysdale in command, now continued on north and, topping a slight rise, came into view of the tractor headlights working on the airfield at the south side of the Hagaru-ri perimeter. This part of the task force seemed unaware that the burning truck in the valley had split the column and that nothing was following them now. Similar stops had occurred frequently during the day, and always before, those behind a temporary break in the column had caught up. Not this time. Left behind in what came to be called "Hell Fire Valley" were about 60 Commandos, Royal Marines; most of Captain Peckham's B Company, 31st Infantry; and just about all the headquarters and miscellaneous service troops in the rear echelons of the task-force column.

As dusk settled, the tanks, followed by Sitter's G Company and part of the commandos, continued on through some scattered enemy fire from the east side of the road until it was within about one and one-fourth miles of Hagaru-ri. Then it came under intense mortar and small-arms fire. An enemy-thrown satchel charge so damaged a tank that it had to be abandoned. Enemy shells set many vehicles afire. Lieutenant Colonel Drysdale was wounded, and Captain Sitter took command. He formed the men and vehicles into a perimeter and repulsed this enemy attack. After he had beat it off, he ordered the column to resume the advance to the Hagaru-ri perimeter, now plainly in view.

Just outside the perimeter stood a number of American pyramidal tents, which Sitter assumed American troops occupied. These were the tents D Company, 10th Engineer Battalion, had erected the day before when they arrived to build the projected X Corps Advance CP. They had left these tents, expecting to return to them, when they were suddenly ordered into the perimeter line on East Hill during the previous afternoon. Chinese had by now occupied them, and from their vicinity they attacked Sitter's column, destroying two trucks and inflicting several casualties. The tanks and G Company eventually overcame this flurry of enemy action and entered the Hagaru-ri perimeter.

At 7:15 P.M. on 29 November Captain Sitter reported to Lieutenant Colonel Ridge, his battalion commander, and the defense commander of Hagaru-ri. Ridge placed Sitter's G Company in reserve, since the expected attack on Hagaru-ri had not materialized. Most of the 41st Commando, Royal Marines, that reached Hagaru-ri came in after the Marine company, some of them as late as 1:30 A.M. on 30 November. The commando group with Drysdale that reached Hagaru-ri that night had lost about 70 casualties during the day and night and 17 vehicles, with many other vehicles damaged. Only a few of the Army soldiers from B Company, 31st Infantry, reached Hagaru-ri. G Company, 1st Marines, and the Commando, Royal Marines, had a night of rest after they reached Hagaru-ri.

Of the nearly 900 men in Task Force Drysdale that started from Koto-

Napalm dropped by F4U Corsairs on an enemy position near the route of the 1st Marine Division withdrawal from Chosin Reservoir in December 1950 (US Marine Corps photograph A-5438)

ri that morning to Hagaru-ri, only about 400 of them got through. They and the 16 tanks that came through with them, leading the column, represented a tremendous reinforcement for the Hagaru-ri defense. The defense perimeter had by now been stretched very thin because of many casualties and the increasing number of enemy on East Hill.[13]

Intelligence later revealed the reasons Hagaru-ri had enjoyed the unexpected respite from enemy attack on the night of 29–30 November.
Marine artillery and heavy-mortar fire was laid down that evening and
night on enemy assembly areas of the CCF 58th Division—their locations as reported by the South Korean agents two days earlier to Lieutenant Carey and Lieutenant Colonel Ridge. Six sorties of planes from
Navy VMF-542 also attacked these assembly areas that night. The night
intruder planes, or night hecklers, as they were commonly called, were
generally Navy-Marine Corsair F4Us, as they proved to be more effective
for this work than the B-26, which was tried for a while. Dropping flares
over suspected enemy assembly areas or depots and railroad and road
targets prior to attack was a common practice, and sometimes they illuminated excellent targets. Lieutenant Colonel Ridge has written of how
he used the Navy-Marine Corsairs at night to help in his defense of Hagaru-
ri: "I had a pair of .50 caliber MGs on each side at night to use tracers
to indicate beyond what point I wished the Marine a/c to drop their ordnance; where the tracers crossed and beyond was their target. I believe
it was quite effective; it probably by intent both depicted initiative of
a nature which was foreign to the CCF and, hopefully, created a bit of
turmoil."[14]

Prisoners said the next day that the CCF 58th Division had planned
an attack during the night of 29 November but that the artillery barrages
and air attacks broke up most of these efforts in their assembly areas and
that many of their units were badly hit during the night. The nearest
approach to an enemy attack was a green flare in front of H and I companies and a number of white phosphorus mortar rounds that fell on their
lines, but nothing more ever materialized.

ORDEAL IN "HELL FIRE VALLEY"

The nightlong ordeal of the troops behind the burning truck that split
the column in the valley just south of Pusong-ni is a classic demonstration of Chinese tactics in 1950 in destroying an enemy column once it
was entrapped and cut off from help. What was at first only a split somewhere near the middle of a three-mile-long vehicular train soon became
a fragmented and disjointed series of groups of men and vehicles of varied sizes. Soon after the initial split, a mortar shell hit an ammunition
truck at the end of the commando column and formed a roadblock between it and the Army troops and Seeley's transportation convoy behind
them. Behind the burning commando ammunition truck and its exploding shells, everything in the column came to a halt.

Lieutenant Catania left his stalled B Company, 31st Infantry, trucks
and went forward along the line of trucks and men to see what the trou-

ble was. The column had halted this time where the road made a gentle
S curve, about halfway between Koto-ri and Hagaru-ri. It was now dark,
the landscape visible only when the moon was directly over the valley.
This part of the valley of the Changjin River was about 500 to 600 yards
wide, flanked by mountains on both sides. On the right of the road the
narrow-gauge railroad was sometimes only 50 yards away, and the slope
of the mountains there started upward immediately from it. Most of the
valley lay to the west, or left, of the road. The Changjin River, a fast-
flowing mountain stream, ran through about the middle of the valley,
and beyond it, sharply inclined mountains rose to the west.

Catania was a few hundred yards from his trucks when he saw five
or six Chinese soldiers walking along the narrow-gauge railroad track.
He could just make out their quilted uniforms. He warned a nearby
truckload of infantry. They began sweeping the area with rifle fire, and
Catania threw a grenade. This burst of fire seemed to act as a signal for
Chinese up and down the rail embankment and on the lower slope of
the mountain eastward. They returned fire with small arms, grenades,
machine guns, and some mortars on the roadbound column. It happened
that there was no concentration of American men and vehicles at this
point—they were scattered at some intervals along the road. Everyone
in the line of fire sought cover. Catania told the men near him to get
behind the trucks on their west side and then to fall back to the fields
west of the road. The intense enemy fire, however, caused numerous casualties. Catania was hit twice, the first time in the back by a shell fragment, and the second time by a .45-caliber bullet, probably from a Thompson submachine gun, that ranged upward through his shoulder, breaking
the collarbone and lodging in his neck. An infantryman bandaged him
and gave him a shot of morphine. Catania propped his head on his helmet and tried to give some control to the situation immediately around
him. One of his more daring truck drivers volunteered (none of the infantrymen would go) to try to retrieve a .30-caliber machine gun and a box
of ammunition from a truck that had come to rest in the field below the
road. He succeeded in getting the gun and ammunition, but not the tri-
pod. This man fired the machine gun from his hip until it ran out of ammunition, and then he threw it into the Changjin River.[15]

This was but one of a multitude of incidents taking place along the
length of the cut-off and surrounded men. Lt. Col. Arthur A. Chidester,
assistant 1st Marine Division G-4, was the senior officer caught south
of the split column after the tanks, Sitter's G Company, and part of
Drysdale's Commando, Royal Marines, had forged ahead. He decided the
best chance for the cut-off part of the task force was to turn around and
try to get back to Koto-ri. Before his order to turn around could be carried
out, however, the Chinese cut the road both in front of and behind his

party. And other Chinese attacks along the road cut the column, badly fragmenting it. There was no chance to attempt an organized return to Koto-ri. Chinese mortars and machine guns emplaced on a bench of land that rose about 20 feet above the narrow-gauge railroad could sweep the road below, not more than 200 yards distant, and for the three-quarters of a mile the convoy was strung out in the valley. Control of the heterogeneous groups of men in the ditches along this stretch was virtually impossible under Chinese fire. But some officers and noncommissioned officers made the attempt.

Lieutenant Colonel Chidester and Maj. John McLaughlin, a X Corps assistant G-3 and the corps liaison officer with the 1st Marine Division, formed a defense line at the north end of the stalled convoy, covering the road to Hagaru-ri. Maj. James Egan assembled some men and took a position at the railroad embankment. McLaughlin took command of the men in his immediate area, including most of B Company, 31st Infantry. At the southern end of the convoy, Maj. Henry J. Seeley took command of the truck transport echelon and all the drivers he could find. There were at least four groups that formed what might be called perimeters. Numerous small parties were scattered along the mile-long surrounded valley, some trying to escape to the hills in the west.

The largest group was in the perimeter formed by Major McLaughlin at the north end and just south of Pusong-ni, where the initial break in the column had taken place. He had about 130–40 men there, including Capt. Charles Peckham and part of his B Company, 31st Infantry. Also included in his group were some Marine military police, some Commando, Royal Marines, and assorted Marine service and headquarters personnel. Three smaller perimeters formed south of McLaughlin. About one-quarter of a mile south of his perimeter, remnants of two Army platoons, with some Marines, were in a drainage ditch. A short distance below them was another group of transportation troops and some Marines about 100 yards farther south. Seeley had at first tried to keep his men together in the transport group, but Chinese attacks had splintered them into small groups.

A fifth group of surrounded men made up two platoons of B Company, 1st Tank Battalion, and a 15-truck convoy that left Koto-ri in late afternoon to join Task Force Drysdale, then only about three miles north of the village. But Chinese fire stopped this column at Hills 1236 and 1182, which Task Force Drysdale had cleared of enemy earlier in the day. Chinese had reoccupied these strongholds after the task force passed on. The Chinese now on these hills split the B Company tank force and escorted trucks into three segments. Tanks and trucks at the rear got back to Koto-ri at 9:10 P.M. In the middle separated segment a large number of trucks suffered extensive damage. Many men with them were wounded, but a considerable number were able to fight their way back to Koto-ri by 2:30 the next morning, 30 November. The tank platoon in the lead, and farthest forward when the Chinese stopped the B Company tank column, reached a point about half a mile south of Major Seeley's stalled truck convoy of the task force. Neither 1st Lt. Herbert B. Turner, commanding this tank platoon, nor Major Seeley knew of the other's location or proximity. Seeley kept hoping through the night that the B Company tanks would come up, as he knew they were supposed to have joined the column that afternoon. But Turner felt forced to put his tanks into a defense perimeter, where, boxed in and protected by artillery fire from Koto-ri, he survived the night with little difficulty. The next morning his tank platoon returned to Koto-ri unopposed. The men trapped just north of the B Company tanks did not know of these events just below them and continued to hope during the night that B Company might arrive and rescue them.[16]

The Chinese were content for a while to remain relatively inactive, but they took care to keep the surrounded men pinned down in the ditches and in their little perimeters. In this interval they set up some mortars on the west side of the road near the Changjin River. They did not try to destroy the vehicles on the road, as they no doubt expected to capture them intact with their stores and supplies. They did set afire and destroy a jeep and three more trucks at the head of the column to make sure the road was effectively blocked. Gradually, Chinese riflemen took positions at the south end of the column, where they could enfilade the ditches, where most of the Americans had taken shelter and where most of the wounded had been placed. But for the most part they held their fire.

During the first part of the night, when the Chinese did not press their attack against the surrounded convoy and the fragmented groups of troops, there was considerable looting in the stalled trucks. In the early hours of 30 November, however, the Chinese began to probe the several American perimeters and, by 2 A.M. had worked to within grenade range of them. The men in McLaughlin's perimeter, the largest one, were out of grenades. Twice, Chinese got into the mortar positions at McLaughlin's position but were driven out both times. An Army crew working a 75-mm recoilless rifle there fired at enemy mortar flashes until all of the enemy mortar crew were killed or wounded and their mortar put out of action.

At 4:30 A.M. on 30 November, the Chinese local commander sent some American prisoners to Major McLaughlin, asking for his surrender. McLaughlin went with a British commando to meet the Chinese and through an interpreter discussed their demand. He hoped to stall the talks long enough to allow some of his men to escape. The Chinese, however, soon tired of this subterfuge and gave him an ultimatum to surrender within ten minutes or they would overrun his position. McLaughlin went back to his men and discussed the matter with his officers. He made the rounds of his able-bodied men, about 40, to learn how much ammunition they had left. Some had none at all, and no one had more than eight rounds of rifle ammunition. McLaughlin returned to the Chinese and said he would surrender if they would allow his more serious wounded to be evacuated. They promised to do so but did not keep their word. Some of the more critically wounded, however, were placed in a hut and allowed to remain there. After daylight they were rescued and evacuated to Koto-ri. The battle was over. Two Marines captured in this action later escaped and said the Chinese captured about 130 men in Task Force Drysdale, including Marines, Army personnel, Royal Commando, and ROKs.

Things had gone somewhat better at the south end of the cut-off column. Major Seeley there knew his men, and they remained under better control, engaged in less promiscuous firing, and saved their ammunition. At one point Seeley joined in the discussions with the Chinese who asked him to surrender his group. The liaison in all these surrender discussions with McLaughlin and later with Seeley was a Sgt. Guillermo Tovar, who had been captured with wounded Major Egan in a position on the railroad embankment near the north end of the surrounded column. Tovar told the Chinese that McLaughlin wanted to confer with Major Seeley, commanding the southern perimeter, before he made a final decision on surrender. The Chinese allowed this. Seeley came forward and stalled with the Chinese as long as he dared, but he told McLaughlin he was not going to surrender, as his men had plenty of ammunition and he believed they could hold out until daylight. He had about 44 men in his group at that time.

Seeley started back to his men. The Chinese took over McLaughlin's perimeter before he got back. Seeley held a hurried conference with his officers. They decided that, once McLaughlin's men had been brought under Chinese control (then in progress), they would have little chance of holding out. They then collected the wounded, crossed to the west side of the Changjin River, and began climbing the steep mountain just beyond. They carried and dragged the wounded. Five hours later they entered Koto-ri.[17]

Lieutenant Catania, when we left him, was twice wounded, with his head propped up on his helmet in a field just west of the road, and a small group of soldiers holding a small perimeter. By 2 A.M. Catania decided his group could stay no longer where they were and ordered them to fall back to the Changjin River. Two and a half hours later he decided they would have to cross the river, then split up and try to get back to Koto-ri. The men, however, seemed lethargic from the cold and showed no desire to move across the river. Catania then decided to move with one or two of his truckers. They had to raise his head and get him on his feet, but once that was done, he could walk. After he had started, the infantry left behind got up, crossed the stream, and started up the mountainside. In climbing the slope, the party split up for various causes, and Catania had three enlisted men with him—two truckers and one infantryman. When they reached the hilltop, dawn had arrived. Only one of the men, a trucker, was not wounded. Catania knew that their feet, soaked in wading the river, would freeze if they were not given treatment. With a knife he cut the frozen laces from his boots. He could not free the heavy inner-liner socks to warm them next to his body; they were frozen to the boots and could not be removed. He threw away boots and socks, and tied strips of blanket around one foot. He put his pile-liner cap on the other foot. The three other men did the same.

They soon joined up with uninjured Marines who were in the vicinity. Catania asked them to hike the approximately three miles to the Marine perimeter at Koto-ri and get help for them, which they agreed to do. But after waiting two hours, Catania decided they could wait no longer and would have to descend to the road and take their chances of reaching Koto-ri. They reached the road after a painful descent and then walked straight south on it. The four men knew that Chinese were all around them and could see their every step. Once from near the road a Chinese crew fired at a helicopter that flew up the valley. The Chinese made no effort to bother the four hobbling men but let them pass unmolested. They made it into Koto-ri.[18]

TASK FORCE DRYSDALE CASUALTIES

An accurate statement of Task Force Drysdale's casualties cannot be given. There was too much confusion and too many were missing in action, some of whom returned to their units days or even a week later. There are numerous discrepancies in several listings of the casualties, so only an approximation is possible. Task Force Drysdale suffered at least 320 casualties in its effort to reach Hagaru-ri. B Company, 31st Infantry, had the greatest number of casualties of any unit, including 100 killed or missing in action and 19 wounded. Sitter's G Company of Marines lost eight killed and 40 wounded. The 41st Commando, Royal Marines, were conservatively given 18 killed or missing and 43 wounded. One source says 22 commandos were captured. The 1st Marine Division Headquarters Battalion had 25 killed or missing and 50 wounded. An American, captured by the Chinese on 28 November, escaped two days later and reported (on 30 November) that the Chinese held 130 Marine prisoners only five miles north of Koto-ri. Also, 75 or more vehicles were lost. Among the wounded and captured were many officers. Both Lieutenant Colonel Chidester and Major Egan were wounded and captured. Major McLaughlin, who was captured when he surrendered the northern group, said later, after the prisoner exchange in 1953, that it appeared from his information that both Chidester and Egan died before they reached a prisoner-of-war camp.[19]

Gen. Oliver P. Smith, the Marine commander at Hagaru-ri, summed up his opinion of the results of Task Force Drysdale: "The casualties of Task Force Drysdale were heavy, but by its partial success the Task Force made a significant contribution to the holding of Hagaru-ri which was vital to the Division. To the slender infantry garrison of Hagaru-ri were added a tank company of about 100 men and some 300 seasoned infantrymen. The approximately 300 troops which returned to Koto-ri participated thereafter in the defense of that perimeter."[20]

A rough approximation would indicate that, of the nearly 900 men in Task Force Drysdale on 29 November, about 400 men and 16 tanks arrived at Hagaru-ri; about 300 men and two tank platoons got back to Koto-ri (including 12 tanks in two platoons of B Company, 1st Tank Battalion, and 15 vehicles and their personnel, who were not counted as part of Task Force Drysdale because they were never able to join it); and about 220 men were casualties—killed, wounded, missing, or captured. In equipment, one tank was lost, and something more than half of the 141 vehicles lost. Drysdale and Sitter estimated that about one Chinese regiment opposed them on the road to Hagaru-ri. It was from the CCF 60th Division.

Marine air reported on 30 November that a group of Army personnel, apparently from the task force, was pinned down and apparently could not extricate themselves from Chinese forces just a short distance south of Hagaru-ri. A tank platoon moved out from the Hagaru-ri perimeter to help them. About a mile south from the perimeter the tanks came under very heavy enemy fire from a group of houses east of the road. The tanks' 90-mm guns let loose on the shacks and decimated the Chinese soldiers inside, who had packed into these structures to escape observation and cold. The tanks found no Army personnel in that vicinity and returned to Hagaru-ri.[21]

The enemy strength around Koto-ri apparently had not lessened during 29 November because of the number of Chinese that were mustered to oppose Task Force Drysdale. Chinese could be observed from the Koto-ri perimeter keeping the area under close observation all that day. Marine air strikes hit Chinese concentrations on the high ground around Koto-ri several times. The Chinese observers apparently thought the northern rim of the perimeter was the most vulnerable part after they had witnessed the departure of B Company, 1st Tank Battalion, and 15 trucks late in the afternoon, as well as the Task Force Drysdale force in the morning. The Chinese commander presumably thought the time was ripe for an assault on the Koto-ri defenses.

Just before dark an increased number of Chinese could be seen assembling on the hills overlooking Koto-ri from the northeast. Enemy mortar fire began hitting E Company's lines at the northern part of the perimeter about 5:45 P.M. This was soon followed by a series of bugle calls and whistle signals. An estimated company of Chinese infantry then attacked from the hill on the northeast, with the remainder of a battalion probably in reserve. The Marines had expected an attack from that quarter and were not surprised. Maj. Clarence J. Mabry, the 2nd Battalion executive officer, was on hand to give encouragement to E Company. The waiting Marines poured a curtain of fire into the advancing Chinese. But the attack was so persistent that 17 Chinese soldiers got inside the perimeter, apparently heading for the warming tents, where wounded lay. All 17 were killed. When the Chinese drew off from the attack about 7 P.M., nearly 150 Chinese dead lay in front of the perimeter in the E Company sector. The Marines lost six killed and 18 wounded. In addition to the approximately 175 Chinese killed, there must have been another 200 wounded. The extent of their loss is also indicated in the enemy weapons captured in the vicinity of the perimeter or inside it: ten heavy machine guns, seven light machine guns, 12 Thompson submachine guns, 76 rifles, four pistols, and 500 hand grenades. Most of these had earlier belonged to the American-armed Chinese Nationalist soldiers of Chiang Kai-shek.[22]

9

SECOND BATTLE OF HAGARU-RI,
30 NOVEMBER–1 DECEMBER

We have already noted that American artillery, mortar, and night air bombing of the CCF 58th Division assembly areas broke up attempts during the night of 29 November for a continuation of Chinese attacks against Hagaru-ri. This reprieve gave General Smith the opportunity during the twenty-ninth to bring in reinforcements from Task Force Drysdale at Koto-ri. Included was Capt. Carl Sitter's G Company, 3rd Battalion, 1st Marines. They rested during the night of 29 November after reaching Hagaru-ri. The next morning, 30 November, they were to attack the Chinese-held East Hill, which overlooked all of Hagaru-ri, and which constituted a threat for major catastrophe.

On the morning of 30 November Captain Sitter formed his company for attack. The part of the 41st Commando, Royal Marines, that had reached Hagaru-ri during the night of 29–30 November was to remain in reserve. Sitter formed two platoons for the attack, which was to pass through Major Myers's defensive lines on the southwest slope of the hill and then assault the southwest slope ridge near the crest. The G Company attack made little or no progress. Captain Sitter then committed his third platoon and two engineer platoons. These additional troops had no success in their attacks. The Chinese on the crest of East Hill held firm, despite daylong pounding of their positions by Marine air and artillery barrages. The Navy Fast Carrier Task Force shifted its efforts on 30 November to the Chosin Reservoir and sent 39 sorties there, with a major effort of 25 sorties against East Hill. The other 14 sorties went to the Army 31st RCT, which was cut off north of East Hill on the east side of the reservoir. Chinese long-range automatic-weapons fire from the crest of East Hill and the difficult, icy slopes frustrated all Marine efforts to gain and hold the hill. Sitter withdrew G Company to the earlier defense lines on the slope that Myers had held. The engineer platoons went back to the foot of the hill.[1]

Tanks Join Perimeter Defense, 30 November

Chapter 5, on the battle actions of the 7th Infantry Division elements and Task Force Faith on the east side of the reservoir, has already discussed in some detail the events that led to Capt. Robert E. Drake's withdrawal of his 31st Tank Company, under orders, from Hudong-ni to Hagaru-ri late in the afternoon of 30 November. As soon as he arrived there, the 1st Marine Division command put his tank company in the defense perimeter. A valuable reinforcement, it was placed on the east side of the perimeter, at the foot of East Hill. Drake placed all of his 16 tanks on the defense line, holding back only his command tank with its communications equipment and 105-mm howitzer (and possibly a second tank with a 105-mm howitzer). These were only a short distance behind the defense line at the tent area the 31st Tank Company occupied for sleeping quarters. The tanks on the line were placed about 50 to 100 yards apart, thus covering about 1,000 yards of the defense line at the foot of East Hill. The southern end of the 31st Tank Company was opposite the highway bridge that carried the west fork of the road through Hagaru-ri toward Yudam-ni, and just north of the southwest spur ridge of East Hill that came down to the Koto-ri road where the Marine Weapons Company had established its strong roadblock. Its northern and middle parts were generally opposite the Marine division supply area inside the perimeter, and northeast of the main part of Hagaru-ri.[2] There were no friendly infantry or ground troops in front of the tanks on the slope of East Hill. Drake's tanks had the whole mountainside for their shooting area.

The CCF Night Attack, 30 November

An enemy attack after dark on 30 November was expected. It came. A little after 8 P.M. men in I Company's positions at the southwest end of the perimeter heard three bugle calls. An hour later they saw a green flare. Half an hour before midnight Chinese from the CCF 58th Division were at hand—their patrols began probing I Company's part of the perimeter for weak spots. They made a bad choice. First Lieutenant Fisher's I Company had defenses of all kinds in front of its lines, and its own foxholes and gun positions were well dug in and sandbagged. At midnight, the enemy probing ended, and enemy skirmish lines approached in assault formation. The assault teams came up against the perimeter in echelon, one after the other, like gusts of rain beating against a wall. Marine firepower had been concentrated for immediate use in front of I Company's position because this was one place they were certain enemy strength would strike. The infantry firepower from their own weapons was supplemented by tank, artillery, 81-mm mortar, and heavy machine-gun fire, which had already registered in on the I Company front. Even so, some of the Chinese attacks carried a few of their soldiers right up to the Marine foxholes. It was a repeat of the well-established Chinese pattern of frontal attack—hit the same place again and again despite ruinous casualties, and eventually there would be a breakthrough and resulting demoralization of the enemy. But it did not work on I Company. The Chinese casualties in front of I Company were tremendous—an estimated 500 to 700. In contrast to the mounds of bodies in the snow-trampled area, I Company defenders had only 12 casualties, of whom two were killed.[3] The Chinese who attacked the south side of the Hagaru-ri perimeter in the I Company area were from the 173rd and 174th regiments of the CCF 58th Division, sister regiments of the 172nd, which had carried the attack in the same area two nights earlier and had been decimated.

CCF ATTACK FROM EAST HILL

While Chinese soldiers from the 173rd and 174th regiments assaulted the southern part of the Hagaru-ri perimeter, an equally formidable enemy attack was launched from East Hill. The Chinese attacks on the night of 30 November–1 December seem to have been better coordinated than they were two nights earlier. The attacks from southwest of Hagaru-ri and from East Hill on the opposite side of the perimeter occurred about the same time.

By dark, Captain Sitter's G Company, after failing in a daylong battle to win the crest of East Hill, had dropped back down the slope to the defense position Major Myers's force had held the night before. Below it to the southwest was B Company of the 1st Engineers, and below it near the foot of East Hill to the northwest was a platoon of A Company, 1st Engineers. At the north end of the perimeter along the base of East Hill was the 1st Platoon, A Company, 1st Engineers; two Marine tanks; and a part of Lt. Col. Charles L. Banks's 1st Service Battalion, which then bent the line westward, south of Chosin Reservoir, from the base of East Hill north of Hagaru-ri. Drake's 31st Tank Company, 7th Infantry Division, occupied 1,000 yards of perimeter south of A Company's Engineers and Banks's service troops.

Just before midnight, a host of Chinese seemed to rise out of the night on the slope of East Hill in front of an engineer listening post on the right side of the defense line. The men in the listening post rushed pell-mell back to the main line, with the Chinese right behind them. A wild, scrambling close-in fight followed. At the same time, well-aimed Chinese mortar fire hit so accurately in the middle of Sitter's G Company line that its 1st Platoon was threatened with extermination. The Marine company gave ground, its left flank bent back toward the road. First Lt. Earnest

Skelt's 3rd Platoon of engineers was pushed off the hill, with the loss of half its 28 men. The fight now spread all along the base of East Hill as Chinese streamed down toward Drake's tanks and Banks's Service Battalion. Artillery and mortar fire from emplacements around Hagaru-ri was concentrated on the area of the enemy penetration in the Marine G Company and engineer positions on the right side of the East Hill defense line and helped check a Chinese exploitation of the penetration there.

At midnight this massed Chinese attack down the west slope of East Hill hit Drake's tank line. The Chinese attacked directly into his position, charging downhill with bugles blowing. The battle lasted all night. The Chinese penetrated past the tanks and entered the tankers' tent area behind the perimeter line. Fighting there was hand-to-hand. At the first sign of daylight the Chinese withdrew from the 31st Tank Company area and started back up the mountain slope. The tank crews fired on them with all weapons. After daylight when the Chinese had withdrawn, Drake said his tank company counted approximately 200 dead Chinese in front of its position. His 31st Tank Company suffered only a few casualties in the night battle. It had plugged a large hole in the Hagaru-ri defenses. Because these tanks arrived at Hagaru-ri so late in the day and went into position just before dark, it is not known to what extent the Chinese knew of their presence prior to their attack headlong down the hill. North of Drake's tanks, Banks's Service Battalion troops had a similar battle at the foot of the hill with Chinese who penetrated their line. These enemy troops were likewise killed or driven off by dawn.[4]

This night battle on East Hill and along its base was at times quite spectacular. In one incident an enemy mortar shell hit and set fire to 50 drums of gasoline in the Marine supply area. The brilliant light from the soaring flames illuminated part of the battle scene on the hill so vividly that General Smith from his frame-house CP doorway could watch the action from two-thirds of a mile away.

By 1 A.M., 1 December, Captain Sitter, up on the northwest slope of the hill, had to ask for reinforcements for G Company. All available men from the CP and any other place within Hagaru-ri were assembled and placed under 2nd Lt. Richard E. Carey's command. He led them up the hill to Sitter's position. Still later, Lieutenant Colonel Ridge sent B Company troops of the 41st Commando, Royal Marines, to the same place to restore a position in Sitter's G Company line. During this close-in and intense Chinese counterattack down the slope of East Hill against Sitter's position, Captain Sitter visited each gun position and foxhole of G Company and its reinforcements, despite being wounded in the face, arms, and chest by grenade fragments. He refused to be evacuated and stayed with his troops throughout the night. Something of his leadership and

determination to hold the slope of the hill, even after the Chinese penetrated to his CP, must have inspired his men to hold on, despite very heavy
casualties. The Chinese did not break through there to the road and
Hagaru-ri, although they engaged in hand-to-hand combat at times in their
frenzy to do so. Captain Sitter won the Congressional Medal of Honor
for his leadership, battle tactics, and personal valor on 30 November and
that night. He and his men had been in 36 hours of almost constant combat for control of the southwestern spur of East Hill.[5]

By his unusual efforts, following his commitment of Sitter's G Company to East Hill, in improvising a series of reinforcements for him as
the powerful Chinese force on the hill threatened to overwhelm Sitter,
Lieutenant Colonel Ridge, the perimeter defense commander, was able
to hold the lower part of the vital southwest spur of East Hill. The Chinese did not get to the Koto-ri road and the Weapons Company roadblock.
But at daybreak, 1 December, Chinese still held the crest of East Hill.
During the night battle, G Company and its reinforcements had lost 60
men killed and wounded. When the Chinese everywhere on the lower
slopes or at the base of East Hill withdrew at daylight of 1 December
toward the crest, the worst was over in the defense of Hagaru-ri, although
no one knew it at the time.

CCF Losses in the Battles of Hagaru-ri

While the first battle of Hagaru-ri, on the night of 28 November, was
poorly coordinated by the Chinese and the attacks from East Hill indicated that only a limited force there was available and engaged, it nevertheless resulted in a severe loss for the 172nd Regiment of the CCF 58th
Division, which attacked the southern part of the perimeter. In the second battle of Hagaru-ri, on the night of 30 November–1 December, the
efforts of parts of two divisions showed some degree of coordination in
that the attacks from the southwest and those from East Hill on opposite
sides of the perimeter started at nearly the same time and rose in intensity in the hours just after midnight. This time the CCF 58th Division
sent its remaining two regiments, the 173rd and 174th, into the battle.
Also involved was the 176th Regiment of the CCF 59th Division. The
59th Division had been identified south of Yudam-ni earlier, and its main
assignment seems to have been to take control of Toktong Pass and the
road between Yudam-ni and Hagaru-ri.

Estimates of enemy losses, based in part on prisoner reports, indicate
that the CCF 58th Division lost approximately 6,800 casualties. Of this
total, the 172nd Regiment, which fought in the first battle, had the heaviest losses, with about 3,300 casualties, or 90 percent of its entire personnel. The 176th Regiment of the 59th Division seems to have had about

1,750 casualties. After the two battles Chinese known dead totaled 1,500. Wounded casualties may be assumed to have been at least three times that number. A factor that increased the number of Chinese losses, according to Chinese prisoners, was that their ammunition supply was just about exhausted after the second night battle of 30 November–1 December.[6] In the frigid weather prevailing in the Chosin area, and with the primitive state of Chinese transport and medical care, it can be assumed that hundreds of wounded Chinese died subsequent to the Hagaru-ri battles, as indeed they did after all the other major engagements of the Chosin campaign.

In the defense of Hagaru-ri from the first enemy attack on the night of 28 November on through the second and more intense battle of 30 November–1 December, Lt. Col. Thomas L. Ridge, the Hagaru-ri defense commander, deserves credit for ably managing the defense with the resources available to him. He used them all. He was a man of imagination and gifted with cool and shrewd common sense in combat. His viewpoint may be expressed best in his own words: "One has to know when to throw away the book and depend on all appropriate variations of military history as thought provokers when facing unusual situations."[7]

AIR EVACUATION OF WOUNDED FROM HAGARU-RI

On Friday morning, 1 December, after the second night battle of Hagaru-ri, Capt. Eugene R. Hering, the 1st Marine Division surgeon, reported to General Smith that there were 600 friendly casualties within the perimeter and that he expected 500 more to arrive from Yudam-ni and 400 from the Army's 7th Division units, east of the reservoir. From 27 November, when the heavy Chinese attacks began, to the morning of 1 December, 152 casualties had been evacuated from the Chosin area, all by helicopters and small observation and liaison planes, the only means available. These men were the more critically wounded, whose lives depended on speedy surgical or medical treatment not available in the combat zone.

After Captain Hering had described the critical situation in trying to care for more wounded at Hagaru-ri, General Smith authorized a trial landing at the airstrip, although it was only 40 percent complete. During the night battles of 28–29 November and 30 November–1 December, the engineers had continued to operate their bulldozers and scrapers under floodlights immediately behind the front-line perimeter positions of H and I companies, 1st Marines, at the southern end of the perimeter. They kept their individual weapons always at hand. Several times these D Company engineers had joined in the battle, and they suffered numerous casualties during the Chinese attacks. By 1 December they had hacked out of the frozen ground a runway 2,900 feet long and 50 feet wide, with a 2 percent grade running northeast. That afternoon, after General Smith had authorized a trial landing, parka-jacketed Marines watched the first Far East Air Force transport, a C-47 two-engine plane, touch down at 2:30 P.M. on the rough, frozen, snow-covered Hagaru-ri airstrip. Half an hour later it took off with 24 wounded and successfully lifted off the short, bumpy runway just as it seemed the plane would run out of room, cleared the hills to the south, and soared off to the Yonpo airfield Clearing Stations established there by the X Corps.

Three more planes landed at Hagaru-ri that afternoon. Two of them took off with about 60 more wounded. The third plane, loaded with ammunition coming in, broke its landing gear on landing and had to be destroyed. Beginning on 1 December, transport planes landed daily thereafter at Hagaru-ri to take wounded as long as American troops held the town.

One of the planes that landed successfully on 1 December and took off with wounded that afternoon was a four-engine plane that Navy pilot B. J. Miller had flown from Japan to Yonpo. At Yonpo, Miller heard of the critical condition of hundreds of wounded at Hagaru-ri. He requested permission to fly there and get a load of wounded. Assuming that he piloted a two-engine C-47 plane, officials gave permission. All of Miller's crew volunteered to go with him. A plane of the type he was flying normally required a runway of 4,000–5,000 feet. Miller landed at Hagaru-ri successfully, to the astonishment of the Marines there, loaded 39 wounded on stretchers in the plane, taxied to the extreme end of the runway, turned on full throttle, and got off the ground, clearing the first ridge by only 30 feet. He piloted the first and only four-engine plane to land at Hagaru-ri during the Chosin campaign.[8]

The estimates of casualties who would arrive at Hagaru-ri needing medical treatment and evacuation from the fighting at Yudam-ni and on the east side of the reservoir proved too low. The biggest immediate problem on 2 December, after the airstrip became usable, was to evacuate the wounded. In overseeing this task, the 1st Marine Division surgeon, Captain Hering, froze both feet, but he kept on with his duties. On 2 December 914 casualties were flown out of Hagaru-ri, and in the next three days the average was more than 1,000 a day. On the morning of 5 December, when plans were under way to start the withdrawal of all troops from Hagaru-ri to the coast just as soon as all the wounded could be evacuated, there were 1,400 casualties still in the perimeter. All of them were flown out during the day. The total number of casualties evacuated by air from 1 December to the end of 5 December was, by Marine count, 4,312. Of these, 3,150 were Marines, 1,137 were Army, and 25 were 41st Commando, Royal Marines.[9]

On 1 December, then, Hagaru-ri was no longer isolated to the same extent it had been previously. Planes from Yonpo on the Korean coast and from Japan could bring supplies and reinforcements on the incoming trip and leave with wounded men on the outgoing trip. The evacuation procedure that X Corps established for the Chosin operation was that the planes would fly the wounded out of Hagaru-ri to the corps Clearing Stations at Yonpo. From there, the less seriously wounded who were expected to require no more than 30 days in the hospital were taken either to the 1st Marine Division hospital in Hungnam, the Army 121st Evacuation Hospital in Hamhung, or the USS *Consolation*, a hospital ship stationed in Hungnam harbor. Those expected to require more than 30 days in a hospital were flown to Japan. Some very critical and special cases were flown directly from Hagaru-ri to Japan.[10]

THE TIDE OF ASSAULTS EBBS ON 1 DECEMBER

Friday, 1 December, might be called "Good Friday" for the Marine and Army men caught in the Chosin ordeal, except for the men of Task Force Faith, who on that day were engaged in their ill-fated breakout attempt from their inlet perimeter on the east side of the reservoir. One can say in hindsight that it was the day the tide turned for the Marine forces in the Chosin area battles. The Marines at Yudam-ni in four days and nights of battle, the Marines and Army troops at Hagaru-ri and along the MSR southward to Koto-ri, and survivors of the ill-fated elements of Task Force Faith of the 7th Infantry Division east of the reservoir, supported throughout by the magnificent air effort of Marine and Army fighter planes and bombers, still held the vital positions. More, they had destroyed the main strength of four Chinese infantry divisions and parts of two others. After 1 December the Chinese assaults grew lighter or became almost nonexistent on the major American perimeters. The fight thereafter became one primarily of battling through Chinese roadblocks and overcoming enemy positions along the MSR, leading southward to the coast.

AMERICAN AIRDROP OF SUPPLIES AT CHOSIN

Although Marine reserve stocks of food and ammunition amounting to six days of rations and two units of fire had been trucked into Hagaru-ri dumps before Chinese cut off the supply road on 28 November, airdrop of food, ammunition, and medical supplies became an important and perhaps vital factor in enabling the troops to sustain a successful defense of their critical positions. Certainly a great amount of supplies was dropped to all the perimeters. It is not known, however, how much of it was actually delivered safely into the hands of the troops—certainly not all of it was, possibly not more than a modest fraction of it. Records do not exist to establish the true amount. It is known that, of what was dropped, an appalling percentage was destroyed or rendered useless because containers broke when they hit the frozen ground. There was some loss in drops that landed in enemy territory, especially at the inlet perimeter of the Army troops on the east side of the reservoir. The breakage rate of the supplies that landed in friendly territory and could be recovered but were not usable ran to about 70 percent of petroleum products at the Marine Hagaru-ri perimeter and 70–80 percent of rations. Of artillery ammunition, about 40 percent was badly damaged, and only 25 percent ever got to gun positions. Less than half of small-arms ammunition, about 45 percent, was usable when recovered. Most of the mortar ammunition requested fell in the drop zones, but the damage rate was about the same as for artillery shells.[11] Even though the damage rate for air-dropped supplies of all kinds was excessively high, the fraction recovered within or at the edge of the Hagaru-ri perimeter was worth all the effort made for its delivery. It may have made the difference in firepower capability that enabled the defenders to sustain their margin of superiority over the Chinese sacrifice attacks.

The main burden of accomplishing this aerial resupply rested on Maj. Gen. William F. Tunner's Combat Cargo Command of the FEAF in Japan. Many packaged units designed to supply a battalion in combat for a day were dropped in the Chosin battleground, and some requests for special supplies were hastily assembled and dropped. This type of resupply to the combat elements at Chosin may be illustrated by Hagaru-ri alone. The Hagaru-ri defenders requested 1,466,740 rounds of small-arms ammunition, 15,168 rounds of 60-mm and 8,544 rounds of 81-mm mortar shells, 2,160 rounds of 105-mm howitzer shells, 10,350 grenades, 46,000 C rations, 11,660 gallons of gasoline, and 200 miles of wire. Available records do not indicate how much of this was actually air-dropped.

HAGARU-RI QUIET, 1–6 DECEMBER

In the five days following the second massive Chinese effort to take Hagaru-ri on the night of 30 November–1 December, there was a strange and unexpected quiet. No enemy soldiers were in sight during the daytime, and activity at and within the perimeter went on with no enemy interference. Even at night there was an absence of enemy attacks, which had characterized almost every part of the Chosin battlefield since 27 November. It seemed plain that the Chinese assault divisions assigned the mission of destroying the Marine and Army troops deployed at the reservoir had simply fought themselves into decimation and exhaustion and that those who remained alive and combat effective had little or no ammunition. It must have been at this time, at the beginning of December, that General Sung started at least two of his four divisions of the CCF 26th Army, the 76th and 77th divisions, toward the battlefield from their reserve position at Linchiang on the north bank of the Yalu River in Manchuria. They were first identified in contact in the vicinity of Hagaru-ri on 5 December.

In evaluating the Chosin battles it must be remembered that, whereas American forces had air capability of resupply by airdrop, the Chinese had none. And their supply of ammunition of all kinds had been less at the beginning of the battles than that of the American forces. They had almost no artillery, only a relatively few 76-mm pieces, and their mortars were far inferior to the Americans'. They had no combat aircraft, in contrast to the formidable ground support of Marine Corsairs and the miscellaneous and bombing aircraft of the Far East Command's Fifth Air Force. And they had no tanks. The few enemy tanks encountered in the Chosin area in the early days of contact with the Chinese had been remnants from the NK Army.

One strange aspect of life at Hagaru-ri at this time was the sudden popularity of candy in any form, particularly the well-known Tootsie Roll of those days. It gave quick energy to fight off cold, and it did not lead to digestive disorders in the frigid weather, which was often caused by eating frozen foods. As happened earlier at Koto-ri, men who seldom touched candy in civilian life in the United States now could not get enough of it.

10

BREAKOUT FROM YUDAM-NI, 1–4 DECEMBER

After the heavy battles around Yudam-ni during the night of 27–28 November and some continuation the following day, there was comparative quiet on the night of 28–29 November. Before midnight of the twenty-ninth, General Smith at Hagaru-ri received an alert from General Almond to prepare to withdraw all Marine forces from Yudam-ni to Hagaru-ri. This order was Almond's immediate follow-up to General MacArthur's order to him that morning in Tokyo to cease all offensive action in the X Corps area and to concentrate his troops in the Hamhung-Hungnam coastal region.

REDEPLOYMENT AT YUDAM-NI, 29–30 NOVEMBER

Planning to disengage from contact with the enemy at the Yudam-ni perimeter began during the night of 29 November after General Smith in the afternoon had ordered the 5th Marines to protect Yudam-ni and the 7th Marines to mount a full regimental attack south along the MSR, clear it of enemy, and reach Hagaru-ri. Later in the evening, General Smith received a X Corps order to do the same thing. To implement these instructions, Colonels Litzenberg and Murray, at 6 A.M. on the morning of 30 November, issued Joint Operation Order 1-50, calling for the two regiments to redeploy during the day and concentrate on the south side of Yudam-ni as the first step in preparing for a breakout attempt. They sent a copy of this order to General Smith later in the day by Lt. Col. J. N. Winecoff, assistant G-3, 1st Marine Division, who had flown to Yudam-ni. Litzenberg and Murray during this changing situation conferred with each other and with Maj. William McReynolds, commander of the 11th Marines (artillery regiment), as they had done during the battle thus far, before issuing their joint orders.[1]

In preparing for the withdrawal from Yudam-ni, General Smith asked that no more 155-mm shells be air-dropped at Yudam-ni for the artillery but that the drops concentrate on 105-mm shells, as more of them could be obtained in this way and they would be more useful than the 155-mm shells. He also asked that the size of air-dropped ammunition packages be reduced to 300 pounds for a 24-foot parachute, as there had been excessive breakage in the airdrops.

During the morning of 30 November the 2nd Battalion, 5th Marines, remained in its positions about three miles west of Yudam-ni. It reported that Chinese were strongly entrenched on the ridge to its front and that the first four roadblocks in front of it were heavily manned. Aerial reconnaissance reported 33 more roadblocks spaced along the westbound road farther on out of sight of the battalion. It also reported three strongly defended Chinese roadblocks between Yudam-ni and Hagaru-ri. That was an understatement. The entire road was actually a Chinese fireblock. Chinese soldiers with automatic weapons were in position along the high ground to deny passage.

As the day advanced, the 5th and 7th Marines continued preparations for moving into new positions on the perimeter, drew rations and ammunition, and prepared to destroy all supplies, ammunition, and equipment that could not be moved from Yudam-ni. By day's end, all units were ready for the movement scheduled to begin the next morning, 1 December.

The 1st Marine Air Wing flew 158 sorties during the 30th, all but seven of them in support of troops in the Chosin Reservoir area. This daylong aerial attack did much to keep the Chinese relatively quiet. It helped greatly in enabling the Marines on 30 November to redeploy their forces to positions south of Yudam-ni, where they would start their breakout effort. It involved execution of a complicated disengagement from the enemy on the hills north and northwest of Yudam-ni by the 5th Marines, in which they would pass through the 7th Marine Regiment, which was now mostly south of the village. The objective was to get both the 5th and 7th Marines south of Yudam-ni. The 11th Marines, the artillery regiment, was already there. The two infantry regiments were then to seize and occupy the strategically situated high ground along both sides of the Hagaru-ri road, which would allow the vehicular column withdrawal to start. Both Litzenberg and Murray agreed it would be necessary to carry out this redeployment in daylight. They would then have the benefit of continuous air observation and protection and of observed artillery fire.

Basically, the redeployment on 30 November required the 5th Marines to withdraw from north and northwest of Yudam-ni to relieve elements of the 7th Marine Regiment, so they in turn could move to new defensive positions south of Yudam-ni that commanded the MSR exit from the village. In carrying out this movement, part of the 3rd Battalion, 5th Marines, had a hard fight with CCF on Hill 1282 on North Ridge. The 2nd Battalion, 5th Marines, however, had the hardest job of the day in withdrawing from Hill 1426 on Southwest Ridge. Marine Corsair air cover and artillery fire support helped it withdraw and move back about one mile, where it relieved elements of the 3rd Battalion, 7th Marines, which then moved 2 miles south of Yudam-ni. Elements of the 1st Battalion, 7th Marines, held Hill 1276 on an eastern spur of South Ridge, where they covered the gorge and road through it one and one-half miles south of Yudam-ni.

The enemy took little advantage of the movements north of Yudam-ni once contact was broken. They were held in check, no doubt, by the certainty of heavy casualties from air strikes and observed artillery and mortar fire if they attempted to move in the open after the withdrawing Marines. Airdrops of supplies were made at Yudam-ni on 30 November.

YUDAM-NI BREAKOUT PLAN

In preparing for the breakout it was essential that all men be organized into fighting units. For this purpose, 26 provisional rifle platoons were organized from artillerymen of the 11th Marines and from Headquarters and Service units. Many of these platoons were attached to regular rifle companies as reinforcements. Some were used as reserve forces. Litzenberg and Murray also formed a provisional battalion from miscellaneous units and placed Maj. Maurice E. Roach, 7th Marine Regimental S-4, in command of it.

Colonels Litzenberg and Murray decided that the dead could not be taken out of Yudam-ni. All vehicles would be needed for the wounded assembled at Yudam-ni from the last four or five days of combat and those they knew who would have to be picked up at Toktong Pass from F Company when the column reached that point and from Davis's 1st Battalion, 7th Marines, which was certain to have many wounded in the breakout fight. Accordingly, a field burial service was held at Yudam-ni on 1 December for 85 officers and enlisted men. The bodies of these dead were retrieved and returned to the United States later under the armistice terms that ended the Korean War.[2]

General Smith approved the plan of march submitted to him by Colonels Litzenberg and Murray for the breakout. These two officers then issued Joint Operations Order No. 2-50 on the morning of 1 December. The troops and the convoyed vehicular column were to move toward Hagaru-ri astride the MSR, with infantry sweeping the adjoining hills and ridges. Lt. Col. Robert D. Taplett's 3rd Battalion, 5th Marines, initially was to pass through the 7th Marines' positions south of Yudam-ni and take the lead in the attack. It was 14 road miles to Hagaru-ri.

The plan meant attacking Chinese positions on the high ground dominating the road. This was to be no running of the gauntlet—it was an

attack south to Hagaru-ri. Only after the high ground was in friendly infantry hands, or entirely neutralized, could the long train of vehicles move
safely along the road. In some instances, after roadblocks had been reduced the column might proceed if only enemy long-range fire was striking sporadically near the road.

The lone tank at Yudam-ni—tank No. D-23—was to be at the point.
Sgt. Russell A. Munsell and another crew member had volunteered to
drive it out. Taplett's battalion was to meet Lt. Col. Raymond G. Davis's
1st Battalion, 7th Marines, at Toktong Pass. At the time the breakout got
under way, Lieutenant Colonel Davis was to lead his battalion on a forced
night march east of the road through the mountains and try to reach Fox
Company at its perimeter above the pass.

The eight tractors and the 155-mm howitzers they pulled were placed
at the end of the vehicular train. They were so large and unwieldy the
chance could not be taken that one or more of them might be knocked
out or disabled in such a way that they would block the road and prevent
the passage of vehicles behind them. Many disastrous roadblocks originated in this way during the Korean War. Only drivers of vehicles and
wounded were permitted to ride. Vehicles and critical equipment were
generally interspersed throughout the middle of the column. The breakout effort was to have maximum air cover, including carrier planes from
Task Force 77 standing by off the east coast in the Sea of Japan. It was
known that on 1 December there would be available 96 shore-based and
184 embarked planes, for a total of 280.[3]

COMMANDERS CONFERENCE AT HAGARU-RI, 30 NOVEMBER

While the officers of the 5th, 7th, and 11th Marine regiments were making final plans and redeployments at Yudam-ni for the breakout attempt
the next morning, a commanders conference on the general situation at
the Chosin Reservoir was in progress during the afternoon at Hagaru-ri.
The conference was held in the two joined pyramidical tents erected at
the Hagaru-ri airstrip. After a busy morning of conferences with Generals Barr of the 7th Division and Soule of the 3rd Division and members
of the X Corps staff, General Almond, X Corps commander, left Hamhung
at 1:40 P.M. with his senior aide, Major Ladd, and flew by L-17 plane to
Hagaru-ri.

There at 2:10 P.M. he began a conference with Generals Smith, Barr,
and Hodes and Colonels Forney and Williams on the Chosin situation.
The conference lasted nearly an hour and a half. In this conference Almond emphasized that the 5th and 7th Marine regiments must be withdrawn from Yudam-ni immediately. He asked Generals Smith and Barr
to submit a plan to extricate elements of the 7th Infantry Division from

east of the reservoir. (The fate of these troops is covered in chapter 5, above.) General Smith told General Almond that evacuating the hundreds of wounded would be the major problem in withdrawing both the Marine and Army units on either side of the reservoir to Hagaru-ri. General Almond interrupted the conference to place a telephone call to Maj. Gen. Clark Ruffner, his chief of staff, to hasten movement of troop reinforcements, particularly Lieutenant Colonel Reidy's 2nd Battalion, 31st Infantry, 7th Division, northward to join Colonel Puller, commander of the 1st Marine Regiment, at Koto-ri. He also asked that experts be flown to Hagaru-ri, including Lieutenant Colonel Carlton, to arrange for airlift of supplies needed in the projected breakout attempt. During the conference General Almond gave General Smith a copy of his X Corps Operations Order No. 8, dated 30 November. This order specified the movements and responsibilities of major units of the X Corps in northeast Korea in concentrating on Hungnam as rapidly as possible.[4] At 3:30 P.M. Almond flew back to his Hamhung CP.

DISENGAGEMENT OF 5TH MARINES, 1 DECEMBER

The 5th Marines' last disengagement action north of Yudam-ni took place on the morning of 1 December. It involved leaving Hills 1282 and 1240 and was the most difficult and potentially the most dangerous for the units involved of all the disengagement movements. The 1st Battalion, 5th Marines, held Hill 1240; the 3rd Battalion held Hill 1282. These were the only Marine troops left north of Yudam-ni on the morning of 1 December. At 8 A.M. the 3rd Battalion started leaving Hill 1282, where contact with Chinese troops was so close that fighting was with grenades. There was danger that Chinese would swarm over the crest as the withdrawal started. This danger was averted by Marine aircraft making a number of dummy runs over the enemy positions, getting them well down in their holes, and then on signal the planes came in for real strafing and bomb runs, at the same time that mortars and artillery barrages from Yudam-ni kept the enemy low. G Company was the last of the 3rd Battalion to leave Hill 1282. The aerial heavy-fire concentration was so successful that G Company disengaged with no loss. The rear-guard unit of the two battalions was B Company of the 1st Battalion, 5th Marines, on Hill 1240, half a mile east of the 3rd Battalion on Hill 1282 on North Ridge. First Lt. John R. Hancock, the company commander, thought his best chance was to slip off the hill with no supporting fires at all. He did this, covering his withdrawal by light machine-gun fire. He, too, got away without loss.

Part of the redeployment on 1 December called for the 3rd Battalion, 7th Marines, to seize Hill 1419, a little more than half a mile east of the road and three and one-half miles south of Yudam-ni. This hill was to serve as one of the jump-off points in the breakout. It also was to be the place where Lieutenant Colonel Davis was to begin his surprise night movement for the relief of F Company at Toktong Pass. The 3rd Battalion had a hard fight with determined Chinese defenders before it won the hill. There was heavy fighting for other hills immediately south of Yudam-ni as the Marines completed their redeployment moves. Chinese were everywhere. If they did not move aggressively in the open on 1 December in pursuit of withdrawing Marine units north of Yudam-ni, they did fight stubbornly in their dug-in positions south of the town as elements of the 7th Marines battled to win key positions to cover the beginning of the breakout effort.[5]

THE BREAKOUT BEGINS, 1 DECEMBER

At 9 A.M. on 1 December, the 3rd Battalion, 7th Marines, started an attack against Hill 1542, which from the west dominated the road two and one-half miles south of Yudam-ni. Opposite Hill 1542 on the east side of the road, Hill 1419 was another enemy bastion. Together, the two hills controlled the road. The Marine vehicular train could not leave Yudam-ni until these two hills had been taken. The 3rd Battalion commander, Lt. Col. William F. Harris, detached H Company to attack Hill 1419.

While the fighting to open this gateway was in progress, three battalions in the rear formed a strong defensive line to hold off enemy from that quarter. It was clear to the Chinese that the Marines were maneuvering to quit Yudam-ni. The Marine rear defensive line slanted from Hill 1542 northeastward over Hill 1276, which controlled passage on the road through the gorge, where it made a twisting turn south from Yudam-ni. The defensive line then bent eastward to the southeast edge of a western arm of the Chosin Reservoir a mile southeast of Yudam-ni. The troops on this rear defensive line were (from southwest to northeast) the 3rd Battalion, 7th Marines, and the 2nd and 1st battalions, 5th Marines. The 3rd Battalion, 7th Marines, was to attack from this defensive line to capture Hill 1542, just below its own defensive position, and Hill 1419, more than a mile away across the road to the east.

Before the 3rd Battalion, 7th Marines, secured Hills 1542 and 1419, Lt. Col. Robert D. Taplett arrived with his 3rd Battalion, 5th Marines, to lead the breakout. Taplett waited as the stubborn fight developed, with his battalion astride the road. But at 3 P.M., with these hills still unsecured, Taplett attacked through Lieutenant Colonel Harris's 3rd Battalion. Tank No. D-23, a platoon of H Company, 5th Marines, and a platoon of A Company engineers led the way. The breakout was in progress, therefore, at midafternoon on 1 December. G Company, 5th Marines, previously

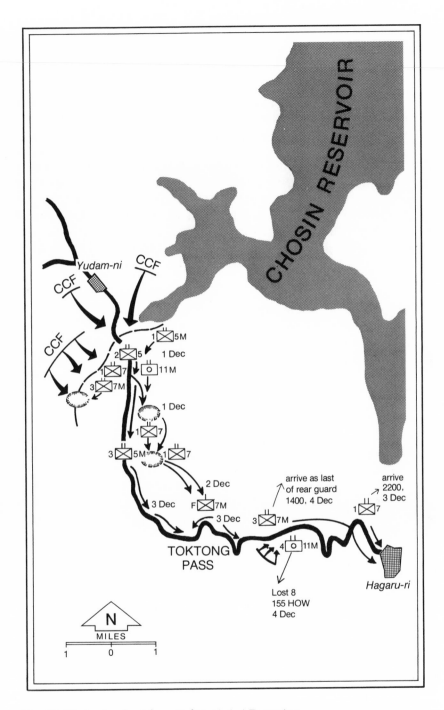

CHOSIN RESERVOIR

Yudam-ni

CCF
CCF
CCF
CCF

1 ⊠ 5M
2 ⊠ 5   1 Dec
1 ⊠ 7   ▢ 11M
3 ⊠ 7M

1 Dec

1 ⊠ 7

3 ⊠ 5M 1 ⊠ 7

2 Dec

3 Dec   F ⊠ 7M

arrive as last
of rear guard
1400, 4 Dec

arrive
2200,
3 Dec

3 Dec

3 ⊠ 7M   1 ⊠ 7

TOKTONG
PASS

4 ▢ 11M

Hagaru-ri

Lost 8
155 HOW
4 Dec

N

MILES

1   0   1

MAP 13. Marine breakout from Yudam-ni, 1–4 December.

on Hill 1282 north of Yudam-ni and on North Ridge, was the last Marine company out of Yudam-ni.

Meanwhile, Chinese soldiers holding Hill 1542 inflicted heavy casualties on G and I companies of the 7th Marines in repeatedly repulsing their efforts to seize the hill. The Chinese appear to have had about a regiment holding it. As dark fell, the Marine attack was stalled on the east slope of the hill. Across the road, H Company likewise failed to gain Hill 1419. It was necessary there to commit A and B companies to Davis's 1st Battalion, 7th Marines, to help H Company take it, and this was not accomplished until about 9 P.M. Only then could Davis's battalion get ready to start its overland march toward F Company at Toktong Pass.[6]

Lt. Col. William F. Harris's 3rd Battalion, 7th Marines, had more than it could handle in trying to dispose of the estimated Chinese regiment holding Hill 1542, and with casualties mounting and the enemy pressing attack after attack on it as the night wore on, Harris committed I Company to the defense line. Some artillerymen had been assigned to the company to build up its strength. One of these, Sgt. James E. Johnson, now had to fight as an infantryman. Soon after I Company went into the line, the Chinese hit Johnson's platoon in a vicious attack. Johnson, a squad leader, had to assume the role of platoon leader in a short time, and he performed the duty with uncommon coolness and valor. Johnson's platoon position was not dug in and was open to attack by the Chinese from their entrenched positions above him. The fight went against the platoon, and it was ordered to withdraw during the firefight. Johnson went among his men, supervising their individual withdrawal, while he covered them with his fire. He took up the most defensible position he could find as his men departed and continued his covering fire against the Chinese. The last of his platoon in its withdrawal saw Johnson, wounded, engaging enemy troops in hand-to-hand grenade exchanges. Johnson was not seen again and was carried as missing in action until he was listed three years later as killed in action on 2 December 1950. (The date probably should have been 1 December.) Johnson had saved many lives in his platoon when he sacrificed his own in covering the platoon's withdrawal. Johnson received the Medal of Honor, Posthumously.[7]

After Taplett started his attack south at 3 P.M., he gained nearly a mile before heavy Chinese fire stopped his advance. Taplett sent H Company west of the road and I Company east of it to destroy the Chinese positions that blocked the way. Only after a prolonged firefight that continued after dark until about 7:30 P.M. did he succeed in clearing the flanks. Taplett gave his 3rd Battalion a brief rest after this fight before he proceeded farther.

As part of the breakout plan, the 1st Battalion, 11th Marines, was to provide supporting fire from the south side of Yudam-ni, and the 3rd Bat-

Soldiers of the 1st Marine Division take advantage of a momentary lull in the fighting on the road from Yudam-ni to Hagaru-ri, 1 December 1950. (US Marine Corps photograph A-5675)

talion, 11th Marines, was to emplace its guns at Sinhung-ni at the northern base of Toktong Pass as soon as that place was in Marine possession. From there it was to give supporting fire for the continuing attack toward Hagaru-ri. Each artillery battalion in the breakout column was to join the last infantry battalion passing its position.

Just before midnight 1 December Taplett ordered his battalion to resume the attack. West of the road H Company met little resistance. East of it I Company approached the western base of massive Hill 1520. There the Chinese had dug in well and in strength. At the time I Company met this wall of Chinese soldiers on the west side of the hill, Davis's 3rd Battalion, 7th Marines, on their way to rescue F Company at Toktong Pass, was fighting its way through some Chinese on the opposite, east side of the hill. Neither Marine force knew of the other's presence on the opposite side of this big hill mass. The huge, mile-high hill completely separated them, and the sounds of their separate actions did not reach the other.

In the battle on the west side of Hill 1520, Capt. Harold O. Schrier of I Company requested permission to withdraw closer to the road, where he still might be able to protect it. His request was approved, but there, alternate Chinese infantry and mortar attacks hit his company. Schrier lost radio communication with Lieutenant Colonel Taplett, and his runners to Taplett lost their way. The company was isolated the rest of the night. Enemy fire wounded Schrier twice, and 2nd Lt. Willard S. Peterson took over command of I Company.

In this night battle on the slope of Hill 1520, S. Sgt. William G. Windrich was platoon sergeant of the 1st Platoon in I Company. At one point when the Chinese seemed about to overrun the forward elements of the company, Windrich organized a squad of men and led them to the top of the threatened knoll. Armed with a carbine, he and his handful of men reached the knoll and engaged in a confrontation close fight with Chinese, who were supported by heavy automatic and mortar fire. The assault team of the Chinese threw grenades. Windrich was wounded seriously in the head by a grenade fragment, and seven of his 12 men were also wounded. Windrich refused to be evacuated and went instead to the main company position and organized a small group of volunteers to return to the knob and evacuate the wounded and dying there. Windrich was wounded there again in the fighting that now continued—this time in the legs. Again he refused evacuation. Sgt. Charles Pearson wanted to dress his wounds, but Windrich replied, "There isn't time. They're only small holes anyway." For an hour more, Windrich continued to lead the men at the knob, going from one to the other to help and encourage them. They repulsed the enemy attacks. Near the end of the fight, Windrich collapsed in the bitter cold from loss of blood, exhaustion, and pain. He lost consciousness and died. Windrich received the Medal of Honor, Posthumously.[8]

Because of I Company's perilous situation, Taplett moved G Company and attached engineer troops up behind it. I Company had been decimated—only 20 able-bodied men remained. After daybreak, G Company passed through I Company's position. It counted 342 dead Chinese in and around I Company's position. G Company now resumed the attack on the west slope of Hill 1520, gaining the crest by noon.[9] Meanwhile, Taplett was forced to call for reinforcements.

When the composite company made up of remnants of D and E companies of the 7th Marines arrived, Taplett put them on the road between G and H companies of his own battalion. A spectacular Corsair strike by ten planes helped greatly in reducing an enemy roadblock established at a blown bridge. His advance halted there until engineers could construct a bypass around the bridge.

THE REAR DEFENSIVE WALL AT YUDAM-NI

The three battalions holding the rear defensive line from the slopes of Hill 1542, a distance of three air miles southwest of the ice of the Chosin Reservoir, with its center about one mile south of Yudam-ni, where it crossed the Yudam-ni–Hagaru-ri road, had hard fighting holding back the Chinese while Taplett's 3rd Battalion, 5th Marines, started the breakout drive south out of the perimeter. In effect, these three battalions formed a rear wall, in front of which the attack south down the MSR was taking place. The long vehicular column moved with the attack as fast as adjacent hills could be cleared of enemy. The critical terrain that had to be held south of Yudam-ni to allow the vehicular column to move out was Hill 1276, near the center of the defensive rear-guard line near and just west of the road, and Hill 1542, at the southern end of the rear defense line, also west of the road but a little more than a mile from it. Lt. Col. Harold S. Roise's 2nd Battalion, 5th Marines, in the center of the defense line, was the rear-guard battalion of the three on the line.

All three battalions received numerous Chinese attacks after midnight of 1 December, and throughout the hours of darkness early on 2 December, they were under almost constant attack. The CCF attack, using their familiar inverted-V formation, was so fierce and persistent against F Company's front on Hill 1276 that at 2 a.m. on 2 December the Marine FAC asked for an air strike by two night fighters. The Chinese positions were marked by 60-mm white phosphorus shells. The resulting air strike of strafing and rockets hit within 200 yards of the Marine line. Three more night fighters joined the two already over the area in making the strike. Roise then tried twice before daylight to retake a lost position. Both failed because of enemy machine-gun fire. After daylight and another air strike, still another attempt to retake the position failed. Then after yet another air strike at 10 A.M. that lasted 25 minutes, with napalm and 500-pound bombs, observers saw some Chinese soldiers leaving their position. But the 2nd Battalion now was nearly due to pull off the hill and take its position as rear guard. So the enemy in the end were left in possession of the hotly disputed crest of Hill 1276's pulverized rubble.[10]

At the right end of the rear defense line near the reservoir, the 1st Battalion, 5th Marines, had an easier time. Shortly after midnight, a force of about 100 Chinese crossed an arm of ice and tried to infiltrate the 1st Battalion position. They were driven back by mortar and artillery fire. Chinese replacements tried ineffectually during the rest of the night to make some gain here. In front of one machine gun 51 dead Chinese were counted. Total Chinese losses during the night at this extreme right end of the line were estimated to be 200. After daylight some Chinese soldiers threw away their weapons and tried to run to safety. Many were killed.

The story at Hill 1542, on the other end of the defense line to the southwest, was a different tale. Captured documents later told the Chinese side of what happened there. The 9th Company, 3rd Battalion, 235th Regiment, 79th Division, 27th Army, and three other companies of the same regiment hit G and I companies of the 7th Marines on the eastern slope of the hill. The two marine companies had received reinforcements of about 100 miscellaneous artillerymen, headquarters personnel, and other rear-echelon men who could be hastily assembled. The Chinese attack came downhill. They had held the crest all day against Marine attack. Their assault struck at 4:30 A.M. with supporting fire. The familiar Chinese inverted-V wedge formation pressed in close, first on one side and then on the other, hoping for a penetration. The left-hand Chinese platoon took a beating, losing its commander and half its men. The other two platoons had heavy casualties also, but they did rout the provisional company of Marine reinforcements. Under the pressing Chinese attack I Company fell back slowly until it was abreast of G Company, which had been only slightly engaged. The two companies now numbered fewer than 200 men. More reinforcements from the Headquarters and Service Company were sent to them. The two companies then formed a defensive arc that reached from the MSR a little more than half a mile up the eastern slope of Hill 1542. They had to hold that position until the main vehicular column passed the hill. Their position afforded only marginal protection, but it did keep effective enemy small-arms fire off the road and prevented the Chinese from closing on the road itself. The provisional company and I Company lost heavily in this battle.[11]

SLOW PROGRESS ON 2 DECEMBER

It was inevitable that, with the rifle companies so heavily engaged on the hills flanking the road and fighting for almost every foot of the way, the vehicular convoy made slow progress. This continued to be the situation during 2 December. The constant air cover kept most of the Chinese a distance from the road itself. In spite of this protection, however, there was a considerable infiltration of snipers who directed their fire on drivers of vehicles in an effort to cripple the movement of the convoy. There had to be many replacements of drivers killed or wounded.

In the afternoon the advance along the road reached a blown bridge that had spanned a rock channel about 300 yards south of Hill 1520, where the road turned east to start climbing into Toktong Pass. Chinese automatic weapons covered the road at the bridge. There it brought the advance of the composite D-E Company astride the road to a halt. A Corsair strike of 12 planes cleared the enemy gunners from the ravine, and another air strike south of the road broke up an enemy force that had stopped H Company. As dusk settled over the scene, engineers finished a hastily built bypass around the blown bridge. The lone tank, still at the point, took the bypass, and the vehicular column behind it started across at 7 P.M.[12] Taplett's troops continued to clear the hills on either flank, and the infantry astride the road kept pace with them.

During the night an enemy attack on the 3rd Battalion of artillery in the train destroyed one howitzer and several vehicles. In general, however, the infantry kept the enemy from the convoy. Taplett's attack halted at 2 A.M. on 3 December, about half a mile short of the top of Toktong Pass and the nearby position of Fox Company. The composite company formed of remnants from D and E companies had suffered heavily in the breakout, fighting adjacent to and along the road. It had lost most of its noncommissioned officers and was now at the end of its endurance. Taplett felt he had to stop for the night. He put his 3rd Battalion into a defensive position about a mile below the top of the pass.

Across Toktong Pass, 3 December

Dawn of 3 December brought a scene of beauty, for six inches of new snow gave a smooth and illusory tranquillity to the landscape. Sergeant Munsell led off in his lone tank when the advance began. Behind it, Sergeant Knox's platoon of engineers served as the infantry point. When the column reached Hagaru-ri, only 17 able-bodied men remained of the 48 who started with this engineer platoon. G Company, 5th Marines, replaced the composite D-E Company astride the road on 3 December. The men of the composite company still combat effective were incorporated into 2nd Lt. John J. Cahill's G Company. The forefront of Taplett's 3rd Battalion advance on the morning of 3 December was nearing the crest of Toktong Pass and an anticipated junction there with F Company, 7th Marines, and also with Lieutenant Colonel Davis's 1st Battalion, 7th Marines. In order to relate that event in the breakout, one must go back to the story of Davis's 1st Battalion, its rescue mission to F Company, and the latter's impressive stand in its perimeter above the road at Toktong Pass.

Fox Company at Toktong Pass

To those who were in the Army or the Marine Corps during World War II or the Korean War, "Fox Company" signifies F Company, according to the military phonetic alphabet then in use. The rifle and weapons companies of the Army battalions were known to the men who fought in them as Able, Baker, Charlie, Dog, Easy, Fox, George, How, Item, King, Love, and Mike. Dog, How, and Mike companies were the Weapons companies, and the rest were rifle companies. (The letter "J" was skipped in this nomenclature, as it was susceptible to being misunderstood over radio and telephone and in some other forms of military communication.) The Marine Corps used letter designations for the three rifle companies in a battalion, but the fourth company was known simply as the Weapons Company. Thus, in the 1st Marine Division the lettered rifle companies in a regiment ran from A to I. The soldiers themselves nearly always referred to their unit and others as "Baker Company," for instance, and not B Company or Company B.

The Fox Company referred to here was F Company, 2nd Battalion, 7th Marines, 1st Marine Division. The beginning of its story here is with the movement of the 7th Marine Regiment to Yudam-ni. It ends when a relief force reached it on 2 December in the breakout from the Yudam-ni encirclement. It is the story of a reinforced rifle company of fighting men, with superb company officer and noncommissioned leadership, under almost constant attack from numerically superior Chinese soldiers for five days and five nights. It held out in a perimeter defense position with the help of airdrop of supplies, Marine Corsair fighter support in daytime, and artillery fire support from Hagaru-ri at night at an extreme range for 105-mm howitzers. It is a story that any army could be proud of, and it teaches the valuable military lesson that most American soldiers sorely need to know, and often did not practice in the Korean War—a numerically inferior force can hold out in a tight and well-chosen perimeter defense against a superior force if it does not panic, fights courageously, and has air and artillery support.

One may well ask what makes men fight this way. Orators, publicists, politicians, and moralists commonly attribute the highest and legendary forms of courage and self-sacrifice on the battlefield to love of country and patriotism. Livy, the early Roman historian of ancient, republican Rome, fostered such interpretation and believed it the duty of historians to invent such examples if they did not in fact exist. But soldiers who fight the battles that so often bring them close to death do not place this interpretation on their own acts. Among junior officers, noncommissioned officers, and the rank-and-file who undergo all the fatigue and dangers that close combat can bring, in hostile terrain and harsh climate, it is common knowledge that it is not the fire of patriotism that sustains them in the ordeal, although there often is patriotism in the background. The principal motivation for courage under stress in battle is personal pride in doing one's share in the company of men one has been associated with and whose respect he values and wants to retain. "Esprit de corps" is a term often used to express this feeling. It is also knowing that, if each one does not do his part, all may be endangered. Personal salvation, as well as buddy and unit salvation, depends upon each man's performing his immediate duty, whatever the danger it poses. This belief, and consequent reaction under stress, is commonplace among the best soldiers of all nations, and no less is it true of American soldiers in the units that make their mark in our military history.

Capt. William E. Barber commanded the 240 men of F Company, reinforced. He had reconnoitered and selected the position at Toktong Pass before he left Hagaru-ri, about midafternoon on 27 November. The first members of the relief force from Yudam-ni entered its perimeter just before noon 2 December. Its ever-present foe during the interval of five days and five nights apparently was elements of the CCF 59th Division. The enemy division's assigned mission had been to close the 14 miles of road between Yudam-ni and Hagaru-ri and to deny American forces any movement on it.

Because F Company was sent to control Toktong Pass, Captain Barber had chosen a position he thought was the best available to protect the top of the pass with the force and weapons available to him. It was an isolated hill just north of the road, about midway through the pass and near the road's highest point. The highest ground close to the road was on the north side of it; the terrain fell away from the road on its south side at the top of the pass to a valley below. In going over Toktong Pass, the MSR ran generally in an east-west direction, with several twists and turns. Once through the pass, going north toward Yudam-ni, the road straightened out and ran nearly due north along a narrow valley floor. Barber had a heavily reinforced rifle company at Toktong Pass. The heavy machine gun and the 81-mm mortar sections of the 2nd Battalion Weapons Company were attached to it. This gave Fox Company great firepower.

Barber placed his rifle platoons in an inverted U-shaped perimeter, with the closed end of the U pointing generally north. The 3rd Platoon, led by 1st Lt. Robert J. McCarthy, was on the summit of the hill, occupying the closed part of the U. It faced north toward higher ground. The 1st Platoon, commanded by 1st Lt. John M. Dunne, was on the right-hand leg of the upside-down U and faced east. The 2nd Platoon, led by 1st Lt. Elmer G. Peterson, occupied the left-hand leg of the U and faced west. Both legs of the U-shaped position fell back down from the crest toward the road. Barber placed all the heavy machine guns with the rifle platoons. The company headquarters group and the rocket squad held a position in the open end of the U. The guns with the 2nd Platoon could sweep the MSR below it westward. Barber established his CP at the base of the isolated hill and near the road. Here also he stationed the 81-mm and

60-mm mortars. A steep embankment on the north side of the hillside road cut here constituted an obstacle to any troops that might try to attack the rear of the perimeter from the road.[13]

In the late afternoon of 27 November, General Almond, X Corps commander, passed F Company in his jeep, on his way from Yudam-ni to Hamhung. Later, after dark, Lt. Col. Olin L. Beall's long truck convoy passed F Company, returning to Hagaru-ri from carrying supplies to Yudam-ni that afternoon. When the rumble of the trucks pulling through the pass ended about 8 P.M., quiet settled over the snow- and ice-bound landscape. Hours later, when Lieutenant McCarthy made the rounds of his 3rd Platoon position a little after 1 A.M., he found the men listless and drowsy from numbing cold. He cautioned his squad leaders to maintain a better alert. On his next round he thought he had achieved it.

At 2:30 A.M. on 28 November, Chinese silently struck the 3rd Platoon's line at the closed end of the U and immediately overran its two forward squads. The Marine loss in this first clash was heavy. Out of 35 men in the foxholes and gun positions, 15 were killed, nine wounded, and three missing. The remaining eight men escaped back to the reserve-squad position. The Chinese now held the topographic crest of the perimeter position. One cannot find anywhere in the records, including the Marine history of the Chosin operation, any suggestion that these men were surprised or asleep in their positions. But the conclusion is inescapable that these men of the 3rd Platoon were not alert. Such a large number of casualties is not inflicted so quickly unless the men are caught inattentive.

Following quickly on this initial success, the Chinese assault force tried to penetrate at the junction of the 3rd and 2nd platoons at the northwest bend of the U. Here the fight was at close quarters with grenades and small arms. The Chinese were thrown back repeatedly and apparently brought up reinforcements to replace the heavy losses in their original attack force. Pfc. Robert F. Benson, Pvt. Hector A. Cafferata, Jr., of the 2nd Platoon, and Pfc. Gerald J. Smith, a fire-team leader of the 3rd Platoon, and his men are credited with turning the tide here and being largely responsible for destroying two platoons of Chinese. Cafferata alone was credited with killing 15 enemy and wounding many others.

During this fight, all members of his fire team became casualties, and Cafferata was left alone at his team's section of the line. There he waged a lone battle with grenades and rifle fire as Chinese groups repeatedly tried to overrun him and penetrate the line. He held out long enough to permit reinforcements to come up and close off the threatened enemy penetration. Later in predawn morning darkness, the Chinese mounted another series of onslaughts at this point of the perimeter. At one point an enemy grenade landed in a shallow entrenchment where some wounded Marines had been placed. Cafferata saw the grenade come in and rushed to it. He picked it up and threw it free of the entrenchment. It exploded just after it left his hand, and fragments cut off one finger and otherwise wounded him in the right hand and arm. Cafferata ignored these wounds and stayed on the hill in the fight. An enemy sniper subsequently hit him with rifle fire, and he had to be evacuated. All his buddies thought that he saved many of them from death or serious injury by snatching the grenade from the entrenchment where they lay wounded and that, throughout the close combat at their corner of the perimeter that night, he had prevented an enemy penetration into the rear of their front line by his impressive combat performance. Cafferata won the Medal of Honor for his heroism with Fox Company on 28 November.[14]

While this fight at the crest was in progress, another force of Chinese came down the road, apparently unaware of the presence there of Barber's CP and the mortar positions. These Chinese, initially surprised, recovered fast and attacked the mortar positions, forcing Barber and the mortar crews to escape up the hill a short distance to a line of trees. The steep road embankment prevented the Chinese from following quickly. When they did climb to the top of the embankment, they were shot down by machine-gun and rifle fire, and those massed at the bottom of the embankment were decimated by grenades the Marines rolled over the embankment. Surviving Chinese tried to run for it. Most of them were gunned down as they broke into the open.

The 1st Platoon, on the east leg of the perimeter, had relatively minor action, but fighting around most of the F Company perimeter continued until daylight. Except for the enemy group that had come up the road, the enemy had come from the high ground of Hill 1653, north of the perimeter.

A flight of Australian F-51 Mustang fighter planes arrived over F Company's positions about midmorning. They bombed and strafed Rocky Ridge of Hill 1653 to the north, which the Chinese by now had made into a bastion of strength. Then they made runs over the valley south of the road. These air strikes caused all Chinese fire to cease.[15]

After daylight, Fox Company counted about 450 dead Chinese within and in front of its perimeter. But F Company had suffered casualties also. It lost 20 killed, 54 wounded, and three missing. None of the missing was ever found. Three-fourths of those killed died in the initial attack against the 3rd Platoon. Later in the day, 28 November, F Company received orders to fight its way out, but with 54 wounded on its hands and, as its daytime patrols disclosed, surrounded by Chinese on all sides, it was unable to do so, and it did not even try. No relief force from either Hagaru-ri or Yudam-ni could get close to it during the day. The enemy controlled the road completely and turned back all efforts to clear it.

During the twenty-eighth, Read's battery of 105-mm howitzers, emplaced at the edge of Hagaru-ri, had been able to register its fire on the enemy position north of F Company and was prepared to fire interdiction missions that night to help the company if it came under attack again, as was anticipated. Airdrops during the day resupplied F Company with ammunition and medical supplies.

The defense lines that night, 28–29 November, were the same as the night before. Now, however, there were 77 fewer men to hold the positions and fight the battles. All was quiet until after midnight. Then the Chinese came. This time no one was caught off guard. Enemy mortar fire on the 3rd Platoon position gave a warning of the coming infantry attack. This mortar fire, 15 minutes after midnight, killed one and wounded two men. F Company's 81-mm mortars replied to this fire and stopped it. There were now 20 men in the 3rd Platoon's central position on the crest.

Chinese skirmishers probed the perimeter and then hit with a concentrated force on both flanks of the 3rd Platoon. About 50 Chinese soldiers broke through its lines and got down the hill behind Peterson's 1st Platoon on the left, or west, flank. Instead of striking quickly and exploiting their breakthrough, the Chinese seemed to lack leadership; the enemy soldiers assembled in a confused mass. This allowed Peterson to turn one of his machine guns around. McCarthy's 3rd Platoon did the same thing. The two machine guns fired into the massed Chinese and virtually annihilated them.

Captain Barber rushed up the hill from his CP during this penetration and joined McCarthy's platoon as it backed down the hill a short distance. Both McCarthy and Barber were hit in the leg by a flurry of fire from the east flank. Barber had his wound dressed and remained in action. On the left, or west, flank of the perimeter, Lieutenant Peterson was wounded a second time, but he stayed with the platoon. The enemy attack here remained strong and was turned back only with the help of mortars and of artillery fire called in from Read's battery at Hagaru-ri. At sunrise on 29 November, a Marine counterattack regained the original position on the crest of the hill. F Company's casualties the second night were five killed and 29 wounded.[16] The Chinese lost about 200 killed. During the hours of predawn darkness that morning, the cries of wounded Chinese around the perimeter sounded until one by one they froze to death.

At midmorning 29 November an airdrop of supplies came in to the perimeter, and a helicopter landed with new batteries for radios. These were vitally important. Among other things, the batteries enabled F Company to keep in constant contact with Read's battery of artillery at Hagaru-ri, which was firing with such deadly accuracy on the Chinese main position on the Rocky Ridge of Hill 1653, and from there directly in front of the F Company perimeter during Chinese night attacks. During daytime, the artillery battery kept up harassing fire on the Rocky Ridge north of the perimeter, which seemed to be the Chinese stronghold.

Airdrops that afternoon by big C-54s of the Cargo Command missed the perimeter, landing about 500 yards west of it. Peterson, twice wounded, led some of his men out to get the supplies. Chinese fire pinned them down, and they got back one by one with some trouble. The airdrops were helping F Company, even though some of the supplies were lost. Some critically wounded Marines had died during the first night of battle because blood plasma had frozen in its containers and could not be administered. After the airdrops, F Company had adequate blanket rations and most other needed items.

During the twenty-ninth, the Marines made hot coffee for themselves. That evening, Barber received word by radio that no help could get through from Yudam-ni or Hagaru-ri and that he would have to hold where he was. He told the others that the Marines at both Yudam-ni and at Hagaru-ri were surrounded, just as they were, and had taken heavy casualties. After dark Barber organized groups to go out to the air-dropped ammunition and supplies west of the perimeter under cover of his own mortar fire and artillery fire from Hagaru-ri on the Chinese position on Rocky Ridge. Two trips brought in all the supplies, apparently without enemy knowledge of it. Badly needed 60-mm and 81-mm mortar illuminating shells and cases of fragmentation grenades were among the supplies recovered.

Two o'clock in the morning seemed to be the time the Chinese surrounding Fox Company chose for their effort to break the will of Barber's men. For the third night in a row, now 30 November, the Chinese went into action at that time. It began when a voice called out in English, telling the Marines that they were surrounded and that, if they surrendered, they would be given good treatment. The Marine answer was O'Leary's mortars firing two 81-mm illuminating shells that lit up the area, upon which Marine machine gunners cut loose in the direction of the voice.

The Chinese then prepared their attack. Thirty minutes later an estimated two companies of enemy came, this time with fixed bayonets, from the valley south of the road. There was little firing from them as they advanced. Usually they had used fast marching fire from submachine guns. Marine mortars fired more illuminating shells, which brought the advancing Chinese into full view. Heavy and light machine-gun fire ripped through their ranks. The mortars adjusted on them. At the same time, Forward Observer 1st Lt. Donald Campbell, attached to F Company, adjusted artillery fire from Read's battery at Hagaru-ri on them. Those who made it to the road huddled under the steep embankment that rose on the north side of the cut. Here, most became victims to grenades the

Marines rolled down on them. Only a few of the estimated two companies of Chinese ever regained the valley south of the road.[17]

After daybreak on 30 November, with the sun warming up the frozen landscape, the men made fires, warmed rations, and made coffee. Their spirits had now risen to the point where they felt they could survive. Captain Barber was still in action with them, although his hobble had become worse, and sometimes he had to be helped to his feet when he sat down. Sniper fire from the Rocky Ridge came in during the day. Barber called for an air strike on the ridge. Soon four Corsairs came in and strafed, rocketed, let loose 500-pound bombs, and then dropped napalm. The ridge spouted flames, and a smoke cloud rose over it. Another airdrop came for the beleaguered company, this time just at dark. The drop was off target and landed 800 yards east of the perimeter—half a mile away. But the resupply of ammunition and other supplies again was recovered without incident. There was now plenty of ammunition for another night. Snow began to fall just after dark, and in four hours three inches of new snow lay piled on the old. Although the temperature was 20 degrees below zero, even the wounded, who had an ample supply of medicines and blankets, were reasonably cheerful.

But an ominous new development now occurred. During the snowstorm, the Chinese had moved four machine guns into firing positions on Rocky Ridge. At 1 A.M. on 1 December they opened up. Barber at once told Lieutenant Campbell, the artillery forward observer, to call in Read's artillery fire on the ridge. Barber's own 81-mm mortars were to coordinate so that they could place illuminating shells on the ridge as the artillery fire arrived. Sgt. Clyde Pitts of S. Sgt. John Audus's 3rd Platoon was to adjust the artillery fire by binoculars from a forward position. Read radioed that four howitzers were ready to fire. The order to fire was given, and the shells were on their way.

Two mortar illuminating shells broke over the enemy position just as the artillery rounds arrived, and then quickly four more put the ridge under brilliant light. Pitts from his forward position astonished everyone by reporting that the four artillery shells had been perfectly on target—that adjusting for further fire was unnecessary. The four enemy machine guns and their crews had been wiped out. There was no further enemy action against F Company that night. Read's artillery had fired from six miles away. This has to be one of the really remarkable—and fortunate—precision artillery firings in the Korean War. It is a good example of what artillery support can do for infantry in a forward combat situation.[18]

On the morning of 1 December, eight Corsairs came over F Company and went on to Rocky Ridge. Their strike left it in flames once more. The Corsairs then worked over the hills east and south of F Company's position while details from the company gathered in supplies just dropped from C-119 Flying Boxcars. In the afternoon a patrol left the perimeter and ventured north and then west toward Rocky Ridge. Heavy enemy fire from the ridge drove the patrol away with one killed and four wounded. During the day, F Company gathered all its dead and placed them near the road embankment, covered with ponchos.

That night, 1–2 December, the fifth in Fox Company's isolated position, the enemy seemed to have run out of steam. For the first time there was no Chinese attack during the night, only long-range sniper fire. Captain Barber had in the meantime learned that the 7th and 5th Marines were preparing to break out of Yudam-ni and that Lt. Col. Raymond G. Davis and his 1st Battalion, 7th Marines, were moving overland during the night in an effort to reach his position.

Lt. Col. Davis's Overland March, 1–2 December

The relief of Fox Company, 7th Marines, at Toktong Pass is an integral part of the Marine breakout from Yudam-ni. Lt. Col. Raymond G. Davis commanded the relief force, the 1st Battalion, 7th Marines, reinforced. His mission was to make a secret night movement around the east side of the Chinese blocking the Yudam-ni–Hagaru-ri road and join F Company at Toktong Pass. It was anticipated he might have to battle some Chinese en route, but he was to avoid heavy engagements if possible. While the main Marine force was to proceed along the Hagaru-ri road, Davis was to start after dark on 1 December from Hill 1419, east of the MSR and about four miles south of Yudam-ni, on a compass route over the hills to F Company's position.

All during 1 December the Marines were shifting their positions around Yudam-ni in a series of battles and movements. Part of the day's objective was to capture Hill 1419 before dark so that Davis's 1st Battalion could move into position near its crest for the departure point of his overland march. But H Company, 7th Marines, was unable to seize the hill during the day. Davis had to commit his A Company to help take the hill, which was finally accomplished about 7:30 P.M. Davis thereupon immediately had all dead and wounded carried from the hill down to the road and the aid station there. He then made his final preparations for the night march.

Each man carried an extra bandolier of ammunition, and extra litters were to be carried. Two 81-mm mortars and six heavy machine guns were taken with the battalion. Each man was to take his sleeping bag. They would be needed for wounded, and for all if enemy should cut them off in the mountains. The route was planned to be generally parallel to the MSR, but about two miles east of it. The temperature quickly dropped after dark to 16 degrees below zero. Troops already wet with perspiration from fighting up the hill would soon be frostbite victims in that temperature if they did not keep moving.

Davis quickly organized his three rifle companies, now reinforced by H Company, which Colonel Litzenberg decided should stay with the battalion on its march. By 9 P.M. on 1 December Davis's column was ready to move out from Hill 1419 on a southeasterly course. His march order placed 1st Lt. Joseph R. Kurcaba's B Company in the lead, followed by Lieutenant Colonel Davis with the 1st Battalion command group, then 1st Lt. Eugenous M. Hovatter's A Company, Capt. John F. Morris's C Company, the battalion Headquarters Company group, and last, 2nd Lt. Minard P. Newton's H Company of the 3rd Battalion.

Davis already had sent patrols out to the southeast, on the course he intended to follow. The patrols reported back that they had found no enemy. At 9 P.M., in a dark night but with a few stars showing above the horizon to the southeast, the column started on its cold, dangerous mission. In some places snow had drifted knee deep and slowed the men. Also, there was much difficulty in keeping on course in the snow-covered mountains. In places the men had to climb finger ridges on hands and knees, and on downhill courses many fell on ice. Davis's movement apparently was wholly unexpected by the Chinese, and it took them by surprise. There was no enemy opposition or encounter with enemy soldiers for some hours.

Davis became aware in crossing the second valley from Hill 1419 that his infantry point was veering too much to the southwest and that, if this continued, it would come out on the MSR, which was to be interdicted during the night by friendly artillery fire. Also, it would very likely run into enemy forces there. Davis tried by radio to correct the point's advance, but he failed to get a response from Kurcaba. After other methods of reaching Kurcaba failed, Davis took off running in the snow to reach the head of the column and stop it. In the darkness he lost his radioman and runner and plunged on by himself. He overtook the point only after a strenuous effort, when Kurcaba had begun to climb the next ridge. There the point had begun to receive its first Chinese opposition—which it stumbled into. Davis had arrived just in time. The point was headed up Hill 1520, which the enemy held.

In order to move ahead, Davis had to organize B and C companies to attack the Chinese positions on the east slope of the hill (1520), supported by his 81-mm mortars and the heavy machine guns. The Marine attack overran a Chinese platoon position where many of the Chinese soldiers were surprised in sleep or were numbed and half-frozen by the cold.

Davis now halted his forces for reorganization. Small-arms fire, almost spent, came in on his men from a long way off, and did no damage. Davis's men, once they had been allowed to halt, began collapsing in the snow, almost at the end of their endurance. They were oblivious to the cold and also the Chinese bullets that ricocheted off nearby rocks. The officers and noncommissioned officers had to go around among the men, shake them, cuff them, and pull them to their feet. Using a compass reading, Davis got them going again on the correct course.

At 3 A.M. in the morning of 2 December, he allowed the column to stop for a rest. The men had been climbing hills and fighting for 20 hours without sleep. Davis put the battalion into a perimeter, had company patrols organized, and kept 25 percent of the men on alert while others slept. He then set up the pack radio and established contact, the first during the march, with Colonel Litzenberg's 7th Marine CP near Yudam-ni. During the night a shell fragment had hit Davis's helmet, knocking him to the ground. Two bullets pierced his clothing.

At daybreak, 2 December, Davis got the men on their feet and started for Hill 1653, about a mile north of the F Company perimeter. Davis was not able to reach F Company by radio. As his column progressed, there were several long-range firefights with enemy on ridges to the east. Davis seemed to have achieved surprise in his approach to Hill 1653, as he encountered little opposition on the western slope of the hill. There was a bad moment, however, when H Company at the rear with the wounded came under a strong enemy attack. The litter cases were carried forward, and then H Company beat off the enemy.

In the advance eastward from Hill 1520 to Hill 1653, C Company covered A and B companies, which had the task of gaining the hill. During this movement, Davis's radio operator established communication with F Company. Captain Barber offered to send out a patrol from F Company to guide the 1st Battalion to his position. Davis declined the offer. But Barber did perform a valuable service in guiding an air strike onto an enemy-held position 400 yards north of F Company, in Davis's path. F Company also directed 81-mm mortar fire on Hill 1653. The air strikes and the mortar fire enabled A and B companies to seize the hill.

At 11:25 A.M. on 2 December the first men of Davis's relief force entered the F Company perimeter. Davis's battalion brought their 22 wounded into the safety of the perimeter. After the nightlong march ordeal, it seemed ironic that, soon after he entered the perimeter, Navy lieutenant Peter Arioli, the regimental surgeon who had accompanied Davis, was killed by a sniper as he attended to wounded. No other member of the relief force was killed during the march or upon arriving at the F Company perimeter. But tragedy did strike in another way. Two men of the column had to be placed in straitjackets when they broke down mentally and physically. Both died before they could be evacuated.[19]

By the time Lieutenant Colonel Davis reached F Company, that company, after five days and five nights in its perimeter, had suffered 118 casualties: 26 killed, 89 wounded, and three missing. Six of seven officers were wounded, some more than once, and nearly everyone who had not been wounded was suffering from frostbite and digestive disorders. Only 82 of Barber's original 220 men were able to walk away from the position they had defended.

After Davis's battalion joined F Company, the units assembled and reorganized. That night the combined force went into five separate company perimeters, mutually supporting. The night passed quietly.

The next morning, 3 December, Davis divided his four companies into two attack forces. They had the task of sweeping the remaining CCF from the eastern and southern parts of Toktong Pass, so that it would be clear when the main Marine force arrived there. Its lead units were expected to arrive during the day unless there were serious setbacks to it along the MSR. There were two known CCF concentrations near F Company in the pass area. One of these was on high ground to the east, in the direction of Hagaru-ri; the other was on a spur ridge running southward. Davis led C and H companies against the CCF to the east. Maj. Thomas B. Tighe commanded A and B companies in their attack against the larger enemy force on the high ground south of the bend in the MSR.

The attack south of the road took the Chinese there completely by surprise. They fell back from their position in some confusion. The Chinese lack of good communication now showed clearly in the fact that they withdrew straight toward the advancing point of Lieutenant Colonel Taplett's battalion, coming up to the pass from the west. Their course would take them directly into the path of H Company, 5th Marines, which was sweeping the high ground south of the road. Colonel Litzenberg received news of the Chinese move by radio from Major Tighe. Litzenberg told Lieutenant Colonel Murray to inform Taplett of the development and for him to be ready for the Chinese.

Taplett, meanwhile, had seen Chinese on the high ground south of the road at daybreak. He called in artillery fire from Hagaru-ri. But the distance was too great, and the shells fell short. Taplett then called for an air strike. Corsairs were soon over the target and hit the confused CCF with rockets and napalm at the same time that 81-mm mortar and heavy machine-gun fire from the 3rd Battalion, 5th Marines, and Tighe's converging force struck them. This fortuitous turn of events in the meeting of the two Marine forces at Toktong Pass resulted in the near annihilation of an enemy battalion by 10 A.M. that morning. It was the greatest single casualty loss to the Chinese in the Marine breakout from Yudamni. H Company of Taplett's battalion continued on and occupied the vacated Chinese positions.[20]

In his attack elsewhere in the pass, Davis cleared the Chinese from the hill northeast of the crest by 1 P.M. The way was now open down the eastern incline of the MSR through Toktong Pass.

Captain (and then Major) William Earl Barber received the Congressional Medal of Honor from President Truman on 20 August 1952 in Washington, D.C., for his leadership of F Company in its five days and nights of battle against the CCF at Toktong Pass.[21] Barber, 30 years old in 1950, had entered the Marine Corps as a private. At Iwo Jima in World War II he earned the Purple Heart and the Silver Star when he disregarded his own wounds and rescued two wounded comrades from enemy-held territory. After being relieved at Toktong Pass on 2 December when Davis's 1st Battalion arrived there, Barber was subsequently evacuated because of wounds and spent two months in a hospital in Japan. Captain Barber was a handsome, pleasant-looking athletic young man with a wife and two children, a fine example of an American soldier—brave, experienced, and a dauntless leader of men.

Three months after Captain Barber received his Congressional Medal of Honor from President Truman, the latter presented one also to Lt. Col. Raymond G. Davis for his leadership and outstanding performance of duty in leading his battalion in its overland night march to the relief of Fox Company. Davis, then 37 years old, with two small sons and a daughter, was a dauntless battalion commander.[22]

Davis Takes Over Advance from Toktong Pass

About 1 P.M. in the early afternoon of 3 December, the lone lead tank and part of G Company, 3rd Battalion, 5th Marines, arrived at the top of Toktong Pass and met F Company, 7th Marines. It seemed certain now that the breakout from Yudam-ni would succeed.

Lieutenant Colonel Davis received orders to take over the lead with his 1st Battalion, 7th Marines, from Taplett's 3rd Battalion, 5th Marines, and clear the rest of the way into Hagaru-ri. He in turn ordered Captain Barber to remain in his F Company perimeter for the time being. Davis formed his battalion with A Company in the lead, followed by B Company, H Company, and C Company. The lone tank again took the lead. Davis's men came down from their hills and fell in behind it. Davis conferred only briefly with Taplett at the pass before he resumed the advance toward Hagaru-ri. The truck column following behind Taplett's infantry stopped at the pass to receive the wounded men of Davis's and Taplett's battalions. The wounded of F Company, 7th Marines, were so numerous that some of the wounded already in the trucks but able to walk had to dismount to make room for the F Company wounded. The wounded who left the vehicles at the pass trudged and hobbled painfully the rest of the way to Hagaru-ri.

DRYSDALE FORCE FAILS TO MEET BREAKOUT COLUMN

Knowing a little after noon on 3 December that the Marine breakout column from Yudam-ni had reached and secured the top of Toktong Pass and should be starting downhill from it during the afternoon, the Marine command in Hagaru-ri decided to send a tank-infantry force toward it in an effort to clear the road and meet it during the afternoon. Lt. Col. Douglas B. Drysdale commanded this force, which included a platoon of his 41st Commando, Royal Marines, and an attached platoon of the Army 31st Tank Company, led by Capt. Robert E. Drake, the tank company commander. Lieutenant Colonel Drysdale rode with Drake in the latter's command tank; the Royal Marine commandos rode on the tank decks. The hastily assembled force left Hagaru-ri about 4:30 P.M. and proceeded west on the Yudam-ni road about three road miles from Hagaru-ri, where it came to a stop just east of the village of Sohung-ni. Enemy positions high up on both sides of the road directed long-range fire at the tank column. Drysdale's commandos left the tanks a few times to make short sorties into areas near the road but encountered no enemy. The enemy forces were so high on the slopes of the mountain mass leading to Toktong Pass that they could not have been dislodged except by a major effort involving far more troops than Drysdale had with him, and even then it would have taken a long time to accomplish. Drysdale turned the column around just before dark and returned to Hagaru-ri. There were no casualties among the commandos and the Army tankers. The Drysdale sortie was poorly planned and started too late in the day. It accomplished nothing.[23]

THE FIRST MARINES REACH HAGARU-RI, 3 DECEMBER

Meanwhile, Davis's 1st Battalion, 7th Marines, now leading the convoy down from Toktong Pass in the afternoon of 3 December, had little trouble. The worst was over for them. Constant, effective close-support air cover overhead was a big factor in its relatively easy advance. In one incident that told much of Chinese conditions, one of his flank patrols came upon a few Chinese soldiers so cold and exhausted that they had abandoned their weapons and were huddled together for warmth.

During 3 December the middle and rear parts of the breakout force had become somewhat scrambled, and there was some intermingling of artillery and service troops and miscellaneous vehicles with the infantry. Every halt of the column, for whatever reason, seemed to increase this disorganization. During daylight, however, with observation planes constantly overhead warning of enemy positions ahead and with Marine fighter planes attacking enemy positions in front of and on both flanks of the road column, the infantry units were able to climb the flanking hills and clear the enemy from them temporarily. Then the vehicle column, with its wounded and the artillery pieces, passed through the protective sleeve.

At midnight of 3 December the bulk of the artillery came over the pass. Lieutenant Colonel Taplett placed G and H companies of his 3rd Battalion, 5th Marines, in the column there for its security. About an hour later, near 1 A.M. on 4 December, the rest of the 3rd Battalion joined the road column. Lieutenant Colonel Roise's 2nd Battalion, 5th Marines, which until now had served as rear guard, passed through Lt. Col. William F. Harris's 3rd Battalion, 7th Marines, which became the rear guard for the last leg of the movement from the pass to Hagaru-ri.

Up front at the head of the breakout column, Lt. Col. Frederick R. Dowsett, executive officer of the 7th Marine Regiment, was with the Weapons Company and Headquarters and Service troops of the 1st Battalion, 7th Marines, as they neared the Hagaru-ri perimeter. All the rifle companies of the 1st Battalion had been left behind at key points to control the last two and one-half miles of road into the Hagaru-ri perimeter. Behind this advance party came the walking wounded, and then the trucks carrying the litter cases and the more severely wounded. Some hundreds of yards from the roadblock at the Hagaru-ri perimeter, the oncoming convoy halted. Those in the vehicles who thought they could walk the remaining distance got out, joined the other wounded already walking behind the point, and formed in column, and then the whole column resumed its forward movement. The beat of the shoepacs on the frozen ground was in cadence as the first Marines from Yudam-ni joined those cheering comrades who had gathered at the Hagaru-ri roadblock to meet them. The time was about 7:35 P.M., 3 December.[24] More than 20 hours passed before the tail of the Yudam-ni column entered the Hagaru-ri perimeter. The arrival of the advance at Hagaru-ri was not the end of the breakout story. Most of the column and all the escorting troops were still strung out on the road for many miles, and there was much fighting still ahead of them before they reached Hagaru-ri and temporary safety.

CHINESE ATTACK YUDAM-NI COLUMN, 4 DECEMBER

Although there were repeated instances of small and scattered Chinese attempts to break up the convoy's progress during the night of 3 December, no serious difficulty developed until after midnight. The troops of the 3rd Battalion, 5th Marines, and of the 4th Battalion, 11th Marines, had entered Hagaru-ri, except for Lieutenant Colonel Taplett and a small body of the 3rd Battalion that remained at Toktong Pass until midnight. Meanwhile, the 1st and 2nd battalions, 5th Marines, took positions east of the pass to protect the vehicular column as it passed through.

All might have continued to go well had it not been that the prime movers pulling the big 155-mm howitzers ran out of fuel at 2 A.M., 4 December, east of the pass. Gasoline had been air-dropped for the trucks, but the prime movers received no diesel fuel, which had been requested at Sinhung-ni, on the west side of the pass. The infantry ahead of the prime movers continued on, unaware of the stalled howitzers. Maj. Angus J. Cronin, in charge of the 4th Battalion, 11th Marine (artillery) vehicular column, including the stalled howitzers, had to round up truck drivers and some artillerymen to beat off a Chinese platoon that initially struck at the stalled artillery pieces.

Capt. O. R. Lodge moved the howitzers off the road to clear it for everything behind them. Lieutenant Colonel Taplett, on his way down from the pass, arrived at the scene. Lieutenant Colonels Stevens and Roise of the 1st and 2nd battalions, 5th Marines, also arrived there. The three battalion commanders of the 5th Marines consulted on the situation. Roise had at hand a platoon of E Company, and Taplett had small elements of the 3rd Battalion. These troops attacked the Chinese position overlooking the road, from which they were placing fire on the stalled convoy. At this juncture, the Chinese succeeded in blowing a small bridge just ahead, thus creating a second roadblock. Enemy fire also seemed to increase at this time. It appears that Chinese reinforcements were arriving to help the initially small force that began the fight. A real threat of Chinese success in creating havoc in the Marine withdrawal now seemed in the making. Two truck drivers were killed by enemy fire while engineers worked to repair the damaged bridge.

A number of truck drivers, including some whose trucks were pulling 105-mm howitzers, gave way to momentary panic in a dash for safety by driving their trucks off the road and across the small ice-bound stream. Officers present pursued some of these men and took vigorous steps to halt the incipient panic. CWO Allen Carlson of the 1st Battalion, 11th Marines, took a leading role in this. He also set up a 105-mm howitzer on the road and directed its fire against the Chinese. Lieutenant Colonel Taplett directed the fire of a 75-mm recoilless rifle. Another howitzer was put into action, as well as a heavy machine gun. This battle around the 155-mm howitzers lasted from 2 A.M. until well after daylight, when air strikes enabled the platoon of E Company, 5th Marines, to overrun the Chinese fireblock position at 8:30 A.M. on 4 December. Other elements of Roise's 2nd Battalion attacked and cleared Chinese from high ground on the left of the road. The convoy now moved on. The eight 155-mm howitzers and their prime movers had to be left behind. This was the most important equipment loss of the Yudam-ni breakout. A 105-mm howitzer had been lost earlier when it skidded off the road. Later in the morning, the 41st Commando, Royal Marines, made an effort from Hagaru-ri to reach the howitzers and rescue them, but the attempt failed. The abandoned howitzers were subsequently destroyed by a Marine air strike, since there was no hope of retrieving them.[25]

A close-up view of this chaotic battle around the stalled howitzers has been left by Cpl. Michael Houston, Message Center chief, Headquarters Battery, 4th Battalion, 11th Marines. His experience was similar to many others there. Houston graduated early from Thomas Jefferson High School, Richmond, Virginia, and shortly after his seventeenth birthday he enlisted in the Marine Corps for a three-year term. He sailed from the West Coast on 15 August 1950 and made the Inchon landing on 15 September. His three-year enlistment was up on 6 November 1950, when his unit was moving toward the Chosin Reservoir. He was in the Marine withdrawal from Yudam-ni, knowing full well that, as rear-echelon artilleryman, he was lucky, compared to the infantry. He went out in a radio jeep. His two assistants became temporary infantrymen. Houston's radio jeep soon had a dozen bullet holes in it, and the radio became useless. He wrote, "There were times when I thought that none of us would ever get through to Hagaru-ri." Sometime in the early hours of 4 December, word came back up the column that the last roadblock had been broken and they were going through. About 3:30 A.M. a liaison officer came along and said they could take it easy—it was only two more miles into Hagaru-ri. He said the road was clear.

Houston obtained a relief driver for his jeep and crawled into his sleeping bag. He fell asleep in seconds. A few minutes later he awakened to the sound of bugles. Huge red flares lighted up the road just in front of him. Men were screaming in pain. The driver of his jeep was missing. He tried, but could not get the other man in the jeep and in his sleeping bag to wake up. Houston struggled out of his sleeping bag, only to find that his right boot was missing. A mortar shell hit near his jeep. His driver now ran past the jeep yelling for everyone to get out—Chinese were on the other side of the road. Houston and two others dove headfirst over the road embankment and landed in a pile on a frozen stream. The jeep had stopped on a bridge—it was the second roadblock mentioned earlier. One of the other two men in the pile was badly wounded. Houston tried to lift him to dry land. Houston then saw a Chinese soldier coming under the bridge toward them. He told the wounded Marine to play dead, and he started to move away. The Chinese soldier came on and caught Houston and two others without weapons—only six to eight yards away. Houston and the others stood paralyzed. Then the Chinese soldier pulled the trigger on his Thompson submachine gun. The other two men fell.

Houston was off running. He got away and finally fell on his face in the partially frozen stream. He got soaking wet; his clothes started to freeze on him.

He crawled away and had gone only a short distance when someone in the darkness challenged him with the words, "Are you a Marine?" He answered that he was and soon joined another Marine, who turned out to be a sergeant from K Battery. He had an M-1 rifle. After discussing the situation, the two of them decided they had better stay hidden in the reeds until daylight. They piled snow around that helped to make them invisible in the darkness. About 5 A.M. a wounded Marine from a 105-mm howitzer battalion joined them. Half an hour later they heard Chinese talking to each other only 25 yards away. After a short time, the Chinese left the vicinity but opened fire on something. A machine gun answered the Chinese fire, traversing and sweeping the area. Bullets cut the reeds over the heads of Houston and his two companions. They heard the Chinese move off, and soon the American machine-gun fire stopped.

About 6:45 A.M. it began to get light. In a few minutes a Marine sergeant stumbled into their hiding place carrying a wounded corpsman on his back. The Marine with the M-1 almost shot the sergeant. The little group, now numbering five, decided that American vehicles and troops were still on the nearby road. They decided to make a run for the road and took off, yelling as loud as they could not to fire at them. They got to the road and found a terrific firefight going on with the enemy on the other side of the road. This continued until about 7:30 A.M., when the Chinese departed, apparently afraid of being caught by an air strike in early daylight.

Tractors now started clearing the road of vehicles. Wounded were gathered up and loaded on the vehicles that had not been destroyed in the battle. Only then did Houston become aware of a strange feeling in his left leg. He saw that his trousers were torn and caked with frozen blood. His knee had puffed up to the size of "a football" and was getting stiff. Houston crawled up on the trailer of a gun as it started to move. He described the scene at that moment:

> What a mess the road was! About half our guns and vehicles were ditched off the road and dead Chinese were all over the place. I didn't count them but there were plenty. I saw my own jeep in the creek where I had first started out a few hours before. The jeep had a huge hole in it and was burning like mad.
>
> We made it back to Hagaru without too much trouble and the next morning I left for Japan. I don't know what the final outcome was. I guess it will be a long time before I find out just what we did lose. However, I know we got it bad.

In Japan, Houston found that one of his buddies in the reeds was also in the hospital, shot six times. Michael Houston, 20 years old, was lucky. He came through the last major fight in the Yudam-ni breakout with nothing more than an injured knee and three frozen toes.[26]

Marine Breakout Completed, 4 December

After the battle around the eight 155-mm howitzers during the morning of 4 December at the eastern side of Toktong Pass, the Marine column had no further trouble in moving on into Hagaru-ri. Air cover gave it security. The last unit of the rear guard, the 3rd Battalion, 7th Marines, entered Hagaru-ri at 2 P.M. on 4 December. This ended the four-day fighting breakout from Yudam-ni. The Yudam-ni Marine column brought 1,500 casualties to Hagaru-ri, a third of them nonbattle casualties, mostly frostbite cases. As Montross and Canzona, authors of the Marine Corps's official history of their part in the Chosin Reservoir campaign, put it, "It had taken the head of the column about 59 hours to cover the 14 miles, and the rear units 79 hours."[27] For some it meant an average of five and one-half hours to the mile. It was not a footrace.

Lieutenant Colonel Taplett's 3rd Battalion, 5th Marines, had led the way out of Yudam-ni, fought the battles at the point of the column, and cleared the hills commanding the road up to Toktong Pass. It had performed in the best tradition of fighting men. The battalion's three rifle companies—G, H, and I—on 1 December had a combined effective strength of 437 men as they started to vacate their defensive positions at Yudam-ni. After they reached Hagaru-ri on 4 December, they counted a combined effective strength of only 194 men, a loss of 243—more than half their number. I Company had taken the greatest loss, falling from 143 men on 1 December to 41 men on 4 December. These losses were combined battle and nonbattle casualties (mostly frostbite cases). These 243 casualties compared to 144 casualties the same units suffered in the four days of fighting at Yudam-ni from 27 to 30 November.[28] These figures give some idea of the nature of the breakout fighting. The Marines had to defeat the Chinese to reach Hagaru-ri.

It would be hard to overestimate the importance of the Marine air wing and 5th Air Force support to the ground troops during the breakout from Yudam-ni to Hagaru-ri and to the less successful effort of the 7th Infantry Division elements on the east side of the reservoir. On 1 December there were 96 shore-based and 184 embarked (carrier) planes available in the Hungnam area, for a total of 280 to support the troops in the vicinity of the reservoir. On that day, three fighter squadrons, at Wonsan, Marine Air Group 12, moved to Yonpo to be closer to the scene of combat. The next day, 2 December, was the last day the carriers offshore split their effort between the east and west sides of the peninsula. Two-thirds of the air strength went to the Chosin area on the second. That night planes were sent to carry out night-heckler missions on the Yudam-ni road. On 3 December the 5th Air Force sent its entire force of light bombers to the Chosin Reservoir area. Marine aircraft made 45 flights using 197 planes in close-support missions that same day. The next day, 4 December, there were 238 aircraft in 68 flights in close support of the ground troops. That morning a flight from the carrier *Leyte* sighted and attacked an estimated 1,000 CCF at the northern end of Chosin Reservoir. Later in the day another flight from the *Leyte* saw troops moving south on all trails. These CCF must have been among the reinforcements that General Sung had called up from Linchiang on the Yalu.[29]

On 4 December Maj. Gen. Field Harris, commander of the 1st Marine Aircraft Wing and the Tactical Air Command, X Corps, flew to Hagaru-ri to watch the Marines come in from Yudam-ni in their successful breakout fight. That night he sent a dispatch to Rear Adm. Edward C. Ewen, commander of Fast Carrier Task Force 77, saying the Marine breakout from Yudam-ni could not have succeeded without the extensive air support they had received in the past few days. He asked for all possible air support in the days ahead, when the breakout to the coast would be continued from Hagaru-ri. He said he would plan to put an air cover of 24 close-support aircraft over the withdrawing column from Hagaru-ri from dawn to dusk, and night hecklers over the downhill road at night. All surplus planes would be placed to the front, on both flanks, and at the rear of the column. From 4 December on, the main mission of Fast Carrier Task Force 77 officially was to support the withdrawal of the 1st Marine Division.[30]

One of the few Corsairs to be shot down by enemy fire in the Chosin operation occurred on 4 December as the last of the Marines from Yudam-ni were arriving at the Hagaru-ri perimeter. Enemy antiaircraft fire hit Lt. (jg) Jessie Brown's plane, and he crashed on the ice of the reservoir. His plane burst into flames, and he was trapped in the burning wreckage. A squadron mate from Fighter Squadron 32, from USS *Leyte*, Lt. (jg) Thomas Jerome Hudner, Jr., maneuvered around the downed plane. He saw that Brown was trapped in the wreckage and could not get out by his own efforts, even if he were still alive. Hudner crash-landed his own Corsair, wheels up, near Brown's burning plane. With only his hands as tools, Hudner tried to pack snow in the fuselage to keep the flames away from the pilot and tried to pull him free. He failed in this effort and ran back to his own plane and radioed for an ax and a fire extinguisher. Meanwhile the Air Control Center at Hagaru-ri received a message that a Navy plane was down on the ice. Capt. Wallace Blatt, a helicopter pilot, took off to go to the crash site. En route he received messages from Navy planes flying over the crash site that an ax and a fire extinguisher were needed. Blatt returned to Hagaru-ri, where he got both, and then took off again for the crash site. He landed and joined Hudner in an effort to put out the flames and rescue Brown from the crushed cockpit. They failed and had to get out of the way when the flames reached the downed plane's fuel tanks. Hudner's devotion to the plight of a downed comrade and his risky effort to save his life earned him the Congressional Medal of Honor.[31]

Redeployment of close air support took place as more than 10,000 men gathered at Hagaru-ri and prepared to continue withdrawal to Koto-ri, and hence down Funchilin Pass to the coast. One Corsair squadron flew to Itami, Japan, to embark on the light carrier, *Bataan.* The day before, the 5th Air Force fighter-bombers evacuated themselves to South Korea. The arrival of the big carrier *Princeton* off the coast near Hung-nam on 5 December in a support role for the Hagaru-ri breakout effort, which was to start on 6 December, more than made up for the loss of the fighter-bombers.

The buildup of air support in the Hungnam-Hamhung area for the X Corps in northeast Korea increasingly became carrier based as the withdrawal from the Chosin Reservoir area proceeded. On 10 December shore-based aircraft numbered 96, and those embarked on carriers numbered 184, for a total of 280 aircraft. All the troops still alive in the Chosin area had successfully withdrawn to the Hamhung-Hungnam perimeter by the close of 11 December. By 16 December there were no land-based support aircraft left in northeast Korea. But there were 318 carrier-based planes supporting the evacuation of X Corps. On 23 December there were 398 carrier-based planes supporting the final stages of the evacuation, which was completed the next day. At its peak, Fast Carrier Task Force 77 used four attack carriers, one battleship, two cruisers, and 22 destroyers in covering the final phase of the X Corps evacuation from Hungnam.[32]

Until 2 December the 5th Air Force officially had been in control of air support for the ground troops in the Chosin area. On 2 December, however, Maj. Gen. Field Harris, commanding the 1st Marine Air Wing, received responsibility for providing close air support for the X Corps. This change was made to give more complete control to General Almond and the X Corps in use of the close-support aircraft available in the planned withdrawal from Hagaru-ri to the coast. There were three squadrons of Marine Air Groups 12 operating from Wonsan, two squadrons of Marine Air Group 33 from Yonpo, and one squadron from a CVE carrier offshore. The carrier-based planes increased in number from that time on, until they provided the total air support for the troops ashore. X Corps remained in control of the 1st Air Wing until 11 December, when the troops from

the Chosin Reservoir and along the MSR southward had been successfully withdrawn into the Wonsan-Hungnam perimeter at the coast, preparatory to evacuation by sea.[33]

In the Chosin Reservoir battles and the role the 1st Marine Air Wing
played in giving superb ground support to the Marine infantry, General
Almond, the X Corps commander, found all the evidence he needed to
become completely convinced that the Marine air-support doctrine for
its infantry ground troops was far superior to that provided by the Army
through the Fifth Air Force. He never failed to laud it and to compare
it favorably with what he had for his Army units. He wanted the same
kind of support for all his troops in X Corps as that given the 1st Marine
Division. This led to heated disputes with the Fifth Air Force and the
United States Air Force headquarters all the way back to Washington.
General Almond never ceased to favor the Marine doctrine of close air
support for its ground forces and to urge its adoption by the Army.

The flow of troops by air was not all in one direction. During the first
five days of December, 537 replacements were flown into Hagaru-ri,
equipped with cold-weather clothing and ready to take their places in
combat units for the breakout fight. Each of the three Marine regiments —
the 1st, 5th, and 7th — received portions of these replacements into their
ranks at Hagaru-ri. Most of these men had been wounded in the Inchon-
Seoul operation in September. Now recovered, they were returning to their
units, fit for duty.

After the last of the Marines from Yudam-ni arrived at the Hagaru-ri
perimeter in the afternoon of 4 December, General Smith decided that
the men of the 5th and 7th Marines were badly in need of a short period
of recuperation. He decided they must have some rest before the withdrawal continued toward Koto-ri and the coast. Their condition, and the
necessity to evacuate all wounded from Hagaru-ri by air before the troops
left Hagaru-ri, caused General Smith to set 6 December as the date the
withdrawal from Hagaru-ri would begin. Almond concurred in this date.
The last of the wounded at Hagaru-ri were evacuated by air on 5 December. Planning for the withdrawal went on feverishly at Hagaru-ri on
5 December. Orders for the general organization of the withdrawal were
completed and issued on that date.[34]

11

BREAKOUT FROM HAGARU-RI, 6–7 DECEMBER

The 1st Marine Division completed planning on 5 December for the breakout movement from Hagaru-ri to Koto-ri, 11 miles distant. It was the first leg of the withdrawal to the coast. On that day, accordingly, Maj. Gen. Oliver P. Smith issued 1st Marine Division Operational Order 25-50, which set forth the plan by which the division and attached Army troops would fight their way to the sea. In the afternoon he called together all the unit commanders at Hagaru-ri and went over the details of the order with them. The withdrawal was planned as a fighting attack southward.

The 7th Marine Regiment was to lead off out of Hagaru-ri at first light on 6 December. The 5th Marine Regiment was to hold the Hagaru-ri perimeter until the 7th Marines and all divisional troops and transport had cleared it, guarding the rear. Then after the 7th Marines had made progress in clearing the way, it was to follow. The hills flanking the road were to be seized, and enemy-held roadblocks overcome, before the long motorized trains at Hagaru-ri were to leave the perimeter and move southward. There was to be no running of the gauntlet. Hard fighting was expected. It was well known to all that Chinese troops held strong points in force along the route southward.

The operational order divided all personnel and vehicles not part of the 7th and 5th Marines into two divisional trains, each commanded by a lieutenant colonel. Only disabled personnel, radio operators, and drivers of vehicles would be allowed to ride. Everyone else would walk at the sides of the vehicles and act as a close-in screen guarding them. This procedure would serve several purposes: it would help to protect the trains from close enemy attack; it would reduce casualties if vehicles were hit by enemy mortar or artillery fires; and it would reduce frostbite by compelling the men to be active. Any vehicle that broke down or was disabled was to be pushed to the side of the road at once, and if not repaired, the last units to pass were to destroy it. When halts were made for any reason, personnel alongside the vehicles were to form a perimeter defense for each motorized serial unit.

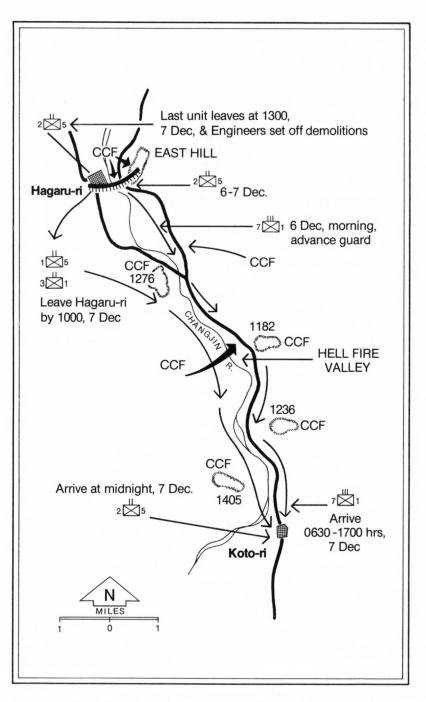

MAP 14. 1st Marine Division and Army units' withdrawal from Hagaru-ri to Koto-ri, 6–7 December.

Lt. Col. Charles L. Banks commanded Train No. 1, which was part of the 7th Marine advance. Lt. Col. Harry T. Milne commanded Train No. 2, which was to accompany the 5th Marine Regiment. All troops were to carry two days' rations—one day on their person, the second in their organic transportation. All supplies and equipment at Hagaru-ri that was excess to needs or could not be taken out was to be destroyed by unit commanders.

Col. Lewis B. Puller's 1st Marine Regiment was to continue to hold Koto-ri and Chinhung-ni, holding these essential stepping stones for the movement to the coast. Thus, for the first leg of the movement, the 1st Marines held Koto-ri, the 5th Marines held Hagaru-ri, while the 7th Marines tried to open the 11 miles of enemy-held ground between the two places. Strong air cover would fly over the column and attack enemy positions during daylight hours. Artillery would give protective fire from both ends of the 11-mile corridor, as well as from a designated point about midway between them when artillery in the 7th Marine column had advanced that far. Tanks were interspersed in both regimental trains, and a platoon of tanks was to lead the advance. More than 14,000 troops and more than 1,200 vehicles were involved in the withdrawal from Hagaru-ri.

A provisional Army battalion of 490 men, 385 of them survivors from the 7th Division's Task Force Faith, commanded by Lt. Col. Berry K. Anderson, 31st Infantry, was attached to the 7th Marines for the breakout. Lt. Col. Thomas B. Drysdale's British Royal Commandos and Lt. Col. Thomas L. Ridge's 3rd Battalion, 1st Marines, were attached to the 5th Marines.[1]

During the four days from 2 to 6 December at Hagaru-ri, Lt. Col. Berry K. Anderson, the senior officer of the 31st RCT, organized the men of the Army combat team into a two-battalion provisional regiment. The men of the 3rd Battalion, 31st Infantry, he placed under the command of Maj. Carl G. Witte and called this group the 3rd Battalion. The men of the 1st Battalion, 32nd Infantry, he placed under the command of Maj. Robert E. Jones and called it the 1st Battalion. The artillerymen of the 57th Field Artillery Battalion who reached Hagaru-ri were divided equally and attached to Jones's and Witte's battalions. Each of these battalions also had from 50 to 100 ROK troops from the KATUSA originally assigned to them. General Smith attached Anderson's Army provisional regiment to the 7th Marine Regiment, and its commander, Colonel Litzenberg, gave Anderson's men the mission of extending the left flank of the Marine point in the breakout on 6 December from Hagaru-ri to Koto-ri.[2]

Jones divided his provisional 1st Battalion into three companies, with 1st Lt. C. G. Smith commanding A Company; Captain Thackus commanding a second company; and 2nd Lt. James C. Barnes, Jr., the forward observer of A Battery, 48th Field Artillery Battalion, who had accompanied the 1st Battalion, 32nd Infantry, to Chosin, commanding the third company.

Witte, similarly, divided his 3rd Battalion into three companies. Capt. George A. Rasula commanded I Company; Capt. Robert J. Kitz commanded K Company; and Lieutenant Boyer commanded L Company. Rasula said his company was made up entirely of artillerymen, with three artillery officers as his platoon leaders.[3]

In preparing for the breakout, the X Corps had organized the largest daily airlift of wounded casualties from Hagaru-ri on 5 December. The attack south would be difficult, and it was important that the troops not be encumbered by large numbers of casualties at the outset. During the day, 38 sorties of C-47 aircraft evacuated 1,580 casualties to Yonpo airfield, near Wonsan on the coast.[4]

ALMOND AND X CORPS COORDINATE EFFORTS

As the X Corps and the 1st Marine Division were preparing plans to withdraw from Hagaru-ri, the CCF, in one of their numerous puzzling acts, released 27 wounded American prisoners (none of whom was an officer) during the night of 3 December at the reservoir. The next day, 4 December, General Almond flew to Hagaru-ri and conferred with General Smith and his staff in the afternoon on their breakout plan. Almond told them he had mustered the full strength of the corps and the Air Force to assist in the expected ordeal. One of the greatest concentrations of air power in the Korean War would be in close support of the ground troops. Marine planes at Yonpo airfield could make about 100 sorties daily, planes from the *Badoeng Strait* 30 more, and planes from Navy fast carriers *Leyte*, *Valley Forge*, *Philippine Sea*, and *Princeton* had abandoned interdiction and deep-support missions for the time being and would contribute at least 100 more sorties daily. On the morning of 5 December the *Princeton*, escorted by four destroyers, would arrive off the coast as part of Task Force 77 and be ready to launch its planes. The US Fifth Air Force and Australian fighter-bombers and medium and heavy bombers would also join the breakout battles. Altogether, the Marine TACPs at Hagaru-ri could control an estimated 248 sorties. Also, beginning on 6 December, the new large Mosquito plane would be over the Marine breakout column to observe the action below and would be capable of better communication than the Mosquitos previously in use.[5] Almond also readied the Army's 3rd Infantry Division to cover the withdrawal south of Chinhung-ni and to protect the coastal area.

The massive air strength mobilized to help in the breakout effort of the 7th Marines on the morning of 6 December was to be used at the same time to support the 5th Marines at Hagaru-ri in a major attack on the morning of the 6th against the Chinese on East Ridge. The CCF still held the commanding ground there, and from it they could threaten the withdrawal and possibly critically slow the 7th Marines in opening a passage southward.

THE CCF CALL UP RESERVES FROM THE YALU

Generals Almond and Smith knew that elements of at least seven CCF divisions were in the vicinity of the withdrawal route. They had been identified in combat in the past week and a half. New intelligence indicated that General Sung had ordered two additional divisions, the 76th and 77th of the CCF 26th Army, which had been in reserve at Linchiang on the north side of the Yalu, to move hurriedly south to join in the Chosin battle. Sung had overestimated the capability of his troops at the reservoir to destroy the 1st Marine Division and X Corps troops there when he launched his attack on 27 November. Now, belatedly, he recognized that his huge losses necessitated use of his other four divisions if he was to win the battle. But it would take at least two to three days of forced foot marches to bring his reinforcements to the scene of battle. As it turned out, only two of them ever arrived in time to take part in the battle. The 78th and 88th divisions, following the 76th and 77th, did not arrive until the X Corps troops had withdrawn to the coast. Had these four divisions been close to Chosin and quickly available for reinforcements, the outcome might have been different. This misconception as to the possible need of the reserve divisions on short notice must be considered a Chinese mistake of major importance.

It is not known precisely when General Sung ordered the divisions of the 26th Army southward from their reserve position at Linchiang, but it must have been about 1 December. By then Sung must have realized that his 20th and 27th armies had been either defeated or stalemated. The first recorded contact with elements of the 26th Army was on 5 December at Hagaru-ri.[6]

At midnight of 5 December the 5th Marines relieved other elements of the 1st Marine Division for the defense of Hagaru-ri, and with Lieutenant Colonel Ridge's 3rd Battalion, 1st Marines, attached, Lt. Col. Raymond L. Murray assumed that task. General Smith and his 1st Marine Division command group remained at Hagaru-ri as action started on the morning of 6 December. Later in the day, upon receiving a favorable report from Colonel Litzenberg on 7th Marine progress, Smith flew to Koto-ri about 2 P.M. and established his Forward CP there.[7]

LITZENBERG LEADS BREAKOUT ATTACK, 6 DECEMBER

Litzenberg's 7th Marines attacked south from Hagaru-ri on 6 December with 300 artillerymen from the 11th Marines and Anderson's 490 Army men, most of them survivors from east of Chosin. He had about 2,200 men for the breakout fight. He disposed his forces so that Lockwood's 2nd Battalion, with a tank platoon in the lead, would be astride the road. On the right (west) of it, Davis's 1st Battalion would clear the ground to the Changjin River. Anderson's composite Army battalion from the 7th Infantry Division had the same mission along the high ground left (east) of the road. Behind the 2nd Battalion, the regimental train would follow on the road as fast as enemy were cleared from its path and flanks. Behind the trains, Harris's 3rd Battalion came next along the road in reserve, with one company on the flanks of the vehicles. And finally, the artillery and Division Train No. 1 completed the 7th Marine column.

Lieutenant Colonel Davis had his 1st Battalion in column at 4:30 A.M. on 6 December, ready to start his attack. First Lt. Kurcaba's B Company led off toward the first objective, high ground southeast about a mile away near the village of Tonae-ri. There was no opposition. Near the village, the company came upon a platoon of 24 Chinese asleep in their foxholes. It killed 17 of them.[8]

From the Marine roadblock at the south end of the defense perimeter, the 2nd Platoon of D Company tanks, 1st Tank Battalion, led off with F Company, 2nd Battalion, as advance guard at 6:30 A.M. Almost immediately three rounds from a 3.5-inch bazooka hit the lead tank. Chinese on high ground to the east of the road, however, allowed F Company to pass unmolested for about a mile. Then they opened up with heavy fire on the remainder of the 2nd Battalion. Fog prevented air strikes at first, but when it lifted, aircraft struck the enemy position. Only a coordinated attack of several hours by E and D companies and the tank platoon, together with the air strikes and artillery fire, finally reduced the CCF position sufficiently to enable the column to proceed. Enemy on the crest were not wholly subdued until midafternoon by D Company of the 5th Marines. In this fight of the 2nd Battalion, 7th Marines, to clear enemy from the first contested position on the withdrawal route, Maj. Webb D. Sawyer, battalion executive officer, and 1st Lt. Robert E. Bey, commanding officer of E Company, were wounded. First Lt. John M. Dunne, the only officer still with F Company from the Toktong Pass battles of a few days earlier and now commanding officer of the company, was killed.

After this initial strong enemy opposition had been overcome, F Company and the tank platoon resumed their advance. Two and a half miles south of Hagaru-ri, enemy fire again stopped the column. Aerial observers could not locate the enemy, although some of the American infantry on the far right could see them clearly. The Marine 2nd Battalion, supported by artillery fire, attacked the enemy fireblock position east of the road. The 1st Battalion, west of the road, had frequent enemy contact but no serious opposition. The 3rd Battalion, in the rear along the road behind the motor convoy, had no enemy action at this time.

The Marine point in the breakout in this first action had run into enemy machine-gun fire from the left side of the road just outside the Hagaru-ri perimeter. Tanks moved up to the front of the column and began firing on the enemy position. This action lasted for about four hours.

The road column had halted about 7:30, an hour after the point had started down the road, and it did not resume movement until 11 A.M. After the column had progressed about two miles, Lieutenant Colonel Anderson committed Witte's 3rd Battalion on the left flank, to extend the Marine flank on that side of the road. He held Jones's 1st Battalion on the road with the motor column.

Anderson sent Rasula's company to the left to help the Marines. The company first built up a base of fire on a high ridge that was within the Hagaru-ri perimeter. Air strikes continuously hit the Chinese who were holding up the road advance, and Rasula called in 4.2-inch Marine mortar fire. After the air strikes had ended, Rasula sent one of his platoons forward in attack on the enemy position. The air strikes and the mortar fire, with supporting machine-gun fire, were so effective that Rasula said his platoon captured 115 Chinese soldiers without losing a man in the attack. He had four men wounded at his base-of-fire position. In this action Rasula had the usual trouble with his ROK troops. They had to be driven into firing positions and held there virtually at bayonet point.

In related action during the early afternoon, Lieutenant Boyer's company had a hard fight with the Chinese in which Boyer was killed. One of his platoon leaders, Lt. Roland Skilton, was hit in the same action— three enemy machine-gun slugs ripped into his stomach. Some men in his platoon carried him down to the road, where he was placed in a Marine ambulance to be evacuated to the Hagaru-ri airstrip. He was carried missing in action in the Army records for a time, as he was never heard from again. His comrades who placed him in the ambulance said he looked very bad at the time.[9] Apparently he died shortly thereafter, and in the hectic situation records on him were lost or never completed.

After this action had cleared the Chinese from the high ground on the left immediately south of the Hagaru-ri perimeter, the road column advanced, and once started again, it moved rapidly south. The Army 3rd Battalion troops caught up with the road column about 4 P.M., where another enemy roadblock on the left of the road had stopped it again. This time an enemy machine gun, protected by a group of enemy riflemen, was causing the trouble.

Lieutenant Colonel Anderson now committed Jones's 1st Battalion to relieve the 3rd Battalion in attacking this fireblock. Jones took his battalion around the Marine point's left flank to build a base of fire there. Lieutenant Smith led the attack with his A Company, and Lieutenant Thackus then extended the Army line farther to the left of Smith's platoon. A joint attack by Lieutenant Smith's and Lieutenant Barnes's platoons overran the enemy position. Barnes played a dominant role in reducing this position. After the enemy machine-gun fire pinned down his platoon, he raced across about 300 yards of open ground, fully exposed to enemy automatic fire, until he reached a bit of cover near the enemy emplacement. From there he destroyed the enemy machine-gun crew with grenades and rifle fire. Smith's and Barnes's platoons captured about 30 enemy in this action.[10] During the night of 6–7 December, the Army's 1st Battalion remained on the left flank of the Marine advance into Koto-ri.

The Chinese opposition to the 7th Marines during the day was so effective that by dark the road column had progressed only about three miles from Hagaru-ri. Thereafter, CCF opposition increased after close air support had to be discontinued. Expected arrival of fresh CCF reinforcements from the north caused the Marine decision to press ahead through the night, even though it was realized that losses might increase. Throughout the long afternoon, long lines of CCF could be seen on the skyline to the east, moving southward and toward the road. Air strikes did not stop them.

While these encounters were taking place, Major Witte was on the road with his battalion command staff, which consisted of a radioman to operate the jeep radio (which turned out to be dead) and three enlisted men who were messenger runners. Lt. Hodges S. Escue also joined him. At times he also had one Marine and a ROK and perhaps a couple of other soldiers with him. Lieutenant Kitz and K Company were behind him on the road, and a couple of Marine tanks had somehow become mixed up in his group and were following immediately behind him after dark. The night was cold, with a temperature estimated to be 20 degrees below zero; two to three inches of snow lay on the ground, and the moon was out.

The Marine point and the Army troops on the left were some distance ahead as Witte's party approached a stone fence that ran down toward a small house that stood on the left side of the road. The house had the usual stone wall around it and its small yard. As Witte's group reached the point where the stone wall came down to the road, an enemy soldier behind it threw a grenade that hit on the road among them. It sputtered and zipped around—and proved to be a dud. Witte and the men with him instinctively ran for the stone wall. Several more grenades came over the wall at them. One of them exploded on Witte's left shoulder, knocking him down. He gained his feet and, with the others, rushed to the wall, knocked down a wooden door in the fence, and raked the inside of the little yard with fire. They killed four to six Chinese, Witte estimated later. The enemy grenades, however, in addition to wounding Witte, had killed his pack radio operator. A Marine tank commander hurried up and joined in the fight.

The tank commander helped Witte to the rear deck of his tank on the road. Witte had been trained as a tanker, so he was at home on the tank and took the gunner's seat, where he was warm. The crew gunner had dismounted to walk about and renew the circulation in his feet. While in the gunner's seat, Witte fired the coaxial gun up and down the stone wall to his left. Witte left the tank when the tanks made ready to move forward with the column. He walked the rest of the way into Koto-ri that night. Medical examination disclosed that he had a shattered shoulder blade. He was air-evacuated to Japan. When gangrene developed in the shoulder, he was flown to the Brooke Army Medical Center, San Antonio, Texas.[11]

7TH MARINES' NIGHT BATTLE, 6–7 DECEMBER

About 10 P.M., and approximately five miles south of Hagaru-ri, a CCF machine gun stopped the advance for about two hours. Army tank fire finally knocked out the enemy gun near midnight. Half a mile farther a destroyed bridge caused another halt. Engineers were able to repair this bridge, but when the advance continued at 2 A.M. on 7 December, only a short distance ahead another destroyed bridge caused still another halt. This bridge could not be repaired quickly. A bulldozer cut a bypass around it by 3:30 A.M.

While the bypass around this destroyed bridge was being prepared, the enemy succeeded in partially splitting the stalled road column. A burning hut brightly illuminated a nearby area on the road. Colonel Litzenberg went forward to direct fire on known Chinese positions. At this time, the Chinese scored heavily on the regimental command party. Capt. Donald R. France and 1st Lt. Clarence McGuinness were killed, and Lt. Col. Frederick W. Dowsett, regimental executive officer, was wounded. In the same area, Chaplain Cornelius Griffin went into an ambulance to give comfort to a dying Marine. There, enemy machine-gun fire shattered his jaw, the bullet traversing his face and entering his shoulder. The same stream of bullets killed Sgt. Mathew Caruso, who was at his side.

The 3rd Battalion headquarters, near the rear of the column, received a close-in Chinese attack. The Chinese came to within grenade range in this brief but furious fight around the battalion headquarters section.

Earlier, the 3rd Battalion had replaced the Army Provisional Battalion as left flank security east of the road, where the enemy pressure was greatest, so the headquarters section of the battalion had a heavy responsibility in protecting the rear of the column. M. Sgt. William J. McClung and Maj. Fred Simpson organized the defense there. Two trucks burned and lighted up an area for the Chinese where several wounded Marines lay. Sergeant McClung hurried to the scene and carried out two of the wounded. He was killed while carrying out a third. Second Lt. Minard P. Newton's H Company now arrived from the rear, deployed, and overran the Chinese force making the attack.

The 7th Marine road column now passed through Massacre Valley, where the Royal Commandos, Marines, and Army troops in Task Force Drysdale had taken such a beating on 29 November in trying to get through to the relief of Hagaru-ri. As they passed this part of the road to Koto-ri, Rasula said of the destroyed or stationary vehicles: "It seemed there were hundreds of them of all descriptions, all with a light coat of snow covering them."

Just south of these vehicles the Marine point was fighting another roadblock. Soldiers of the 3rd Battalion, 7th Marines, were now mixed among those of the Army 3rd Battalion. They all sat in the ditches while the roadblock was being reduced.[12]

This roadblock began when a tank stalled sometime after 2 A.M. on 7 December at a bridge bypass and the 2nd Platoon of I Company there came under heavy fire, one of the enemy machine guns sweeping the road. Sgt. Leland Ehrich led a squad in a charge across the road from the west side toward the enemy gun. Enemy fire killed him, but others in the squad wiped out the Chinese gun crew. Finally, at 5:30 A.M., 1st Lt. Robert E. Bey's E Company, now in the lead, made contact with the 1st Marine perimeter outside Koto-ri, nine miles from, and 22 hours after, the start from the edge of the Hagaru-ri perimeter. Then came daylight, the fighting stopped, and the 7th Marine road column entered Koto-ri, half a mile from where it had been halted.[13]

About the time First Lieutenant Bey's advance Marine company began arriving at the Koto-ri perimeter, Lt. Col. William F. Farris, the 3rd Battalion commander, disappeared back near the rear of the 7th Marine regimental column. A search for him was fruitless, and it was learned later that he had been killed. Maj. Warren Morris, the battalion executive officer, assumed command of the battalion. The bulk of the 3rd Battalion at the end of the column reached Koto-ri about 7 A.M. on 7 December.

Four hours later, Colonel Litzenberg ordered Morris and Lockwood to take the 3rd and 2nd battalions back up the road to establish blocking positions below Hill 1182 to keep the road open there and to help the 5th Marine Regiment get through. While there, the 2nd Battalion helped rescue 22 British soldiers of Drysdale's commandos who had been stranded in enemy-held territory for eight days and nights. An American artillery observation pilot had seen them on 4 December, but they could not be rescued then. Ten of the 22 commandos had to be carried out on stretchers.[14]

Although the 7th Marines all were in Koto-ri by 7 A.M. on 7 December, Division Train No. 1, following behind the infantry regiment, was strung out behind it during the night. It encountered a lot of trouble. The train had more casualties than the infantry who were in front and who were supposed to clear enemy from its path. CCF closed in around the division train after the 7th Regiment had fought its way through. The miscellaneous personnel of Division Train No. 1 themselves had to fight as infantry. The train finally got through, after suffering many casualties in a nightlong battle with the CCF.

Train No. 1 started to move from Hagaru-ri at 4 P.M. on 6 December, much later than expected, because the 7th Marines made only slow progress during the day and an earlier start for the vehicular column was not warranted. By dusk on 6 December, G and H batteries of the 11th Marines were just over a mile south of Hagaru-ri when CCF mortar and small-arms fire hit the column. The artillerymen repulsed this attack. Less than a mile farther a second firefight flared in which CCF mortars set several vehicles afire, blocked the road, and brought the column to a halt. The artillery of G and H batteries were emplaced between trucks as Chinese formed for an assault at daybreak. The howitzers fired at point-blank ranges of 40 to 800 yards during a two-hour enemy assault. The gunners estimated that no more than 50 of more than 500 Chinese escaped death or wounds.[15]

The Marine Division Headquarters Company likewise had its share of woe during the night. It repeatedly had firefights with Chinese groups, and its progress was slow. After midnight, Chinese mortars and rockets set several of its vehicles afire. Headquarters personnel, walking alongside the vehicles, went into the roadside ditches to return the enemy fire, and a number of Marine Division bandsmen worked two machine guns, which helped keep the CCF away from the vehicles. At 2 A.M. the cloudy sky cleared enough to allow Marine night-heckler planes to come over and make strikes on the Chinese. Despite this considerable help, a company-sized group of enemy got to within 30 yards of the road just before dawn, and a close-in fight took place. In this fight 1st Lt. Charles H. Sullivan, six feet, four inches tall and weighing 240 pounds, emptied his carbine into charging Chinese and then hurled his bayoneted weapon like a javelin. The bayonet pierced the breast of a Chinese soldier only 15 feet away. Two night-fighter planes came over and risked strafing runs only 30 yards from the convoy troops. Their fire pinned down the Chinese. At dawn four planes dropped four tons of bombs, rockets, and napalm cannisters on the pinned-down Chinese. They broke and ran for cover. Headquarters Company lost six killed and 14 wounded in this action.[16]

ESCAPING CCF PRISONERS KILLED

Just ahead of Headquarters Company, the Military Police Company guarded about 160 Chinese prisoners that were able to walk. The CCF prisoners who were unable to walk when the withdrawal from Hagaru-ri began were left behind there under shelter with food and fuel. During the CCF night attack on the Division Train No. 1, Chinese prisoners were made to lie down on the road. The attacking CCF were aware of their presence, shouted to them, and also directed fire on them. In the midst of all this, some of the able-bodied prisoners jumped to their feet and tried to run for it. Marine fire, as well as that from some of their own people, now tore into them. In this wild melee, 137 of the Chinese prisoners were killed.

The convoy got under way again only after daylight, under an umbrella of close air cover. It reached the Koto-ri perimeter about 10 A.M. on 7 December.[17] At that time, with part of the 5th Marine Regiment still in Hagaru-ri, elements of the withdrawing troops stretched back 11 miles, all the way from Koto-ri to Hagaru-ri.

Wednesday, 6 December, was the last day wounded were evacuated from Hagaru-ri—most of them wounded from the 7th Marines and the attached Army troops in the breakout fighting of that day and from the 5th Marines and their attached Army troops who were trying to capture East Hill from the Chinese and protect the MSR from Hagaru-ri for the last elements there to withdraw. Col. Robert Forman, director of operations for the Combat Cargo Command, accompanied by two enlisted men and two correspondents, flew to Hagaru-ri just before noon of 6 December. He noted on his approach to the small landing field that smoke from napalm and artillery shells ringed the perimeter within which the short runway was still operational. C-47s were still flying in for cargoes of dead or wounded soldiers. The 5th Marines were still fighting hard for control of the slopes of East Hill. Forman could see enemy soldiers on high ground east of the town, and they disappeared from view only when air strikes came in on them. Forman decided at 4 P.M. that the last two transport planes should leave the field. He did not leave in the second plane, however, until an hour later, because he waited for one more critically wounded man to be brought to the field for evacuation. By dusk of 6 December the last evacuation plane flew from the C-47 airstrip at Hagaru-ri.[18]

THE REAR-GUARD 5TH MARINES AT HAGARU-RI

When the 7th Marines started their attack south from Hagaru-ri on the morning of 6 December, Lieutenant Colonel Murray's 5th Marine Regiment not only took over defense of the entire Hagaru-ri perimeter, but it also had the difficult task of seizing East Hill from the Chinese. CCF troops had held the crest of this hill mass ever since they occupied it after midnight on 28 November. The critical terrain of East Hill was in the general shape of a horseshoe, with the toe of the shoe pointing north. The two sides of the shoe were high, sharp ridges that met at their northern ends in a saddle—the toe of the shoe. The westernmost ridge, running southwest, lay just above Hagaru-ri. The eastern ridge and that side of the horseshoe descended from the heights east of the saddle in a succession of knobs to end just above the road, railroad, and the Changjin River at the southeastern edge of the Hagaru-ri perimeter, and south of Hagaru-ri itself. This latter ridge was perhaps the most critical terrain of East Hill because, if the Chinese could hold all of it, they could intercept the only escape road south from Hagaru-ri just below the town. This southern spur ridge dominated the withdrawal route from Hagaru-ri. The Hagaru-ri defenders had been barely able to hold this spur ridge and thus protect the vital southeastern part of the perimeter. As a part of the withdrawal plan, it was considered important that the Marines strengthen their hold on this spur and drive the Chinese troops off the top of East Hill.

In preparation for the attack on East Hill, to coincide with the 7th Marines' lead-off in the withdrawal on 6 December, Colonel Murray at 10 P.M. the preceding night ordered Lt. Col. Harold S. Roise's 2nd Battalion to seize the crest of East Hill in the morning. A 4.2-inch mortar barrage on the hill was set for 7 A.M. A series of air strikes was to hit the enemy positions on the hill at the same time. The mortar preparations were on time, but the air strikes that followed did not have napalm. The rockets, bombs, and strafing seemed to have little effect on the CCF. When 1st Lt. George A. Sorenson's 3rd Platoon of D Company led off in D Company's attack at 9 A.M., it advanced only 50 yards before CCF fire stopped it. Sorenson was wounded. Lt. John R. Hurd replaced him. When McNaughton's 2nd Platoon moved up, Chinese fire stopped it. Lieutenant Johnson's 3rd Platoon was then committed. All three platoons now made a concerted attack. CCF resistance at the crest suddenly ended about 11 A.M. When D Company reached the crest, it found only 30 CCF dead there — a figure that seemed low after all the barrages and air strikes that had hit the position. During the day, 76 aircraft aided in the battle for East Hill.

D Company's initial success about noon was just the beginning of the battle for East Hill. At the same time, the 7th Marines on the road below were making only slow progress in their withdrawal attack toward Koto-ri. At 11:30 A.M. Roise ordered F Company to relieve D Company on the northeast crest of East Hill so that D Company could attack the high ground across the saddle, 500 yards to the southeast. Capt. Samuel S. Smith started D Company's attack about 12:30. After two hours of battle, it gained the high ground. Smith then placed his three platoons in three positions along this spur — the southern, or right-hand, side of the horseshoe. From these positions he controlled the withdrawal road from Hagaru-ri.

Late in the afternoon, Chinese were seen massing in the saddle. F and D companies had left it unoccupied. An air strike was called in on these Chinese, and all F and D companies' weapons within range opened up on them at the same time. From D Company, Lieutenant McNaughton led his platoon against the CCF caught in the saddle. The 220 Chinese survivors there surrendered en masse to him. This was the highest number of CCF prisoners taken at one time by X Corps troops in the Chosin campaign.[19]

Captain Smith now requested that another Marine force be sent to relieve McNaughton's platoon and to occupy the saddle. In response to this request, Murray sent 42 men from the Antitank Company and the 4th Signal Company, including two officers. This force then occupied the saddle between D and F companies.

The 1st Marine Division at Hagaru-ri had by now been receiving reinforcements that were flown in from Japan. Many of the Marines wounded in the fighting at Inchon and in the capture of Seoul had recovered from their wounds of a month earlier sufficiently to be returned to their units, and these men came in at the Hagaru-ri C-47 airstrip. The total number of these Marines returned to duty for the final battles around Hagaru-ri and in the breakout from there to the coast is not known. But they were a significant number and made a valuable contribution to the successful outcome.

CCF COUNTERATTACK, NIGHT OF 6–7 DECEMBER

After dark on 6 December the CCF counterattacked the Marines on East Hill in a spectacular and determined show of force. Again and again, after successive repulses, the Chinese returned to the attack, continuing the fight until midnight. Then after a two-hour lull, they came on once more against all three companies of the 2nd Battalion, 5th Marines, and also against C Company of the 1st Battalion at the base of the hill northeast of Hagaru-ri.

During the next three hours, until just before dawn, perhaps the most fiercely contested battle of the Chosin Reservoir campaign took place on and around the northwest base of East Hill. The veterans of Yudam-ni said they had never seen the CCF come in such numbers and return again and again with such persistence. Tracer bullets left their bright tracks in a crazy crisscross of multitudinous bright streaks against the darkness. At intervals an illuminating shell burst overhead to reveal Chinese attack groups coming forward at a trot, as they deployed into skirmish lines before falling in heaps before the concentrated fire of artillery, rockets, machine guns, and small-arms fire. The dogged fatalism that seemed to inspire these Chinese soldiers as they pressed forward into death awed the Marines into respect for their efforts. Some Chinese got to within grenade range before they fell. At the same time that the Chinese infantry pressed their attack, enemy mortar and machine-gun fire pounded the Marines. D Company was hard pressed, and all three of its platoons were riddled with casualties, including many officers. This was the same company that had played the crucial role in the attack on the hill complex northwest of Seoul in September, less than three months earlier. In that battle the company had come out of it with only 26 able-bodied men, and 1st Lt. Karle F. Seydel its only unwounded officer. But this night Seydel's chain ran out. He died on East Hill. D Company and the group in the saddle lost 13 killed and 50 wounded. The survivors had to fall back to F Company's position on the west side of the saddle.[20]

After daybreak a group of six men ventured out of the lines to recover Seydel's body and 16 others. Chinese on the high ground east of the saddle watched but did not interfere.[21]

During the intense battles on the crest of East Hill during the night of 6–7 December, E and C companies, 5th Marines, at the northern base of the hill, had relatively easy success in beating back CCF attacks. There the CCF had to cross nearly level ground, and the Marines, with the help of three Army tanks from the 31st Tank Company, had good fields of fire and destroyed the assault groups. Farther west and north of Hagaru-ri other CCF attacked A Company and made a penetration, forcing one platoon back to the place where the 1st Marine Division CP had stood only a day earlier. B Company helped in a counterattack that restored the lost position by 6 A.M. The 1st Battalion in this fight had ten killed and 43 wounded. Counted CCF dead in front of A and B companies the next morning numbered 460. On the south side of the perimeter, G Company beat off a relatively minor attack, killing 60 and capturing 15 Chinese.

Daylight of 7 December revealed a scene of slaughter on and around

East Hill. Estimates of CCF dead in front of the 2nd Battalion on the hill reached 800. Although there was never any precise count of enemy dead from that night's battles at East Hill, it would seem that the 5th Marines killed perhaps 1,000 Chinese soldiers. They did win a victory in this showdown battle. After daylight came to the scarred hill, aircraft returned to the scene. The Chinese, as usual in such circumstances, sought cover, and quiet descended on that part of the snow-covered landscape.

THE 5TH MARINES WITHDRAW, 7 DECEMBER

During the night, Colonel Murray had ordered the 3rd Battalion, which was not engaged in the night's battles, to lead off after daybreak in the regiment's withdrawal. Division Train No. 2 would follow it; then in succession the 1st Battalion and Ridge's 3rd Battalion, 7th Marines. Roise's 2nd Battalion, which had been battered in the night battle on East Hill, would hold its positions there while the rest of the regimental movement was in progress. Then it would come off the hill, and with the Army's 31st Tank Company, under Capt. Robert E. Drake, and the engineers still in Hagaru-ri, would be the last United States units to leave the ruins to the enemy.[22]

While the 2nd Battalion, 5th Marines, was fighting on East Hill during 6 December, Division Train No. 2 had formed in Hagaru-ri during the afternoon. It did not leave the perimeter, however, until after dark. By midnight it had progressed only a short distance. Lt. Col. Harry T. Milne, the train commander, then requested infantry support before advancing farther. Murray assigned Taplett's 3rd Battalion, which had only two companies at hand, to accompany the train. These troops and Division Train No. 2 traveled nearly the entire distance to Koto-ri after daylight on 7 December under constant air cover and met only slight enemy resistance. The leading elements of Division Train No. 2 and Taplett's 3rd Battalion entered Koto-ri at 5 P.M. on 7 December, and all of the column had arrived there by midnight.

Daylight of 7 December saw probably the greatest concentration of UN aircraft in the Chosin Reservoir area of any time during the fighting there. Three fast carriers, *Philippine Sea*, *Princeton*, and *Leyte*, from just off the coast put 125 sorties into the air during the day, more than half the total number of 216 used. Forty of the sorties were used against villages in the hills near Koto-ri. There were few enemy sightings in the villages, but refugees said the CCF crowded into all available housing there during the day for cover from the weather. In many cases when air strikes hit these villages and set the houses on fire, CCF soldiers in large numbers erupted from them and ran for any other cover that was nearby.[23]

After reaching Koto-ri during the predawn darkness of 7 December, the 1st Battalion of the Army troops had little chance for a rest. At 7 A.M. Lieutenant Colonel Anderson alerted it for a return back up the road to help the 5th Marine Regiment, which was having trouble. The 1st Battalion, and possibly some from the 3rd Battalion, moved out with the expectation of going about two and one-half miles back toward Hagaru-ri to protect the left flank of the approaching 5th Marines. It met the Marines about three miles up the road and deployed to hold the left flank for the road column. The 1st Battalion stayed there until relieved later in the day by combat elements of the 5th Marines. Jones's battalion then returned to Koto-ri and remained there that night.[24]

Anderson's provisional regiment had suffered several casualties on the breakout fight from Hagaru-ri to Koto-ri, but many more men had become combat ineffective because of cold and frostbite. This depleted situation in his Army force caused Anderson to form the remaining men into two companies, the 31st Company, which Captain Rasula commanded, and the 32nd Company, which Captain Kitz commanded.

Following Taplett's 3rd Battalion and Division Train No. 2, the 1st Battalion, 5th Marines; Ridge's 3rd Battalion, 1st Marines; and the British Royal Commandos moved out in that order on the morning of 7 December. They all departed Hagaru-ri as rapidly as possible when the road ahead cleared. By 10 A.M. only Roise's rear-guard 2nd Battalion was left at Hagaru-ri, along with 1st Lt. Vaughan R. Stuart's tank company, 1st Engineer Battalion, and CWO Willie S. Harrison's Explosive Ordnance Section of Headquarters Company, 1st Engineers. The engineers and Ordnance Section had the task of setting off demolitions at Hagaru-ri when Roise's battalion left the perimeter. The demolition teams already had prepared for destruction heaps of mortar and artillery ammunition that could not be transported out of Hagaru-ri and piles of clothing and miscellaneous equipment. Buildings at the Hagaru-ri railroad yard were also to be destroyed, and lastly, the bridge over the Changjin River in Hagaru-ri was to be blown.

On 6 December bulldozers had smashed cans and crates of food in the rations dump and the men had soaked everything with gasoline so that it could be put to the torch in the final moments. Colonel Roise was to give the order for all demolitions and destruction of supplies and equipment when he was ready for it. But fires mysteriously broke out in Hagaru-ri before he had ordered any fires to be set. These were burning as the 2nd Battalion pulled back off the southern tip of East Hill. Dense smoke blotted out views of most of the Hagaru-ri area, and enemy movements could not be observed at this time. Premature explosions now took place as engineers were still setting fuses for demolitions. Rockets and shells exploded, and fragments rained down together with great chunks of earth. Roise was greatly angered, since his withdrawing troops were endangered.

Miraculously, the 2nd Battalion came off East Hill without casualties, and they started south on the road. The battalion passed Captain Drake's Army 31st Tank Company, which had taken position at the southern edge of the perimeter. All day it watched unit after unit leave the perimeter and head south toward Koto-ri. This Army tank company was to be the final rear guard for the entire withdrawal. After the 2nd Battalion passed, only the engineers were left in Hagaru-ri. They ignited their time fuses and hastily departed. One great explosive charge destroyed the bridge over the Changjin River.

Captain Drake and his 31st Tank Company then left the southern edge of the perimeter. Drake described these last moments before American troops left Hagaru-ri and the Chosin Reservoir forever:

> The rear guard action was performed at or close to the positions marked on your sketch map. There was indeed a very effective Marine infantry force holding the southern end of East Hill. We watched the demolition operation from our positions. The light was bright enough to read our maps in the middle of the night! All through the early morning there was enough tracer fire in addition to make the area look like a 4th of July. I do not recall seeing or firing upon any CCF. Someone in the miles long column which passed through our positions for hours on the road, said to me that they were the last element. At this point, I ordered my company to prepare for rear guard action and we joined the long motor column to Koto-ri. To the best of my knowledge, nobody was behind us except the CCF who were, I later learned, busily looting the remains of stores left behind. This was their major mistake—they could have jumped our vulnerable column and scored another big victory![25]

The few who looked back saw, in the rifts of smoke that allowed momentary glimpses into the burning and destroyed village, Chinese soldiers already there searching for food.

Roise's rear-guard 2nd Battalion and attached troops, including Drake's 31st Tank Company, encountered almost no opposition on the way to Koto-ri—only a little scattered small-arms fire in Hell Fire Valley, the scene of Drysdale's ordeal earlier, and a few mortar rounds when he briefly halted the column. Engineers at the rear blew each intact bridge after they had passed over it. Great numbers of Korean refugees followed at the tail of the column. Although warned about the bridge demolitions, some of the refugees undoubtedly were caught in some of them. By midnight of 7 December the last of the 1st Marine Division and attached troops had reached Koto-ri.

The withdrawal from Hagaru-ri to Koto-ri on 6–7 December, including the battles on East Hill, had cost 616 American casualties: 83 killed, 20 dead from wounds, 506 wounded, and 7 missing in action. It had taken 38 hours for the approximately 10,000 men and more than 1,000 vehicles to traverse the 11 miles. The service troops in Division Train No. 1, in-

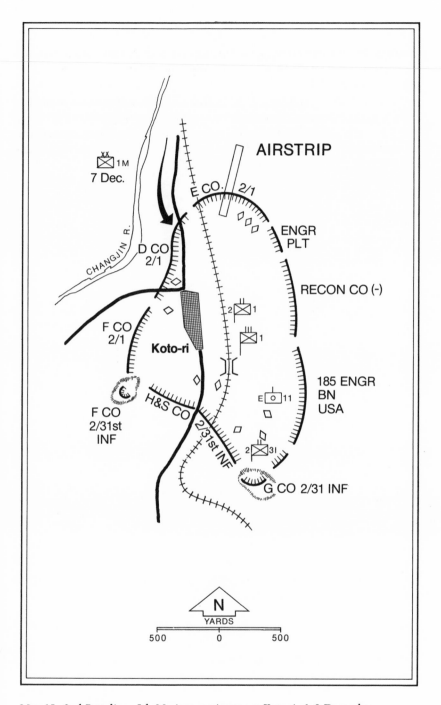

AIRSTRIP

XX
⊠ 1M
7 Dec.

E CO. 2/1

CHANGJIN R.

D CO
2/1

ENGR
PLT

RECON CO (-)

2 ⊠ 1

III
⊠ 1

F CO
2/1

Koto-ri

185 ENGR
BN
USA

E ▭ 11

H&S CO

F CO
2/31st
INF

2/31st INF

2 ⊠ 31

G CO 2/31 INF

N
YARDS
500   0   500

MAP 15. 2nd Battalion, 5th Marines, perimeter at Koto-ri, 6–8 December.

cluding the 3rd Battalion, 11th Marines (artillery), had suffered losses proportionally heavier than those of any other unit or group—15 killed and 117 wounded.[26]

Now, just ahead and facing the withdrawal force, was what many believed might be the worst ordeal of all—descending Funchilin Pass from Koto-ri to Chinhung-ni. It was to begin immediately. But before taking up that story, it is necessary first to describe briefly the situation then confronting the rest of X Corps.

12

THE X CORPS SITUATION, 8 DECEMBER

In early December 1950, the bulk of the X Corps—(other than the 1st Marine Division) the Army 7th Infantry Division, the Army 3rd Infantry Division, the ROK 1st Marine Regiment, and the ROK I Corps (consisting of the ROK 3rd and Capital divisions)—was scattered over several hundred square miles, with a 400-mile front, all the way to the Manchurian border, some in regimental and battalion combat groups. The 3rd Infantry Division was operating in a zone around Wonsan, south and west of Hungnam. The 7th Infantry Division was far to the northeast, with its 17th Regiment on the Yalu around Hyesanjin. The ROK 3rd Division was striking inland toward the border from the coast at Kilchin and was in the vicinity of Hapsu. Still farther northeast on the coastal road, the ROK Capital Division was 18 miles north of Chongjin, and only 38 miles from the Soviet border. None of the American or ROK troops near the border met any Chinese units—only North Korean Army remnants. These X Corps troops were advancing rapidly in their zones against only light and scattered resistance.

It will be recalled that CCF forces counterattacked the Eighth Army in the west, beginning on the night of 25 November, two days before CCF forces counterattacked the X Corps in the Chosin Reservoir area of northeast Korea. In the intervening two days, 26–27 November, the CCF in the west defeated and threw into utter confusion the Eighth Army right flank, which consisted of two ROK divisions, and at the same time they struck hard blows at the Eighth Army center along the Chongchon River. These surprising and swift enemy assaults on Eighth Army caused the entire army to start south in precipitate retreat. Just as this was taking place in the west, the CCF on the night of 27 November unleashed attacks in great strength against the X Corps troops at Chosin Reservoir.

These events in Korea in the three days from 25 to 28 November caused General MacArthur in Tokyo to call General Walker, the Eighth Army commander, and General Almond, the X Corps commander, to a hurried meeting in Tokyo the night of 28–29 November, as related in chapter 5. The meeting lasted until well into the early morning hours of 29 November. Before he started on his return trip to Korea that day, Almond received orders from MacArthur to withdraw the X Corps troops from their advanced positions and to concentrate them at Hungnam. This order to Almond in Tokyo on 29 November set the stage for the events that followed in the X Corps zone of operations.

Maj. Gen. Clark Ruffner, the X Corps chief of staff, was greatly worried about the situation and, in conversation with Major General Soule of the 3rd Infantry Division, said, "I don't know whether we will be able to save the Old Man's [Almond's] corps." Lieutenant Colonel McCaffrey, deputy chief of staff, X Corps, had the same misgivings, as did many of the X Corps staff.[1] Most of the corps's widely scattered battalions and regiments were not within supporting distances of each other and could not expect much help if they suddenly came under attack. The only favorable element of the situation as the corps began its hectic scramble to reassemble its scattered forces was that Chinese soldiers had not appeared in northeast Korea east and north of the Fusen Reservoir. The opposition there was North Korean Army remnants retreating northward and some guerrilla action.

To provide a bit of perspective for events in northeast Korea after 29 November, it may be useful to remember that General Walker's Eighth Army had fallen back rapidly in the west, and by 5 December, the day before the 1st Marine Division started its withdrawal from Hagaru-ri, Eighth Army had passed through Pyongyang, evacuating that city, and was entirely out of contact with Chinese forces. It was heading for the Imjin River line, north of Seoul.

When Almond started troop movements designed to concentrate the X Corps at the coast, his plan was thrown into some confusion by the situation that developed in the 3rd Infantry Division. Almond commented as follows: "The concentration of Corps units was appreciably slowed when the 3rd Infantry Division, after having initiated a move to Hamhung, was ordered by CINCUNC [MacArthur] to concentrate on Wonsan. At that time it was planned to attempt employing the 3rd Infantry Division to help plug the gap in the center of the Korean Peninsula between X Corps and Eighth Army."[2]

ALMOND CALLS IN SCATTERED X CORPS

The order to concentrate the 7th Infantry Division at Hungnam posed a problem because it was widely scattered in regimental and battalion groups, reaching all the way to the Manchurian border. As previously noted, certain units of its 31st and 32nd regiments were assembled on the east side of the Chosin Reservoir by 27 November and there suffered great losses to the CCF 80th Division. Task Force Kingston, which reached the Yalu River at Singalpajin in the afternoon of 28 November, was part of the 3rd Battalion, 32nd Regiment. Singalpajin is about 20 air miles west of Hyesanjin, where the 17th Regiment had reached the Yalu eight days earlier. Task Force Kingston did not remain long at the border. The day following its arrival there, 29 November, it received orders to withdraw posthaste, and by 3 P.M. it started south. By nightfall it was 12 miles below Samsu.[3]

The main line of withdrawal for units of the 7th Infantry Division near the border, and in northeast Korea above the Fusen Reservoir, was by way of Pungsan to Pukchon near the coast, and hence southwest to Hungnam. The troops rode trucks part of the way, marched on foot for some miles, and traveled the last miles on the railroad that ran from Pukchon to Hamhung. The terrain was mountainous, the weather frigid, often 25 to 35 degrees below zero. The roads were narrow and icy. One officer present in the 7th Division withdrawal said later that the roads were so icy in places that track-laying vehicles could not stay on them and that trucks stalled. Even though the vehicles were hampered by such a simple thing, there was not enough time to correct the problem, and the men "had to push vehicles over to the side." The ten-minute break planned for every hour was often dispensed with in favor of more frequent but shorter breaks to avoid allowing men to stiffen up from the cold and to reduce sweating in the heavy, cold-weather clothing.[4] Division units encountered little enemy opposition in their withdrawal. Their difficulties involved mostly the mountainous terrain and weather conditions.

Although no Chinese troops appeared on the withdrawal route of the 7th Infantry Division, there was certainly some fear that they might. A manuscript left by 1st Lt. James H. Dill, executive officer of B Battery, 31st Field Artillery Battalion, 7th Infantry Division, makes that concern clear. The 31st Field Artillery Battalion was composed of 155-mm howitzers, pulled by track-laying tractors. Colonel Welsh, commanding the 31st Battalion, was ordered to send one battery with the division force that had been dispatched to reach the Yalu at Hyesanjin. He chose B Battery. Captain Klaniecki commanded the battery, and Dill was second in command of the battery. Dill's manuscript covers the conditions and experiences the battery of six 155-mm howitzers met from the time it started from the coast at Iwon on 11 November until its withdrawal to Hamhung on 1 December. In that period it traveled a one-lane, dirt road that switchbacked over high mountain passes and endured temperatures that frequently were 32 to 40 degrees below zero. The tractor-drawn howitzers did not travel over the icy roads as well as did the 105-mm howitzers of the 57th Field Artillery Battalion, which were drawn by 2½-ton trucks as support for the 31st Infantry Regiment, to which it was attached. As for its sister FA battalions, the 48th supported the 32nd Infantry, and the 49th supported the 17th Infantry Regiment. Dill's B Battery of 155-mm howitzers never quite reached the Yalu but did get to the ancient walled town of Kapsan on 23 November, only 30 miles south of the Yalu at Hyesanjin. Kapsan had been almost completely destroyed in earlier fighting with withdrawing remnants of the North Korean Army ahead of the 17th Infantry, which entered Hyesanjin on 21 November.

The artillery battery passed north through Pungsan on 17 November and on 19 November received instructions that its support of the 31st Infantry was ended and that it was moving farther north to support elements of the 32nd Infantry Regiment, which had already arrived near the Yalu to extend the 17th Regiment's line to the west of Hyesanjin and farther down the Yalu.[5] B Battery, 31st Field Artillery Battalion, at Kapsan, 30 road miles from the Yalu, was the only battery of 155-mm howitzers to reach that far north during the Korean War.

Meals during this period inevitably consisted of canned hashed corn beef. On the twenty-fourth, however, B Battery had its Thanksgiving Day dinner. Dill wrote that, on this day, the dinner "was an unbelievable joyous break from hashed corn beef and bread." The battery was told on this day "that the war was almost over, and that we should prepare for a return to Japan. The advisory also included an example of how forms should be made up for returning our ROK's to their own army. We were told to tell them that most would soon be discharged and sent home. An unofficial note was added to brush up on close order drill since the 7th Division would be expected to take part in a Grand Victory Parade as soon as we reached Japan."[6]

The 31st Field Artillery Battalion, headquarters at Pukchon, 100 road miles southward, recalled Captain Klaniecki to its headquarters on 25 November and left Dill in charge of the battery. That night, 25–26 November, Lieutenant Dill was abruptly awakened in the middle of the night by the duty sentry and told that division headquarters wanted him on the phone. The conversation that followed went approximately thus:

Div. G-3: You are to move your battery to So-dong at once. Get moving.
Lt. Dill: Where is So-dong? I've never heard of it.
G-3:   It's south of Division Headquarters at Pungsan. Stop by on the way for further orders.
Lt. Dill: Good God, Sir! That's over eighty miles. Can't I wait until morning? I'm not sure the gun tractors can make it down the road at night. The mountains are covered with ice.
G-3:   Stop arguing and get moving, Lieutenant. Leave with your advance party at once and have your guns follow as soon as

they can march-order. If something cannot be moved, blow
it up.

Lt. Dill: Blow it up?

G-3:   You heard me. I'll tell you more when you get to Pungsan, but
          those howitzers of yours have got to start long before day-
          break.

Lt. Dill: Yes, Sir. March orders at once.[7]

Because the division headquarters had called him direct, bypassing all
intervening echelons, Dill knew something was up but had no idea what
it was.

Dill wrote that he would never forget the cold on that trip south from
Kapsan. Twice he stopped at MP checkpoints and warmed himself at their
fires. Once the ¾-ton truck behind honked its horn, and he stopped to
run back to see what was the trouble. Two of the men had passed out
from the cold. Dill ordered everyone out and set them to cutting down
bushes with their bayonets. With the aid of gasoline he soon had two
fires going, and in their heat the two men revived. They loaded up again
and continued down the road. Dill believed the two men would have died
if he had not made this stop and revived them. His own driver kept driving but moaning as he drove. Dill himself was near collapse when he
reached division HQ. The temperature there registered 36 degrees below
zero. In the mountains it must have been under 40 below.

The division HQ was in a schoolhouse, always the most substantial
building in a Korean village or town. Dill reported at once to the war room.
The G-3 was still up. It was about 4:30 A.M. He gave Dill a cup of hot
coffee and told him to sit next to the stove. He explained to Dill what
had happened. Dill said he recalled his exact words: "We had a message
brought in to our forward outpost by relays of Korean runners. It was written in Korean and was from the headman of a village downriver [west]
from Hyesanjin. In it he says that thousands and thousands of Chinese
are crossing the Yalu near his village and heading due south."[8]

Lieutenant Dill expressed some incredulity at such information. The
G-3 told him that it did not matter what he thought, that General Barr,
the division commander, believed it. According to the message from the
outpost, the Chinese were crossing the Yalu and headed south into the
gap between the Marines and Army troops at Chosin and the 7th Division on the next road northeastward. They could either bear right and
strike the Chosin area or bear left and cut the 7th Division road east of
Fusen Reservoir. General Barr feared they might do the latter and catch
nearly the entire division in a trap. The G-3 told Dill that, from Barr's
experience in China as advisor to Gen. Chiang Kai-shek, the general was
convinced that there was no terrain that Chinese troops could not cross,
regardless of the weather.

While they were talking, General Barr walked in. He had apparently been up all night. He greeted Lieutenant Dill courteously and explained his actions. He said the 17th Infantry would leave Hyesanjin the next day at dawn, and he just had to get the unwieldy tractors and medium howitzers out ahead of them. Unless this were done, he feared that they would hold up the main column and might even block its march. If placed at the rear, the B Battery would probably be left behind and lost to the enemy.[9]

The G-3 then explained the next position B Battery was to take, one about a mile southwest of Undam. An ox trail came in there from the west from the Fusen Reservoir. If the Chinese turned east at the Chosin Reservoir to interdict the 7th Division's MSR, they would travel over this track. General Barr had placed the 1st Battalion, 31st Infantry, across this track, and B Battery was to fire support for it together with C Battery of the 57th Field Artillery, which had not gone with Colonel MacLean to the Chosin Reservoir. Dill had two quad-50s of D Company, 15th AAA Battalion, with him. Dill reached the Undam position about dawn of 26 November.

It must be pointed out that these events all occurred before General Almond issued his orders to the 7th Division to withdraw to Hamhung, following his orders from General MacArthur in Tokyo on the morning of 29 November. The message from the village headman that reached a 7th Division outpost, apparently on the twenty-fifth, and was then radioed to the 7th Division HQ must have reported on the observed crossing of the Yalu by Chinese of the 27th Army of the IX Army Group, Third Field Army, at Linchiang. Linchiang was the easternmost crossing site of any Chinese troops into North Korea. The 27th Army included four divisions, two of them being the 79th and 80th divisions, which marched due south to the Chosin Reservoir and attacked the Marines and Army troops there on the night of 27 November. Hyesanjin is about 70 air miles southeast, up the Yalu, from Linchiang. It appears that General Barr had early notice of an unidentified but large body of Chinese troops that had crossed the Yalu and had headed south in the last part of November. The X Corps apparently never received this information, nor did the Marines and Army troops at Chosin Reservoir. There is no record that General Barr ever informed the X Corps of this message from a Korean village headman near the crossing site. Barr, according to Lieutenant Dill, accepted the message at face value, but it is doubtful if higher headquarters would have accepted it without further confirmation.

B Battery went into firing positions at Undam, but nothing happened there. On 28 November it was ordered to move farther back near the coast. On the twenty-ninth, it left for Chori by way of Pukchon. There was heavy snow. The battery reached Pukchon, the 7th Division Rear CP, at noon and from there was ordered to Hamhung.

On the way down from near the Yalu, B Battery men had to use picks to break up the ice on steep and ice-slick sections of the road. They had another stretch of such road near the coast. The entire battery was put to work chopping the ice so the tractors could get traction. On a steep curve, overlooking a 50-foot cliff, one of the tractors and its 155-mm howitzer slipped over the side. Heavy snowdrifts saved the men from serious injury. Later a recovery vehicle pulled the howitzer back to the road, but the tractor was irretrievable. Lieutenant Dill went down to the coast, where a small town called Yanghwe had a railroad station but no loading dock or ramp. Dill and Captain Klaniecki had decided in a conference that day, 1 December, that they would never get the tractors and howitzers to Hamhung over the rough coastal road, that the only way to save them would be to transport them on railcars. Lieutenant Dill arranged through the village headman for the villagers to build a loading ramp out of railroad ties at the site, which they did during the night. Dill went back to Pukchon and reported the situation to Colonel Welsh, the battalion commander, and asked him to arrange for rail transportation of the artillery battery. A train arrived at Yanghwe and loaded the artillery and larger vehicles on flatcars. A boxcar was available to carry most of the men. The rest would have to ride the remaining vehicles that would go by road. The train arrived at Hamhung at 4 P.M., one of the first units of the 7th Infantry Division to reach the concentration point of Hamhung-Hungnam from their far-flung positions when the order to withdraw was issued.[10] It arrived there that early only because General Barr had ordered it back several days before X Corps issued its general withdrawal order on 29–30 November.

At Pukchon, the battery heard exaggerated and often untrue tales of what had happened to the 57th Field Artillery Battalion, D Battery, of the 15th AAA AW Battalion, and the others caught on the east side of Chosin Reservoir. These reports put all the men in a somber frame of mind. This day, 1 December, happened to be the very day those troops were engaged in making their breakout from the inlet perimeter in an attempt to reach Hagaru-ri.

According to Graves Registration officer, 7th Infantry Division, Maj. Jacob W. Kurtz, 50 American and 24 ROK dead were not evacuated from Pukchon, the 7th Division Rear CP, but were buried in a division cemetery that he established half a mile south of the town and half a mile from the MSR.[11]

General Barr with a small party had established an Advance CP at Hungnam by the morning of 30 November. The 7th Division Rear CP left Pukchong with all operational vehicles at 10 A.M. on 6 December. According to their own records, they destroyed 350 tons of low-priority ammunition, 100,000 gallons of diesel fuel, 171 inoperable vehicles, and other equipment at that time. In the afternoon of 7 December, when General Almond visited the ROK I Corps Headquarters, he learned that the ROK 26th Regiment of the ROK 3rd Division, then at Pukchon, had reported that the US 7th Division had left numerous supplies there when it withdrew. Almond ordered the ROK 26th Regiment to bring these supplies with them. He also sent a X Corps staff officer to Pukchon to help supervise the movement.[12]

ROK I CORPS TROOPS ORDERED BACK

On 30 November General Almond ordered the 3rd and Capital divisions of the ROK I Corps, the major units farthest north under X Corps command and making rapid progress toward the Chinese and Soviet borders, to turn back. At the time, the ROK 3rd Division was at Hapsu, and the ROK Capital Division was above Chongjin on the east coast. Almond's orders called for all ROK troops to retire on Songjin. The destroyer USS *Noble* and two merchantmen left Wonsan on 5 December to outload the ROK I Corps at Songjin, which was a lumber-export port on the east coast that had an 1,800-foot-long quay with 27 feet of water alongside, allowing large ships to pull up alongside it. Another merchantman and an LST arrived at Songjin on 9 December and loaded out some of the ROKs and then sailed for Pusan. The ROK I Corps HQ and about half the troops loaded out on the first ships and LSTs to arrive and were brought to Hungnam. By 8 December two regiments of the Capital Division and the ROK 26th Regiment of the ROK 3rd Division also had arrived at Hungnam. They were placed on the right flank of the X Corps perimeter there under the command of Gen. Kim Pac Il, the ROK I Corps commander. The other ROK troops, initially headed for Pusan, were put ashore instead at Samchok, a coastal port south of the 38th Parallel.[13]

THE 3RD INFANTRY DIVISION

The 3rd Infantry Division was the last of X Corps troops to land in northeast Korea. One of its regiments, the 65th, was composed mostly of Puerto Ricans. It had been in Korea for three months, having landed at Pusan on 22 September. The other two regiments and the division headquarters sailed from San Francisco at the end of August and on 2 September. The division was understrength. In Japan it took in 8,500 South Korean draftees. Some squads consisted of eight Koreans and two American enlisted men.

The 2nd Battalion of the 65th Infantry joined X Corps in northeast Korea at Wonsan on 5–6 November, and on 10 November the 3rd Division Advance CP opened at Wonsan. The 15th and 7th regimental combat teams unloaded there between 11 and 17 November. Initially, the 3rd Division's main mission was to relieve the 1st Marine Division in the Wonsan area and south of Hamhung and to block the main roads in the southern part of the X Corps zone against guerrillas and North Korean regular-unit remnants moving up from the south. The 26th Regiment of the ROK 3rd Division was attached to the division for a time, thus giving it a four-regimental combat team. The ROK 26th Regiment and the 15th Regiment of the 3rd Division, west of Wonsan in the Majon-ni and Tongyang areas, had numerous skirmishes and ambush fights with North Korean groups and guerrillas in the last half of November.[14]

The 3rd Infantry Division was one of the oldest and most prestigious infantry units in the United States Army. It had an enviable reputation in World War II, in which it suffered 250 percent casualties. Its members won 29 Medals of Honor, and the division was awarded 17 Presidential Unit Citations and ten Battle Stars—a record unmatched by any other division. Lt. Audie Murphy was one of its Medal of Honor winners.

Two of the division's regiments, the 7th and the 15th, had special historical distinctions. The 7th Infantry dates back to 1798. The 3rd Division's shoulder patch, which represents a bale of cotton, comes from the 7th Infantry's participation with Andrew Jackson in the Battle of New Orleans in 1815. The 7th Infantry, under the command of Col. John Gibbon, arrived at the Little Bighorn in Montana just after Custer's defeat there in 1876, discovered the bodies of Custer's men, and brought out the surviving wounded of Reno's and Benteen's groups. The 15th Infantry served 26 years in China, from 1912 to 1938. While there it adopted its "Can Do" motto. Gen. George C. Marshall commanded the regiment for a period in China.

Maj. Gen. Robert H. Soule commanded the 3rd Infantry Division when it arrived in Korea. He was an old China hand. In 1918 he was a young engineer second lieutenant with the Siberian Expeditionary Force. Before the outbreak of the Korean War, he had been the US military attaché to Chiang Kai-shek's Nationalist China at Chungking from 1946 to 1949. Soule assumed command of the 3rd Infantry Division in the United States only a month or two after leaving his military-attaché post in China. General Soule knew Chinese Communist military tactics thoroughly as they had been practiced during the Chinese civil war. He believed the best way to combat the Chinese was to keep them tactically off balance, since they were used to fighting according to a plan that had been worked out well in advance. He also knew their biggest problem was logistics.

Maj. Gen. Robert H. Soule, commanding general of the 3rd Infantry Division, northeast Korea, 1950 (National Archives 80-G 371280)

Their basic transportation was still the horse and cart, about the same as in 1905. The cart carried about one ton at a speed of from three to five miles an hour.

One of the 3rd Division's first tasks after landing in Korea fell to its engineer unit. It had to revise the 1917 and 1934 Japanese maps of northeast Korea for US military operational purposes. No up-to-date maps were available. One of the difficulties in the old Japanese maps was the use of three different place-names for all towns: Japanese, Korean national, and Korean local. These diverse names in the first maps the X Corps used in northeast Korea led to confusion that still exists between place-names that appear in 1950 US Army and Marine military records of the time and more modern map nomenclature. In its effort to revise the military maps of the region, the 3rd Division engineers used aerial photography.

BATTLE AT SACHANG-NI, 28–29 NOVEMBER

Perhaps the largest single contact with Chinese troops in the 3rd Division sector in November took place on the night of 28–29 November at Sachang-ni, where the 1st Battalion, 7th Infantry, held a defensive, blocking position at an important road intersection, about 80 road miles northwest of Hamhung. The Sachang-ni–Hamhung road was a twisting, mountainous road of poor quality. It continued on west to Pyongyang, the North Korean capital. Another mountain dirt road ran south from Yudam-ni on the western side of the Chosin Reservoir to Sachang-ni. The enemy force that appeared at Sachang-ni undoubtedly came from Yudam-ni along this road. Yudam-ni was about 25 air miles north of Sachang-ni.

A sizable enemy force of Chinese, variously estimated to be from 800 to 1,500 strong, but probably no more than a battalion, attacked the 1st Battalion, 7th Infantry, during the night of 28–29 November. This engagement has already been mentioned in connection with the CCF concentration at Yudam-ni and will be mentioned only briefly here. By morning the 1st Battalion was surrounded. Casualties were heavy on both sides, but the Chinese breached the 1st Battalion's outer perimeter. Battery A, 10th Field Artillery Battalion, attached to the infantry battalion, supported it effectively during the night. Artillery forward observers brought down the fire of the battery's six howitzers on the outer perimeter area where the Chinese made penetrations. Prisoners identified the attacking force as being from the Chinese 89th Division, 20th Army. During the afternoon of 29 November a 3rd Division relief force of two rifle companies broke through a Chinese roadblock and joined the beleaguered 1st Battalion with a resupply of ammunition.

It is of interest to note that the CCF 20th Army, to which the Sachang-ni force belonged, had concentrated near Yudam-ni earlier and was at this very time heavily engaged with the 5th and 7th Marine regiments at Yudam-ni. One may speculate that this Chinese battalion from the 89th Division was on a reconnaissance-in-force mission to test X Corps position and strength west of Hamhung and Hungnam.[15]

At midafternoon, 29 November, another enemy force, North Korean or guerrillas, ambushed a platoon of A Company, 15th Infantry, and a convoy trying to reach Majon-ni and the 3rd Korean Marine Corps (KMC) Battalion at Tongyang, near the Eighth Army border, 70 air miles south of Sachang-ni. There had been many ambushes on this stretch of road in late November—so many that it was known as "Ambush Alley." In this action on 29 November, Sergeant Griffis won a Silver Star by recovering a jammed machine gun his men had abandoned and putting it back into action against the enemy.[16] Guerrilla groups were very active inland from Wonsan in the southwest corner of the X Corps zone.

3RD INFANTRY DIVISION ORDERED TO SOUTH KOREA

On 1 December an event took place that threatened the ability of X Corps to extricate its surrounded troops in the Chosin Reservoir area, to concentrate the remainder of the corps in Hungnam, and to defend successfully there on a perimeter for the evacuation of the corps from northeast Korea. GHQ in Tokyo ordered General Almond to assemble the 3rd Infantry Division at Wonsan for movement immediately to South Korea, where it would come under Eighth Army command to reinforce that threatened force. Apparently General MacArthur and his staff considered the danger there to be significant. Almond started action at once to carry out the order. But he also thought it very dangerous for his own X Corps. He decided to send two emissaries at once to Tokyo to seek a reversal of the order. His emissaries were Col. Edward H. Forney, the ranking US Marine officer on his staff, and Lt. Col. William W. Quinn, the X Corps G-2. They were charged with presenting his case for retaining the 3rd Infantry Division in X Corps. Almond had a conference with the two officers at his headquarters at noon on 2 December before they left for Tokyo.

Forney and Quinn met with Maj. Gen. Doyle Hickey, MacArthur's acting chief of staff, at once on their arrival in Tokyo. The next day MacArthur revoked his order of 1 December and informed Almond he would retain the 3rd Infantry Division to prepare to assist the withdrawal of the Marine and Army troops cut off in the Chosin Reservoir area.[17]

Colonel Forney was a good emissary to send on this particular mission. He was generally recognized as the foremost Marine expert on amphibious assault. He said little as a rule, but he was very gravely concerned that the 1st Marine Division might not get out of the Chosin entrapment. He had spoken to General Almond several times on the subject, even before the CCF attacked in strength at Chosin on 27 November. He felt, along with Gen. Oliver Smith, that the Marines were being placed in a perilous position so far inland in the mountains in the dead of winter without adequate support on their flanks and feared that Chinese might attack them in force. It is certain that his arguments were strong, and possibly decisive, in securing the continued use of the 3rd Infantry Division in the crucial days ahead in helping to get the 1st Marine Division and the Army troops at Chosin withdrawn to the coast.[18]

At 10:25 P.M. on 1 December a telephone call from X Corps ordered the 3rd Infantry Division to halt all northward movements. A few minutes after midnight X Corps published its Operational Instructions No. 21, which included instructions for the 3rd Division, minus the 7th Regiment, to concentrate in the Wonsan area to protect the port and Yonpo airfield and to send the 1st KMC Regiment to Hamhung to cover the withdrawal of troops from the Chosin Reservoir area. The division was also instructed to hold a regiment in readiness for deployment north of Hamhung. On receipt of this order, the 3rd Division HQ returned to Wonsan, and immediate action was taken to implement that order. On 4 December, after MacArthur rescinded the order for the 3rd Division to move to South Korea, the division moved to the Hamhung area as fast as available transportation permitted.

MacArthur's order of 1 December, and Almond's moves to implement it, for the concentration of the 3rd Infantry Division at Wonsan brought shipping there to move the division. On 3 December the *Saint Paul* arrived there from its duty station off northeastern Korea, and four APAs and one APD arrived from Japan. Loading of the 3rd Infantry Division began at once. When Almond won MacArthur's cancellation of the order to move the division to South Korea on 3 December, most of the division started by road and railroad for Hamhung the next day, 4 December. But the shipping at Wonsan brought about 4,000 men and 12,000 tons of division gear by water to Hungnam.

By 7 December all the troops in the Wonsan area had left for the Hamhung-Hungnam area except one Korean Marine battalion. One empty Victory ship still lay in the harbor. It eventually loaded Korean refugees that were fleeing the area in the face of the Chinese Communist threat. By 9 December the beaches at Wonsan were clear, and the final withdrawal from the port was covered by a United States destroyer. The next day, 10 December, the last ships departed. Naval records indicate that 3,800 troops, 7,000 refugees, 1,146 vehicles, and 10,000 tons of cargo were removed from the Wonsan area by water between 3 and 10 December. All the troops and most of the cargo were taken to the Hungnam area for use in the perimeter defense there prior to X Corps evacuation of all northeast Korea.[19]

At this time, and indeed from the beginning of the massive CCF counterattack in the Chosin area, many officers in X Corps despaired of being able to save the corps and reassemble it at the coast. The prospect was indeed frightening. The 1st Marine Division and some 7th Infantry Division troops were trapped, surrounded at the Chosin Reservoir, and fighting desperately at all their perimeters. Their only escape route was cut behind them for 30 miles at innumerable places. Other elements of X Corps were scattered over northeast Korea for several hundreds of miles in regimental and battalion combat units. The weather itself was a relentless enemy. Snow and ice were common on the roads and country-side, and temperatures of 25 to 30 degrees below zero prevailed in the more northern and mountainous regions. General Almond was just about the only one in the X Corps headquarters confident of his ability to withdraw his troops and save the corps. After 28–29 November Almond was fully aware of the danger to his troops, but he did not despair. When Gen. Clark L. Ruffner, Almond's chief of staff, said to General Soule, "I don't know whether we will be able to save the Old Man's corps," Soule had replied, "Yes, we will be able to do it."[20]

Almond's deputy chief of staff, Lt. Col. William J. McCaffrey, has related a conversation he overheard during this period between Vice Adm. C. Turner Joy and Almond. Joy was conferring with Almond at the latter's headquarters at Hamhung about X Corps withdrawal plans. The 1st Marine Division was still surrounded and fighting in the reservoir area. The equivalent of one regiment of the 7th Infantry Division had been destroyed. Admiral Joy told Almond he could get transports in to Hung-nam in a few days to outload the troops, but that it would take 3 to 4 weeks to get shipping there to bring out supplies and equipment. Almond replied that he wanted to bring it all out. Joy replied to that remark in effect, "But if the enemy breaks your perimeter while you are trying to outload your gear, the American people will never forgive you for the loss of lives." Almond, undaunted, rejoined, "I came in like a soldier; I'm going out like a soldier."[21] He did that. Once the corps had assembled at Hungnam, the task proved to be relatively easy, but it did not appear that way at the time of the conversation between Joy and Almond. It must be stressed, however, that Maj. Gen. Oliver P. Smith, commanding general of the 1st Marine Division, a calm, far-seeing commander, never doubted the ability of the Marine division to fight its way out of the enemy entrapment.

It is worth recording that Almond's experience with the 1st Marine Division in Korea made him a staunch supporter of its concept of including a Tactical Air Control Group as an organic unit of infantry battalions for close ground support. For fighting on extended fronts and in rough terrain, he became convinced that only such air groups, physically present with the infantry, would ensure efficient and effective close air support in ground combat. Certainly in the Chosin Reservoir campaign it was of incalculable value. Army personnel experienced in ground combat have typically envied the quantity and quality of the Marine close support.[22]

An aerial view of the road through Funchilin Pass south of Koto-ri, December 1950. Some troops can be seen on the road through this difficult terrain. (US Marine Corps photograph A-130513)

Task Force Dog

X Corps planning realized that the 1st Marine Division faced a near-impossible task of fighting its way down from the Koto-ri plateau over the twisting, steep road through Funchilin Pass and of bringing their vehicles and equipment with them. CCF troops held strong positions all the way down, and they must have felt confident the long Marine and Army trains would never get through. All planning officers and the commanders involved thought it would be necessary for the 1st Battalion, 1st Marines, which constituted the main defensive force at the Chinhung-ni perimeter, at the foot of the pass, to attack uphill along the road and its adjacent ridges and overlooking hill positions at the same time that the bulk of the 1st Marine Division left Koto-ri to fight its way down.

In order to free the 1st Battalion, 1st Marines, for this task, General Almond ordered the Army's 3rd Infantry Division to form a special task force to relieve the Marine battalion in its defensive perimeter at Chinhung-ni. This task force became known as Task Force Dog.

General Almond discussed the proposal with General Soule, 3rd Infantry Division commander, on the morning of 5 December and informed him that the order would be issued during the day. It was issued at 6:52 P.M. as Operational Instruction 26. The 3rd Division received its copy at 8:30, with notice for the task force to be ready to move on six hours' notice after 6 A.M. on 6 December, from Majon-dong to Chinhung-ni. The purpose stated in the order was to help the 1st Marine Division to withdraw from Koto-ri into the Hamhung-Hungnam defense perimeter.[23] The 3rd Division implemented the corps order by issuing its own Operational Order No. 4 at noon the next day, designating the units of the task force, which would be under the command of the assistant division commander, Brig. Gen. Armistead D. Mead. The organization was subsequently slightly augmented. As finally constituted it consisted of the units listed in table 4.

The task force assembled at Majon-dong, nine miles south of Chinhung-ni, by noon of 6 December and there awaited orders to proceed. The order came at 2:30 A.M., 7 December. The task force started for Chinhung-ni at 11 A.M. that day and arrived there without enemy contact at 2:20 P.M. that afternoon.

On the way, however, it passed 13 trucks the Chinese had destroyed the previous afternoon. They were from a Marine convoy of 15 vehicles. Most of the personnel in the convoy had been lost. There were no American troop positions along this nine-mile stretch of road between Majon-dong and Chinhung-ni. Occasional patrols from Chinhung-ni came down the road, and some supply convoys had risked passing over it. This nine-mile stretch of road followed a narrow valley northward from Majon-dong to Sudong, where it turned abruptly west for half a mile and then continued north. Much of this road was cut into a rock wall and crossed from one side to the other of the stream it followed as terrain dictated.

Just north of Sudong the point of Task Force Dog met a small Marine patrol from Chinhung-ni as it rounded a blind corner. Both groups scrambled from their vehicles to deploy but almost immediately recognized each other as friendly forces. The Marine patrol was on its way to recover the bodies of the men lost in the previous day's truck-convoy ambush.[24]

Upon arriving at Chinhung-ni in the afternoon of 7 December, the task force turned over to the 1st Battalion, 1st Marines, A Company of its 73rd Engineers to help them in their upcoming attack up the pass. Information given to the task force at this time was that several thousand CCF troops were located about five miles west of the Chinhung-ni perimeter. The day before, enemy had forced a Marine reconnaissance patrol away

TABLE 4.
Task Force Dog

Unit	Commanding Officer
3rd Bn., 7th Inf.	Lt. Col. Thomas A. O'Neil
92nd Armored FA Bn. (SP), 155-mm howitzers	Lt. Col. Leon Lavoie
A Co., 73rd Comb. Eng. (X Corps)	
3rd Plat., 3rd Recon. Co.	Lt. John N. Norton
2 sections, C Btry., 3rd AAA AW Bn. (SP)	Lt. Charles W. Boykin
17th Ordnance Bomb Disposal Unit	Captain Randel (X Corps)
Elements of 52nd Trans. Truck Bn.	Lieutenant Colonel Winston (X Corps)
Platoon of 560th Ambulance Co. (X Corps)	Lieutenant Davis
a TACP	—
a detachment from the 3rd Signal Co.	—
a platoon from A Co., 10th Eng. Comb. Bn.	—
a HQ group from the 3rd AAA AW Bn.	Lt. Col. Alvin L. Newberry

SOURCE: 3rd Inf. Div., Comd. Rpt., Dec 1950, p. 8; Lt. Col. Alvin L. Newberry, exec. off., Task Force Dog, "Springing the Chosin Reservoir Trap," 9 pp. (undated typescript MS written in early 1951), copy in author's possession.

from a village only two miles west of the perimeter. Korean refugees from the village came into Chinhung-ni during the night and reported large numbers of CCF in the vicinity. But the night of 7–8 December passed quietly at Chinhung-ni. The breakout effort from Koto-ri was to start early the next morning, 8 December.

ARMY CHIEF OF STAFF COLLINS VISITS X CORPS

On 6 December Gen. J. Lawton Collins, the Army chief of staff and representative of the Joint Chiefs of Staff for the Korean War, visited the X Corps, coming from Japan, where he had conferred with General MacArthur. He was to report his firsthand impressions of the Korean situation to the Joint Chiefs of Staff and through them to President Truman. Collins was in the X Corps area about four and a half hours. During this time he visited the 3rd and 7th Infantry Division headquarters and flew by plane with Almond over the MSR to the Chosin Reservoir as far as Sudong. Commanding officers and staffs briefed him at all stops. He seemed relieved in finding a prevailing opinions that X Corps had the combat situation in hand and that the withdrawal from Chosin Reservoir and the subsequent evacuation of the corps from northeast Korea would be executed successfully. But a surprising revelation came out of his conversation with General Almond as the latter accompanied him to Yonpo airfield, where he was to board his plane for return to Tokyo. Collins asked Almond why the Marines happened to be involved in the Chosin Reservoir area, implying it would seem, that it was no place for them to be. Almond replied that GHQ in Tokyo, in an effort to help Eighth Army in the west, had ordered the Marine advance and that X Corps was complying with that order.[25]

THE WITHDRAWAL ROUTE SOUTH OF CHINHUNG-NI

Before continuing the story of the last leg of the withdrawal from the Chosin Reservoir to the coast, a brief sketch of conditions prevailing along the route south of Chinhung-ni, the last defense perimeter held by the Marines and Army units under command of General Smith, is necessary. From Chinhung-ni southward to the edge of the Hamhung-Hungnam perimeter, which General Almond established with 7th and 3rd Division units and elements of the ROK I Corps between 1 and 6 December, there was a long stretch of road subject to almost daily enemy ambushes of convoys and to attacks on US patrols which were trying to keep harassing enemy groups away from the MSR and to stop them from blowing bridges and cratering the road. Almond had sent the 65th Regiment (less one battalion) of the 3rd Infantry Division northward to a base at Majon-dong for this purpose. From Majon-dong it was to patrol and try to control this stretch of road and make it safe for travel. But the 65th Regiment was unable to establish control of the road for the entire distance to Chinhung-ni. Especially subject to enemy action was the vicinity of Sudong, six miles south of Chinhung-ni and seven miles north of Majon-dong—about halfway between the two places.

As early as 2 December the Chinese blew up the narrow-gauge railroad between Majon-dong and Pohu-jang, eight miles northward, and thereafter supplies could not reach the railhead at the latter place. The next day, 3 December, all northern movement of supplies by rail was suspended on the MSR. And the following day, 4 December, all supplies then at Majon-dong considered as excess to the withdrawal needs were reloaded and sent back to Hamhung. The narrow-gauge railroad was actually in use only for about a week, between 25 November and 2 December. During this time the railroad carried 1,350 tons of supply to the railhead at Pohu-jang. Truck transportation was the main method of supplying the troops in the Chosin Reservoir operation, supplemented in the final critical days by airdrop and airlift.

During the last days of November and in early December, Chinese parties at night blew up virtually all the bridges and cratered the road north of Majon-dong. Engineer parties were kept busy in daytime, often under infantry and air protection, trying to rebuild bridges or construct by-passes and filling road craters. Except for the perimeter defense zones at Chinhung-ni, Koto-ri, Hagaru-ri, and Yudam-ni, the Chinese virtually controlled the MSR north of Chinhung-ni after 28 November, and north of Majon-dong after 2 December.

Perhaps the most critical point on the entire MSR was the bridge over a mountain chasm at the gatehouse in Funchilin Pass where penstocks carried water from the Chosin Reservoir down the mountain to Power Plant No. 4. The Chinese made a point of destroying this bridge as fast as it could be repaired. The 73rd Engineer Battalion had placed an M-2 steel Treadway bridge there after an earlier temporary wood crossing had been improvised when the original bridge was destroyed. During the night of 5 December the Chinese destroyed this steel Treadway bridge. On the morning of 6 December X Corps thus faced a dilemma. Unless this place could be bridged, not a single vehicle could escape from the Chosin Reservoir area.[26]

13

BREAKOUT FROM KOTO-RI, 8–11 DECEMBER

By 28 or 29 November it was well known to General Almond and his X Corps staff at Hamhung and to General Smith at Hagaru-ri, and to most of the unit commanders of the troops cut off at the reservoir, that Chinese soldiers in force held virtually all the hill and ridge positions along the steep and twisting eight miles of one-way road from the Koto-ri plateau down through Funchilin Pass to Chinhung-ni. From the plateau the road dropped about 3,500 feet in elevation to the valley below. The most dominating and critical enemy position on the way down was Hill 1081, about midway between Koto-ri and Chinhung-ni. It rose on the east side of the road, its crest overlooking the hairpin curve of the mountain road where the cable car from the valley to the plateau passed over the road. About two-thirds of a mile higher up the pass and west of the place where the cable car passed over the road, the road passed over the floor of a gatehouse on the side of a cliff, where penstocks carried water from the Chosin Reservoir to turbines in Power Plant No. 4, which generated electric power in times of peace. This point on the road was the only way out for vehicles, and it was vulnerable to complete destruction at any time.

CCF Strength and Positions South of Koto-ri

Adding to the apprehensions of General Smith and the X Corps commander was the knowledge that heavy Chinese reinforcements had been arriving in the Chosin area, with most of them moving into positions around the south of Koto-ri. It will be recalled that, while the four divisions of the CCF 20th Army and at least two divisions of the 27th Army attacked the Marines and elements of the 7th Infantry Division at the reservoir, the CCF 26th Army of the CCF IX Army Group had been held in reserve at Linchiang on the north side of the Yalu River at the Manchurian border. When it became apparent near the end of November that the UN forces at the Chosin Reservoir had not been defeated, much less

The break in the road at the power plant in Funchilin Pass, south of Koto-ri, December 1950 (US Marine Corps photograph A-5376)

destroyed, General Sung, in command of the IX Army Group, started the 26th Army south to join in the fight. Only two of the four divisions of the 26th Army, the 76th and 77th divisions, reached the field of battle in time to take part in the action during the UN withdrawal to the Hungnam perimeter. These two divisions first had contact with American troops on 5 December at Hagaru-ri, but their heaviest engagements were to be farther south in the vicinity of Koto-ri, in the battles for control of Funchilin Pass and the descent to Chinhung-ni. The other two divisions of the CCF 26th Army, the 78th and 88th, did not arrive in time to play a role in the Chosin Reservoir campaign.

When Gen. Sung Shih Lun held one-third of his IX Army Group far to the rear in the almost trackless wastes of North Korea, he made a crucial mistake. This error of judgment on his part must have grown out of his belief that he would not need those troops in the destruction of the X Corps troops in the Chosin Reservoir area — and if he did need them, he could bring them up in time to finish off what he concluded would be a decimated remnant of the X Corps forces unable to escape his trap. When his calculation proved wrong, he was unable to get his reserve divisions to the battle area quickly enough to be a decisive factor.

The CCF 76th Division surrounded Koto-ri from 5 December on, but because of fatigue from their forced marches, the intense cold, and the unceasing American artillery barrages and air strikes on their assembly areas, which were generally about two to five miles west of Koto-ri, they were unable to mount any serious assault on the Koto-ri perimeter. The division was in fact decimated without engaging in much heavy fighting. Only a small part of the 76th Division survived the campaign.[1]

Capture of Chinese prisoners also clearly demonstrated that the bulk of the CCF 60th Division, after initial contact with Marines at Yudam-ni, had moved to Koto-ri and Funchilin Pass and was heavily engaged there in various actions between 1 and 10 December. It appears that elements of this division defended Hill 1081. A Chinese captain of the 180th Regiment of the 60th Division, captured near Koto-ri on 9 December, said his regiment had lost half its men between 1 and 9 December. Half of these heavy losses were due, he said, to frostbite and trench foot, the remainder mostly to air attack and artillery fire. Inadequate food rations and near-starvation conditions also had lowered Chinese morale and stamina, he reported.[2]

PLANS FOR BREAKOUT FROM KOTO-RI

Planning for the breakout from Koto-ri to Chinhung-ni, to begin on the morning of 8 December, was essentially the same as that from Yudam-ni to Hagaru-ri, and from the latter to Koto-ri. Infantry was to seize and hold the high ground on either side of the road, after which the long vehicular trains, tanks, and artillery would move southward over the icy road. Artillery from either end would support both the infantry and the trains. At the same time, if weather permitted, air cover would help in close support of the infantry fighting in the hills dominating the road and would provide protective cover over the trains on the road. Snowstorms, if they came, would seriously hamper artillery and air support and might stop the latter entirely. The arrival of darkness would also end close air support, except for the limited availability of night-fighter planes.

There were about 14,000 men assembled at the Koto-ri perimeter for the breakout, consisting of approximately 4,200 troops that constituted the Koto-ri garrison and about 10,000 that had survived the withdrawal fight from Hagaru-ri.[3] The CCF below Koto-ri had blown every bridge on the road down the mountain, had blown craters in the road, and had caused landslides. Included in their destruction of bridges was the one over the penstocks in Funchilin Pass. The Chinese had constructed bunkers from which they could deliver mortar, automatic, and small-arms fire on these vulnerable spots, and indeed their emplacements enabled them to cover with fire nearly all the road down the pass. The Chinese command must have thought that no Marine or Army vehicle could ever make it down the mountain to Chinhung-ni and that the UN troops who might get there would be stragglers, making their way by good fortune on foot through the snow-covered and icy hills—survivors from a general rout.

Each side knew the eight miles from Koto-ri through Funchilin Pass was the showdown. For the CCF it was their last chance to destroy the X Corps in North Korea. For the UN troops in the Chosin Reservoir area, it was simply a case of their survival.

General Almond had supported General Smith's request for control of all supporting aircraft during the withdrawal of his troops. In addition, Almond told Smith he could count on every possible assistance from the X Corps. General Almond realized fully that the Chosin Reservoir fighting, and extricating his Marine and Army troops there, was really a fight to save his X Corps.

While the defensive battles were being won at the reservoir by superb discipline and sacrifice of the troops, those actions were also buying time for other elements of X Corps, spread over a 400-mile front in frigid northeast Korea, some of them on the Yalu and others within 38 miles of the Soviet border. Now they had to withdraw from their exposed positions and assemble at the Hamhung-Hungnam perimeter. This action could not be accomplished overnight.[4]

During the night of 7–8 December arrangements were being made at both Koto-ri and at Chinhung-ni for attacks to start at dawn from both places in the breakout effort from Koto-ri. The 1st Battalion, 1st Marine Regiment, would attack north from Chinhung-ni with the objective of seizing Hill 1081, the critical high ground at Funchilin Pass east of the road. The main withdrawal force would attack down the road from Koto-ri. The two forces would execute a pincer movement; they hoped to meet in the vicinity of Hill 1081, about halfway between the two starting points. While the road distance between Koto-ri and Chinhung-ni was about ten miles, this was reduced to approximately eight miles if one counts from the edges of the two perimeters.

Because of its special mission, the southern force was to move earliest on 8 December. Its progress, therefore, will be followed before turning to the breakout attack from Koto-ri.

1st Marines Attack North from Chinhung-ni, 8 December

In the darkness of early Friday, 8 December, Lt. Col. Donald M. Schmuck, commanding officer of the 1st Battalion, 1st Marines, formed his battalion in a column of companies in an assembly area south of Chinhung-ni. His battalion had an approach march on foot of six miles up the road before it reached the point of deployment for attack at 8 A.M. Its first objective was to seize the southwest nose of Hill 1081. The battalion started its approach march at 2 A.M. It was well rested and fresh, having engaged thus far in the relatively inactive defense of the Koto-ri perimeter. A swirling snowstorm filled the air with dustlike powdery flakes, which reduced visibility almost to zero in the five hours before daybreak. The only vehicles in the column were a radio jeep and two ambulances. During the predawn march the snow clung to the men's parkas, giving them nearly complete color camouflage. This camouflage on the men continued in the low visibility following daybreak.

Capt. Robert P. Wray's C Company took the lead. Wray was to seize and hold the southwest nose of Hill 1081, while the other two rifle companies continued toward the crest. Capt. Robert H. Barrow's A Company had the hardest job. It was to attack through C Company, east of the road, and go for the crest of 1081. Capt. Wesley Noren's B Company was to attack along the left flank of A Company and between it and the road. C Company took its objective soon after daybreak with little resistance. For a period, Noren's men followed the road, and with the help of A Company, 73rd Engineer Combat Battalion, it quickly overcame successive enemy roadblocks. The heavy snowstorm helped them. The Chinese in the roadblocks could not see the approaching Marines and engineer troops.[5]

While Noren's B Company and the Army engineers were overrunning the first series of roadblocks, Colonel Schmuck set up the battalion's 4.2-inch mortars and 81-mm mortars in the position of Wray's C Company, on the spur ridge running down from Hill 1081. These mortars were to support the attack on Hill 1081. He also placed five Army self-propelled quad-50 and dual-40 gun carriers on a rise to the left of the road. From there these weapons covered the road as it climbed upward under towering Hill 1081 as far as the destroyed bridge over the penstocks at the clifflike face of the mountain.

The main assault on Hill 1081 began about 10 A.M. B Company continued its advance up the road and the western slope of the mountain. On its right, Captain Barrow's A Company made the main assault up the steep hogback spur ridge that led to the summit from the south. They knew from intelligence reports that elements of the CCF 60th Division that had survived the Chosin fighting thus far had moved into the prepared positions on Hill 1081. Newly arrived elements of the 76th and 77th divisions of the 26th Army on forced marches from Linchiang on the Yalu border had relieved them along the east side of the road south of Hagaru-ri. The 60th Division had one of the best reputations in the Chinese Communist Army.[6]

On the western slope of the mountain, B Company surprised Chinese in a bunker complex and captured the bunker position after a short but violent fight. The largest bunker here was a strong log and sandbag structure that apparently had been an enemy command post. A kettle of rice was cooking at the time of capture. Lieutenant Colonel Schmuck established his CP there as daylight faded.

Meanwhile, Barrow's A Company, out of physical contact with B Company, was laboring to climb the icy white hogback's narrow spine. There was no room for deployment. The snowstorm that had continued through the day benefited the Marines. In effect, it blinded the Chinese defenders in their bunkers and dug-in positions. Visibility was about 25 feet.

Barrow and T. Sgt. King Thalenhurst were in the lead when they suddenly heard Chinese soldiers talking a short distance from them. They stopped. The snowstorm swirled to form a brief rift, and through it Barrow saw Chinese soldiers moving about on a knoll directly ahead. Thalenhurst quickly dropped back and warned Jones's platoon to be quiet. A Company had spent two hours of hard climbing to reach this point. Barrow's brief glimpse of the knob indicated it held a couple of bunkers and was probably strongly held, constituting a main defense of the crest against an approach from the south along the hogback spur ridge the Marines had climbed.

Before deciding on a plan of action, Barrow carefully reconnoitered the vicinity. Only a squad could deploy on the top of the narrow hogback. On either side, east and west, the edge dropped off in very steep inclines. Barrow set up the 60-mm mortars behind the company. Lieutenant Jones then led his platoon forward toward the knob. Only three or four men could crawl in the skirmish line, so narrow was the approach. They got so close to the Chinese that the latter heard rather than saw them and began firing wildly at the sounds they heard. Only a few of the Marines could fire back. It became apparent to Barrow that this kind of attack would likely prove disastrous. He called off Jones's approach along the hogback and directed him to take two squads of the 2nd Platoon and worm their way around to the left, below the hogback. Lieutenant McClelland's 1st Platoon was to perform a similar movement on the right of the hogback. Lieutenant Roach's 3rd Platoon would lead a frontal attack. When Jones and McClelland had reached their places just below the knob on either side, Barrow would give the signal, and all three platoons would leap to their feet and charge for the crest. It took Jones and his squad an hour to crawl 150 yards.

When the groups were in position, Barrow gave the signal. The men in the three assault forces scrambled to the top, those from the two sides of the knob yelling wildly as they burst out on top. The Chinese in the bunkers seemed stunned as the shadowlike figures emerged from the snowstorm. One enemy machine-gun crew, however, had not lost its alertness and poured a destructive stream of bullets into the attackers, causing most of their casualties. Cpl. Joseph Leeds killed most of the crew and silenced the gun. Leeds himself was mortally wounded in this assault. The rest of the men in his squad quickly finished off the enemy soldiers still in the bunker.

Most of the demoralized CCF fled their bunkers, some straight into the fire of the Marines; others were shot down as they ran away. More than 60 CCF soldiers lay dead in the bunkers on this knoll or in the snow outside. When the shouting and shooting died down, the Marines found they had paid a price—10 killed and 11 wounded.[7]

The conditions that assault groups had to overcome in fights such as Barrow's on Hill 1081 are hard to visualize. One who participated in some of them has left this description:

> Some of these ice-covered ridges were so treacherous that when a rifle company attacked, it was a squad from the leading platoon that went along the only avenue of approach, the well-beaten path along the ridge line. Why? Because a Rocky Mountain goat could not have scaled the slippery sides of these rocky ridges without falling. Sure, the enemy had this path zeroed in, but when there was only one approach the rifle squad had to use it, with the remainder of the company charging along in column behind.[8]

This form of attack characterized many, many assaults in Korea, by both Marine and Army troops throughout the war.

Darkness was approaching when Barrow's men had won the bunkers on Hill 1081. Barrow put his A Company into a tight perimeter on the knob for the night. From this steep, icy pinnacle it took four-man litter teams four hours to get a wounded man to the bottom of the hill. Lower down the slope, Noren's B Company received orders to dig in and hold for the night. They halted where they were about 4:30 P.M. after the engineers reduced a third enemy roadblock on the road.

That night of 8–9 December was bitterly cold, and especially so on Hill 1081. From the Chinhung-ni perimeter, Marine and Army artillery kept up a nightlong interdiction fire on enemy positions and protective fires around Barrow's position. The fire from the Army's Armored Field

Artillery Battalion's 155-mm howitzers of Task Force Dog was particularly effective. The only enemy action during the night on Hill 1081 was a platoon attack about midnight against Barrow's position. The Chinese lost 18 killed in this futile attack.

On balance, the heavy snowstorm of 8 December was a stroke of good fortune for the 1st Battalion, 1st Marines, in its attack up the southern slope of Hill 1081. It helped B Company and the engineers advance north up the road and along the lower slope of Hill 1081. And it was a critical factor in enabling Barrow's A Company to surprise and eventually overwhelm the Chinese strongpoint on the spur ridge knob below the crest. When dark fell, the military crest of Hill 1081 still remained in Chinese possession. The task of taking it would still face the 1st Battalion when dawn broke on the ninth. Before resuming that story, it is necessary to note what had happened during the day to the main Marine and Army force attacking south out of Koto-ri.

7TH MARINES LEAD ATTACK SOUTH FROM KOTO-RI, 8 DECEMBER

About the same time that the 1st Battalion, 1st Marines, left its line of departure at the south end of Funchilin Pass to attack north up the spur ridge of Hill 1081, the 3rd Battalion, 7th Marines, at 8 A.M. led the attack south out of the Koto-ri perimeter. The same snowstorm cut visibility to short distances, and close air support was impossible during the day. The snowstorm hurt the efforts of the 7th Marines, whereas it had helped the attack from the south. General Smith's plan required Marine and Army infantry to sweep and seize the high ground on either side of the road before vehicular trains, artillery, and tanks could move out southward down the road into the steep incline of Funchilin Pass. He also decided, apparently after issuing 1st Marine Division Operational Order 26-50 the evening before, that the tanks would be at the rear of the column because of the narrow road with its numerous sharp curves down the long, steep pass. He wanted to avoid having a stalled tank block the way to all other vehicles behind it. And he also wanted to get the division's 1,000 vehicles over the Treadway bridge he expected to be installed over the blown bridge site where the water-power penstocks passed over the road in Funchilin Pass before tanks were entrusted to it. There were bound to be many wounded in the fight through the pass to Chinhung-ni, and these wounded would have to be transported in the trucks. If the bridge could not be replaced and held as the column moved across it, only the walking, able-bodied men would have any chance of escaping, and the chances of saving wounded would be slim.

On the morning of 8 December, when the attack southward from Koto-ri began, there was no bridge over this clifflike chasm, and enemy soldiers held the high ground commanding the site. Plans to install a bridge had been made if the attack went well and the bridge site could be seized. The story of the Treadway bridge will be told later. But it was not to be a factor on 8 December. The Marine attack from the north was doomed not to reach that point during the day.

The way ahead for the withdrawing troops was not an easy one geographically. About two miles south of Koto-ri the road left the high 4,000-foot plateau and started the steep descent of Funchilin Pass. In a distance of ten miles from Koto-ri, the elevation dropped about 3,500 feet, to approximately 500 feet at Chinhung-ni in the valley below. From there the road ran generally south along the walled valley of the Hungnim and Songchon rivers to Hamhung. The route then crossed the flat river delta for another ten miles to the port of Hungnam on the Sea of Japan.

Maj. Warren Morris with his 3rd Battalion, 7th Marines, led out with the objective of capturing Hill 1328 on the west (right) side of the road. A mile south of Koto-ri the CCF opened fire on the lead elements of the battalion. In trying to overcome the enemy position, the 3rd Battalion made very little progress.

Meanwhile, the 1st Battalion, 7th Marines, was supposed to move along the road for a little more than a mile from Koto-ri and then wait for the 3rd Battalion attacking on the west of it to come abreast. Maj. Webb D. Sawyer now commanded the 1st Battalion. It had met no opposition when it stopped to wait for the 3rd Battalion. Sawyer sent a patrol down the road, however, and it received CCF fire as it approached Hill 1304, which was one and one-half miles farther south. Sawyer ordered A and C companies out in an envelopment maneuver westward against the hill. B Company advanced down the road in support of the patrol that was under fire. It ran into a heavy crossfire from its front and from Hill 1304 to the west. In this action 1st Lt. Joseph R. Kurcaba, the commanding officer, was killed, and two of his officers wounded. A and C companies succeeded in overcoming the defenses on Hill 1304 about dusk, and the 1st Battalion dug in for the night.

Early in the afternoon, Colonel Litzenberg committed the 2nd Battalion to help the stalled 3rd Battalion in its fight for Hill 1328. By 6 P.M. E and F companies had joined on the northeast slope of the hill. Darkness was near. The attack was halted at that time, short of the first objective. The troops dug in and held there for the night.

Meanwhile, Lieutenant Colonel Stevens with the 1st Battalion, 5th Marines, was scheduled to follow the 7th Marines out of Koto-ri and attack on order. This order came about noon. He followed the road for about a mile and then turned east up the steep slope of Hill 1457. B Company occupied some intervening high ground and from there covered the attack of C Company against the crest. In this attack, C Company met elements of the Army Provisional Battalion, Captains Kitz's and Rasula's companies, advancing from the north. The combined forces seized the top of Hill 1457 about 3:50 P.M. They repulsed a CCF counterattack. The 1st Battalion, 5th Marines, and the two Army companies set up perimeter defenses there for the night.

Back at Koto-ri, the 7th Marine truck convoy meanwhile had moved out to follow the 1st Battalion, 7th Marines. It had to stop for the night less than two miles from Koto-ri. The vehicles backed up to the edge of the Koto-ri plateau and there went into a defense perimeter.

A little more should be said about the Army Provisional Battalion's efforts in the attack on the east side of the road out of Koto-ri on 8 December. The now-reorganized Provisional Battalion in two companies moved out of Koto-ri at 7:30 A.M. in attack to seize high ground a mile south and 600 yards east of the road. They took the high ground without resistance and went into a defensive position there to guard the road. In this action, Captain Rasula had two platoons, each consisting of about one and one-half squads with Lieutenant Polari leading one and Lieutenant Holcomb leading the other. Lieutenant Escue remained behind in Koto-ri to round up as many other men belonging to the 31st Company as he could find. Bringing more men, he eventually caught up with Rasula's company. These men were integrated with others into three platoons. Captains Rasula and Kitz remained in this position for about two hours. Then they received an order to move to higher ground for about two hours. Then they received an order to move to higher ground on the left, Hill 1457, overlooking Funchilin Pass.

Snow began to fall, in Rasula's words, "like I've never seen it snow before—couldn't see twenty-five yards." Control of the men was difficult in this situation, but the companies got to the highest ground they could see and started digging in for the night.

Soon after they started this work, two enemy submachine guns and several automatic carbines suddenly delivered fire on them. At first the group thought it came from a Marine patrol. But one of the artillery officers saw a Chinese soldier covered with a white blanket crawling toward him. He shot the enemy soldier. That started a close-in fight. The unidentified artillery officer quickly assembled some men at his end of the line and led them in a quick assault that killed about a dozen Chinese; others disappeared in the snowstorm. This attack cost one man killed and four wounded. But it disclosed that the Chinese had been on ground slightly higher than that the 31st and 32nd companies had occupied. These two companies immediately moved into the Chinese holes and worked for several hours improving the position—a hard task in the frozen ground.

That night the temperature dropped to 10 degrees below zero. Rasula said the two companies lost more men that night because of the cold and frostbite than they had to all causes all the way from Hagaru-ri.[9]

Because of the falling snow and low visibility on 8 December, Chinese soldiers in their observation posts around the Koto-ri perimeter probably could not see a ceremony that occurred within the perimeter. General Smith attended services at which 117 dead Marines, Army soldiers, and British Marine Commandos were buried in a mass grave. The frozen ground made digging individual graves prohibitive in the short time available. Since all available space in planes and vehicles was needed for the wounded, it was decided that the dead could not be taken out in the withdrawal from Koto-ri. These buried dead were later recovered by the United States under terms of the Korean armistice of 27 July 1953.[10]

PLANNING FOR THE TREADWAY BRIDGE

During the night of 5 December Chinese for the third time had blown and destroyed the bridge three and one-half miles south of Koto-ri in Funchilin Pass that passed over the four steel penstocks that emerged from the concrete gatehouse. This gatehouse, which had no floor, had been built by the Japanese years earlier on the uphill side of the cliff. Water from the Chosin Reservoir was carried by a tunnel down the mountainside to the gatehouse, where it entered the four steel pipes to drop down the mountainside to Power Plant No. 4, where the surging water generated electricity. The bridge, in short, carried the road over the steel pipes and the chasm immediately below the gatehouse. This spot was nearly two-thirds of a mile uphill and west of the place where the cable car overpassed the road, on the west side of a hairpin curve in Funchilin Pass. The destroyed bridge left a gap in the road of 16 feet, or 24 feet if the abutments on either side are included.

US Army engineers had first built a wooden structure, and later an M-2 steel Treadway bridge, at the site after Chinese had destroyed the original span. Enemy soldiers destroyed both these replacement bridges.

General Smith had Lt. Col. John H. Partridge, commanding officer of the Marine 1st Engineer Battalion, make a detailed study of the bridge site from the air on 6 December. Partridge thought four sections of an M-2 steel Treadway bridge could span the gap. A section of the bridge was 18-feet long and weighed 2,900 pounds. Special trucks with special equipment were needed to handle, join, and put in place two sections of such a bridge. As luck would have it, a platoon of the Army's 58th Engineer Treadway Bridge Company, with four Brockway trucks, was in the force cut off at Koto-ri. Two of the trucks were operative. If the sections of the bridge could be delivered to it at Koto-ri, they could transport them to the bridge site and install them over the gap, providing the infantry could cut a way through the enemy and hold the high ground along the road down the pass and at the bridge site. Enemy forces had by now taken positions near the bridge site and covered it with automatic weapons and other fire. There was only one way to get the needed bridge sections to Koto-ri—by airdrop.

X Corps engineers and a liaison officer from the Marine Engineer Battalion worked all night studying aerial photographs, trying to determine the precise length of bridging required and, most important, how to deliver the bridging by air undamaged so that it would be usable. All agreed that a bypass road could not be cut behind the gatehouse and that there was no chance of building a ledge on the lower side to support a road. Captain Atkins of the X Corps Engineering Intelligence staff kept suggesting that the bridge could be lowered from the air, two sections then linked together and launched over the chasm. It appeared that a Treadway bridge had never been dropped from an airplane before. The idea had to be tried. There seemed to be no alternative.

Time was short. The troops were expected to be at the bridge site in the next two days if their breakout effort succeeded. Combat Cargo and Quartermaster aerial supply teams at Yonpo airfield, near Wonsan, had the task of rigging and loading the bridge sections. The Air Force commander at Yonpo requested that they make a trial drop at Yonpo before undertaking the drop at Koto-ri. One bridge section was rigged with a G-1 24-foot parachute, the largest at hand. When dropped, the bridge section crumbled and buried itself deep in the ground—one source said 20 feet deep. A message was sent at once to Ashiya airfield in Japan for better equipment. Capt. Cecil W. Hospelhorn of the 8081st Army Quartermaster Airborne Air Supply and Packaging Company and a detachment from Ashiya flew at once to Yonpo with a supply of 48-foot parachutes. An experimental drop with the 48-foot parachute was successful. Hospelhorn and his men worked all night rigging each of eight Treadway bridge sections with two of the big parachutes. Eight C-119 Flying Boxcars were detailed to carry one each of the bridge sections. An Army–Air Force briefing discussion on the problem decided that, at 1,000 feet above the ground, seven feet of each section would be moved so as to protrude past the rear opening of the plane, thus aiding in obtaining a fast drop into the small 300-yard-long drop zone. The drop was to be made from 800 feet. A margin of safety was provided in dropping double the number of sections needed.

On 7 December at 9:30 A.M., three C-119 planes dropped three bridge sections within the Koto-ri perimeter, which were recovered by the Brockway trucks. The other five sections were dropped by noon. One fell outside the perimeter into Chinese hands, and another was damaged in the drop. Plywood panels also were dropped at Koto-ri to make a floor over the center sections of the Treadway bridge to carry any type of wheeled vehicle. Tanks could cross on the metal spans.

By midafternoon of 7 December all the necessary bridging material had been assembled at Koto-ri. In a staff meeting that evening, Colonel Litzenberg and Colonel Bowser, the 1st Marine Division G-3, agreed that the Brockway trucks with the Treadway bridge sections should accompany the 7th Regimental Train out of Koto-ri. First Lt. Ewald D. Vom Orde's 1st Platoon of D Company, Engineers, was named escort for 1st Lt. Charles C. Ward's platoon of the Army's 58th Treadway Bridge Company, and they were to lead the train column with the Treadway bridge sections on Ward's Brockway trucks. Ward and his men were very well trained in the installation of Treadway bridges, having had much experience in the work in Italy during World War II. Both engineer groups were to cooperate in installing the bridge once they reached the site. The bridge trucks moved out of Koto-ri about 2 P.M. on 8 December, but the slow progress of the infantry that day in advancing south and clearing the way for the trains forced Ward to return to the tank park and perimeter that evening near Koto-ri.[11]

The story of how the Treadway bridge was made ready for use in Funchilin Pass is told here at some length because it illustrates so well how competent service troops, together with higher-command coordination (in this case, X Corps and the 1st Marine Division) can affect the outcome of battle and save the lives of hundreds, perhaps thousands, of soldiers and their equipment. It also illustrates how ingenuity of officers and subordinates using sophisticated military technology can affect the outcome of battle. The Chinese forces at Chosin Reservoir had none of these capabilities, and therein was one of the factors that finally decided the outcome.

1st Marines Take Hill 1081, 9 December

Hill 1081 glittered and sparkled under its new snow mantle as 9 December dawned. The sky was clear. The snowstorm had passed. Air support, observed artillery fire, and the use of all supporting weapons could aid the infantry. It portended some trying moments for the Chinese in their dug-in positions and bunkers.

On the western slope of Hill 1081, dawn disclosed to Captain Noren's B Company that it was one ridge short of its objectives—the northwest slope of the hill, from which it could cover the MSR below in the vicinity of the hairpin curve and the cable-car overpass. The company moved forward to this position without opposition.

On the morning of 9 December, when the Marines relieved the two

Withdrawal through Funchilin Pass continues after Treadway bridge sections are installed over the break in the road at the power plant. (US Marine Corps photograph
A-5408)

Army companies on Hill 1457, where high ground overlooked the road
descent into Funchilin Pass, Captain Rasula's company moved to a knob
closer to the road, and Captain Kitz's company moved farther down the
road into the pass to a point just above the destroyed bridge at the penstocks on the mountain side. There it joined the troops protecting the
engineers who were working to install a new bridge over the chasm. That
night was cold and windy, but there was no enemy action for them.[12]

It was quite a different situation for Barrow's A Company, higher up
on the spur that led to the topographical crest of Hill 1081, about half
a mile distant from Captain Noren's B Company. Late on the previous
afternoon, it will be recalled, A Company in a fierce, close-in battle in
the snowstorm had overcome the first strong complex of bunkers and

related positions guarding the approach to the crest along the southern spur. Now, on the morning of 9 December, after a bitterly cold night on the hill, Captain Barrow had his men test-fire their weapons as they prepared to renew the attack. The test-firing showed that some of the weapons' mechanisms had frozen and had to be thawed out before they became operable. The Chinese in the bunker complex on the crest and its approaches were now fully aware of the presence just below them of the Marines and of an impending continuation of their attack.

Air strikes and artillery and mortar barrages worked over the enemy positions on the crest of Hill 1081 before A Company started to climb upward in a column of platoons. McClelland's 1st Platoon led. The heavy volume of small-arms fire that poured out of Chinese camouflaged sand-bag and log bunkers seemed to indicate that the air strikes and artillery fire had not done much damage to their defenses. The 1st Platoon in its approach took many casualties from this fire. S. Sgt. Ernest J. Umbaugh and a squad on the platoon left finally worked their way to within about 200 yards of the crest. There Umbaugh led a grenade attack on the nearest bunker, wiping out its defenders.

About 500 feet of open slope, swept clear of snow in places by strong wind, now separated the 1st Platoon from the crest. This was a field of deadly fire for the Chinese gunners in protected bunkers on top. Captain Barrow, after careful observation, thought this field of fire could possibly be skirted by working around a shelf that at one point projected from the crest. He prepared for the effort by bringing up his 2nd and 3rd platoons under cover of an air strike by four Corsairs and a heavy barrage from his 60-mm mortars. McClelland, helped by the shelter of some scrub trees, moved below and around the projecting shelf to gain the rear of the enemy bunkers. Jones's 2nd Platoon set up its machine guns and built up a base of fire to support a frontal assault by Roach's 3rd Platoon. With everything ready, Barrow signaled the assault. McClelland attacked from behind the bunkers as Roach's men scrambled up the slope. The two-platoon assault culminated in a close, fierce battle around the bunkers. The remnants of McClelland's 1st Platoon finished off the last two CCF bunkers by throwing grenades through the firing embrasures. Sergeant Umbaugh was killed in this final action. The CCF still did not surrender, and the fight continued. By midafternoon A Company had seized its objective, the crest of Hill 1081. It had been a tough fight. The CCF defenders had resisted to the last man. The count of enemy dead on Hill 1081 in the path of Barrow's A Company's attack was 530. But at the close, Barrow had only 111 able-bodied men left on the crest of Hill 1081 of the 223 who had started up the hill the previous morning.[13] While A Company held the crest, B Company below it started moving up the northwest slope of Hill 1081 along the cable-car route above the road, clearing out pockets of Chinese soldiers as it proceeded.

The attack north from Chinhung-ni by the 1st Battalion, 1st Marines, had captured the crest of Hill 1081 by midafternoon on 9 December. The seizure of this dominant and key terrain above the road through Funchilin Pass was of the greatest significance in the breakout effort of the 1st Marine Division and its attached Army troops. One might well consider this operation by the battalion as a classic example of combat operation under adverse conditions against a well-prepared enemy in a strong position. The A Company attack by maneuver and determined assault was especially noteworthy.

THROUGH FUNCHILIN PASS, 9–10 DECEMBER

General Smith's plan for the withdrawal on 9 December remained the same as it had been the day before. In its simplest form it was for the 7th Marines to go first, followed by the 5th Marine Regiment, while the 1st Marines held Koto-ri and covered the rear of the withdrawing troops and their trains. The divisional trains would follow the 1st Battalion, 7th Marines, after it had cleared the road to the bridge site. When the bridge had been placed over the chasm at the gatehouse in the pass, the divisional trains would start down from the Koto-ri perimeter. The tanks would follow the 1st Marine Regiment out of Koto-ri, with the 2nd Battalion of that regiment and the Reconnaissance Company the last to leave. Lieutenant Colonel Schmuck's 1st Battalion, 1st Marines, would hold Hill 1081 until all units from Koto-ri had passed on the road below it. Then the battalion would come off the hill and cross the Treadway bridge. While all this was happening, it was certain that the CCF would have to be driven from the high ground along the road and kept from closing in on the long column from side and rear. That there would be bloody episodes in this march was a foregone conclusion. But there was no alternative.[14]

The resumption of the 7th Marines' attack on the morning of 9 December started with conditions far different from those that had prevailed the previous day. Now the sky was crystal clear, visibility was good, and there was an umbrella of air cover over the troops as they moved out toward their objectives. All units seized their first objectives quickly—Hill 1304 on the west of the road and the high ground opposite it, east of the road. Still farther east, the 1st Battalion, 5th Marines, held its positions on Hill 1457 all day. The success of the 1st Battalion, 1st Marines, in seizing the crest of Hill 1081, farther south and the dominating ground east of the road, had important—perhaps decisive—effect on the inability of the CCF to prevent the steady advance of the 7th Marines on the morn-

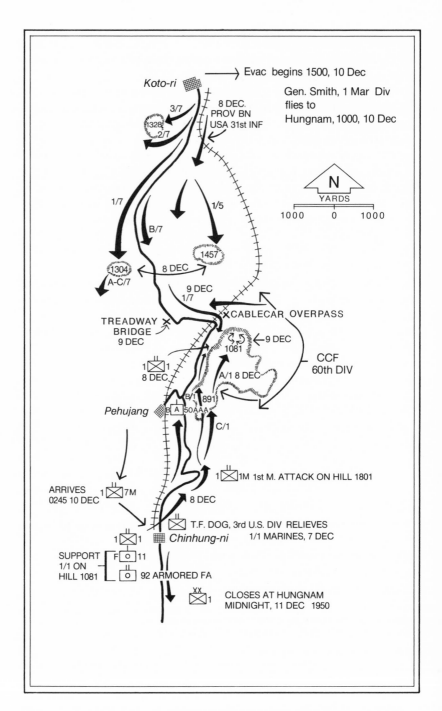

MAP 16. 1st Marine Division and Army units in Funchilin Pass, 8–10 December.

ing of 9 December. Also, the constant air strikes and artillery barrages on their positions began to demoralize the CCF.

Capt. John F. Morris's C Company and a platoon of B Company, 7th Marines, moved down the road to the Treadway bridge site and gained control of the immediate area after a brief firefight. Morris divided C Company into six outpost groups of eight men each and placed them in protective positions around the bridge site. While this was being done, the B Company platoon crossed behind the gatehouse at the bridge site to gain the south side. On the way, the platoon suddenly came upon about 50 CCF soldiers in foxholes. They looked like sitting statues. In fact, they were so nearly frozen to death they could not move. Maj. Webb D. Sawyer, the 1st Battalion commander, in describing later what happened said, "The men simply lifted them from the holes and sat them on the road where Marines from Charlie Company took them over."[15] The Chinese soldiers' fingers and hands were so frozen to their weapons that in disarming them their fingers had to be physically bent and broken from the rifles they grasped. These Chinese were numb and dazed from fatigue and cold. Interrogation later revealed they were members of a force, numbering into the hundreds, that in the snowstorm the day before had been hurried southward as reinforcements, often at a run, to this critical area. Despite the cold temperature they had sweated. When they were halted and put into positions along the road, they had literally frozen during the night in their own sweat. Some of those interrogated said the subzero weather of the Chosin Reservoir region had taken extremely heavy toll of the CCF, in some units almost 100 percent.[16]

PLACING THE TREADWAY BRIDGE ACROSS THE CHASM

Even though the 7th Marines, together with the 1st Battalion, 1st Marines, on the crest of Hill 1081 above them, now controlled the bridge site, this control did not extend very far downhill along the road. A 7th Marine patrol sent down the road in an effort to contact the 1st Marines was driven from the road by CCF fire but later made its way into 1st Marine lines on the slope of the hill.

Sawyer informed Lt. Col. John H. Partridge that the 1st Battalion held the bridge site. Partridge then brought the Brockway trucks with sections down the mountainside, guarded by the Weapons Company of the 1st Battalion. The engineer troops set to work at once to get the bridge in place. First, they had to rebuild the southern side abutment, which the Chinese had destroyed along with the last bridge. They did this by building a base of sandbags and timbers. Engineer officers Ward, Vom Orde, and 1st Lt. David D. Peppin coordinated the work of about 100 men, including some Chinese prisoners, in constructing the abutment and then laying the Treadway bridge sections with one of the Brockway trucks. The work started shortly after noon and was completed about 3:30 P.M. Colonel Partridge drove in his jeep to the top of the pass at once and told Lt. Col. Charles L. Banks, commander of Division Train No. 1, he could start the descent. Partridge returned to the bridge site. About 6 P.M. on 9 December, the first vehicles of the division train crossed the Treadway bridge on their way to Chinhung-ni.[17]

While the bridge was being constructed, the 1st Battalion, 7th Marines, was busy driving back Chinese soldiers trying to reach the bridge site. In the advance of the UN troops and the huge divisional train down the mountain, not a single enemy mine was encountered. This probably indicated the CCF had no mines to use. Had they been able to mine the road, the damage and destruction in the column would probably have been extensive and the loss of life considerable, because the train would not have been able to move rapidly, as it did most of the time after it successfully crossed the bridge.

There was near disaster at the bridge, however, soon after the vehicles began crossing it. Wood flooring had been laid to allow wheeled vehicles to pass over the bridge, and a tractor towing a piece of earth-moving equipment broke through the plywood center panel between the steel treadways. Now, none of them could cross, and there was the problem of getting the tractor off the broken part of the bridge. T. Sgt. Wilfred H. Prosser, an expert tractor driver, succeeded in backing it off the bridge.

Colonel Partridge then calculated that, if the treadways were relaid as far apart as possible, he would have a total width of 11 feet, 4 inches, which would give a margin of two inches for the M-26 tanks on the treadways and one-half inch for jeeps, using the 45-inch interval between the inner steel lip edges of the treadways. The treadways were successfully relaid, and at dusk traffic resumed with vehicular lights on and engineer troops guiding the vehicles across the bridge with flashlights. The 1st Battalion, 7th Marines, succeeded in keeping Chinese from closing in on the bridge site during the night.

All that night of 9–10 December Marine and Army troops and vehicles streamed south across the Treadway bridge. The sound of crunching feet and turning wheels in the frozen snow was continuous. The number of CCF prisoners increased during the night until there were more than a hundred of them. Some had gangrene in frozen limbs. Others were in various stages of malnutrition and starvation.

Shortly after midnight of 9–10 December Major Sawyer, commander of the 1st Battalion, 7th Marines, came down from the Koto-ri plateau and reached Lieutenant Colonel Schmuck's CP bunker on Hill 1081. Some Marines from one of Sawyer's patrols had reached Schmuck's lines on the mountain earlier in the night. Thus, the two attacking Marine combat forces, one from the north and the other from the south, met during the night.

Breakout Column Reaches Chinhung-ni, 10 December

The lead elements of the withdrawing column, members of the 1st Battalion, 7th Marines, arrived at the foot of the mountain, at Chinhung-ni, at 2:45 A.M., 10 December.[18] With an escort from the Reconnaissance Platoon, Task Force Dog, 3rd Infantry Division, they continued on south. Some parts of the 7th Marine Regiment were still a mile and a half north of the bridge at 4 A.M. A halt in the traffic occurred, this one lasting three hours, when two trucks stalled in a bypass around a blown bridge more than a mile below the Treadway bridge. The bypass was cleared, and the trains began to move again about 7 A.M. The first vehicle in the column reached Chinhung-ni at 8:30 A.M. on 10 December. Both regimental trains got through to Chinhung-ni with their escorting troops without trouble, as did nearly all the troops after crossing the Treadway bridge.

The two companies of the Army's Provisional Battalion also passed over the Treadway bridge on the tenth and reached the coast that night. After daylight on 10 December, the companies of Captains Rasula and Kitz continued on down the pass above the Treadway bridge. Friendly troops held the ridgelines along the road, and they reached Chinhung-ni, at the foot of the pass, without enemy action. There they entered the Army's 3rd Division perimeter and found plenty of food in a ration dump. Trucks were also waiting there that carried them the rest of the way to Hamhung.[19]

Maj. Robert E. Jones, leading the Army's 1st Battalion, 32nd Infantry, survivors from the Hagaru-ri breakout, arrived with his men at a 7th Division assembly area at Hamhung at midnight on the tenth. This tragic remnant included three officers—Major Jones, 1st Lt. Cecil Smith, and Second Lieutenant Barnes—with 18 enlisted men and four ROKs. The next afternoon these men moved to the Service Company, 32nd Infantry, area where 29 more men and three ROKs arrived in small groups to join them, 57 men in all. The 1st Battalion, 32nd Infantry, survivors embarked at Hungnam on 13 December for the Pusan area.[20]

Only at the rear of the column, near Koto-ri, was there a Chinese attack in any force along the road. About 350 enemy attacked G Company of the 1st Marines during the night but were driven off. The CCF seemed defeated, numbed by fatigue and cold.

Large groups of enemy, however—apparently reinforcements arriving from the north—were sighted after daybreak of 10 December moving south in company- and platoon-column formation half a mile east of Hill 1051, parallel to the road. Lieutenant Colonel Schmuck, on Hill 1081, called down air strikes and artillery barrages on these formations of marching Chinese soldiers. For an hour air strikes and artillery, as well as automatic fire from the Army self-propelled quad-50s and the dual 40-mm AAA guns attached to Schmuck's battalion, wreaked havoc in these closely packed columns. But the survivors stoically held rank and continued southward.[21]

GENERAL SMITH LEAVES KOTO-RI, 10 DECEMBER

At 10:30 in the morning of 10 December, General Smith and some of his staff left the 1st Marine Division Forward CP at Koto-ri and flew by C-47 plane and helicopter to the division's Rear CP at Hungnam, which now became the division's main CP. All that day troops and trains descended the mountain road from Koto-ri. By dusk of 10 December both division trains, all elements of the 7th Marine Regiment, and three battalions of the 11th Marines (artillery) had reached Chinhung-ni. There the infantry climbed into waiting trucks for the final miles to Hungnam. The 5th Marine Regiment followed the 7th down from Koto-ri, two battalions arriving at Chinhung-ni close behind the 7th Marines. They had one firefight at the top of the pass with a Chinese force. The 1st Battalion of the 5th Marines was not relieved in its defensive position on Hill 1457 at the top of the pass until just before dark and did not reach Chinhung-ni until after midnight.

Lt. Col. Alvin L. Newberry, executive officer of the Army's 3rd Division Task Force Dog, which was responsible for holding Chinhung-ni during this phase of the Marine withdrawal, described the scene at Chinhung-ni when the withdrawing troops streamed through on 10 December: "All day they marched through, both foot and motor elements moving at the 2-mile per hour pace of Atley Trailers and the dog-tired riflemen. Every inch of every vehicle was covered with material or men, including many casualties. Trains were well organized, and those fortunate enough to have escaped frostbite but not lucky enough to have caught a ride were still carrying all their equipment. They were weary to exhaustion, but they were intact, proud, and fit to fight."[22]

The 1st Marine Regiment was the last major unit to leave Koto-ri. Its 3rd Battalion held the high ground just south of Koto-ri at the head of the pass, and Schmuck's 1st Battalion continued to hold vital Hill 1081 on the east side of the road halfway down the mountain. The 1st Battalion was to move down to the road and join the tanks at the end of the column and act as rear guard. The 1st Marine Regiment began pulling out of Koto-ri at 3 P.M. on 10 December. The 2nd Battalion of the 11th Marines (artillery) fell in behind Headquarters Company, and following it came a detachment of the Army's 185th Combat Engineers. Then followed in sequence the Army's Provisional Battalion, 31st Infantry; the 2nd Battalion, 1st Marines; the Marine Division Reconnaissance Company; and finally Lt. Col. Harry T. Milne's tank column, with tanks of B and D companies, 1st Tank Battalion; Capt. Drake's Army 31st Tank Company; and the tank platoon of the 5th Marines Antitank Company— 46 M-26 tanks in all. It was near midnight when the tank column left Koto-ri.

As the last elements of the withdrawing US forces left Koto-ri, the big 155-mm howitzers of the Army's 92nd Field Artillery Battalion of Task Force Dog at Chinhung-ni, ten miles southward, opened up with heavy interdiction fires on Koto-ri to prevent Chinese from closing in on the tail of the column. Under the protection of this fire, the tail of the column got out of Koto-ri with only a scattering of small-arms fire from enemy soldiers who had intermingled with a mass of Korean refugees gathered there. Chinese soldiers among the refugees who followed the withdrawing troops were to be a continuing problem during the night.[23]

Final acts of American troops at Koto-ri included the placing of about 50 wounded Chinese prisoners in a heated house after giving them first aid for their wounds and frostbite and providing food and water. The Americans placed a Red Cross panel on the house. They expected these Chinese soldiers would be recovered by their own forces after the UN troops had all departed. In a sense, this action was a "thank you" for similar treatment enemy Chinese had given to American prisoners two weeks earlier.[24]

The comparative smoothness with which the withdrawal had proceeded thus far on 10 December near Koto-ri, under the protection of infantry units holding the key high ground adjacent to the road and the constant umbrella of close air support and observation overhead of enemy movement, did not continue throughout the night. Some severe setbacks were yet to come.

CCF Ambush at Sudong

During the two weeks of attacks in the Chosin Reservoir area, the CCF had also been active in the vicinity of Sudong and had carried out many ambushes of small parties and supply convoys between there and Chinhung-ni, the southernmost perimeter held by combat forces of the 1st Marine Division. By 7 December General Almond had made the Army's 3rd Infantry Division responsible for the MSR south of Chinhung-ni. Task Force Dog, as we have seen, became responsible for the security of Chinhung-ni, and two battalions of the 3rd Division's 65th Infantry Regiment took positions to protect the road south of it. The 65th Infantry positions centered on Majon-dong, but the two battalions simply did not have the strength to outpost and hold all the high ground south of Chinhung-ni in the narrow, steep-walled valley the road followed south toward the coast, including that around Sudong. General Mead, commanding Task Force Dog, noted from his position at Chinhung-ni the exposed and dangerous route in the vicinity of Sudong. There was poor radio communication between Task Force Dog and the 65th Infantry headquarters at Majon-dong and between the task force and the 3rd Division headquarters at Hamhung. The narrow gorges and steep hills between the several CPs made radio communication often inoperative as the FM radios had very little range there. But General Mead finally got a message through to the 3rd Division, which then instructed the 65th Infantry to extend its protection to the Sudong area.

The regiment responded by sending its G Company, all it could spare, to Sudong on 8 December. One platoon of the company went into position on the north side of Sudong. The rest of the company took positions on the hills west of the road, about a mile south of Sudong. The two groups soon lost radio communication with each other when their radios failed. And neither, apparently, had any knowledge that an enemy force had occupied the hill just west of Sudong until the afternoon of 10 December.

Task Force Dog's patrols south out of Chinhung-ni discovered part of this enemy force digging in on the north face of the hill. When the Reconnaissance Company's patrol called for artillery fire from the 155-mm howitzers at Chinhung-ni, the 92nd Field Artillery Battalion sent an observer to the scene to direct fire, but the 155-mm shells did not stop the enemy force from continuing to dig in on its positions. Only a few of the enemy soldiers took shelter on the reverse slope of the hill.

Just after dark on 10 December a force of Chinese, estimated to number about 200, attacked G Company, 65th Infantry, in its position a mile south of Sudong. The enemy lost heavily in this attack and withdrew. That part of the withdrawing Marine column that was then approaching this place halted while the fight was in progress. After it had ended, the Marines continued on unmolested. Meanwhile, when news of the Chinese attack south of Sudong was received at Chinhung-ni, all road traffic south from there was halted. It resumed shortly after dark when Colonel Snedeker, Marine liaison officer there, received word that the road was clear below Sudong. There was no further incident in that area until just after midnight.

Before describing this development it will be useful to mention the artillery's effort during the night from Chinhung-ni to neutralize the enemy force on the hill west of Sudong. After dark, 155-mm fire was continued hourly during the night on the hill west of Sudong. Only after daylight the next morning did observers discover that the artillery bursts had hit 250–300 yards west of the target area because of meteorological change that took place during the night, and corrections could not be made because of technical problems. So the nightlong artillery fire had had no effect on the enemy strongpoint just west of Sudong.

From this hill an estimated 50 or more Chinese soldiers infiltrated the village of Sudong during the night. Shortly after midnight these Chinese ambushed a part of the 1st Marine Regimental Train as it entered Sudong.[25] Chinese assault groups suddenly burst from behind huts near the road, firing burp guns and throwing grenades into the vehicular train of the 1st Marine Regiment that was then passing southward through the village. This quick attack killed several truck drivers and set several vehicles ablaze. The flickering and shadowy light from burning trucks only partially lighted the scene as the column halted. A confused fight erupted. There was no infantry present. The transportation and service troops of the train column had to fight their own battle. At first there was no American leadership to organize and guide the fight. But at some point soon after the battle erupted, Army Lt. Col. John Upshur Dennis Page, an artillery officer, emerged to assume leadership. He and two Marines who followed him charged from someplace back up the road to the front, where the column had halted and several vehicles were burning on the road in the village. One of the Marines stopped to fire at some enemy. The other man, Pfc. Marvin L. Wasson, stayed with Page. They ran past burning vehicles and tripped over bodies in the road but reached the head of the stalled column, where enemy soldiers held the road. Page put his carbine on automatic and charged straight at a group of about 30 Chinese, firing into them as he ran forward. Most of this group, astounded at what was happening to them, broke and ran for the shadows. One of them threw a grenade as the others took off. Fragments from it knocked Wasson down with wounds on his head and one arm. Page ordered him to go back and said he would cover him. Wasson obeyed and staggered back to the column, turning once to see Page charging on after the running Chinese. Page did not return. The two-man assault broke the spell, disrupted the Chinese assault, which had demoralized the column and was spreading death and destruction, and gave those back of the leading vehicles time to get their courage in hand and to organize a counterattack.

Another Army officer, Lt. Col. Waldon C. Winston, commanding officer of the 52nd Transportation Truck Battalion, took over leadership at Sudong and organized a Marine and Army service-troop counterattack. In this counterattack, Wasson was back in the fight, his wounds dressed, manning a 75-mm recoilless rifle. A machine-gun crew covered him. Wasson fired several white phosphorus shells at a hut that seemed to be a Chinese strongpoint. The building erupted in flames. Chinese soldiers inside made a dash from it to escape, but machine-gun fire cut them down. Jeep driver Wasson then helped to push trucks of exploding ammunition off the road. The Chinese gradually were driven off as Lieutenant Colonel Winston succeeded in organizing the defense. But the fight had lasted several hours, and it was daylight of 11 December before the road was cleared so that traffic resumed. This CCF ambush at Sudong killed eight men and wounded 21, and it destroyed nine trucks and an armored personnel carrier.

When the column started on and passed through Sudong, just beyond (south of) the village the point came upon the body of Lt. Col. John Page in the road. There was a scattered heap of Chinese bodies—16 of them—near him.

Lieutenant Colonel Page had been in the war only 12 days when he was killed. Forty-six years of age, he was a professional soldier from New Orleans, where his wife and children remained when he departed for Korea in October 1950. He had always wanted combat assignments, but his reputation for being able to get units in shape for combat had kept him at Fort Sill during World War II. He was assigned to X Corps artillery upon his arrival in Korea and was then attached to the 52nd Transportation Truck Battalion.

Page's performance at Sudong the night of 11 December was no fluke. He had been doing the same kind of thing for 11 days in the defense of Koto-ri and in the descent from there through Funchilin Pass. Page had arrived at Hamhung on 27 November. Two days later he led a special mission north from Hamhung to establish communication points on the now-dangerous road toward the Chosin Reservoir. He and his jeep driver, Cpl. David E. Klepsig, got into Koto-ri the night of 29 November only after a series of heroics by both men, who fought their way past a Chinese machine-gun crew at a blown bridge site. Upon reaching Koto-ri, Colonel Puller, the 1st Marine Regimental commander there, gave Page responsibility for extending the airstrip 1,000 yards beyond his perimeter into no-man's-land, an area covered by Chinese snipers. Page got the job done, but often he had to mount a tank and personally operate the topside machine gun and direct the tank's crew in direct attacks on Chinese forces firing on the workers from nearby hills. The Marines at Koto-ri marveled at his courage and audacity.

When the withdrawal column started down from Koto-ri, Page was in it. Twice in descending through Funchilin Pass, Page was responsible for getting his part of the column moving when enemy fire stopped it. Once he grabbed a machine gun in his arms and scrambled up an incline to a point from which he brought the enemy position under fire and silenced it. He was on foot, looking for his jeep in the column, when the Chinese ambush at Sudong stopped the column again. He was close enough to the front that he was able to rush forward, as already described, and break up the enemy group on the road at the head of the column.

No one who saw Page in action those 12 days of late November and early December 1950 ever had any doubt that the lieutenant colonel fresh from the States was truly a combat soldier. The Marine Corps gave Page its highest award—the Navy Cross. His story was not widely known or publicized immediately, and he was not an early recipient of the Congressional Medal of Honor. When the facts of his short but momentous combat career became known in 1957, an act of Congress was necessary, because of the lapse of time, to grant him that honor posthumously.[26]

Many Marines, and some Marine writers on the Chosin Reservoir campaign, have criticized the Army units involved and the X Corps command for not securing their withdrawal route in the Sudong area. But one can easily cite instances where the Marines themselves, north of Chinhung-ni, for example, failed to provide complete security, for reasons comparable to those that limited the Army units south of Chinhung-ni. One cannot always deny the enemy their successes with the kind of difficult terrain, conditions, and limited resources that characterized the Chosin battles and the related withdrawal to the coast.

A CCF SUCCESS AT THE HEAD OF FUNCHILIN PASS

While the setback at Sudong was taking place in the narrow valley below the pass, another disaster occurred at the very rear of the withdrawing Marines near the top of the pass. This one also developed largely because of lack of infantry protection, which in turn grew out of confusion in the march order of units out of Koto-ri and some lack of clarity in orders from Colonel Puller, commanding officer of the 1st Marine Regiment, to Lieutenant Colonel Schmuck, commanding the 1st Battalion. The withdrawal plan had called for the 1st Battalion to come off Hill 1081 and be the last troops in the withdrawal, following the tanks, over the Treadway bridge before it was blown. At Koto-ri the tanks were held back behind all the other vehicles so that, if any stalled or were knocked out by enemy action and blocked the road, they would not trap other vehicles behind them. Schmuck's final rear-guard battalion of infantry could walk out around any tanks that might become immobile or block the road. But as it turned out, there was no final battalion of infantry behind the tanks to protect them.

As the withdrawal from Koto-ri entered its final phases in the afternoon of 10 December, the 1st Marine Regiment leapfrogged infantry units from one defense position to another down the road until it in turn was relieved by another behind it. The withdrawal proceeded in an orderly fashion throughout the day and into the evening past Hill 1081, where Lieutenant Colonel Schmuck's 1st Battalion still held that vital position above the pass.

About midnight 10 December approximately 40 M-26 tanks departed their perimeter near Koto-ri, following the 3rd Battalion, 1st Marines, in column formation, and started the descent of Funchilin Pass. First Lt. Jack Lerond's platoon of tanks was last in line. Only Maj. Walter Gall's Reconnaissance Company was left to accompany it. His platoons were interspersed at intervals in the tank column. Lt. E. C. Hargett's Reconnaissance Platoon of 28 men were with Lerond's tank platoon, the last ten tanks in the column.

Following the tail end of the tank column out of Koto-ri was a dense mass of hundreds of refugees, who kept as close as they dared. CCF soldiers had infiltrated among them — an enemy practice by now well known to all US soldiers. It was thus necessary to keep the refugees at a distance — by weapons fire if necessary. Hargett's Reconnaissance Platoon had this responsibility. The tanks proceeded slowly. The Funchilin Pass road curves were sharp and frequently icy. The tanks had their lights on to help the drivers as much as possible. Some crewmen were on foot, guiding with flashlights.

Approximately at 1 A.M. on 11 December, the ninth tank from the rear stalled, its brakes locked or frozen. All the tanks behind it had to stop, for 45 minutes. This accident occurred southwest of Hill 1457, which was one and one-fourth miles short of the Treadway bridge. The rest of the tanks ahead and their Reconnaissance Company escorts kept going, unaware of what was happening behind them. This action is a bit hard to understand, as it would seem that any break in a column of this kind would soon be observed by those ahead. But whatever the facts in this respect, the last nine tanks and Hargett's Reconnaissance Platoon were left all alone. Their radio communication also failed at this time.

Soon after the last nine tanks stopped, Hargett, who was at the extreme rear, holding back the crowd of refugees, saw five CCF soldiers emerge in file from the refugees. Someone in the mass of people there called out in English that the five CCF wanted to surrender. While Cpl. George Amyotte covered him with a BAR, Hargett walked carefully toward the five Chinese, holding his carbine ready for use. Suddenly, the leading CCF stepped aside, and the four behind him pulled hidden burp guns and grenades from their clothing. Hargett pressed the trigger on his carbine, but the mechanism had frozen. A big, strong man, Hargett charged, swinging his carbine. He crushed the skull of the leading Chinese. At the same time, an enemy grenade exploded and wounded him. It was in reality a planned ambush, as enemy fire now erupted from the side of the road and from farther to the rear. Meanwhile, Amyotte shot down the four remaining CCF near Hargett before they could act. A melee followed, with Hargett and his platoon falling back. The last tank and its crew were engulfed by the CCF. The crew in the second tank from the rear had closed its hatches, and they could not be stirred when Hargett's men pounded on the hull with their rifle butts. While Hargett was trying to get this tank's crew out, an enemy explosive knocked him nearly unconscious, and blew Pfc. Robert DeMott, who was with him, over the steep side of the road. DeMott landed unconscious on a ledge below the road.

Amyotte, who was wearing a fiberglass body jacket, covered with his BAR fire the further withdrawal of Hargett and others in the platoon. It must have surprised the Chinese to see that, when a grenade landed squarely on Amyotte's back (who was then firing from a prone position), its explosion had no effect on him. He just continued cutting them down with his BAR. As the platoon withdrew past the stalled tanks, the men noticed that the tank crews had abandoned the next five tanks. Their hatches were open, and the men gone. They also saw that crewmen of the lead stalled tank had freed its brakes and had driven off. The next one behind it then also drove off down the road.

Before he fell back from the second tank from the rear, Hargett and five men tried to go back to the last tank and rescue its crew, but enemy machine-gun fire swept the road. Quickly, two of his men were wounded. Hargett realized that he had no chance of rescuing the tank crew and that he would have to pull back or all his small party would be sacrificed. As they turned back, Chinese soldiers set the last tank afire. Hargett's platoon by now had several wounded. He sent them ahead down the road as he and the others fell back more slowly.

Many men of Hargett's platoon still lived because they were wearing the new fiberglass body armor. About 500 of these protective jackets had been airlifted to the 1st Marine Division for field tests, but only the 50 issued to the Reconnaissance Company were being worn in combat at this time. Hargett's platoon, with two killed, one missing in action, and 12 wounded, got down to the Treadway bridge. The demolition team, waiting there for the last of the tanks to pass, then blew the bridge when they learned that no more tanks would be crossing and that probably there would be no more stragglers to reach the bridge.

But one man did make it—Private First Class DeMott of Hargett's platoon, who had been blown unconscious over the side of the road by a Chinese explosive charge of some kind near the next-to-the-last tank in line. He regained consciousness later, found that he was only slightly wounded, climbed back to the road, and there mingled with a party of Korean refugees going south. He walked with them through the gatehouse above the blown Treadway bridge and came down to Chinhung-ni.[27]

The question remains, What had gone wrong to deprive the tank column of its expected infantry protection? Lieutenant Colonel Schmuck's 1st Battalion, 1st Marines, coming off Hill 1081 was supposed to fall in behind the tanks and be the rear guard and last unit over the Treadway bridge to clear the pass. But the loss in men and tanks took place before they reached Hill 1081 and Schmuck's position. Who was supposed to protect the tanks from Koto-ri to Schmuck's position? The stalled tank and the Chinese attack there occurred more than a mile north of where Schmuck's lines came down to the road and where his battalion was to fall in behind the tanks.

Schmuck later said that he did not receive a copy of the 1st Marine Division operation order on the details of the withdrawal, but only a fragmentary order designating his battalion as the rear guard. That was supplemented by a hasty 30-second conference with Colonel Puller, he said, when the regimental command group passed through his lines. Puller told him at that time, he said, that the tanks were following the 1st Marines, whatever that meant, and that the Army's 2nd Battalion, 31st Infantry, was bringing up the rear. Puller made no mention in this hasty conference of the Reconnaissance Company. Thus, as soon as the 2nd Battalion, 31st Infantry, passed, Schmuck fell in behind it, assuming he was the rear guard. Schmuck had established a checkpoint where the incline railroad passed over the road below Hill 1081. There he checked off each unit at it passed. He said there had been a great deal of intermingling of units by the time they reached this point and went through his lines.

Schmuck's 1st Marines Leave Hill 1081

When Schmuck saw the lights of approaching tanks about 3 A.M. on 11 December, he gave the order for A Company to start withdrawing from Hill 1081 so that he could consolidate the battalion before daybreak for its rear-guard action. When the tanks reached his lines, he learned to his surprise that the 2nd Battalion, 31st Infantry, was not with or behind them and that only the Reconnaissance Company was covering the tanks' withdrawal. The tanks and the two platoons of the Reconnaissance Company that passed through his checkpoint had no knowledge of what had happened at the tail of their column, and Schmuck at the time did not know of it either. It is obvious that Schmuck did not wait for the last of the tanks—perhaps he thought the leading group of 30 or more tanks constituted the whole column—and after they passed, he started his battalion down the hill toward Chinhung-ni, which it reached without major incident. But we know that the demolition party was still at the Treadway bridge when Hargett's men came through later.

It is apparent, however, that there was considerable confusion in the last phase of the 1st Marine Regiment's withdrawal, that many, if not most, of the final group were anxious to get through the pass with little checking on what was happening behind them. And it would seem that there was some carelessness and haste at regimental command level, involving Colonel Puller himself.

General Smith's order of 7 December establishing the march order out of Koto-ri, beginning the next morning, had not specified that all the tanks would be held in one group and would be the last major element out of Koto-ri at the very end of the column, and it did not specify any infantry unit as guard for the tanks in the move. It is not clear who, and at precisely what time, decided that the tanks would be held together in one body and whether, when that decision was made, an infantry protecting force was assigned to accompany it. We do know that the Provisional Battalion of the 31st Infantry was not the rear guard. It followed the 2nd Battalion, 11th Marines, and the 185th Engineer Combat Battalion detachment in the march order through the pass to Chinhung-ni, and the 3rd Battalion, 1st Marines, followed it. The 3rd Battalion, 1st Marines, left its positions on Hill 1304 and the high ground opposite on the east side of the road at the head of the pass about 9 P.M. on 10 December, fell in on the road, and proceeded down to Chinhung-ni. It seems to have been the last major infantry unit in the 1st Marines' withdrawal north of Schmuck's positions on Hill 1081. The tanks and the Reconnaissance Company were the only elements still left in the vicinity of Koto-ri. Thus, when these units began their withdrawal, they were on their own, at least as far as halfway down the mountain, where Schmuck's battalion still held its defensive positions.[28] It is a bit hard to understand why Colonel Puller, commanding the 1st Marine Regiment, thought that the Army 2nd Battalion, 31st Infantry, was at the end of the column, and why General Barr, commanding the 7th Division, later said that battalion was rear guard for the Marine units.

FROM CHINHUNG-NI TO HAMHUNG AND THE COAST

As the withdrawing troops reached Chinhung-ni, the infantry elements and any others on foot loaded into waiting trucks and were hurried south. Others got onto waiting railroad cars at Sontang. But there was not sufficient transportation at Chinhung-ni for all, and many units had to continue on foot as far as Majon-dong, 13 miles farther south. Lieutenant Colonel Sutter's 2nd Battalion, 1st Marines, for instance, slogged it all the way from Koto-ri to Majon-dong, 23 miles in 20 hours, with pack, parkas, individual weapons, and sleeping bags.[29]

In preparing to transport the withdrawing Marines and Army units the last part of the way to Hamhung and Hungnam, after they had fought their way down the mountain from Koto-ri, the X Corps assembled at Sontang all the rail equipment available. Sontang was two miles below Majon-dong, the farthest point north where it was safe to assemble the rail equipment. On 7 December there were ten locomotives and 58 cars in service on the narrow-gauge railroad. The G-4 of X Corps ordered that no evacuation trucks would proceed north of Sontang, except on orders of General Smith. By 8 December an eight-car hospital train was waiting at Sontang to carry wounded to the coast, and 60 other railcars had been assembled there to transport soldiers to Hamhung-Hungnam. There were 32 more cars at Oro-ri, about 12 miles farther south. The hospital train left first with wounded and was followed by other trains that carried about 4,000 men into Hamhung.[30] The remainder of the surviving Chosin Reservoir force was transported on trucks waiting at Chinhung-ni or Majon-dong.

Hargett's platoon, the last of the Reconnaissance Company at the rear of the withdrawing force, arrived at Chinhung-ni about 11 A.M., 11 December. The last elements of the Marine and Army troops withdrawing from the Chosin Reservoir left Chinhung-ni at 1 P.M. By 5:30 that afternoon they had cleared Majon-dong, the last point on the road to the coast where enemy action posed a serious threat. By 9 P.M. that night, 11 December, all elements except the tanks had arrived at their assembly areas in the Hamhung-Hungnam perimeter area. Just before midnight of 11 December the tanks arrived at Hungnam. The memorable breakout fight from the Chosin Reservoir was now history. Only Task Force Dog of the US 3rd Infantry Division had stayed behind to cover the final hours of the withdrawal.

In the withdrawal phase from Koto-ri to Chinhung-ni, 8–11 December, the 1st Marine Division had suffered 347 battle casualties. This number included 51 killed, 24 who died of wounds, 16 missing in action, and 256 wounded.[31]

TASK FORCE DOG AT CHINHUNG-NI AND THE REFUGEES

Back at Chinhung-ni, Task Force Dog had a problem after the last of the withdrawing troops had passed through. It inherited what had been the special worry of Hargett's platoon in the descent of the pass—the several thousand Korean refugees that were strung out behind the withdrawal force, eager to escape south. Security and traffic control for the American troops required that these refugees be kept at a distance. The head of the valley approaching Chinhung-ni had been heavily mined, and the area strung with barbed wire. This was part of the perimeter defense line, and in the final hours was also covered by automatic weapons fire, some of it being from the self-propelled AAA quad-50 and dual-40 vehicles. But even the mines and the automatic-weapons fire did not stop some of the refugees from trying to come on in. Consequently, there were many Korean civilian refugee casualties on the edge of Chinhung-ni, most of them in the mine fields. Task Force Dog had no other alternative. The problem was most acute when the task force prepared to blow up remaining supplies on 11 December, just before it withdrew. Only cannon and machine-gun fire from the Reconnaissance Company tanks across the refugee front held them back long enough for the engineers to set off the demolitions.[32]

Task Force Dog began its preparations to leave Chinhung-ni when the last vehicle of the Marine rear guard, an Army quad-50 (M16) of the 15th AAA AW Battalion (SP) of the 7th Infantry Division, cleared the town at 2 P.M. on 11 December. Engineers led, followed by the artillery and the task-force HQ. All but drivers and vehicle commanders had to walk with weapons in hand. Any vehicle that became inoperative was pushed to the side of the road, and if it could not quickly be made operational, it was burned.

When the task-force column was ready to move out of Chinhung-ni, the 3rd Battalion, 7th Infantry, moved up to the ridgelines on either side of the road to protect the column. Army air reconnaissance overhead was continuous. As Task Force Dog neared Sudong, where enemy ambushes and attacks had been persistent for several days, a firefight in progress south of the town could be heard. When the column passed through Sudong, those on the road saw five trucks still smoldering at the roadside and four American dead, three of them badly burned, still lying there. The column halted at the south edge of Sudong.

Immediately south of Sudong the road ran through a narrow valley that resembled a trough—deep and straight. Those awaiting at the head of the task-force column could see .50-caliber and 40-mm automatic-weapons fire hitting about 300 yards west of the road, where it crossed the stream. The column soon started on but was brought under CCF small-arms fire, and a few enemy mortar rounds fell just after it crossed the stream. The gunfire from both sides was mutually ineffective. Four Marine Corsairs came overhead at this time, rocketing and strafing the CCF hillside positions. With the CCF fully pinned down by this aerial attack, Task Force Dog vehicles and men got around a bend in the road and out of the enemy line of fire. Two miles farther down the road, Task Force Dog arrived at the X Corps truck head in time to see the last of the Marines load into a truck and go rolling away from Hungnam.[33]

When the main part of Task Force Dog and its infantry elements had departed Chinhung-ni, Captain Randal and a X Corps demolition party, protected by a platoon of the Reconnaissance Company and some AAA quad-50s, began destroying the supply dumps left behind. These contained various items that could not be used or could not be hauled away because of a shortage of trucks. About 23,000 B rations, a large quantity of PX supplies, and drums of fuel and lubricants were destroyed by explosives or burned. About 31 tons of small-arms ammunition, grenades, and rockets, enough to load 20 2½-ton trucks, were destroyed in one great explosion. In the first miles on the road after Captain Randal's party left Chinhung-ni, it burned 24 vehicles the withdrawing force had been forced to abandon when they became inoperable. Chinese troops around Chinhung-ni made one last effort as Randal's party cleared the town, opening up on it with automatic fire. This proved a mistake, at least for one enemy machine-gun crew. A quad-50 nearby fired on it with its tremendous volume of .50-caliber from its four automatic machine guns and quickly settled the issue. The quad-50s and dual-40s of the AAA AW Battalion were perhaps the most successful weapons used by American ground troops in silencing enemy close-in fire during the entire withdrawal operation from Chosin Reservoir. They were heavily used, particularly from Chinhung-ni to Majon-dong. Randal's party caught up with the tail end of Task Force Dog at Sudong. The task force arrived at Majon-dong and entered the 65th Infantry perimeter there at 8 P.M. on 11 December. Its mission finished, it was disbanded.[34]

In retrospect, one can make an overall judgment that the successful defensive battles of the 1st Marine Division in the Chosin Reservoir area and its subsequent fighting withdrawal to the Sudong valley and on to the coast, with its attached Army units, was one of the great military operations of United States history—many would say in world military history. It has properly been compared favorably in some aspects with the famous march of the 10,000, immortalized in Xenophon's writings.

14

THE HUNGNAM EVACUATION

By day's end, 11 December 1950, the once-scattered X Corps troops had found relative safety within the protected perimeter arc around Hamhung and the port of Hungnam. Five divisions of troops and supporting service units had moved from an area of 35,000 square miles in northeast Korea and over distances as great as 300 miles, much of it in subzero weather, over poor roads, and through icy and snow-covered passes to their huge assembly area at Hungnam. In the next two weeks nearly all these troops with their equipment and supplies were loaded on ships and evacuated by sea to South Korea. As the last of its far-flung units closed into the Hungnam perimeter on 11 December, X Corps intelligence estimated that the CCF would concentrate their forces there and assault the perimeter.

THE HAMHUNG-HUNGNAM PERIMETER

The Hamhung-Hungnam perimeter at first was expansive, describing an arc that encompassed Yonpo airfield on the coast 10 miles south of Hamhung and 5 miles southwest of Hungnam, then curving northward to Oro-ri, 20 miles north of Hungnam, hence bending southeast to the coast near Toejo, about 15 miles northeast of Hungnam. Oro-ri, at the center of the arc, was on the MSR leading from the Chosin Reservoir. It also was the important road juncture where a main road and narrow-gauge railroad ran northeast through the Sinhung valley and from there climbed through the mountains to the Fusen Reservoir, some 20 air miles east of the Chosin Reservoir. This latter communication line had always been a source of concern to the X Corps, since it offered one of the few access routes from the north and the interior to the Hungnam coastal area.

The Hungnam perimeter was held on the east along the coast by elements of the ROK I Corps; west of it the US 7th Infantry Division spread along the major roadnet leading into Hamhung from the northeast and south of the Sinhung valley; and west of the 7th Infantry Division, the

A party of riflemen from the 65th Regiment, US 3rd Infantry Division, on their way to relieve others at the Hungnam defense perimeter. Typical thatched huts are visible in the background. (US Army photograph 3D 298-6)

US 3rd Infantry Division and the 1st KMC Regiment completed the perimeter arc in its southwest segment.

Included in its segment, the 3rd Division covered the MSR from the Chosin Reservoir, beginning at Oro-ri and continuing southward. It also included the area westward from the Songchon River, past Chigyong and Yonpo airfield to the coast. The 3rd Division had the hardest part of the perimeter to guard, the area where the CCF were most likely to move against it in force.

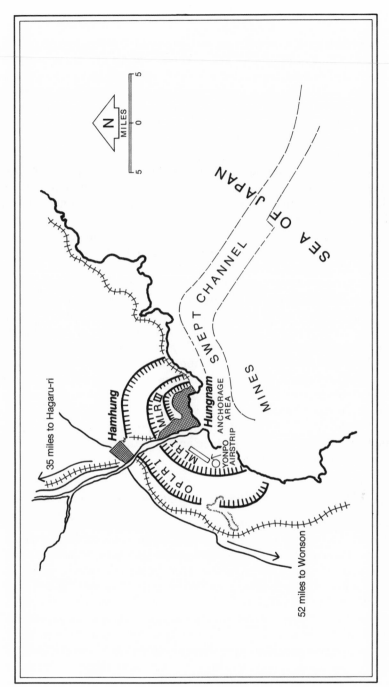

MAP 17. Evacuation of Hungnam, 11–24 December.

The perimeter defense plan had an Outpost Line of Resistance (OPLR) and a Main Line of Resistance (MLR) behind the OPLR. There was also a phased withdrawal plan that would bring the perimeter ever closer to Hungnam and the beach. The plan had three main phase lines as troops within the perimeter outloaded on ships and the perimeter could be allowed to shrink. The evacuation plan called for the 1st Marine Division to outload first, followed by the ROK I Corps, then the US 7th Infantry Division, and finally the US 3rd Infantry Division. As the perimeter shrank, the 3rd Division would be its final protector.[1] General MacArthur sent a message outlining the withdrawal plan to the Joint Chiefs of Staff on 12 December, after his visit with Almond at Yonpo airfield in Korea the day before.

The size and form of the initial perimeter was the subject of discussions among General Almond, his staff, and division commanders. Almond at first favored a rather small, tight perimeter around Hamhung and Hungnam. General Soule of the 3rd Division argued in favor of a larger perimeter that would permit trading space for time as the outloading progressed. Such a perimeter would also keep the CCF off balance in preparing for an assault against it, if they concentrated for that purpose, as expected. Soule pointed out that, as quickly as they had reconnoitered and probed a UN perimeter defense position and prepared their assault of it, it would have changed, nullifying their plans. His viewpoint was adopted for the perimeter, and it worked admirably. The initial perimeter was an arc about 20 miles long, a semicircle, with Oro-ri at the middle and northern tip of the arc. The CCF were never able to mount a strong and determined attack against any of the three phases of the perimeter during the X Corps evacuation of Hungnam.[2]

MacArthur Flies to X Corps, 11 December

On 11 December, the day the last of the troops from the Chosin Reservoir were closing into the Hungnam defense perimeter and the successful evacuation of the X Corps seemed assured, General MacArthur flew into Yonpo airfield shortly before noon for a conference with General Almond. Generals Hickey, Wright, and Whitney and Colonel Canada came with MacArthur from Tokyo. In the pilots' briefing room at the airfield, Almond explained the current situation in northeast Korea and the plans for outloading the X Corps. Almond told MacArthur that X Corps would be ready to report to Eighth Army in South Korea on 27 December. MacArthur questioned Almond and his G-2, Lt. Col. William W. Quinn, on their estimate of the enemy in the X Corps zone. After the briefing, MacArthur paid high tribute to X Corps on its operations. MacArthur and Almond then held a short private meeting.

MacArthur's purpose in this private meeting with Almond was to ask him whether he wanted to return to Tokyo as chief of staff of the Far East Command or to remain in command of X Corps and report with it to Lt. Gen. Walton H. Walker, commander of Eighth Army, in South Korea. Almond replied that he wanted to remain with X Corps.[3]

In response to a direct question to General Almond at his home at Anniston, Alabama, 28–29 April 1977, Almond said that, in the Yonpo airfield conference, MacArthur made no reference to a possible future removal of Walker from command of Eighth Army. It was widely believed in Eighth Army in 1950 that General Walker had no liking for General Almond, believing that he influenced General MacArthur unduly in favor of X Corps for priority in supplies and seeking MacArthur's favor in command decisions, to the detriment of Eighth Army. General Almond denied that he tried to influence General MacArthur in this way, but he did say he did everything possible to get what he needed for his troops. Many persons in Eighth Army would have guessed that General Almond would not have wanted to serve under Walker's command.

It seems that General Almond did not in fact influence MacArthur nearly as much as was commonly supposed in his decisions concerning the Eighth Army and X Corps but that MacArthur himself made these decisions because that is the way he wanted it. Almond apparently preferred the role of a combat soldier and commander to any other. He was an aggressive and able corps commander and was willing to serve the Eighth Army commander.

Even after Almond told MacArthur that he wanted to remain with X Corps in Korea, MacArthur did not make Maj. Gen. Doyle O. Hickey, acting chief of staff, FEC, the chief of staff. He may have had in mind putting Almond back in that position once the Korean War ended. Both General Hickey and General Ridgway in 1951 in Tokyo said privately that, only when Ridgway succeeded MacArthur as commander in chief, Far East, in April 1951, did Hickey then become FEC chief of staff. Ridgway mentioned privately that this was the first official act he performed relating to the Far East Command staff after he became FEC commander. There is no evidence that Almond had anything to do with MacArthur's actions in this matter.

General MacArthur and his party took off from Yonpo airfield at 12:40 P.M. for Kimpo airfield, near Seoul, for a conference with General Walker. After MacArthur had departed, Almond and Major Ladd, his senior aide, flew up the corps MSR as far as Koto-ri on reconnaissance.

In order to avoid confusion in dealing with enemy actions around the Hamhung-Hungnam perimeter and the simultaneous outloading of X Corps in the period from 11 to 24 December, it seems best to separate these two aspects, even though it may result in limited repetition. The separation of the two can be done because at no time did enemy action threaten to halt or seriously interfere with the outloading of X Corps. Outloading began 11 December with members of the 1st Marine Division. The division had proceeded directly to the Hungnam docks as it arrived from Chosin Reservoir. The rather feeble and ineffective effort of the CCF to attack the X Corps perimeter will be sketched first.

CCF Actions against the X Corps Perimeter

General MacArthur ordered General Almond on 8 December to evacuate all of X Corps from northeast Korea. This evacuation took place from three ports: Songjin, farthest north; Hungnam; and Wonsan. Only ROK troops embarked from Songjin, and it was without enemy opposition. Wonsan, 50 air miles south of Hungnam, was evacuated next, with only minor enemy threats, most of it from North Korean units and guerrillas. Lastly, Hungnam was evacuated. It was there that the great bulk of X Corps concentrated. The X Corps expected the CCF to attack and try to break the defense perimeter and prevent an orderly evacuation. It was possible that severe fighting might take place there during the evacuation and heavy losses be inflicted on X Corps. Intelligence disclosed that CCF forces were moving down from the Chosin area and the Koto-ri plateau toward the corps perimeter. Aerial observers reported small groups were also moving down the Sinhung valley from the northeast.

In preparation against expected enemy attacks, Navy and Marine aircraft were always at the ready on the carriers offshore, and naval gunfire from ships in Hungnam harbor and elsewhere offshore kept the perimeter under its protection. This naval and air firepower would become increasingly potent as the perimeter shrank. One must remember that there was a great concentration of infantry and infantry support weapons on the perimeter at all times. Among the most potent close-support weapons were the quad-50s and dual-40s of the Antiaircraft Automatic Weapons battalions. The awesome firepower of these self-propelled weapons was most formidable against infantry at close and medium ranges. The four .50-caliber machine guns of the M16 quad-50s, for instance, could throw out 2,200 rounds a minute. This did not equal the rate of fire from a Skyhawk Minigun aerial cannon (which delivered explosive 20-mm bullets at a rate of 100 rounds a second and sounded like a buzz saw) used 15 to 20 years later in the Vietnam War, but it was still enormously destructive of enemy infantry in the open.

The Chinese really had no answer to the firepower that would confront them from the ground, the air, and the sea at the Hungnam perimeter. Any realistic appraisal of the situation would have to conclude that the Chinese could not mount a successful attack against the X Corps perimeter, and if they seriously tried it, they would be slaughtered. General Almond always maintained—with good reason—that he and the X Corps could have held Hamhung and Hungnam against the Chinese and North Koreans as long as desired by higher authority if supplied from the sea.

On 11 December the X Corps G-2 intelligence estimate was that the Chinese would attack the X Corps perimeter and beachhead. The next day there was no enemy contact, and air reconnaissance disclosed no significant close-in enemy movement toward the defense perimeter. On the thirteenth, however, 7th and 3rd US infantry division patrols made light enemy contact. And at dawn that day, about 200 enemy attacked E Company, 7th Infantry, 3rd Division. In this attack the Chinese surprised the defenders somewhat because they wore American parkas and uniforms. The fight lasted four hours, with 50 enemy killed. One new enemy division, the CCF 81st, was identified; and another, the 79th, which had been out of contact for many days but previously had been in action at Yudam-ni, was identified as present near the perimeter. At least two Chinese divisions or elements of them were thus approaching the corps perimeter.[4]

In early hours of darkness, 14 December, there was a CCF attack estimated to number 400 men against B Company, 65th Infantry, 3rd Division, at the northern edge of the perimeter. The attack overran one platoon and forced B Company to withdraw. Artillery fire, however, broke up the attack, and B Company reoccupied its positions after daylight.

THE CCF CLOSE ON PERIMETER BY 15 DECEMBER

By 15 December sizable Chinese forces had moved close to the perimeter. Enemy action increased. The ROK I Corps received minor attacks near Toejo on the coast, east of Hungnam, but the main enemy effort was against the 7th and 15th regiments, 3rd Division, north of Hamhung. There, as usual in the past, the attacks came after midnight. Chinese assault teams hit four or five outposts of G Company, 2nd Battalion, 7th Infantry, at 3 A.M. A numerically superior force of Chinese surrounded one of G Company's platoons near Singhang-ni, northwest of Hamhung. A task force from F Company of the 7th Infantry, commanded by 2nd Lt. Charles L. Butler, was organized to go to its assistance. Enemy ambushed him and his men before they reached the G Company platoon. In a hard, close-in fight, the enemy turned back Butler's relief force. In this fight, Butler was wounded twice, in the left arm and in the abdomen. But he remained in command of his men throughout. When he received orders to break off the fight and withdraw, he was able to walk. He instructed his men to place him on a tank, where he could fire the deck machine gun and help cover the withdrawal, which was carried out successfully.[5]

Artillery fire helped to break up this attack against G Company. But later, B Company, 1st Battalion, which was reinforcing the 2nd Battalion, received heavy attacks from a strong force of Chinese, estimated as numbering about 1,000 men. This fight began about 7:30 A.M. on 15 December. The 3rd Platoon of B Company, although surrounded, held its position by determined fighting.

Capt. John J. Powers, Jr., commanding B Company, informed that his 3rd Platoon was cut off and engaged in desperate combat, organized a relief force of a reinforced infantry platoon and three medium tanks about 9:30. He got halfway to the 3rd Platoon's position when his own force came under very heavy automatic-weapons and small-arms fire from his front and right flank. Powers deployed his tanks and men and pushed back the CCF on his right. Then he advanced frontally and for a brief period had some success. But suddenly mortar and automatic-weapons fire from his left hit with great force. Powers was wounded but continued to supervise the action and to direct fire. His relief force took many casualties at this juncture, but Powers urged it on. Mortar fire wounded him again, this time seriously, but he refused evacuation. The Chinese now assaulted his relief force, and Powers was wounded a third time. Powers realized now that he could not reach his 3rd Platoon. He reorganized his force, got the wounded loaded on tank decks, and started a withdrawal. Only then did he take a place on one of the tanks. His group withdrew successfully to the B Company perimeter. Powers received the Distinguished Service Cross for his leadership in this action. Late that afternoon, the surrounded 3rd Platoon fought its way back to the B Company position.[6]

Other enemy estimated to number about 400 men attacked outposts of L and F companies, 7th Infantry, at 8 A.M. but were beaten off. All these attacks against the 7th Infantry, 3rd Division, came from northwest of Hamhung. Another attack against I Company, 65th Infantry, came from northwest of Hamhung. It was repulsed. Artillery fire destroyed two enemy trucks in a column there.

During 15 December the 7th and 65th infantry regiments, 3rd Division, were ordered to withdraw to Phase Line 2. The 7th Infantry Division, east of Hamhung, had no enemy contact during the day, but it too withdrew as planned to Phase Line 2. At noon, the 3rd Division CP moved from Hamhung to Hungnam. The X Corps G-3 informed the 7th and 3rd divisions in the afternoon that there would be further withdrawals on the 16th and 17th and that the 3rd Division would assume responsibility for the entire perimeter on 17 December.[7]

The 1st KMC Regiment, which had been protecting Yonpo airfield, had now withdrawn for evacuation. Shortening the perimeter line on 15 December allowed the 3rd Division to cover this vital point long enough to complete evacuation of supplies still at the airfield.

The role of artillery and of the quad-50s and dual-40s in supporting infantry units in Korea in a perimeter defense has been well described by Maj. Gen. William F. Marquat. His description is so applicable to the Hungnam defense perimeter during the evacuation period that it is quoted below:

> Out at the forward positions the infantry would entrench on top of the hills covering the direct enemy approaches. The field artillery would be located to place plunging fire in front of the infantry positions and over the hills on the flanks. The antiaircraft automatic weapons would be emplaced to cover the tops of the hills occupied by the infantry for the purpose of driving out hostile elements which might displace our troops during a night or surprise attack. In the few instances where this type of action was called for, the automatic weapons never failed to make the hilltop positions untenable to the enemy until our infantry could regain them. The antiaircraft guns also were sited to sweep the ravines on the flanks which were avenues of approach for hostile flanking movements. In other words, the high angle fire trajectories and the flat trajectories of the automatic weapon habitually were integrated into a perfectly coordinated pattern of artillery fire power.[8]

BRIDGE AND ROLLING STOCK DESTROYED, 15 DECEMBER

On 15 December the long bridge on the south side of Hamhung was destroyed as part of the evacuation plan. B Company, 185th Engineer Combat Battalion, had received orders to destroy this 2,100-foot-long railroad bridge of 29 spans, eight of which were constructed of wood-tie cribbings to the deck level. All the railroad rolling stock in the Hamhung-Hungnam area was also to be destroyed. There were 15 locomotives and about 275 cars on the tracks and in the yards. B Company decided to destroy the bridge and rolling stock at the same time. Each span of the bridge would be destroyed separately, and then as many cars and engines as possible would be pushed into the open space below the break. The first, southernmost, span was blown at 3:45 P.M., and ten cars and several locomotives were pushed into the void. Some cars were loaded with gasoline, and engines had steam up. The wreckage caught fire. This procedure was followed with each span. When the demolition reached the section of the bridge built with wood cribbing, several carloads of gasoline, diesel fuel, and oil were pushed onto the bridge span together with a locomotive. The cribbing was then set on fire. The heat eventually became so intense that the iron of the engine became cherry red and the steam whistle started blowing. The whole bridge section soon crumpled. One accident occurred in destroying the bridge and rail equipment. A boxcar loaded with explosives was pushed by mistake into some burning wreckage. In the explosion that followed two men were injured.[9]

7TH AND 3RD DIVISIONS WITHDRAW TO PHASE LINE 2, 16 DECEMBER

On 16 December, the 7th Infantry Division withdrew to Phase Line 2, and the 3rd Infantry Division continued its withdrawal to that line. The 15th Infantry Regiment of the 3rd Division relieved all elements of the ROK I Corps still ashore. This now left only the 3rd and 7th divisions on the defense perimeter, since all the 1st Marine Division had loaded out and the ROK troops were mostly loaded by the end of the day. There had been an attack early in the morning against C Company, 15th Infantry, 3rd Division, near Chigyong, eight miles southwest of Hamhung. It was repulsed. Before dawn a larger force, estimated at 400 men, had attacked A Company, 65th Infantry, near Songhung-ni, six air miles farther southwest. The Chinese achieved a penetration there. Reserves were hurried to the scene and in a counterattack restored the position. In this action 27 Chinese prisoners were captured. All these attacks were carried out apparently by elements of the Chinese 81st Division.[10] By this time, elements of three Chinese divisions were at the X Corps defense perimeter—the 81st Division on the northwest, the 79th Division at the north, and the 76th Division on the east. Most of the attacks against the perimeter came from the northwest.

The withdrawal of the X Corps perimeter to Phase Line 2 on 16 December put some space between it and the Chinese, and there was a resulting lull on 17 December, while the Chinese were moving up to reestablish contact. This was a process General Soule earlier had said would take place. Artillery and naval gunfire and air strikes during daylight laid down harassing and interdiction barrages on all roads, trails, and access routes toward the perimeter. Only F Company, 32nd Infantry, 7th Division, received any serious attack. It lost its OPLR but regained it with the help of the 7th Division Reconnaissance Company.

As yet, there had been no coordinated enemy attack against the perimeter. The pattern of strong local attacks and probing reconnaissance continued on 18 December. At 1:30 A.M. about 400 CCF, supported by mortar fire, attacked the 1st Battalion, 15th Infantry, 3rd Division. This fight lasted more than two hours before the CCF were driven off. The 1st Battalion was helped by naval and artillery barrages. In this battle, 75 enemy were killed and 23 prisoners taken. The 2nd and 3rd battalions,

15th Infantry, repulsed three different attacks during the day. They were in company or greater strength. During the day, numerous air strikes hit enemy positions. There were 165 sorties. There is no doubt that air strikes and naval and artillery barrages greatly hindered the enemy in concentrating and deploying troops for effective action.[11]

The 3rd Infantry Division pulled in its left flank perimeter during 18 December so that it no longer included Yonpo airfield. It mined and booby-trapped the airfield heavily before it left.

Just after midnight 19 December, the Chinese made their heaviest attack thus far against the X Corps perimeter. It lasted until dawn, 19 December. The enemy penetrated the OPLR, but the MLR held. One prisoner captured during the night said his regiment was reduced to battalion strength by naval gunfire before it reached the perimeter. One five-man machine gun squad of the 17th Infantry, 7th Division, held its position on the OPLR for two hours in the battle after midnight. It withdrew only after it ran out of ammunition. Artillery fire previously registered on the position now hit the area in repeated barrages. American infantry retook the position at dawn. They counted 102 Chinese bodies there, killed either by the machine-gun crew or by the subsequent artillery fire.[12]

THE 3RD DIVISION MOVES TO PHASE LINE 1, 19 DECEMBER

During 19 December the 3rd Infantry Division relieved all elements of the 7th Division on the perimeter, except the 17th Infantry and part of the 15th AAA Battalion, of which it assumed command. The 3rd Division moved to Phase Line 1, east of the Songchon River during the day, thus drawing the perimeter ever closer and tighter around Hungnam. Naval gunfire was increased to that provided by two cruisers and three destroyers. These in turn had specific assignments to support a given regiment on the line. The 7th Division continued outloading, and its division CP opened on the USNS *Breckenridge*. Intelligence reported enemy forces continuing to move down from the reservoir. X Corps intelligence now stated that four Chinese divisions and an unidentified cavalry unit, totaling an estimated 23,000 enemy troops, were at the perimeter.[13]

Although the evidence is meager concerning North Korean soldiers being present at the Hungnam perimeter during the X Corps evacuation, it is possible there may have been a few of them there. If any were there, they played no significant role in action. It is known that remnants of North Korean divisions that reached the Yalu River area in the vicinity of Kanggye during October began to take in recruits and to attempt re-organization so that they could reenter the fight alongside the Chinese at some future date. There is a report that the North Korean 1st Division during November was one of the units undergoing such reorganization near the border as part of a new North Korean III Corps and that in mid-December it was moved to the vicinity of Hungnam to aid in a planned attack on the X Corps perimeter there. It may have engaged in a few skirmishes along the perimeter outpost line, but as already indicated, the Chinese and any rehabilitated North Korean units that may have joined them were unable to mount an effective attack against the UN perimeter at Hungnam.[14]

There was a lull on 20 December, when little enemy activity occurred. The 3rd Division relieved the 17th Infantry, 7th Division, on the line by noon. The 3rd Division now assumed control at 5:50 P.M. as the infantry force responsible for the entire perimeter and for all remaining X Corps elements ashore. With the bridge over the Tongchon River south of Hamhung destroyed, the 3rd Division now had the river as its western boundary for five miles north from the Sea of Japan from a point a mile west of Hungnam. The perimeter then arched eastward for six miles, and then bent south to the coast again about two miles east of Hungnam. The center of the perimeter arc was two miles north of the city and about three miles from the docks and beaches of the harbor.[15] The 3rd Division had its 7th Regiment on the left (west) side of the perimeter along the Tongchon River, the 65th Regiment on the northern (middle) part of the arc, and the 15th Regiment on the east (right) flank.

CCF UNABLE TO CLOSE IN ON THE PERIMETER

During the next three days, 21–23 December, there was no enemy activity against the perimeter. The only contact was when 3rd Division patrols left the defense line to enter no-man's-land to scout to the front. On these occasions they sometimes encountered enemy patrols. These encounters were usually about a mile away from the perimeter. Enemy forces simply could not approach the tight 3rd Division perimeter on the last four days without the probability of dying. Naval gunfire and artillery barrages saturated the ground in front of the perimeter. Aircraft in daytime were always overhead to spot anything that moved and ready to bring down observed fire. During the last day X Corps troops were ashore at Hungnam and on the beach, there was no enemy contact. As it turned out, the enemy attacks on 19 December were not only the strongest the Chinese launched against the X Corps perimeter, they were also the last. The slaughter of their troops then proved to be their final major sacrifice in North Korea. A measure of the firepower the Chinese faced in the last six days at Hungnam is reflected in the figures of 3rd Division artillery-shell fire. A partial tabulation follows:

19 December	5,099 rounds
20 December	5,800 rounds
21 December	6,648 rounds
22 December	9,964 rounds
23 December	7,967 rounds
24 December	10,806 rounds

There was also additional fire from other UN artillery still on shore. At the same time, naval guns from ships offshore fired an average of more than 2,000 rounds a day during this period.[16]

The US Navy started active gunfire for land support at Hungnam on 15 December, when Admiral Hillenkoetter's Gunfire Support Group, using the cruiser *Saint Paul*, fired eight-inch shells for deep support and interdiction of enemy movements. Two days later the cruiser *Rochester* took up the pattern of firing nightly harassing and illuminating missions. Rocket ships placed plunging fire on reverse slopes of hills, and on 21 December they directed plunging fire on reported troop concentrations on the east side of the perimeter. The Navy established stations for fire-support ships in the Hungnam swept channel that now extended for ten miles on each side of the port.[17]

General Almond and his X Corps staff moved aboard the *Mount Mc-Kinley* on 19 December. Even though a small X Corps CP was left on shore until 24 December, responsibility for the defense of Hungnam passed on the nineteenth to Admiral Doyle. The 7th Infantry Division completed loading on 20 December and sailed at first light the next morning. All the major units were now loaded out and afloat except the 3rd Infantry Division. General Soule, commander of the 3rd Division, insisted on staying ashore until the last day, 24 December, when the evacuation was completed. The beaches were lined with seven LSTs and many LVTs. The naval gunfire zone barrages were one mile wide outside the 3,000-yard perimeter. In the final naval shelling at Hungnam, the battleship *Missouri* fired 162 rounds from its big 16-inch guns.

At 2:05 P.M. on 24 December all beaches at Hungnam were cleared and secured. At 2:10 P.M. Admiral Doyle ordered the underwater demolition teams to blow up the Hungnam port facilities, including docks and cranes, and it was done. At 2:36 P.M. all American personnel were off the beaches and were afloat to leave Hungnam forever. As the ships prepared to sail south, observers aboard could see CCF troops some three miles inland coming over a hill. Some of the ships fired a few rounds at them as a last gesture.[18]

Ashore, on the last two days, some details of how the last troops actually left the now narrowly constricted perimeter may be of interest.

On 23 December the covering force of the 3rd Division withdrew to its last inner perimeter line at 4:30 P.M. This force consisted of one battalion from each of the three regiments. The next morning, Sunday, 24 December, the last three battalions ashore of the 3rd Infantry Division began to move to the beaches at 9:30 A.M. Just ahead of them, and among the last to load out in LSTs, were elements of the 3rd Reconnaissance Company; B Company, 64th Tank Battalion; and three provisional platoons of eight quad-50s each, and one platoon of eight dual-40s of the 3rd AAA Battalion. The infantry withdrawal was covered by the 39th Field Artillery Battalion, which loaded at 11 A.M.

The final infantry covering force was taken off the Hungnam beach in LVTs. Those carrying 7th Infantry troops cleared the beach at 12:30; those carrying 65th Infantry troops at 12:37; and those carrying 15th Infantry, the last to depart, at 2 P.M. The 3rd Division CP closed ashore and opened aboard the USS *Bayfield* at the same time, 2 P.M.[19] As the last troops stepped into the waiting LVTs on the afternoon of 24 December, there was not an enemy in sight.

LOADING OUT OF X CORPS FROM WONSAN AND SONGJIN

The evacuation of X Corps from northeast Korea took place from three ports — Songjin, Wonsan, and Hungnam — and from Yonpo airfield. The evacuations from Songjin and Wonsan were first, on 9–10 December. That at Hungnam, by far the largest, was not completed until 24 December. Wonsan was the first port to be evacuated that had been held from the beginning of X Corps operations in northeast Korea. Marine units began outloading there on 2 December while a battalion of the newly arrived 3rd Infantry Division, B Company, 64th Tank Battalion, and the 1st and 3rd battalions of the 1st KMC Regiment provided protection of the harbor area. Marine air cover and naval gunfire also were available.

There was virtually no enemy effort to hamper the evacuation of Wonsan. Loading was completed in the evening of 9 December. The port was evacuated on 10 December after more than 3,800 troops, 7,000 Korean civilians, 1,146 vehicles, and about 10,000 bulk tons of cargo had been outloaded, most of it bound for Pusan, Korea.[20] The evacuation of Wonsan was initially part of General Almond's effort to concentrate X Corps at Hungnam and to support the hard-pressed 1st Marine Division and 7th Infantry troops at Chosin Reservoir after the Chinese counterattacks started there.

Songjin, a minor port on the Sea of Japan, was about 100 air miles northeast of Hungnam. It was conveniently located for lifting most of the ROK I Corps troops by water from their scattered and isolated positions far to the northeast of other elements of X Corps. Major elements

US military installations at Wonsan are burned and destroyed after troops evacuate.
(US Army photograph SC 354094)

of the ROK Capital Division and the ROK 3rd Division were assembled
as quickly as possible at Songjin. LSTs beached there, and on 9 December ROK troops went on board them and several merchant ships.

Their initial orders were to sail for Pusan. But at midnight, six to nine
hours after the vessels had left Songjin, new orders directed them to put
in at Hungnam. The merchant ships received the new orders, but the
LSTs did not respond to the radio orders. Finally the orders got through
to two LSTs. The vessels arrived at Hungnam on 11 December. The ROK
26th Regimental Combat Team of the 3rd Division and the ROK Capital
Division unloaded, and for a time went into the line as parts of the X
Corps perimeter defense on the right flank, east of Hungnam. The remainder of the ROK 3rd Division and the ROK 18th Regiment of the
Capital Division remained on the ships in the harbor.[21]

General Almond had decided to put the ROK I Corps ashore in the
Samchok area to block the east coastal road against enemy advance southward on the extreme east flank of any line Eighth Army might establish

across South Korea. Accordingly, an advance party of the ROK I Corps already at Hungnam took the space vacated by the 26th Regiment aboard a merchant ship. The next day, 12 December, the ship *Southwind* left Hungnam with 13,700 ROK troops of the ROK 3rd Division, less the 26th Regiment; the 18th Regiment, Capital Division; and the ROK I Corps Advance Party. The ship sailed for Samchok, an east-coast port some 40 miles south of the 38th Parallel. An LST with 900 ROK patients from a ROK hospital accompanied it.

The remainder of the ROK I Corps landed a few days later at Mukho, a village just north of Samchok, where a breakwater enclosed a small harbor. The US Navy swept and buoyed a channel there between 15 and 18 December. On 16 December, Captain Jarrell, back from Pusan with a flotilla of vessels, took charge of bringing the rest of the ROK I Corps from Hungnam to Mukho. He used the *Henrico*, one APA, one AKA, three merchantmen, and two LSTs. They sailed from Hungnam at noon on 17 December. The landing at Mukho was uneventful. Maj. Gen. Kim Pac Il (Kim Paik Il, to many) commanded the ROK I Corps; Brig. Gen. Chong Chan Rhee commanded the ROK 3rd Division; and Brig. Gen. Yo Chan Song ("Tiger" Song, to many) commanded the ROK Capital Division. There were now 25,000 ROK troops with 700 vehicles in the Samchok area.[22]

THE EVACUATION FROM HUNGNAM

The great bulk of X Corps evacuated northeast Korea from Hungnam. This was a tremendously complicated undertaking of logistics and had to be coordinated with the tactical defense of the port at the same time the outloading of personnel, equipment, and supplies was going forward. Every aspect of the operation had to be synchronized with all others involved. Assembling the necessary shipping in a short time was not the least of the many things that had to be accomplished. Marine Col. Edward H. Forney, liaison officer on General Almond's X Corps staff for amphibious operations, was the recognized expert who was responsible for overall management of the evacuation.

The success of any evacuation of X Corps from Hungnam obviously depended upon the Navy. As early as 28 November, only one day after the strong CCF attack began in the Chosin Reservoir area, Vice Adm. C. Turner Joy, commander of US Navy Far East, alerted Rear Adm. James H. Doyle, commander of Task Force 90, to prepare for a possible evacuation of X Corps from northeast Korea by sea. Furthermore, the next day, 29 November, Admiral Joy advised Admiral Doyle that events at the Chosin Reservoir made it desirable that ships of Task Force 90 be on a six-hour notice whether they were in Korean waters or at Sasebo, Japan. Admiral

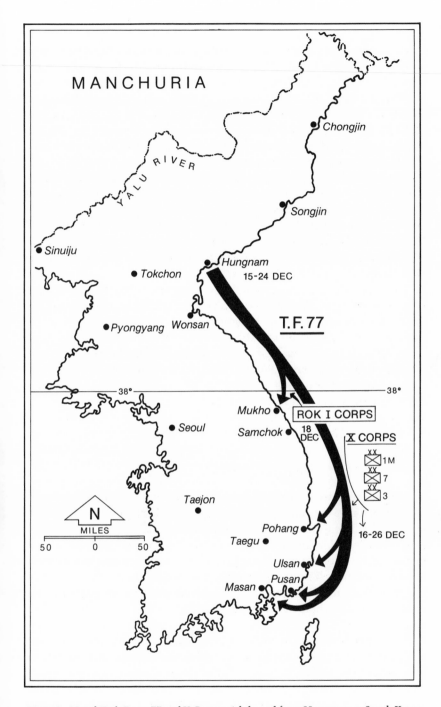

MANCHURIA

Chongjin

YALU RIVER

Songjin

Sinuiju

Hungnam
15-24 DEC

Tokchon

T.F. 77

Pyongyang Wonsan

38°   38°

Mukho ●

ROK I CORPS

Seoul ●

Samchok ●   18
DEC

X CORPS

XX
☒ 1M
XX
☒ 7
XX
☒ 3

Taejon ●

Pohang ●

16-26 DEC

N
MILES
50   0   50

Taegu ●

Ulsan ●

Pusan

Masan ●

Map 18. Naval Task Force 77 and X Corps withdrawal from Hungnam to South Korea, 15–26 December.

Doyle and his staff of Task Force 90 began planning immediately for either an emergency or an administrative outloading of X Corps from northeast Korea.[23]

When General MacArthur on 8 December ordered General Almond to redeploy X Corps to South Korea and report there to Eighth Army, the Navy Far East had plans far advanced for the evacuation by sea. On this day, General Smith was under orders to place the 1st Marine Division in the Hungnam perimeter defense arc on the southwest of Hungnam in the area of the Yonpo airfield and Chigyong. But events in the Eighth Army zone in western Korea actually determined the orders given to X Corps. So when the orders came to redeploy X Corps to South Korea and there to come under Eighth Army control, General Almond on 10 December sent orders to General Smith to bring the 1st Marine Division immediately to the docks for outloading as fast as they arrived at Hungnam.

The change in orders caused no delay or difficulty for the Marine division. As a matter of fact, the division began outloading at Hungnam during the first day its advance elements arrived there, 11 December. This was a special day for General Almond; it was his fifty-eighth birthday.[24]

By 9 December the evacuation plan had proceeded far enough to call for all available AKAs and APAs and one LSD to sail from Inchon for Hungnam. Admiral Joy was instructed to provide ten empty cargo ships daily at Hungnam. Ships that had been scheduled to sail from Wonsan to Pusan were now ordered to come first to Hungnam and unload the Marine Shore Party and Military Sea Transport Service (MSTS) control personnel.

HUNGNAM HARBOR FACILITIES

The Hungnam harbor had four concrete wharves with seven ship berths alongside. Inside the main pier and breakwater there were beaching slots for 14 LSTs. The evacuation plan used the expedient of double-banking cargo vessels and loading inboard from the wharf and loading the outer one by lighter. This doubled the capacity for outloading from the wharves. Troops could march from the wharf across the first vessel to the second. In the outloading operations 1,200 Japanese stevedores assisted in the work. They used their mother ship, the Shinano *Maru*, for sleeping accommodations.[25]

The Hungnam docks formed three sides of a rectangle; the fourth side was open to the harbor. Dock No. 1, which had a breakwater extending from it into the harbor, could berth four ships; Dock No. 3 could berth two ships; and Dock No. 4 could berth one or two ships. Dock No. 2 was short and was used mostly for landing small boats. Green beach was immediately east of the docks. Extensive beach areas lay to the west and east of the three-sided dock area. They were divided into Pink Beach, Blue Beach, Green Beaches 1 and 2, and Yellow Beaches 1, 2, and 3. Green Beach was the most extensively used. LSTs, LSUs, and other types of landing ships and crafts loaded there. The larger ships of the evacuation flotilla anchored out in the stream and were loaded by small craft operating from shore.[26]

PROCEDURE FOR OUTLOADING

Before indicating how and when the X Corps outloaded its major units at Hungnam, it will be useful to indicate overall control and organization of the operation. Vice Adm. James H. Doyle on 10 December, as commander of Task Force 90, assumed control of all naval functions after a conference of Navy and X Corps officers approved the loading plans. Colonel Forney, the ranking Marine Corps officer on the X Corps staff, and serving as deputy chief of staff to General Almond, was appointed the X Corps evacuation control officer. No unit could go to the docks or beaches for loading without his approval.

The Army's 2nd Engineer Special Brigade was responsible for operating the dock facilities and traffic control. There were times when as many as 5,000 Korean and Japanese civilian laborers worked at helping load the ships. The planners knew that 105,000 troops, 17,500 vehicles, and 350,000 measurement tons of cargo would have to be moved from the X Corps zone. There were also thousands of Korean refugees to be evacuated. The planners estimated that it would take ten days to outload this number of men and the massive amount of cargo once outloading began.

One of the most important factors was to maintain a balance ashore of tactical combat troops to prevent enemy from overrunning the beachhead perimeter and to give them in turn adequate logistic support, which would fail if service troops ashore became too few at any given time. These two related problems involved primarily the X Corps G-3 (operations) and the G-4 (logistical, supply) staffs. It became a standard operating procedure that, once the corps G-3 and G-4 agreed on the evacuation of a unit, that unit would be informed. It would then send a liaison officer to Colonel Forney, the control officer in charge of coordinating the loading of ships. Colonel Forney had the task of working with the Navy to maintain a reserve of ships in Hungnam harbor on which the outloading could take place without delay.[27]

Virtually all of X Corps troops, equipment, and supplies unloaded at Pusan and a few other small ports at the southern end of the peninsula, except for ROK troops of the ROK I Corps and their equipment, which unloaded at Samchok and Mukho on the east coast below the 38th Parallel. In order to receive the troops and their equipment at Pusan and to move them quickly from the port area to assembly points outside the city, X Corps sent a control group there under the command of Lt. Col. Arthur M. Murray. Unloading time for a ship at Pusan was reduced from a normal three days to one day. Many of the ships had to make a turn-around for a second loading at Hungnam.

The first large infantry unit to outload at Hungnam was the 1st Marine Division. It began outloading on 11 December and completed it on the fourteenth. Altogether the division required five naval ships, seven merchant ships, 13 LSTs, and three LSDs—28 vessels. At 10:30 A.M. on 15 December the *Bayfield*, with General Smith aboard, and the convoy sailed for Pusan. The Marines loading out at Hungnam numbered 22,215.[28]

During 15 December, the ROK I Corps loaded 4,000 men and 400 vehicles. General Almond visited and inspected the ROK loading during the day. Colonel Forney had informed him that the ROK loading was being kept separate from other X Corps activities and that it was being carried by lighter to ships in the harbor. On 17 December the ROKs at Hungnam finished loading. The next day the ROK I Corps sailed for Samchok, where nearly 14,000 of its troops had already landed. Among the ROKs that had not loaded at Songjin to the north were some units of the Capital Division, which marched down the coastal road to Hungnam. Their special mission during this movement was to blow up railroad tunnels along the way.[29]

By close of 16 December most of X Corps Headquarters personnel and equipment were aboard ship. The 7th Infantry Division loaded between 17 and 20 December as it withdrew from the perimeter defense. The worst weather of the outloading period was 17 December. Winds reached 40 knots. Four LSTs were set adrift and blown into minefields. From 5 P.M. to midnight small-boat traffic in the harbor was halted. The entire period of the evacuation, however, had cold weather. Inoperable and broken-down vehicles filled four Victory ships. An original count of 5,000 drums of petroleum products turned out to be 29,500 outloaded. About 200 drums were left behind. Approximately 9,000 tons of ammunition were outloaded and 1,000 tons of ammunition were left behind; about one-half of this tonnage was frozen dynamite too dangerous to handle.[30]

Meanwhile, during this period, as ships loaded rapidly in Hungnam harbor, Yonpo airfield was destroyed and evacuated. On 15 December Marine VMF-311, the first Marine jet squadron to fly in combat, flew from Yonpo, which had been its base, to Pusan. On 16 December elements of the 65th Infantry, 3rd Infantry Division, which had held a defense perimeter around the airfield, departed for Hungnam. It left some squad tents standing and abandoned some aviation gasoline, ammunition, and food. Something like 500 tons of petroleum products and 500 tons of ordnance items—bombs, rockets, tentage, and bedding—littered the area. One disabled plane stood on the runway. B Company, 185th Engineer Battalion, destroyed these supplies on 17 December. It departed on 19 December, leaving the destroyed airfield to the elements and to the enemy.[31]

On 20 December, General Almond and his staff went aboard Admiral Doyle's flagship of Task Force 90, the *Mount McKinley*, and responsibility for the defense thereby passed to Admiral Doyle. Ashore, General Soule and his 3rd Infantry Division now occupied all the land defenses. Two cruisers and three rocket ships were assigned to help the 3rd Division defend the shrinking perimeter.

Beginning on 20 December and extending to 24 December X Corps Ordnance loaded 9,000 tons of ammunition and 400 unserviceable tanks and vehicles. By close of 22 December all the corps artillery was on ships, and the 3rd Infantry Division began loading its vehicles. The division completed loading them during the night of 23–24 December. During the twenty-third, demolition teams of the 10th Engineer Battalion destroyed bridges and other installations of military value in Hungnam, and the port facilities were prepared for demolition. On the morning of 24 December, the last supplies and equipment were taken aboard ship, and the last elements of the 3rd Infantry Division ashore prepared to evacuate their final defense positions. H hour was set for 11 A.M., 24 December.

It is interesting to note that, at this time, when the CCF were so overwhelmed by UN firepower that they seldom showed themselves anywhere near the American perimeter and were unable to interfere with the Hungnam evacuation, press stories in the United States stirred up fears of disaster at Hungnam; reflecting the influence of the press, letters from home expressed parents' fears that a "Dunkirk" was taking place in northeast Korea. To cite only one example of this development, Lieutenant Colonel Bowsell, executive officer of the 7th Infantry Regiment, 3rd Division, told General Soule on 23 December of letters that men in the regiment had recently received and asked him to do all he could to set the matter straight for people back in the United States.[32] The Hungnam evacuation had no similarity of any kind to the British evacuation of Dunkirk in World War II.

LAST OF X CORPS LEAVES, 24 DECEMBER

On the morning of 24 December seven LSTs beached at Hungnam at 8 A.M. to evacuate the 3rd Infantry Division troops. Men of the three regiments loaded so rapidly that soon each regiment was reduced to one battalion ashore. These battalions then left their positions for the beaches, leaving behind seven reinforced platoons at strongpoints. After a search for stragglers, these platoons went aboard waiting LSTs. The 32nd Field Artillery

Battalion was off the beach at 12:30 P.M. The evacuation in the final hours was marred only by an accidental explosion of an ammunition dump on the beach that killed two men, wounded 21 others, and destroyed three LVTs.

Marines of the 1st Amphibious Amtrac Battalion, covering the last of the Army withdrawals from the beach, apparently were the last to leave the beach at 2:36 P.M., on Sunday, 24 December. No doubt everyone aboard the ships that Christmas Eve in Hungnam harbor considered leaving behind them the coastline of northeast Korea a good Christmas gift.

Relatively few supplies had to be left behind. Among them, however, were 1,000-pound bombs. Some 500 of these bombs were detonated, which helped create the tremendous roar and the huge cloud of black, swirling smoke and flashes of flame when the entire Hungnam waterfront erupted in one great explosion as the final demolitions were set off. In a final note of defiance, the *Mount McKinley* fired her five-inch guns into the smoldering rubble of Hungnam and set sail. Not a single enemy was in sight as the X Corps completed its evacuation of Hungnam.[33]

In the greatest evacuation movement by sea in US military history, the Navy had removed 105,000 soldiers, 17,500 vehicles, and 350,000 measurement tons of bulk cargo from northeast Korea. In addition to the military evacuation, 98,100 Korean refugees were evacuated to South Korea — 7,000 from Wonsan, 4,300 from Songjin, and the rest from Hungnam. Five Korean and Japanese freighters, two Victory ships, and six LSTs carried them. One of the Victory ships carried 14,500 refugees, not including babies on mothers' backs, and one of the LSTs had 10,500 refugees aboard. General Almond had made special efforts to evacuate as many Korean refugees as possible. In making this movement by sea from northeast Korea to South Korea, the Navy used 109 ships in transporting 192 shiploads.[34]

It seems appropriate to mention one of General Almond's characteristics in connection with the Chosin Reservoir campaign — a characteristic he also exhibited subsequently in his command of X Corps in South Korea in 1951 during several massive CCF attacks there. He took pains to see that his staff prepared special historical reports setting forth and trying to explain the military operations his command had participated in. These special reports, not called for by Army regulations, included not only text but also maps, charts, and illustrations. They are of great value to scholars of the Korean War, even though on occasion they omit certain facts, may exaggerate the importance of some event, or evaluate actions differently than would others outside the X Corps. In ordering these reports prepared at the time of the events, or immediately afterward, General Almond did a service to history in maintaining a special record of the times. It would be well for other commanders to emulate

The docks at Hungnam are blown as the last LCVTs leave the beach, 24 December 1950. (National Archives, USN 80-G 424299)

him in this practice. No other commander of a major unit in the Korean War during the period under consideration in this work—army, corps, or division—prepared such operational reports.

KOREAN REFUGEES

One of the tragic aspects of the Korean War was the great number of displaced and miserable civilians who followed the American and UN soldiers in every reverse and withdrawal the fortunes of war forced upon them. This phenomenon was the same in the Eighth Army zone as in the X Corps withdrawal from northeast Korea. But it was especially striking along the withdrawal route of the 1st Marine Division and the 7th Division elements from the Chosin Reservoir to Hungnam. The great mass of homeless people, fleeing from the Chinese and, indirectly, their former North Korean Communist masters, led eventually to nearly

An LST takes aboard Korean refugees during the evacuation of Hungnam. (US Army photograph SC 354789)

100,000 of them being evacuated from Hungnam, Wonsan, and Songjin to South Korea. The size and extent of this refugee movement in the dead of winter had not been anticipated by X Corps. It constituted an immediate serious military threat because enemy troops habitually infiltrated these civilian groups, either as spies and saboteurs or to launch sudden disruptive attacks whenever the opportunity arose. It seemed that no hardship or danger was too severe or too great for the refugees to risk in an effort to escape. The problem became a severe one for X Corps and the 1st Marine Division from Koto-ri southward.

General Almond established the policy, once evacuation of X Corps had been ordered, that all Korean civil officials and their families, other prominent Koreans, and any Koreans who had cooperated with the UN authority in North Korea in trying to establish and maintain local government and order should be evacuated as far as available shipping would allow. This was done. But thousands upon thousands of Koreans followed the soldiers down to the port for evacuation. Even in the midst of a military crisis, the American response was generous in humanitarian terms.

The enormity of the problem is shown by what happened when X Corps was completing the evacuation of Hamhung, ten miles from the coast. As the last train from there for Hungnam was loading for departure, 50,000 refugees tried to get aboard. Front-line troops received firm orders that no refugees were to be permitted inside the perimeter. Many refugees were killed on the way down from Koto-ri to Hungnam because they risked passing through minefields and tried to pass through American fields of fire at the front lines, although fully warned of the danger. In their panic, they often seemed crazed. Chinese reportedly occasionally fired on them with mortars and used them to precede and screen some of their attacks.

On 12 December a rumor, possibly originating from an enemy source, spread among the refugees in the Hamhung area that the United States would provide water transportation for all of them from Hungnam. This started a mass movement toward Hungnam and threatened to clog the main road between the two places. The X Corps provost marshal had to take measures to turn them back. Even the Korean city officials of Hungnam left their posts and joined the refugee movement. The provost marshal, with the help of military police and counterintelligence agents and Korean soldiers from the ROK I Corps, diverted many of the refugees to the village of Soho-jin. The ROK I Corps was particularly instructed not to allow any refugees to enter the corps perimeter.

In spite of all efforts to keep them back, refugees continued to arrive in front of the perimeter from the north between 14 and 20 December. Even harder to control was the large number of the population of Hamhung and Hungnam that gathered at the port for evacuation. The 5th KMC Battalion was moved into Hamhung to control the ever-increasing number of refugees there. During this period, many refugees were placed on small South Korean Navy vessels and small fishing boats and sent south. Rice and barley had to be distributed to the refugees to prevent starvation. Eventually, when the X Corps evacuation neared completion, the 3rd Infantry Division had to deal with the refugee problem as well as to hold the final perimeter.

Altogether, from 9 through 24 December, the South Korean Navy with the help of American Navy, Marines, and Army outloaded a total of 98,100 refugees from northeast Korea. Many more who could not find space onboard any kind of boat started trudging south with their babies and pitifully meager worldly possessions packed on A-frames and bundles carried on their backs. Near the end, when thousands of refugees were unable to find room on any ships, a temporary surplus of shipping for the evacuation of X Corps developed on 23 December. Colonel Forney on this occasion brought in three Victory ships and two LSTs and on them loaded 50,000 of the refugees that were evacuated from Hungnam by sea.[35]

Those who saw the thousands of refugees jammed and packed into the LSTs that carried many of them south, exposed on open decks to freezing weather for three or four days, did not forget the sight. These refugees had to be desperate to take such physical torment and punishment. It was part of the war and should be recorded as such.[36]

15

RESULTS OF THE CHOSIN CAMPAIGN

CASUALTIES

The figures of X Corps casualties — American, British, and South Korean — in the period from 27 November to 24 December 1950 are hard to determine with any exactness. There are wide variations, for instance, between those given by the 1st Marine Division and those tabulated by X Corps for the 1st Marine Division. The figures given here must be considered approximate and indicative rather than exact.

The 1st Marine Division was the major combat element involved in the Chinese counterattack for this period in northeast Korea. It gives its battle casualties as 604 killed, 114 dead of wounds, 192 missing, and 3,485 wounded — for a total of 4,395. Its nonbattle casualties, principally frostbite, digestive disorders, shock, and nonbattle injuries, it gives as 7,338. The bulk of these casualties occurred between 27 November and 11 December. Between 12 and 24 December, for instance, only one Marine was killed and 19 wounded, and 14 or 15 of those wounded received their wounds after embarkation from Hungnam and after arrival in South Korea.

The heaviest single day of battle casualties for the Marines was 28 November, the first full day of the CCF counterattack, when 95 were killed, three died of wounds, 17 were missing, and 539 were wounded — 654 battle casualties. The next day, 29 November, 60 Marines were killed, 14 died of wounds, 43 were missing, and 396 were wounded — 513 battle casualties. Marine casualties remained heavy through 8 December, after which they dropped sharply. Nonbattle casualties were heaviest on 4–5 December, 582 and 469 on those two days, respectively. But nonbattle casualties ran consistently heavy throughout the entire period the 1st Marine Division was in northeast Korea.[1]

In contrast to the 1st Marine Division casualty figures, the X Corps in its table of casualties for all major units of the corps from 27 November through 10 December gives 1st Marine Division losses as only 393 killed, 76 missing, and 2,152 wounded, for a total of 2,621. The Marine

Division, however, gives 454 killed, 94 dead of wounds, 179 missing, and 2,844 wounded, for a total of 3,571—almost a thousand more, or more than 35 percent greater, than the corps figures.[2] One must assume that the 1st Marine Division figures are more nearly correct. The division simply did not have knowledge of its casualties on the day following action. When it learned later what had happened, it recorded them but did not submit revised figures to X Corps.

An interesting feature of the X Corps battle casualties is that those of the Army 7th Infantry Division exceeded by 139 those of the 1st Marine Division and were the heaviest for any division in the corps. The total number of Marine casualties is given as 2,621; that of the 7th Infantry Division as 2,760. But it will be noticed that, if the 1st Marine figures are accepted, then the 4,395 Marine casualties far exceed those for the 7th Division. The 1st Marine Division figures in fact appear to be the more accurate. The great bulk of the 7th Division casualties is in the missing-in-action category. These numbered 2,505, with only 70 killed and 185 wounded. It is known beyond any doubt, however, that hundreds more were killed or died of wounds than are indicated in the corps figures. The bulk of the 7th Infantry Division casualties, and particularly the missing in action, came from the 1st Battalion, 32nd Infantry; the 3rd Battalion, 31st Infantry; the Headquarters group of the 31st Infantry Regiment; and the 57th Field Artillery Battalion—all of which were engaged with the CCF 80th Division on the east side of Chosin Reservoir, 27 November to 3 December, where they were cut off and virtually destroyed. This battleground was never regained by UN forces, so X Corps had to carry most of the killed and many wounded there as missing in action.

The Republic of Korea soldiers (KATUSA) attached to the 3rd and 7th divisions of X Corps also show a high number of missing in action, 1,789. It has already been noted that the figures for the 1st Marine Division are not considered reliable, and instead the figure of 4,395 is considered approximately accurate. Table 5, giving cumulative battle casualties, is based on X Corps figures, despite the knowledge that they are not accurate—but they are the best figures available from an official source.

The Army's 7th Infantry Division had the greatest number of casualties in field-grade officers—15. Of these, seven were from the 3rd Battalion and the Headquarters group of the 31st Infantry Regiment; four were from the 1st Battalion, 32nd Infantry; and four were from the 57th Field Artillery Battalion. They included one colonel, the 31st Regimental commander; four lieutenant colonels, and ten majors—one killed, six wounded, five missing, and three unknown. Fourteen of the 15 were casualties east of the Chosin Reservoir, between 28 November and 3 December. The 1st Marine Division had the second highest casualties in

TABLE 5.
X Corps Battle Casualties, 27 November–10 December 1950

Unit	KIA	WIA	MIA	Total
X Corps HQ and Service Troops	5	20	15	40
X Corps Combat Troops	3	8	0	11
1st Marine Div.	393	2,152	76	2,621 (or 4,385)[a]
41st Royal Marine Commandos	8	31	39	78[b]
Marine Air Wing	2	2	2	6
3rd Inf. Div.	50	206	147	403
KATUSA attached to 3rd Div.	17	76	94	187[c]
7th Inf. Div.	70	185	2,505	2,760
KATUSA attached to 7th Div.	1	41	1,560	1,602[c]
1st KMC Regt.	13	80	0[d]	93
ROK I Corps HQ	1	3	0	4
ROK Capital Div.	126	318	334	778
ROK 3rd Div.	15	127	6	148
Total	704	3,249	4,778	8,731 (or 10,495)

SOURCE: Adapted from HQ, X Corps, Comd. Rpt., 27 Nov–10 Dec 50, p. 97.
[a]The number in parenthesis represents the official total given by the 1st Marine Division. It appears to be more reliable than the number given by X Corps.
[b]Total casualties for the commandos were undoubtedly much higher than the official total given.
[c]KATUSA casualties were almost certainly higher than the figures given here.
[d]The zero here is questionable.

field-grade officers with 14, including one colonel, four lieutenant colonels, and nine majors—one killed, ten wounded, and three missing.[3]

TANK LOSSES

X Corps tank losses were far greater in northeast Korea than they had been earlier in South Korea in the Inchon-Seoul area fighting. Prior to its landing at Wonsan in northeast Korea, the corps had 67 tank casualties, but only seven of them were permanent losses. In northeast Korea the X Corps suffered 86 tank casualties (destroyed or damaged), but 50 of them were permanent losses. Only one tank in northeast Korea was lost to mines, another indication that the Chinese had no mines there other than a few improvised ones. Of the tank casualties in northeast Korea, 54 were due to mechanical failure, and 17, all of them total losses, were due to terrain. A listing gives only three tanks as being lost to enemy infantry attack, but this figure seems to ignore the tanks lost to Chinese action at the very end of the column leaving Koto-ri. The number actually destroyed by enemy was somewhat larger, and it also begs the question, in a sense, since we know that many more were abandoned by their crews because of Chinese infantry attack and were subsequently destroyed by the Chinese or by American air strikes. Enemy attack must be credited with destroying them, either directly or indirectly. A better estimate would be that enemy attack destroyed about 15 American tanks in northeast Korea.[4]

Sometimes tanks were lost at night when infantry fell back without notifying and coordinating with the tank crews. Such behavior exposed the tanks to close-in enemy attacks using satchel charges, pole charges, grenades, bazookas, and small-arms fire. Small arms could knock out periscopes, antenna bases, and other external features. The larger weapons were concentrated against tank tracks and engine compartments. One thing infantry learned in fighting close to tanks was that the muzzle brakes of a 90-mm tank gun could deflect the muzzle blast to the side and inflict serious injury to any men near it.

UN EQUIPMENT AND ARMS LOSSES

The number of vehicles, trucks of all kinds, lost in northeast Korea was very large, but there is apparently no complete listing of such losses. Large numbers of trucks simply wore out or could not be repaired because of a lack of spare parts and were abandoned. Many others were victims of enemy ambushes and attack. Perhaps the single largest loss of vehicles was the complete loss of the trains of the 1st Battalion, 32nd Infantry; those of the 3rd Battalion, 31st Infantry; those of the 57th Field Artillery Battalion as well as all the guns of the latter battalion; and those of part of Headquarters Company, 31st Infantry Regiment. These were all lost in action east of the Chosin Reservoir. The number of small arms and automatic weapons captured by the enemy was also considerable, but no complete tabulation has come to light. It is known that elements of the 7th Infantry Division lost most of their weapons in the action east of the Chosin Reservoir.

CCF LOSSES

The tremendous Chinese losses in the Chosin Reservoir are amply attested by captured enemy documents, some captured several months after the evacuation of Hungnam; by hundreds of Chinese prisoner statements in interrogations; by some authentic body counts on the battlefield; by estimates of forward artillery observers; and by reports of fighter and bomber pilots. It is impossible to give verifiable specific statistics of Chinese losses. Air reports, for instance, can be only estimates in nearly all cases, and experience has shown they are usually exaggerated. Artillery estimates of enemy casualties also are usually exaggerated. When the battleground was not held or regained by UN forces, there was no possibility of a body count of enemy dead or wounded. In any case, many of the wounded either were carried away by their own units, or they walked or crawled off by their own power.

While it is not possible to be precise about enemy losses in northeast Korea, it is known that Chinese losses were crippling to the IX Army Group and that several divisions were decimated. Their losses were many times greater than those of X Corps. A large part of these losses were caused by the arctic weather. The Chinese soldiers were not nearly as well prepared to withstand the subzero temperatures as were the Americans. The latter had relatively good winter clothing and protection for hands, feet, and body that the Chinese soldiers did not have. And whereas the X Corps troops had ample food most of the time, the Chinese did not—they starved, they were weak from loss of strength, and they developed crippling stomach ailments. The Chinese soldiers did not receive a single known resupply of food or ammunition in the Chosin campaign after they crossed the border and headed south toward the Chosin Reservoir. Their medical facilities were either primitive or nonexistent in the Chosin fighting. Relatively few received immediate battlefield treatment for critical wounds, there was only slow evacuation (where there was any) to hospitals in China, and most of the frostbite cases received no treatment at all.

The simple fact is that the terrible winter weather of the Chosin Reservoir area took a far greater toll of Chinese lives and military effectiveness than it did of the X Corps. It should not be forgotten that the Chinese soldiers who were thrown against the X Corps in northeast Korea were mostly from the south of China and were not inured to the severe Siberian type of climate they were forced to fight in. It was different for many of the CCF units from the 4th Field Army that fought against Eighth Army in the west. They were used to the cold weather of Manchuria in northern China.

A few prisoner reports will indicate the magnitude of Chinese losses in northeast Korea during November–December 1950. Fu Won Shu, a member of the Chinese 76th Division, 26th Army, was captured at Koto-ri on 5 December. His division was one of those rushed south from Linchiang on the Manchurian border to reinforce the 20th and 27th armies when it was apparent that they had failed at Yudam-ni and the Chosin Reservoir to destroy the X Corps. Fu said his division marched only at night, thus escaping the devastating air attacks of daytime. He said that on the way south they saw CCF wounded and stragglers with trench foot going north toward the border. At Koto-ri, he said, his division and other CCF troops already there had surrounded the UN units, but they were able to do little fighting because of the severe air attacks and the heavy artillery shelling, which caused severe casualties among them. Fu said the 76th Division suffered crippling losses and was practically annihilated, and those that retreated left their weapons behind. The 76th Division had bolt-action rifles, and each rifleman carried 100 rounds of ammunition and five hand grenades. Their machine guns had approximately 800 rounds of ammunition and were horsedrawn. There was no resupply.[5]

On 7 December a Chinese second lieutenant from the 179th Regiment of the 60th Division was captured near Chinhung-ni. He said that his company had 30 casualties, 20 from air attacks and 10 from frostbite, and that previously altogether one-half his company had suffered from frostbite of hands and feet, but not severe enough to cause their evacuation and to be counted as casualties. He said his division had had no resupply and had to live off the country and what it captured from American forces.[6]

Lui Kin Ju, a private in the CCF 89th Division, was captured on 9 December, 11 miles south of Koto-ri. He said the men in his 3rd Battalion, 266th Regiment, suffered from frostbite and were unable to walk. They either were sent to the rear or deserted. About 20 percent of his battalion had frostbitten hands. His division, he said, was noted for its complete indoctrination in the Communist cause and in its suicidal charges in combat. According to him, no alcohol or narcotics were given to the Chinese soldiers before such attacks.[7]

On 9 December, a Chinese captain who was a political officer of the 3rd Battalion, 180th Regiment, 60th Division, was captured near Koto-ri. He said the 20th Army, of which his division was a part, had failed in its mission because the firepower of tanks and air strikes enabled the UN troops cut off in the Chosin Reservoir area to join those to the south and allowed American troops from the south to reinforce those to the north. He also stressed that Chinese troops were demoralized and that combat effectiveness had deteriorated because of frostbite, trench foot, and inadequate food.[8]

One Chinese prisoner captured later estimated that 20,000 of his fellow soldiers had starved or frozen to death since November. Hospitals in northern and central China were filled with wounded. Air attacks and freezing had caused the heaviest casualties, he said. Frostbite was reported by nearly all Chinese prisoners as being a cause of heavy casualties in their ranks and for noneffectiveness of units. Some said that 50 percent in their units had frostbite. Trench foot was the most common cold-induced injury. Combat wounded among the Chinese had priority for evacuation; frostbite victims had to stay. When they were no longer able to walk, they were generally left to shift for themselves, and many subsequently died of exposure. The soldiers' inability to keep their feet dry

Chinese prisoners taken near Sudong in early November 1950, wearing typical quilted cotton uniforms, fleece-lined caps, and low-cut rubber shoes. These soldiers, like most Chinese troops, did not have gloves. (US Marine Corps photograph 16-11)

and the forced night marches caused much exhaustion and many injuries from cold.[9]

CLOTHING OF THE CCF

The typical clothing worn by the Chinese soldier of the IX Army Group in the Chosin Reservoir campaign consisted of several layers of underclothing worn under an outer uniform of heavy cotton-quilted reversible material, khaki or olive, and white. This and a heavy wool or fur-lined cap with earflaps gave good cover for body and head. There was an inadequate supply of gloves, however. Sometimes Chinese captives had their bare hands frozen to their weapons. But the most serious weakness in the Chinese winter wear was the shoe. They were merely brown rubber and canvas tennis-type shoes worn with two or three pairs of wool socks. The shoes were not waterproof. Often the feet and lower legs of prisoners were frozen solid. In one case, south of Koto-ri, on a night when the wind in the mountain pass was unusually strong and the temperature dropped 30 degrees in a few hours, a Chinese prisoner said his entire battalion became combat ineffective from frostbite.[10]

The Chinese soldier had no overcoat. Some of them carried a form of shawl among items in their small packs. Those lucky enough to obtain an American parka or overcoat on the battlefield wore it.

After the end of the Chosin campaign, and when a study had been made of the multitudinous enemy prisoner interrogation reports and of captured enemy documents, together with American battle reports of enemy killed and wounded (which have to be discounted in varying degrees), one intelligence analysis concluded that the Chinese troops of the IX Army Group in northeast Korea suffered the greatest number of casualties from the weather—just plain freezing—and second, from battle losses in attacks against the American troops. It was estimated that more than two-thirds of the 20th Army and one-third of the 27th Army became casualties. In the 20th Army, the 60th Division was virtually destroyed, the 59th Division lost about half its men, and the 58th Division lost about two-thirds of its men. After these extremely heavy losses in the first week of the Chosin Reservoir fighting, the 26th Army, which had been held in reserve near the border, was marched south to relieve the 20th Army. Its advance units arrived at Hagaru-ri just before the American withdrawal from there began. These CCF 26th Army reinforcements were engaged in the fight along the MSR to Koto-ri and on south through Funchilin Pass. Two of its divisions were the main force engaged near Hamhung and Hungnam during the evacuation.[11]

The 1st Marine Division estimated that, from 27 November through 12 December, during its active part in the Chosin Reservoir campaign, there were 12,000 CCF killed in battle by ground action and that 7,500 more were wounded—a total of 19,500 battle casualties from ground combat. For the same period, the 1st Marine Air Wing, Fleet Marine Force, estimated that it had killed and wounded at least 10,313 Chinese soldiers by air action. These estimates total more than 29,800 enemy soldiers killed or wounded. If one strikes a balance of one-third of all other Chinese in action as victims of various kinds of frostbite, one must add another 20,000–25,000 casualties. Thus, one would have a total Chinese casualty figure of 50,000 to 55,000 of a total force of about 72,000 Chinese engaged.[12] These claims probably exceed the actual number of Chinese casualties. But captured enemy documents amply support the claim that

Chinese casualties were very heavy in the Chosin campaign. One such document, issued by the 27th Army Headquarters, lists nonbattle casualties for the 27th Army alone from 27 November to 31 December 1950 as about 6,200 troops, of which 5,900 were from frostbite. Another enemy document, covering the same period from the 21st CCF Hospital, gives a total of 8,000 combat and noncombat casualties treated in the hospital. About 3,000 of these were frostbite cases. Except for a small number of nonbattle casualties from other causes, the rest were battle casualties.[13]

CCF STRENGTH COMMITTED IN THE CAMPAIGN

Most American sources state that at least 100,000 Chinese soldiers were engaged in the Chosin Reservoir campaign. They reach this figure by assuming that at least ten Chinese divisions were committed to action and that each division was at full strength of 10,000 men. It appears, however, that probably the Chinese divisions in combat against the X Corps in northeast Korea averaged about 7,500 to 8,000 men.[14] There were only nine Chinese divisions firmly identified as being in contact and engaged with X Corps forces in the Chosin Reservoir campaign. Three of the 12 divisions in the CCF IX Army Group were never identified in battle contact during the campaign. Two of the divisions, the 78th and 88th of the 26th Army, apparently did not reach the battle scene in time to be committed to action. The third uncommitted division of the IX Army Group was the 90th, of the 27th Army. It may have been held in reserve somewhere in the Chosin area but never committed, or if elements of it were committed, they were never identified.

The nine known committed Chinese divisions in the Chosin Reservoir campaign from the Chinese IX Army Group were the following (cf. Table 1 in chapter 2, above):

20th Army: 4 divisions committed—58th, 59th, 60th, and (attached from 30th Army) 89th;
26th Army: 2 divisions committed—76th and 77th; not committed—78th and (attached from 30th Army) 88th;
27th Army: 3 divisions committed—79th, 80th, and 81st; not committed—(attached from 30th Army) 90th.

The 26th Army was the last of the three armies to be committed. The other two armies, the 20th and 27th, were in the fight from its beginning on 27 November to the end, although the 20th Army was almost totally ineffective by 10 December, and the 27th Army was no more than one-third to one-half effective by that date.[15]

CCF ANALYSIS AND SELF-CRITICISM

The Chinese Army was nearly always brutally frank in its after-action analysis of what its successes and failures were in battle with the UN forces in Korea. This is shown in captured Chinese Army documents. The first of these captured indicated the Chinese rated the American Eighth Army infantry as being poor in the Unsan battle in October 1950 but gave great respect to American artillery, tank, mortar, automatic firepower, and air power.

In analyzing the Chosin Reservoir campaign, the CCF 26th Army commented on its own weaknesses:

> A shortage of transportation and escort personnel makes it impossible to accomplish the mission of supplying the troops. As a result, our soldiers frequently starve.
>
> The troops were hungry. They ate cold food and some had only a few potatoes in two days. They were unable to maintain the physical strength for combat; the wounded personnel could not be evacuated. . . . The firepower of our entire army was basically inadequate. When we used our guns there were no shells, and sometimes the shells were duds.

The 20th Army had telling comments on battle conditions (it suffered more battle casualties than the other two armies in the IX Army Group). Its critique said in part:

> Our signal communication was not up to standard . . . it took more than two days to receive instructions from higher level units. Rapid changes of the enemy's situation and the slow motion of our signal communications caused us to lose our opportunities in combat and made the instructions of the high level units ineffective. . . . We succeeded in the separation and encirclement of the enemy, but we failed to annihilate the enemy one by one. The units failed to carry out the orders of the higher echelon. For example, the failure to annihilate the enemy at Yut'an-ni [Yudam-ni] made it impossible to annihilate the enemy at Hakalwu-ri [Hagaru-ri]. The higher level units' refusal of the lower level units' suggestion of rapidly starting the combat and exterminating the enemy one by one gave the enemy a chance to break out from the encirclement.[16]

In its critique, the 27th Army said, "The tactics were mechanical. . . . We underestimated the enemy. . . . Reconnaissance was not conducted strictly; we walked into the enemy fire net and suffered heavy casualties." As to why they failed to destroy the 1st Marine Division at the Chosin Reservoir, the 27th Army document commented, "Our troops encountered unfavorable conditions . . . and the troops suffered too many casualties."

Perhaps the most telling and bitter comment from the 27th Army concerned the weather:

> The troops did not have enough food. They did not have enough houses to live in, they could not stand the bitter cold, which was the reason for the excessive non-combat reduction in personnel (more than 10 thousand persons), the weapons were not used effectively. When the fighters bivouacked in snow-covered ground during combat, their feet, socks, and hands were frozen together in one ice-ball; they could not unscrew the caps on the hand grenades; the fuses would not ignite; the hands were not supple; the mortar tubes shrank on account of the cold; 70 percent of the shells failed to detonate; skin from the hands was stuck on the shells and mortar tubes.[17]

After the X Corps evacuated Hungnam on 24 December 1950, a great intelligence silence surrounded the CCF IX Army Group. American commanders expected it to move rapidly across Korea to join units of the Fourth Field Army in a continuing attack on the US Eighth Army. But weeks and months passed, and none of its units showed up there.

Had the UN command known the facts, there would have been no cause for all the anxiety about the Chinese IX Army Group during the months after the Hungnam evacuation. Intelligence collected later told the story. The 20th Army, after the Hungnam evacuation, moved to the Oro-ri–Sinhung area north and northeast of Hungnam and bivouacked; the 26th Army moved to the Kowon-Wonsan area south of Hungnam and bivouacked; the 27th Army remained in the Hungnam-Yonghung area and bivouacked. In all these places the Chinese divisions rested, took in replacements, reorganized, and reequipped. The 90th Division was deactivated, and its remaining troops were divided among the 79th, 80th, and 81st divisions as replacements.[18]

What had happened to the Chinese IX Army Group remained a guessing game in the UN command until March and April 1951. Then some of these units began showing up on the east-central front. The simple fact was that the IX Army Group was so used up in the Chosin Reservoir campaign that at its close the army group was not combat effective and could not be committed anywhere for several months.[19]

Who Won the Chosin Reservoir Campaign?

Who won the Chosin Reservoir campaign—the Chinese IX Army Group or the X Corps? Each can claim victory in a certain sense. One rule of thumb in deciding who wins is to ask, Who holds the battlefield after the fighting is over? In this respect the Chinese claim has a finality that cannot be denied. The CCF IX Army Group of the Third Field Army did force UN forces from all of northeast Korea and an evacuation from there by sea. It did fully protect the left flank of the CCF Fourth Field Army divisions, which attacked Eighth Army in the west, and it prevented the X Corps from helping that army as Lin Piao's veterans drove the US Eighth Army out of North Korea in a near-panic retreat. These were great successes. But the IX Army Group did not destroy the 1st Marine Division, which was its avowed mission, and it did not defeat the X Corps in the series of battles extending from 27 November to 12 December 1950 and the subsequent minor actions around the Hungnam perimeter during the evacuation, which was completed on 24 December.

The X Corps can claim a battle victory in the Chosin Reservoir in the sense that, as a military operation, it defeated the CCF IX Army Group in a series of battles that enabled it to withdraw most of its forces as effective combat tactical units to the seacoast and to proceed with an orderly evacuation, retaining unit integrity, saving and retaining virtually all its equipment (excepting the US 31st Infantry Combat Team of the 7th Division), and constituting upon evacuation a battle-ready force that could be committed to action elsewhere.

X CORPS ANALYSIS OF CHINESE ATTACK OPTIONS

In its evaluation of Chinese action in the Chosin campaign, X Corps criticized the CCF strategic and tactical decision to attack in the Chosin area. It postulates that the Chinese had three options in counterattacking the X Corps in northeast Korea. First, it could attack the X Corps from its southwest flank through the 3rd Infantry Division (which had just landed at Wonsan) from the Sachang-ni area, with the purpose of seizing the Hamhung-Hungnam area, and at the same time it could cut off the 1st Marine Division and elements of the 7th Infantry Division that were 60 miles northward in the Chosin Reservoir area. It then could defeat the scattered elements of X Corps elsewhere in detail.

A second option was to attack from north of the Fusen Reservoir on the Pungsan axis to the coast, cutting off and destroying elements of the 7th Infantry Division to the north and already on the Yalu River and the ROK I Corps along the northeast coastal road. Or, third, it could attack in the center against the greatest concentration of strength in the X Corps area—the 1st Marine Division and part of the 7th Infantry Division in the Chosin Reservoir area—destroy it, and then push down the Hagaru-ri–Hungnam axis to the X Corps base of supply at Hungnam and subsequently destroy the scattered remnants of the X Corps.

The X Corps analysis states that the CCF commander made two major errors in attacking the 1st Marine Division in the center rather than acting on either of the other options it describes. First, the CCF attacked

X Corps strength instead of a weakness, and second, they underestimated the strength of the 1st Marine Division and the power of American air support and other support weapons' firepower in the battle area.

One can grant that the Chinese underestimated the strength of the 1st Marine Division, but it must also be understood that the Chinese considered the 1st Marine Division the most powerful infantry division in the US Armed Forces. The Chinese did underestimate American firepower in support of American infantry in the reservoir area (air, artillery, mortar, tank, and automatic weapons) when properly coordinated for infantry support.

I believe that the CCF chose the right strategy, the only one that might have enabled the Chinese to destroy the X Corps in northeast Korea. Let us consider briefly the second option, the one most unlikely to produce important results from the Chinese viewpoint. A CCF attack east and southeast from the vicinity of the Fusen Reservoir might have reached Pungsan and cut off elements of the 7th Infantry Division that were on and near the Yalu River to the north, and it might have reached the coast at Hongwon and Sinchang, thereby also cutting off the ROK Capital Division, far to the north on the coastal road, and possibly some elements of the ROK 3rd Division that generally were following in the wake of the US 7th Infantry Division for the purpose of taking over control of part of the northern border region. The ROK Capital Division could have been evacuated by sea quickly by the US Navy, as indeed it was as a result of the Chosin operation, if it had been cut off, and probably most of the ROK 3rd Division would have escaped in the same way. Only a part of the 7th Division would probably have been lost if the CCF had exercised this second option. But while this was taking place, the bulk of X Corps, including the 1st Marine Division, the US 3rd Infantry Division, and three battalions of the 7th Infantry Division could have withdrawn from their advanced positions and concentrated in a strong perimeter around Hamhung, Hungnam, and Yonpo airfield. The Chinese would have gained little by acting on this option.

The first option, in the X Corps analysis, postulated a CCF attack from Sachang-ni through Huksu-ri against the scattered 3rd Infantry Division, which would then continue on to seize the Hamhung-Hungnam supply base and communications center. Sachang-ni lies about 22 air miles directly west of Chinhung-ni and about 45 air miles northwest of Hungnam. It is about 30 air miles slightly west of south of Yudam-ni, where the Chinese did actually concentrate against the 1st Marine Division. A poor dirt road ran from Yudam-ni to Sachang-ni, and from there a somewhat better dirt road ran through Huksu-ri, eight miles to the east, where the road turned southeast to Chigyong, and hence to Hamhung and Hungnam. This axis of attack was certainly a possibility and might have offered great chance of success in favorable circumstances, the most important of which would have been the ability of the CCF to concentrate a large attack force there undiscovered and able to launch a swift, surprise attack toward Hungnam.

The difficulty with this option for the CCF was that undiscovered concentration and a swift surprise attack from Sachang-ni were beyond CCF capability after the middle of November. By that time, UN forces were in the area in some strength. First there were ROK troops, then 1st Marine Division units and the 1st KMC Regiment, and lastly the 3rd Infantry Division and the 1st Capital Division. These forces successively fought numerous engagements and skirmishes and dealt with ambushes by North Korean guerrillas and remnants of defeated North Korean divisions retreating northward from the old battlefields in the south. The principal road centers and towns of this area were garrisoned, or at least outposted, by UN forces. The CCF could not have concentrated in this area without having been discovered. They could not have achieved a major surprise attack from there at the end of November. They were able to do so at Chosin Reservoir only because the UN had no troops there at all while the Chinese were concentrating in the vicinity. The evidence indicates that most of the IX Army Group initial attack force arrived there only shortly ahead of the X Corps troops and much too late to have moved undiscovered in large numbers farther south and southeast to Sachang-ni and Huksu-ri.

At least one CCF battalion (or larger force) from the 89th Division did in fact go down the road from Yudam-ni to Sachang-ni on what probably should be considered a reconnaissance in force. When it arrived at Sachang-ni on the night of 28 November, it found the 1st Battalion, 7th Infantry, 3rd Division, holding the town. In battle lasting through the night and following day, the Chinese were defeated with heavy casualties and had to retreat northward.

The moment a Chinese concentration became apparent, or was seen to be under way, in the Sachang-ni area, the X Corps would undoubtedly have drawn in the outlying 3rd Division units in a concentration to protect that approach to the Hamhung-Hungnam area and the MSR running north to the 1st Marine Division. And it would also at that point probably have ordered the 1st Marine Division back to the Hamhung area. This could have been accomplished rather quickly. At the same time, the X Corps presumably would have ordered the scattered 7th Infantry Division also to concentrate on Hungnam. Yonpo airfield, only eight miles from Hamhung and five miles from Hungnam, would have provided a quick turnaround for fighter-plane support, and the Marine carrier fighter planes at sea just off the coast would have had optimum conditions for giving maximum fighter and bomber close support for any UN troops engaged there. Naval gunfire from just off the coast could have added powerfully to the defense of any perimeter in the Hungnam coastal area. In summary, by the time the CCF forces of the IX Army Group arrived in the Chosin Reservoir area, from which they might have proceeded on to Sachang-ni in an attempted approach close to Hungnam, it was too late to consider this option with any chance of success.

The Chinese planners and commander of the IX Army Group, or higher authority, did in fact make the best choice of operations available to them in deciding to attack the 1st Marine Division at the Chosin Reservoir, 60 miles by a mountainous, poor road from its supply base and communications center at Hamhung-Hungnam. This road had two difficult mountain passes, and part of this dirt road was passable only to one-way traffic. Numerous bridges and cliff overhangs offered the chance to create roadblocks. The CCF was able to concentrate undiscovered at least six divisions in the vicinity of the Chosin Reservoir before the 1st Marine Division arrived there in any force and advanced from Hagaru-ri to Yudam-ni. The big Chinese counterattack, beginning on the night of 27 November there and elsewhere around the reservoir, did achieve surprise. If their plan to destroy the bulk of the 1st Marine Division at the Chosin Reservoir had succeeded, the CCF could have poured down the Hagaru-ri road to Hungnam with a good chance of success. And had the Chinese properly coordinated their attack at the reservoir, especially attacking Hagaru-ri in strength on the first night, and if they had initially moved their four reserve divisions closer to the scene of battle, they might well have succeeded in their goal. The concept was good; the execution was bad.

The Chinese reckoned as part of their plan that there was only one escape road from Chosin Reservoir, and they would cut this road behind the 1st Marine Division at the same time they attacked it frontally, having sufficient forces in place to prevent considerable numbers of their enemy from escaping the trap. If they could defeat the enemy's main strength, 60 miles from its base, the Chinese commander of the IX Army Group, General Sung, apparently believed the piecemeal destruction of the scattered remnants of X Corps would follow.

WHY DID COMPLETE VICTORY AT CHOSIN ELUDE THE CCF?

Why did not the Chinese IX Army Group's plan of attack at Chosin Reservoir succeed? What errors of judgment, if any, may be charged against the Chinese command in the Chosin battles? Because of a lack of reliable information, we cannot answer all these questions, but some comments can be made.

First, it is desirable to place the strength of the contestants and their respective qualities and methods of fighting in perspective. Two general misconceptions must be corrected for one to understand the basic situation that prevailed between the UN forces and the CCF engaged in the Chosin Reservoir combat in November and December 1950.

It was the fashion at the time in the press, at the Pentagon, in the Far East Command, and also in X Corps itself to speak of the Chinese as having a huge numerical superiority of troops over X Corps. This was not true, except that the CCF tried to have a superiority at the precise point selected for attack; generally they favored a three-to-one superiority there if they could manage it. But in the general area of combat, they often did not have superiority, or not a very large one.

For instance, the 1st Marine Division had an effective strength of 25,473 men on 27 November 1950, the day the CCF counterattack began at Yudam-ni.[20] At that time, there were two Marine infantry regiments there and nearly all of the artillery regiment, the 11th Marines. The bulk of the actual combat forces of the division was at Yudam-ni, perhaps about 13,000 to 14,000 men. Two Chinese divisions (or elements of two divisions) attacked the Marines at Yudam-ni that night. A CCF division at full strength was supposed to number 10,000 men, but the official Marine history of the Chosin Reservoir campaign accepts the actual strength of the CCF divisions there as being about 7,500 each. Two CCF divisions, therefore, would number about 15,000 men — no great superiority numerically, and possibly none at all. If heavy weapons support is counted in the balance, the CCF attacking force could be said to have been actually inferior to the defending Marines. In general, it must be recognized that the 1st Marine Division was about three times the numerical strength of a CCF division — perhaps about equal to a Chinese army (usually three divisions, but four in the Chosin campaign); and a US Army division, lower in strength than the 1st Marine Division, was about double the strength of a CCF division. Although the CCF used six divisions (or parts thereof) in the first few days of fighting at the Chosin Reservoir, about 45,000 men at a maximum, against about 30,000 US troops (1st Marine Division and three battalions of the 7th Infantry Division), they did not concentrate these divisions in any one battle but scattered them over 40 miles of battle front, which included five UN perimeter defenses and 40 road miles on the X Corps lines of communication. The greatest single CCF concentration for attack was two divisions at Yudam-ni; the next greatest was one division against the three battalions of the 7th Infantry Division east of the reservoir and one division at Hagaru-ri.

We know that the X Corps evacuated 105,000 UN troops from northeast Korea in December 1950. Firm identification of CCF units engaged and in contact with UN forces throughout the Chosin campaign from 27 November to 24 December 1950 shows nine divisions. A tenth division or part of it might have been present. Counting a full 7,500 men for each division on average would give a total CCF strength of only 67,000 men.

In reading the published literature, only a few books but many magazine articles and newspaper stories during 1950–51, one can come across all sorts of variants as to the strength of a Chinese infantry division, ranging from 10,000 on down to 7,000. It seems certain that no Chinese division in combat at Chosin Reservoir numbered 10,000, if indeed that was the theoretical full strength of a Chinese division, which some claimed. The 1st Marine Division itself, and obviously the organization in the best position to know, estimated at the end of the fighting there, basing its estimate on the intelligence gained in the fighting itself and that gained from Chinese prisoners and captured documents, that the Chinese divisions it faced had an average strength of about 7,500 men. In March 1951, a few months later, the Eighth Army, then encompassing all of the Korean combat zone, in a special report estimated that the Chinese divisions that had fought in Korea up to that time averaged about 8,000 men. The judgment of the 1st Marine Division in northeast Korea in late 1950 and the judgment of the Eighth Army three months later for all of Korean combat up to that time were very close to each other—jointly they agreed that the Chinese infantry divisions they had faced numbered 7,500 to 8,000 men. After having engaged in combat a few days, these enemy divisions numbered much less than that, for they had no means of immediate troop replacements. Many Chinese divisions in the heat of combat numbered no more than 4,000 to 5,000 men.[21]

Readers will be better able to understand the Chinese military organization, and how it actually fought in Korea, if they realize that it was a triangular organization, much like that of the American division: the division had three regiments; each regiment had three battalions; each battalion had three rifle companies and a support weapons company with machine guns and mortars; each rifle company had three platoons and a mortar squad; and each platoon had three rifle squads of ten men each. If one wishes to know how many rifle squads at full strength there would be in a Chinese rifle division, a little arithmetic will give the number as 243 squads, consisting of 2,430 soldiers. In attack, the Chinese squad was often organized into two or more fire teams of three to five men each. At company level, the Chinese were supposed to have a mortar squad of two 60-mm mortars and a signal section of messengers. It might have one telephone. While the men in the rifle squads, who actually led the fight in the ground action, actually numbered far less than the division's 8,000 men, it must be recognized that in battle nearly all the soldiers of a Chinese division in Korea in 1950–51 would eventually be engaged in direct combat—a far higher proportion than in an American infantry division. As commonly expressed by the soldiers themselves, "the administrative tail of the Chinese division was far shorter than that of an American division." About half the men in the Chinese divisions fighting in Korea in 1950 and the first part of 1951 had been in Chiang Kai-shek's Nationalist army until it was defeated in 1949 in the Chinese civil war. In some cases entire Nationalist divisions were incorporated into the Chinese Communist Army thereafter. They were indoctrinated to the Communist cause, but their cadre was always Communist, and they were watched closely on the battlefield to ensure their loyalty. Even so, there were many desertions of former Nationalist soldiers to UN forces in Korea.

THE MYTH OF CHINESE "HUMAN SEA" TACTICS

Why do we have the myth of the Chinese "human sea" or "human wave" attack tactics against American troops in the Korean War? The metaphor was journalism's rhetorical attempt to convey to readers the concept that American soldiers were attacked and defeated by immense, overwhelming numbers of the enemy. The metaphor of a gigantic human sea or neverending waves rolling in and over everything offered an easy but misleading picture of Korean battle—a myth. It had no basis in fact. But the American press and the soldiers themselves were fond of the term and used it repeatedly in describing the odds UN forces faced in battle with the Chinese. It was also used frequently in Pentagon releases and in Army communiqués. One could compile hundreds or thousands of such references. The Headquarters, X Corps, Special Report on the Chosin Reservoir itself uses this language, saying that the CCF struck with its "human wave" tactic against the 1st Marine Division.[22]

What then was the method employed by a Chinese unit in a typical attack? In a strong and determined attack, the Chinese usually attacked initially in small groups, fire teams of four or five men, or in squad size, or sometimes platoon-sized skirmish parties. If the first squad perished, there was another behind it to take its place and continue the advance in the same track, and still another if needed. The Chinese hit the same spot of a defense line or a perimeter repeatedly until they had worn down the defenders of a small sector, who may have exhausted their ammunition or suffered continuing casualties in repelling repeated squad-sized skirmishers. Finally, a succeeding Chinese group would make a penetration at this point and quickly plunge ahead to the enemy rear or fan out to the flanks. Then larger numbers of waiting Chinese plunged through the small penetration. They seldom tried to annihilate an enemy group they had penetrated or overrun. Rather, their purpose was to create confusion and spread panic. When this happened, other Chinese forces that had passed around or infiltrated to the rear of the enemy position cut off the escape route or road running to rear communications and thereby created further casualties and more panic by ambushing those trying to withdraw.

In short, the Chinese tactic was to attack repeatedly on a narrow front in a deep column of platoons and, despite heavy early casualties, to continue doing so until a penetration had been effected. This tactic required that a Chinese company or battalion echelon itself in a column of squads and platoons to maintain the attack. In the meantime, an equally strong force tried to reach the enemy rear and cut off its line of communications and escape route and intercept reinforcements trying to reach the point of enemy frontal attack. These tactics won victory for the CCF in the Chinese civil war so recently ended. These tactics had also succeeded in the first CCF intervention in their Phase 1 battles in Korea in October 1950, when units of the CCF Fourth Field Army had destroyed two ROK divisions and one American regiment north of the Chongchon River in the Eighth Army sector. These same tactics worked well against Eighth Army in late November and early December in the west at the same time that Sung's divisions of the IX Army Group were preparing the trap at the Chosin Reservoir for the 1st Marine Division. The Chinese counterattack against Eighth Army sent it reeling back south of the Chongchon in near panic, with that army seeking only to leave the Chinese far in its rear. But the 1st Marine Division did not react that way. It could not have done so even had it wanted to. It did not have an open rear. Therein lay a difference.

CHINESE IX ARMY GROUP'S INITIAL SUCCESS

Sung's divisions had great initial success at Chosin Reservoir. They laid their trap well, concentrating their attack forces without discovery. In the first night and day of battle, they surrounded every one of the four perimeters in which the 1st Marine Division was concentrated but divided in order to protect vital, separated points on the MSR stretching south toward Hungnam. They also surrounded the fifth perimeter, in which three battalions of the 7th Infantry Division attempted to defend themselves. Furthermore, the Chinese had cut off each of the five perimeters from each other, occupying numerous roadblocks at many points for 40 miles on the only line of communications the Americans had to their rear. The Chinese plan had worked like clockwork that far, and success for them seemed possible if not probable. But the 1st Marine Division did not try to flee from its perimeters. It stayed in them and fought the first series of battles there. And the Chinese had made a fatal and far-reaching mistake in not attacking Hagaru-ri in overwhelming strength on the first night of their counterattack, 27–28 November.

THE CCF FATAL MISTAKE AT HAGARU-RI

On the very first night of the CCF counterattack, the Chinese made two mistakes that might be considered as having large consequences later in their ultimate failure. The X Corps opened its planned attack to the west on 27 November from Yudam-ni, with the object of cutting the Chinese main supply line on its main axis of attack against Eighth Army. Lt. Col. Raymond L. Murray's 5th Marine Regiment attacked west from Yudam-ni on the secondary dirt road that had to be its route of advance. The Chinese had the chance to let the regiment advance with little or no resistance until by dark it would have been separated from the 7th and 11th Marines at Yudam-ni by several miles. That night they might well have cut it off from help by the 7th Marines. But the Chinese were never known in the Korean War to adapt rapidly to a developing situation that they had not planned for. So, according to their prepared plan, they contested the advance of the 5th Marines during 27 November from prepared positions just west of Yudam-ni so effectively that the 5th Marines made virtually no gain during the day, and when night came they were on positions that became part of the Yudam-ni perimeter. Thus, at the outset, the Chinese lost the opportunity to separate the 5th Marines from the other Marine forces in the Yudam-ni area.

But the greater failure on the night of 27 November, when the CCF were everywhere in movement around the reservoir and were attacking in great strength at Yudam-ni and on the east side of the reservoir against elements of the 7th Infantry Division, was the failure to attack in overwhelming strength against the key position of Hagaru-ri at the southern end of the reservoir. An enemy attack did not materialize at Hagaru-ri until the second night and therefore did not have the element of surprise. Two Chinese divisions had the mission of attacking and capturing Hagaru-ri as a part of the great counterattack of the IX Army Group on the night of 27 November. The CCF 80th Division was to attack Hagaru-ri from the east side of the reservoir. But it ran into the three battalions of the 7th Infantry Division in two perimeters on the way down that side of the reservoir and attacked them that night. It did not get to Hagaru-ri. And a second enemy division, the 58th, circling southeast in an arc from Yudam-ni, was to attack Hagaru-ri from that direction the same night, that is, from the west or southwest.

Why this division did not attack on the night of 27 November is not clear. But it appears that the commander of the 58th Division must have thought that its reconnaissance was not complete or that the division was not in the most desirable position from which to launch its attack. It was a marked characteristic of Chinese operations that they did not like to attack until all preparations had been carefully made. It seems probable that the 58th Division was not quite ready to attack on the night of the twenty-seventh. When it did attack the next night, 28–29 November, it compounded its failure of the night before by attacking in only regimental strength with its 172nd Regiment, and when that attack failed before midnight, it launched a second attack after midnight with another regiment, the 173rd, which failed after some penetrations to break the defenses. The 58th Division attack against Hagaru-ri did not mass its strength for a decisive assault, which might have succeeded. It did not use the 174th Regiment at all that night but kept it in reserve.

Lt. Col. Thomas L. Ridge's astute gathering of intelligence about the 58th Division's location and attack plan was also a reason for the failure of the two regimental attacks against his 3rd Battalion, 1st Marine, infantry perimeter. A well-coordinated Chinese attack against Hagaru-ri by the two Chinese divisions on the night of 27 November should have succeeded, for it was defended at the time by only one infantry battalion, two batteries of artillery, and some miscellaneous service troops. Holding Hagaru-ri was the key to the 1st Marine Division's ability to escape the trap that enclosed it at the reservoir. The CCF command should have made certain that it fell at the outset of their attack, when it was weakest, even if it had cost them sacrificial losses.

MARINE TACTICS NULLIFY INITIAL CHINESE SUCCESS

Only after it had won the battle of the Yudam-ni perimeter did the 1st Marine Division begin its long attack to the rear—40 miles of it—from Yudam-ni through Hagaru-ri and Koto-ri to Chinhung-ni. And it won that week-and-a-half continuing battle, and salvation, by adhering to an indispensable basic tactic. All along the way it climbed the hills flanking the road and cleared the enemy there before allowing its trains to move ahead on the only road by which they could reach safety. And their rear guard meanwhile held off enemy pressing from the rear. This was indeed a retreat, but it was planned as an attack and executed as such. The Marines and attached Army troops had to fight and defeat the Chinese for every mile of the way, or they would never have reached the coast.

General Oliver Smith, commander of the 1st Marine Division, and his unit commanders must have been close students at some points in their careers of Xenophon's *Anabasis*, or *The March Up Country*, as it is variously known. The Marines' fighting retreat from the Chosin Reservoir through enemy-held territory is a textbook application of Xenophon's lessons. No better analysis and exposition of the tactics of retreat has ever been written than Xenophon's account of the escape of 10,000 Greeks in 401 B.C. from Asia Minor. Xenophon commanded the rear guard. The prime lesson, if there was a single most important one, was that enemy-held high ground along the route of march must be seized before a column attempts to pass below it. The Marines and the attached X Corps troops did this. It is a pity that the Eighth Army, fighting in the west at the same time, did not do it in the Kunu-ri area.

It is fair to quote his own view of the situation that confronted General Smith and his division in November 1950. He said:

> Only by reason of the precautions taken by the 1st Marine Division that the division was in a position to maintain its integrity when the Chinese struck in massive strength; was able to evacuate its casualties and those of the Army from the coast; had sufficient supplies to sustain combat until those could be supplemented by air drop; and was able to inflict ruinous losses on the 9th Chinese Army Group, thus ensuring minimum interference with the orderly evacuation of the X Corps from Hungnam.[23]

It must be added that General Almond, X Corps commander, had frequently fretted and had been irritated by what he considered Smith's excessive caution and slowness in implementing his orders, which in turn were based on General MacArthur's orders to him from the Far East Command, to advance rapidly to the Chosin plateau once the 1st Marine Division had been committed to reach that objective. But once the CCF counterattack developed there against the 1st Marine Division with a resulting crisis, no commander could have given more full-hearted support or showed more determination to use his own energies and capabilities to spring these troops from the CCF trap than did Almond. He drove his X Corps associates, staff officers, and support troops unmercifully to this end and in organizing the evacuation from Hungnam. Almond knew it had been a close call. In evaluating Almond's performance as commander of X Corps in northeast Korea in 1950, one must be aware of his own deep sense of loyalty to and belief in MacArthur. Sometimes he may have let this interfere with his own independent judgment of developing and threatening military events.

In a calm and objective appraisal, one may say the 1st Marine Division, from top to bottom, through regimental, battalion, company, and platoon level, showed professional skill and courage. The noncommissioned officers demonstrated high leadership courage in showing the way for rank-and-file, themselves highly dedicated professional, veteran troops. The rank-and-file showed sacrificial courage in following their small-unit commanders. When necessary, there was always someone to emerge from the ranks to grasp leadership and lead the way. Major General Smith's tribute to the 1st Marine Division at Chosin upon the conclusion of its march to the sea is a deserved one. He said at that time:

> The performance of officers and men in this operation was magnificent. Rarely have all hands in a division participated so intimately in the combat phases of an operation. Every Marine can be justly proud of his participation. In Korea, Tokyo, and Washington there is full appreciation of the remarkable feat of the division. With the knowledge of the determination, duty, and self-sacrifice displayed by officers and men of this division, my feeling is one of humble pride. No division commander has ever been privileged to command a finer body of men.[24]

THE CCF ACHIEVEMENT

Looking to the other side of the hill, as Wellington was wont to do, one cannot withhold some admiration, and humanitarian sympathy, for the Chinese peasants who made such great effort and sacrifice in trying to carry out their orders. One must say of them that Sung's IX Army Group did some spectacular things. It fought without air support, it had no tanks or artillery and almost no heavy mortars, it had poor and almost nonexistent ammunition after the first day or two of battle and no food or ammunition resupply once it crossed the Yalu River and headed south for its rendezvous with battle, and it possessed no adequate footgear for feet or mittens for hands of its soldiers in an arctic clime. Think of a soldier going through the entire Chosin Reservoir campaign with only 90–100 rounds of rifle ammunition and four or five grenades, unless he could manage to resupply himself on the battlefield. In his limited circumstances, he had to face neverending air strikes from the powerful supporting air arms of the X Corps and Fleet Marine and Far East Command (napalm, bomb, rockets, and strafing fire), concentrated tank fire from several of the perimeters it attacked, always a heavy and far-reaching artillery fire supported by the infantry's heavy mortars and its lighter mortars, the close supporting automatic fire of light and heavy machine guns, and the killing fire of BARs. Add to this the fact that the Americans usually had a reasonably good resupply of ammunition available by airdrop if necessary, a generally adequate supply of food, and excellent winter clothing.

In fact, the operations were a mismatch of a fine modern, mechanized body of soldiery against a peasant army of light infantry—but one that was highly mobile and expert at night fighting. The best weapons the Chinese possessed were the American Thompson submachine guns, 81-mm mortars, grenades, and rifles they had captured from Chiang Kaishek's armies during and at the conclusion of the Chinese civil war, a year earlier. Yet, they did drive the X Corps completely out of northeast Korea and occupied and held henceforth that part of the country. No American troops ever returned there.

COULD X CORPS HAVE EVACUATED OVERLAND?

One question remains for some discussion before passing on from the X Corps venture into northeast Korea in the fall and winter of 1950 to the main effort of Eighth Army in the west. Could X Corps have evacuated northeast Korea by an overland route?

The X Corps, at the time the evacuation was ordered, considered briefly the possibility of a land evacuation but decided almost at once that it could not have been done successfully. Only air and sea evacuation were considered practicable. As we have seen, the evacuation was almost entirely by sea. Had evacuation been attempted by land, it would probably have been south along the east coastal road. But by far the most pregnant undertaking would have been to cross the peninsula to arrive on the Eighth Army right, or east, flank in the central part of Korea, in the strategic Iron Triangle area, and to seize it before the main Chinese force got there. Remnants of defeated North Korean units, guerrillas, and some reconstituted North Korean units up to regimental size were in the immediate vital region at the time the X Corps began evacuating from Hungnam by sea in the middle of December 1950.

General Almond has tersely stated why any plan for movement overland from northeast Korea was discarded immediately after MacArthur ordered the evacuation on 8 December. It involved obstacles, he said, of "direction of march, adequacy of the road net for five divisions, resupply of the column, time available to complete the move, and the probable fighting effectiveness of the units at the end of the movement."[25] He said the direction was limited to the south because of enemy penetration of the Eighth Army front. The Eighth Army front had been penetrated, to be sure, and some Chinese had advanced in the west coastal area a considerable distance south of the Chongchon. He said the roadnet was inadequate for the movement of three US infantry divisions and their 12,000 vehicles and the ROK I Corps (two divisions) and their vehicles. He said much equipment would have had to be abandoned if the troops were motorized and rode the trucks. Supply depots and supply points could not have been moved. The base at Hungnam would have had to be abandoned, and there would be no land base available for resupply. The truck columns could not have carried enough supplies to see them through to their destination. The direction and force of the CCF advance during a X Corps land movement could not be predicted with accuracy. Having no base of supply would greatly reduce the combat effectiveness of the corps, at a time when it was vital to keep it at a maximum. And finally, Almond said, "By the time the 1st Marine Division had extricated itself from the Chosin Reservoir pocket, the routes to the south were blocked."[26] By 8 December Eighth Army was indeed in retreat already many miles south of Pyongyang.

Any movement overland from the X Corps position to join with the right flank of Eighth Army in west Korea would have had to follow the roadnet across the waist of Korea—from Wonsan on the east coast to Pyongyang near the west coast, or variants south of it to the Iron Triangle. But already the Chinese held Pyongyang, and North Korean troops were concentrating in the Iron Triangle and had a strong hold on it. The UN and the Joint Chiefs of Staff had suggested several times earlier to Mac-Arthur that he should establish a defense line at the waist of Korea. The British favored such a defense line and opposed proceeding farther north into North Korea. But accepting such a proposal would have meant that all of Korea could not be liberated and unified. MacArthur always opposed taking up such a defense line. The suggestion to do so was made again strongly after the Chinese counterattacks at the end of October and early in November 1950. Pressure to withdraw to such a line and hold there was strong, but only from the United Nations and Washington.

MacArthur on 3 December 1950 sent a message to the Joint Chiefs of Staff voicing his opposition to the proposal of a defense line across the waist of Korea. His message was long and argued with his usual fluency and conviction. Only parts of it can be quoted here, but they will be sufficient to give the direction of his thinking on this subject. His and Almond's views were almost identical. In his 3 December message to the Joint Chiefs of Staff, MacArthur said in part:

> There is no practicability, nor could any benefit accrue thereby, to attempt to unite the forces of the Eighth Army and the X Corps. Those forces are completely outnumbered and their junction would, therefore, not only not produce added strength but would jeopardize the free flow of movement that arises from the two separate logistical lines of naval supply and maneuver.
>   . . . a defense line across the waist of Korea is not feasible because of the numerical weakness of our forces as considered in connection with the distances involved; by the necessity of supplying the two parts of the line from ports within each area; and by the division of the area into two compartments by the rugged mountainous terrain running north and south. Such a line is one of approximately 150 miles. If the entire United States force of seven divisions at my disposal were placed along this defensive line, it would mean that a division would be forced to protect a front of approximately 20 miles against greatly superior numbers of an enemy whose greatest strength is a potential for night infiltration through rugged terrain. Such a line no doubt would have

little strength, and as a defensive concept would invite penetration with resultant envelopment and piecemeal destruction. Such a concept against the relatively weaker North Korean forces would have been practical, but against the full force of the Chinese Army is impossible.[27]

X Corps knew very little about the roadnet from Wonsan to Pyongyang and the other two routes through the Iron Triangle area to Sibyon-ni, aside from some aerial observation of the roads. No one actually drove over these roads south of Pyongyang to Wonsan over their full length to learn their condition on the ground.

There had been limited reconnaissance of these roads from Wonsan during the very early period when Lt. Col. William J. McCaffrey, deputy chief of staff, X Corps, was already in the Wonsan area, and the Navy was conducting minesweeping activities in the harbor. It was not until 27 October that the X Corps began an administrative landing at Wonsan.

While McCaffrey was in command of the X Corps Advance CP, he drove part of the Wonsan-Pyongyang road and flew in a Navy reconnaissance plane over the rest of it. There were no enemy troops in the cross-peninsular corridor then — only some ROK troops. Along the road in the latter half of October, McCaffrey noticed there were many small defensive positions prepared along most of its course through the hills. He thought their locations at the eastern end of the road had been built to repel an amphibious landing at Wonsan. Many of the positions consisted of 15–20 foxholes staggered along the road. Later, guerrilla parties or small groups of North Koreans would occupy one or another of these positions in staging ambushes of single vehicles or small parties, which occurred at the eastern end of the road. McCaffrey thought the road was so poor that an American infantry division could not get through on it in winter if it had any heavy fighting in the course of the effort. He thought the distance too great, the logistics too difficult, the troops insufficiently trained, and the necessary confidence between troops and commanders was lacking at that time to undertake such a precarious effort.[28]

When the 187th Airborne Regiment dropped on 20 October about 30 miles north of Pyongyang, in an effort to cut off troops trying to escape north after the American and ROK capture of that city, Lt. Col. Olinto Barsanti with a party of three jeeps drove across the peninsula from Wonsan on the road all the way to contact with the 187th Airborne Regiment near Sukchon, according to McCaffrey.[29] There is no other known American crossing from Wonsan to the Pyongyang area by vehicles and no known American crossing from the Wonsan area to the Iron Triangle area and to Sibyon-ni in vehicles by road. It is clear that American officers and troops knew little about these roads and had not even tried to reconnoiter them for possible troop movements. They were terra incognita to American ground forces.

It must be concluded that, by 8 December, if for no reason other than that Eighth Army by that time had withdrawn far below the waist of Korea (that is, the Wonsan-Pyongynag line), there was no possibility of the X Corps, or of any part of it, making a successful crossing overland from the Hungnam-Wonsan area to establish contact with the east, or right, flank of Eighth Army. What could have been done a month or two earlier had now become an impossibility. Also, by this time reorganized North Korean units and guerrillas had occupied the Iron Triangle area in considerable strength. All subsequent efforts to drive them out failed disastrously.

By the time the X Corps was ready to begin evacuation, a date that must be set as 11 December, Eighth Army had retreated so rapidly from the Chongchon River battle area in the west that it was taking positions on the line of the Imjin River only 20 miles north of Seoul. On a parallel line, this was a distance of 125 air miles south of Hungnam, which would have to be considered the departure point from the east coast for an overland movement. There were two possible routes southwest toward Eighth Army from there: west from Wonsan to the headwaters of the Imjin River and then southwest along it in very mountainous gorge country to Ichon and Sibyon-ni, where it might hope to contact the right flank of Eighth Army in that vicinity; or south from Wonsan on the road to Pyonggang (at the apex of the Iron Triangle in the interior of Korea, not to be confused with Pyongyang, the capital of North Korea), which paralleled a narrow-gauge railroad line. Pyonggang was a key road junction town at the north end of the Iron Triangle, and from it roads ran on either side of a relatively open triangular-shaped bowl to Kumhwa on the east and Chorwon on the west. From Chorwon, the ancient invasion route ran south to Seoul and South Korea. Another road from Chorwon ran west to Sibyon-ni, a major roadnet center of very considerable military importance. The UN forces in fact should have made every effort to seize the Chorwon–Sibyon-ni–Kumhwa–Pyonggang area in early or mid-December 1950, after the CCF successes farther north, and to hold it. But was it possible?

Eighth Army, in whose sector the Iron Triangle lay, made only feeble attempts to occupy it in December during its withdrawal from the Chongchon River front, chiefly with ROK troops. The enemy forces there at the time were fragments of previously defeated North Korean units in South Korea, guerrillas, and some reconstituted North Korean units. There were no Chinese troops there. A determined Far East Command might have considered having the US Navy, with the help of ground troops, hold a base at Wonsan for a short time, if not permanently, and then sending at least part of X Corps — perhaps two infantry divisions — overland from there along the narrow-gauge railroad and road to Pyonggang and the Iron Triangle. It should have been possible for two divisions to reach that objective at that time — a distance of about 50 air miles but somewhat farther by road. The direction from Wonsan was a little west of south. Once in command of the Iron Triangle, these troops could have established contact with the right flank of Eighth Army. The Iron Triangle was well connected to Seoul by a railroad and a good road and could have been supplied from there. Supply by air was also feasible from the south. Supply and communications from Wonsan might not have been feasible after a month or two. But determined command leadership and good soldier morale were necessary to accomplish the task. There is evidence, however, that neither was present.

The seizure of the Iron Triangle area and its merger into the UN line across Korea in December 1950 would have gained control of the heart of the Korean central communications system north of the 38th Parallel and have made very difficult the ensuing series of CCF attacks against Eighth Army in the west, and especially those against the X Corps, which, after it moved up into the UN line following its evacuation from northeast Korea, went into the mountainous central part of Korea. Although, during the next spring and summer of 1951, the Eighth Army made strong efforts to win control of the Iron Triangle area, it never succeeded in winning and holding it. The UN forces might have won it in early December 1950, with enormous effect favorable to the UN command in the future course of the war.

The UN command in Korea and Tokyo should have made strong, even desperate, efforts in December 1950 to establish its defensive line along the Wonsan–Pyonggang–Ichon–Sibyon-ni lower Imjin River line. But it did not. Evidently, it never even considered it. At the time, from the middle of December on for the next month, the prevailing opinion in Eighth Army, in the Far East Command in Tokyo — and even at the Pentagon in Washington — seemed to be that it would be necessary to evacuate Korea. If this was indeed the case, then obviously no one was going to try to establish a Wonsan–Pyonggang–Imjin River line on which to hold and defeat the CCF.

In reflecting on this matter, one should remember that, when General MacArthur decided to send the X Corps to the east coast of Korea after the capture of Seoul, he intended that it would attack west from Wonsan across the waist of Korea to Pyongyang to aid the Eighth Army in capturing that capital city. All that happened later in changing the mission of X Corps derived from the fact that, by the time the X Corps arrived at Wonsan by sea movement, the ROK I Corps had marched up the east coastal road and captured the Wonsan area and the Eighth Army had captured Pyongyang without the need for help. The rapid, long withdrawal of Eighth Army in December after the Chinese counterattack struck it along the Chongchon River dictated just about everything that the higher command decided on in the further use and deployment of the X Corps after it withdrew from the Chosin Reservoir to the southern end of the peninsula.

Notes

Special abbreviations used throughout the notes include: CG = Commanding General; Comd. Rpt. = Command Report; DIS = Daily Intelligence Summary; PIR = Periodic Intelligence Report (G-2 Daily Intelligence Report); POR = Periodic Operations Report (G-3 Daily Operations Report); SAR = Special Action Report; and WD = War Diary

CHAPTER 1

1. Roy E. Appleman, *South to the Naktong, North to the Yalu* (Washington, D.C.: GPO, 1961), pp. 684–86.

2. Ibid., pp. 684–85.

3. Ibid., pp. 686–87; X Corps, WD, Diary of CG, 30 Oct. 50; *Pertinent Papers on the Korean Situation*, 8 vols., II, 318–19, Msg C7881, 31 Oct 50. *U.S. News and World Report*, 13 Feb 1953, carried an article based on an interview with Lt. Gen. Almond about his interview of the 16 Chinese prisoners, but many of the dates given are erroneous.

4. Appleman, *South to the Naktong*, pp. 741–44; Lynn Montross and Capt. Nicholas A. Canzona, USMC, *The Chosin Reservoir Campaign*, vol. 3 in *U.S. Marine Operations in Korea, 1950–1953*, Historical Branch, G-3, HQ, US Marine Corps (Washington, D.C.: GPO, 1957), pp. 101–24. This is an excellent and detailed study of the 1st Marine Div. and attached troops in the Chosin Reservoir campaign in November and December 1950. Capt. Canzona was a combat engineer officer and served in the Hagaru-ri perimeter defense as a platoon leader. He was personally familiar with the terrain and the conditions prevailing in that frozen and forbidding land. The authors used official Marine records of the combat units involved. They conducted many interviews with officers and men engaged in the various episodes and aspects of the campaign and used many affidavits of experiences prepared by participants. It is an indispensable source for any study of the Chosin Reservoir campaign, and I have relied on it heavily, as citations will show. This work's greatest limitation is that it does not give adequate coverage to the Army troops involved with the Marines in the operations, particularly the elements of the 7th Inf. Div. on the east side of the reservoir. The Marine volume needs to be heavily supplemented in this respect.

5. Office of Research Operations (ORO)-R-1, FEC, 8 Apr 51, "Employment of Armor in Korea," I, 64.

6. Appleman, *South to the Naktong*, pp. 732–37. See map 25, opposite p. 731, for lines of X Corps advance, 25 Oct to 26 Nov 50.

7. My analysis is based on diverse maps of Korea, Manchuria, and other parts of China, with special reference to railroad and highway bridges across the Yalu and rail routes through northern China and Manchuria, in addition to intelligence from Chinese documents and prisoner-of-war interrogations about Chinese troop movements from China and Manchuria into Korea.

CHAPTER 2

1. The comments on the CCF forces and their commanders in the IX Army Group are based largely on the FEC DIS No. 3233, 17 July 51, Box 491. (All official US records of the Korean War are in Record Group 407 in the National Archives, Federal Records Center, Suitland, Maryland. To avoid repetition, all such records will be identified only by box number.) HQ, FEC, *Intelligence Digest*, no. 6 (2 Sept 51): map A-3, p. A-10; FEC, *Order of Battle Information, CCF Third Field Army*, 1 Mar 51, pp. 26–27, Box 413; FEC DIS No. 3082, 16 Feb 51, Box 401; Montross and Canzona, *The Chosin Campaign*, pp. 397–98. The route of the 42nd Army when it moved from the Chosin Reservoir area southwest to the Chinese XIII Army Group front in the Tokchon area in front of the right flank of Eighth Army is not known with certainty. By 29 November Eighth Army and the Far East Command believed that all three divisions of the 42nd Army were in front of the right flank of Eighth Army in the vicinity of Tokchon. See FEC DIS No. 3007, 2/3 Dec 50; Map of Korea, scale 1:250,000, AMS L552, 1950.

2. Korea Road Map, scale 1:1,000,000 (Japan), AMS 3, 1951, sheet 4, and AMS 5, 1961, sheet 4. The 1961 edition of this map is much clearer in delineation of railroads, roads, and topographic features than are the earlier editions.

3. FEC, "Histories of CCF Army Groups Active in Korea, Part II, Ninth Army Group," *Intelligence Digest* 1, no. 3 (16–31 Jan 1953): 32–37, Box 225; Andrew Geer, *The New Breed: The Story of the U.S. Marines in Korea* (New York: Harper and Brothers, 1954), pp. 223–24.

4. When the 26th Army moved south to join the Chosin battles, it apparently moved from Linchiang to Kanggye. There it turned east along the narrow-gauge railroad that crossed the mountains to the Changjin River, which it reached about 30 air miles north of the Chosin Reservoir. From there it proceeded up the river to the reservoir and along its west side to Yudam-ni.

5. X Corps, WD, 24–26 Nov 50, POR Nos. 59–61. X Corps POR No. 59, 24 Nov 50, gave the Marines' strength as 25,323.

6. For a detailed examination of this subject, see Appleman, *South to the Naktong*, pp. 745–48.

7. X Corps, WD, 25 Nov 50, app. I, Intelligence Estimate to Annex A to Operational Order No. 7, 24 Nov 50; *Employment of Armor in Korea—The First Year* (Fort Knox, Ky., 1952), I, 6ff.

8. Map of Korea, scale 1:1,000,000, AMS, ed. 5, sheet 4, Series L302, 1961.

9. The early maps of the Chosin Reservoir area used by the X Corps troops were hastily printed from old Japanese maps whose data had been collected in about 1916. Accordingly, the terrain data were generally reliable, but the human features, such as villages, often had changed in the years between 1916 and 1950. Where there had been villages and place-names for them in 1916, the reproduced maps for use by the American troops still had the place-names, but some of the villages had all but disappeared, and some new ones not shown on the 1916 maps (e.g., Changjin, Sinhung-ni, and Hudong-ni) had taken their places. Also, the narrow-gauge railroad had been built only a few miles up the east side of the reservoir in 1916 but by 1950 had almost reached the Fusen Reservoir. Later, the Army Map Service editions of these maps made corrections and brought them up to date, dropping many village names and other place-names that appeared on the early maps, entering new names not on the first maps—thus leading to endless confusion in identifying place-names. Often map searchers could not find them at all, causing errors in reporting geographic location among students and writers who did not have copies of the early maps and who relied wholly on later editions of maps of Korea. Names on these later maps did not always correspond with the names in the military records of the units whose reports recorded events and actions of late 1950 and were based on the place-names and related data in the older, earlier maps actually used by the troops at the time. I have found it essential to use the early maps for geographic data to know what the military records of the period are talking about. Information from later maps has also been used where it seemed helpful.

10. X Corps, Special Report on Chosin Reservoir Campaign, X Corps, WD, 25 Nov, Summary; Montross and Canzona, *The Chosin Campaign*, pp. 95–98; Geer, *The New Breed*, pp. 260–61; Map of Korea, scale 1:250,000, AMS 1, 1950, Series L 552. The name "Hagaru-ri" does not appear on this map but is carried as "Changjin." There are discrepancies in map nomenclature on maps of Korea, depending on their date. The first maps used by the UN forces carried three names for each place: Japanese, local Korean, and national Korean. Changes such as "Hagaru-ri" are used only when the troops themselves used the names and the official records of the campaign used that terminology. The terminology used in this manuscript is contemporary to that used by the troops themselves.

11. HQ, X Corps, Special Report on Chosin Reservoir, 27 Nov–10 Dec 1950, X Corps, Plans and Orders 9–10; X Corps, WD, 25 Nov 50, Annex A to POR No. 60, Operational Order No. 7.

12. X Corps, WD, Nov 1950, pp. 19–21.

13. Quoted from 1st Marine Civil History Diary, Nov 1950, in X Corps, WD, Monthly Summary, 1–30 Nov 50, p. 10.

14. X Corps, WD, Nov 1950, pp. 19–21.

15. X Corps, "Enemy Tactics and Equipment," Intelligence Bulletin No. 1, in Gen. Matthew B. Ridgway Papers, Box 17 (US Army Military History Research Collections, Army War College, Carlisle Barracks, Pa.); 1st Marine Div., SAR, 8 Oct–15 Dec 50, vol. 1, Annex Baker, p. 16; Robert B. Riggs,

Red China's Fighting Hordes (Harrisburg, Pa.: Military Service Publishing Co., 1951), p. 63.

16. X Corps, WD, 26 Nov 50, PIR No. 61, p. 2.

17. HQ, X Corps, Special Report on Chosin Reservoir, 27 Nov–10 Dec 50, pp. 6–7.

18. FEAF Operations History, vol. 2, 1 Nov 50–28 Feb 51, p. 82; X Corps, WD, 26 Nov 50, POR No. 61, p. 1; Montross and Canzona, *The Chosin Campaign*, p. 151.

19. X Corps, WD, 26 Nov 50, PIR No. 61, p. 4; 1st Marine Div., SAR, 8 Oct–15 Dec 50, vol. 2, Annex Charlie, pp. 55–57, 26 Nov 50.

20. X Corps, WD, 26 Nov, PIR No. 61, p. 3; HQ, X Corps, Special Report on Chosin Reservoir, 27 Nov–10 Dec 50, p. 35; Montross and Canzona, *The Chosin Campaign*, p. 149.

21. X Corps, WD, Diary of CG, and POR No. 61, p. 1, 26 Nov 50; Lt. Gen Edward M. Almond, Ret., letter to author, 29 Oct 1975; Lt. Gen. William J. McCaffrey, Ret., letter to author, 5 Dec 1975; Lt. Col. E. L. Rowney, in *The Military Engineer* 43, no. 295 (Sept–Oct 1951): 315ff. Rowney, in commenting on the Hagaru-ri airfield, said it was "standard practice in X Corps to build C-47 aircraft fields at division command posts." The one at Hagaru-ri was begun long before it became evident that it would be vital to the withdrawal of the troops at Chosin Reservoir.

22. X Corps, Diary of CG, 26 Nov 50.

23. X Corps, WD, PIR No. 61, p. 1, 26 Nov 50; Montross and Canzona, *The Chosin Campaign*, p. 151.

CHAPTER 3

1. The sketch of General Almond's military career is based on a number of sources, including *Hearings before the Subcommittee to Investigate the Administration of the Internal Security Act and Other Security Laws of the Committee on the Judiciary, United States Senate, 83rd Congress, 2nd Session, on Interlocking Subversion in Government Departments*, testimony of Lt. Gen. Edward M. Almond, Ret., 23 Nov 1954, part 25, pp. 2048–53; War Department Summary on Almond, brought up to date as of 23 Jan 1947, 3 pp. mimeographed; Biographical Data, Edward Mallory Almond, 2 pp. mimeographed, 15 Oct 1973 (apparently by Gen. Almond); William C. Barnard, "10th Corps's Almond Is No GI's General," *Washington Post*, 24 June 1951; Gen. Almond, interview with author, 28–29 Apr 1977; Almond, review comments on "Escaping the Trap" MS, 27 Sept 1978.

The question of how long Almond held the post of chief of staff, Far East Command, while at the same time serving as commanding general of X Corps in the Korean War is a matter of interpretation. In the biographical statement of 15 Oct 1973, cited above, Gen. Almond says of himself: "Chief of Staff, GHQ, Far East Command and Supreme Commander, Allied Powers-Japan, February 1949–April 1951; also Chief of Staff, GHQ United Nations Command, July 1950 to Sept. 1950." Apparently he believed he ceased to be chief of staff, GHQ, United States Command, on 11 Sept. 1950, when he became commander of X Corps, but actually he continued to hold the post of chief of staff, FEC, and supreme commander, Allied Powers-Japan, until he was relieved on 15 April and then rotated back to the United States in July 1951. Maj. Gen. Doyle O. Hickey told me in interviews in his office in the Dai-Ichi Building, Tokyo, 14 July and 10 Oct 1951, that he was never the chief of staff, only the acting chief of staff, and did all of the chief of staff's work under MacArthur, and that he became chief of staff when Gen. Ridgway appointed him to that post after Ridgway succeeded MacArthur as commander of FEC in April 1951. Gen. Ridgway confirmed this sequence in an interview with me in his Dai-Ichi Building office in Tokyo, 9 Oct 1951, in response to my direct question on the subject. Ridgway said that one of his first official actions when he succeeded MacArthur in command at Tokyo was to appoint Gen. Hickey chief of staff—that up to that time Hickey had been only acting chief of staff. Almond never took an action as chief of staff after 11 Sept 1950, when he took command of X Corps.

After completing a term as commandant of the Army War College, Gen. Almond retired from the Army on 31 Jan 1953, after 37 years of active service. He then returned to civilian life in Anniston, Alabama. Gen. and Mrs. Almond (the former Margaret Crook, of Anniston, Alabama), had a daughter and a son, Capt. Edward M. Almond, Jr. An infantry company commander, he was killed in action in Europe during World War II. Gen. Almond died in Brooke Army Medical Center, Fort Sam Houston, San Antonio, Texas, aged 86, on 11 June 1979, and was buried in Arlington National Cemetery.

2. Appleman, *South to the Naktong*, pp. 515–41; Lt. Gen. William J. McCaffrey, Ret., letter to author, 10 Sept 1978.

3. Appleman, *South to the Naktong*, p. 764; Lt. Gen. McCaffrey, letters to author, 11 Dec 1976 and 30 Mar 1978. Both Gen. Ruffner and Lt. Col. McCaffrey were present at this conference and heard Willoughby's remarks.

4. Lt. Gen. Oliver P. Smith, Ret., review comments on "South to the Naktong" MS, transmitted in a letter to Maj. Gen. Richard W. Stephens, chief of military history, dated 15 Nov 1957, copy in author's possession (hereafter cited as Smith, Comments).

5. Montross and Canzona, *The Chosin Campaign*, p. 159.

6. Smith, Comments; Col. S. L. A. Marshall, interview with Col. Alpha L. Bowser, Jr., G-3, 1st Marine Div., 2 Jan 1951, copy in author's possession; Montross and Canzona, *The Chosin Campaign*, p. 151.

7. 1st Marine Div., SAR, 8 Oct–31 Dec 50, vol. 2, Annex Charlie, p. 57, 27 Nov 50; X Corps, WD, 27 Nov 50, POR No. 62, p. 1, 27 Nov 50, PIR No. 62, p. 4.

8. Montross and Canzona, *The Chosin Campaign*, map 12, pp. 153, 260–61; Lynn Montross, "Breakout from the Reservoir," *Marine Corps Gazette*, Nov 1951, pp. 24–25.

9. Geer, *The New Breed*, pp. 267–68; Lynn Montross, "March of the Iron Cavalry—Marine Tanks in Korea," *Marine Corps Gazette*, Oct 1952, pp. 47ff.

10. Gen. Edward M. Almond, Diary, 27 Nov 50, copy in author's posses-

sion (hereafter cited as Almond, Diary); X Corps, WD, 27 Nov 50; Geer, *The New Breed*, p. 368.

11. Montross and Canzona, *The Chosin Campaign*, pp. 154–57; Geer, *The New Breed*, pp. 262–66.

12. X Corps, WD, 27–28 Nov 50, PIR No. 62, p. 2, and Summary of Operations, p. 3; 1st Marine Div., SAR, 8 Oct–15 Dec 50, vol. 1, Annex Baker, pp. 29, 31–32.

CHAPTER 4

1. The description of the Marine positions at Yudam-ni on the evening of 27 Nov is based principally on Montross and Canzona, *The Chosin Campaign*, pp. 152–60 and maps 12 and 13; Geer, *The New Breed*, pp. 262–70; 1st Marine Div., SAR, 8 Oct–15 Dec 50, vol. 2, Annex Charlie, 27 Nov 50, also was used. Throughout this chapter I have relied heavily on Montross and Canzona's *The Chosin Campaign*, easily the best printed source on the subject. I have examined, however, most of the official Marine Corps records and sometimes cite them directly.

2. Montross and Canzona, *The Chosin Campaign*, pp. 167–68; Geer, *The New Breed*, pp. 277–79.

3. Montross and Canzona, *The Chosin Campaign*, pp. 168–69, 172–75.

4. Ibid., pp. 182–86.

5. Ibid., pp. 186–87; Geer, *The New Breed*, pp. 286–88.

6. Montross and Canzona, *The Chosin Campaign*, pp. 162–64 and maps 12 and 14.

7. Ibid., pp. 165–66, 187–88; Geer, *The New Breed*, p. 271.

8. Geer, *The New Breed*, p. 276.

9. 1st Marine Div., SAR, 8 Oct–15 Dec 50, vol. 2, Annex Charlie, p. 61, 28 Nov 50; Montross and Canzona, *The Chosin Campaign*, pp. 170–71 and map 15.

10. X Corps, WD, 28 Nov 50, Summary of Operations, p. 1; Montross and Canzona, *The Chosin Campaign*, pp. 187–89.

11. McCaffrey, review comments on "Escaping the Trap" MS, undated letter received 19 May 1979.

12. HQ, X Corps, Special Report on Chosin Reservoir, 27 Nov–10 Dec 50, p. 70; 1st Marine Div., SAR, 8 Oct–15 Dec 50, vol. 2, Annex Charlie, p. 59, 28 Nov 50; X Corps, WD, 28 Nov 50, PIR No. 63, p. 3.

13. Montross and Canzona, *The Chosin Campaign*, pp. 178–79, 189–90, and map 12.

14. Robert F. Futrell, *The United States Air Force in Korea, 1950–1953* (New York: Duell, Sloan and Pearce, 1961), p. 239.

15. Geer, *The New Breed*, pp. 265, 293; Montross, "Breakout from the Reservoir," p. 27.

16. Montross and Canzona, *The Chosin Campaign*, app. E, 1st Marine Division Casualties, p. 382.

17. 1st Marine Div., SAR, 8 Oct–15 Dec 50, vol. 1, Annex Baker, p. 19.

CHAPTER 5

1. This chapter is based on my book *East of Chosin: Entrapment and Breakout in Korea, 1950* (College Station: Texas A&M University Press, 1987), a detailed study of the 31st RCT on the east side of Chosin Reservoir. Appleman, *East of Chosin*, pp. 1–19.

2. Ibid., pp. 28–30; Maj. Wesley J. Curtis, "Operation of the First Battalion, 32nd Infantry Regiment, 7th Infantry Division, in the Chosin Reservoir Area of Korea during the Period 24 November–2 December 1950: Personal Experience of the Battalion Operations Officer," 23 pp. (typescript MS, with map sketches), copy of first draft provided to author by Col. Curtis, USA, Ret. (hereafter cited as Curtis, MS).

3. Appleman, *East of Chosin*, p. 36; Col. Carl Witte, letters to author, 16 Nov 1978 and 26 May 1980; Lt. Gen. William J. McCaffrey, USA, Ret., review comments on "East of Chosin" MS, 27 Feb 1981.

4. Appleman, *East of Chosin*, pp. 40–43; letters to author from: Maj. James R. McClymont, 11 May 1980; Col. Ray O. Embree, USA, Ret., 18 Mar 1979; Lt. Col. Earle H. Jordan, USA, Ret., 5 Jan 1979; Col. Robert E. Drake, USA, Ret., 17 Nov 1977; and Brig. Gen. William R. Lynch, Jr., USA, Ret., 19 Dec 1976 and 21 Jan 1977.

5. Lt. Col. Crosby P. Miller, "Chosin Reservoir, Nov–Dec 1950," 25 pp. (typescript MS, October 1953, with marked map of east side of Chosin Reservoir; hereafter cited as Miller, MS); Appleman, *East of Chosin*, pp. 47–48.

6. Capt. Edward P. Stamford, USMC, "Statement on Action East of Chosin" (typescript MS, undated, but prepared in Jan and early Feb 1951; hereafter cited as Stamford, MS); Appleman, *East of Chosin*, pp. 60–65.

7. Lt. Col. Erwin Bigger, USA, Ret., letter to author, 6 July 1980, and telephone conversation with author, 8 May 1980; Appleman, *East of Chosin*, pp. 70–71.

8. Capt. Hugh R. May, "Chosin Reservoir," Report, 28 Oct 1957; 1st Sgt. Richard B. Luna, B Co., 32nd Inf., Statement (undated, but made apparently on 2 or 3 Dec 1950 at Hagaru-ri); Appleman, *East of Chosin*, pp. 74–77.

9. Capt. Robert J. Kitz, CO K Co., 3rd Bn., 31st Inf., Affidavit, presumably given on 3 Dec 1950, the day after his escape to Hagaru-ri, attached to 7th Div. Chosin Reservoir Comd. Rpt., Box 3172; Appleman, *East of Chosin*, pp. 79–80.

10. 1st Lt. Thomas J. Patton, A Bty., 57th FA Bn., Personal Statement (undated, but apparently prepared in April or May 1951), copy in author's possession; Appleman, *East of Chosin*, pp. 81–82.

11. Mrs. Celeste B. Reilly, undated letter to author received 22 Feb 1977, and newspaper clipping, undated, Barre, Vt., carrying news story datelined 21 Dec 50, copy of letter signed "Bill, Jr." (Lt. Col. William R. Reilly), addressed to "Dearest Mother and Dad," 17 Dec 1950, from Osaka Army Hospital, Japan, in which he describes the nature of the wounds he received at his CP on 28 Nov 50; Appleman, *East of Chosin*, pp. 83–84.

12. Jordan, letters to author, 5 Feb 1979 and 28 Feb 1980; Appleman, *East of Chosin*, pp. 84–85.

13. Lynch, letter to author, 19 Dec 1976; Appleman, *East of Chosin*, p. 87.

14. Maj. James R. McClymont, letter to author, 11 May 1980, p. 4 (hereafter cited as McClymont, Letter); Appleman, *East of Chosin*, pp. 89–92.

15. McClymont, Letter; Appleman, *East of Chosin*, pp. 93–98.

16. Lt. Col. James O. Mortrude, "Autobiographical Chronology of Chosin Reservoir Operation" (typescript MS), pp. 3–4 (hereafter cited as Mortrude, MS), with letter to author, 23 Oct 1980; Appleman, *East of Chosin*, pp. 104–106.

17. Col. Robert E. Drake, USA, Ret., letters to author, 28 June 1978, 19 Jan 1977, 17 Feb 1977, and 1 Feb 1977; Brig. Gen. William R. Lynch, Jr., USA, Ret., interview with author, 12 June 1978; Appleman, *East of Chosin*, pp. 112–15.

18. McClymont, letter of responses to author, 7 July 1980; Appleman, *East of Chosin*, pp. 121–22.

19. Sfc. John C. Sweatman, K Co., 31st Inf., Statement, 19 Apr 51.

20. Appleman, *East of Chosin*, p. 126; Miller, MS, pp. 7–8; Col. James G. Campbell, letter to author, 9 Apr 1981; Appleman, *East of Chosin*, pp. 129–30.

21. Curtis, letter to author, 1 Jan 1977; Campbell, review comments on "East of Chosin" MS, 9 Apr 1981; See Appleman, *East of Chosin*, pp. 138–44, for details of the 1st Bn. withdrawal to the 3rd Bn. position.

22. Bigger, narrative statement to author, 6 July 1980; Appleman, *East of Chosin*, p. 146.

23. Bigger, letter to author, 11 May 1981, with sketch map of route of Col. MacLean's crossing of the inlet; Appleman, *East of Chosin*, p. 146.

24. See Appleman, *East of Chosin*, pp. 146–48, for more details of this incident and MacLean's status in the War Department records during the years following his disappearance.

25. Maj. James R. McClymont, letter to author, 7 July 1980; Col. Robert E. Drake, letter to author, 10 Jan 1977; Stamford, interviews with author; Appleman, *East of Chosin*, p. 154.

26. Almond, Diary, 29 Nov 1950; Lt. Gen. McCaffrey, USA, Ret., interviews and correspondence with author, 24 Apr 1977 and 1976–1980. See Appleman, *East of Chosin*, pp. 168–71, for more detail on this sudden turnaround in MacArthur's plan.

27. McClymont, letter to author, 7 July 1980; Mortrude, MS; Stamford, Narrative of Action of Cpl. Myron J. Smith on 30 Nov and 1 Dec 50; Capt. Hugh R. May, Report, Chosin Reservoir, 28 Oct 1957 (hereafter cited as May, Report), and letter to author, 14 Mar 1982; Appleman, *East of Chosin*, pp. 177–78.

28. Almond, Diary, 30 Nov 50; Appleman, *East of Chosin*, pp. 180–82.

29. Appleman, *East of Chosin*, p. 182.

30. Lt. Gen. McCaffrey, USA, Ret., interview with author, 4 Feb 1976; Appleman, *East of Chosin*, pp. 183–87.

31. Col. Alpha L. Bowser, G-3, 1st Marine Div., Statement to S. L. A. Marshall, 2 Jan 1951, in interview with Marshall (transcript of interview in author's possession); Appleman, *East of Chosin*, p. 186.

32. Drake, memo to CO, 31st Inf., 12 Dec 1950; Appleman, *East of Chosin*, p. 187.

33. Lynch, interview with author, 12 June 1978; Appleman, *East of Chosin*, p. 187.

34. Drake, letter to author, 8 May 1978; Appleman, *East of Chosin*, p. 187.

35. Curtis, MS, pp. 16–17; Appleman, *East of Chosin*, pp. 191–93.

36. Campbell, letter to author, 13 Dec 1980; Curtis, MS, p. 17; Russell A. Gugeler, *Combat Actions in Korea: Infantry, Artillery, and Armor* (Washington, D.C.: Association of the US Army, Combat Forces Press, 1954), pp. 75–76; Bigger, letter to author, 6 July 1980; Appleman, *East of Chosin*, pp. 192–93.

37. Curtis, MS, pp. 17–18; Appleman, *East of Chosin*, p. 194.

38. Stamford, interview with author, 28–29 Oct 1980; Appleman, *East of Chosin*, p. 194.

39. Author's correspondence with Curtis, Miller, Jones, and McClymont and interviews with Curtis and Stamford; see MSS of Curtis, Miller, and Stamford, and May, Report; Appleman, *East of Chosin*, pp. 196–98.

40. Stamford, memo prepared for author at his request, 3 Oct 1979, describing the air strike, and interview with author, 3 Oct 1979; Appleman, *East of Chosin*, pp. 206–11.

41. Miller, MS, pp. 15–16; Curtis, MS, p. 20; Appleman, *East of Chosin*, pp. 219–20.

42. Kitz's statement, written at Hagaru-ri, ca. 3 Dec 1950; Appleman, *East of Chosin*, p. 222.

43. May, undated letter to author, received 22 Aug 1981; Appleman, *East of Chosin*, pp. 227–31.

44. Jones, report to 7th Div., 4 Dec 1950, p. 2; Appleman, *East of Chosin*, p. 228.

45. Stamford, MS, p. 11; Appleman, *East of Chosin*, p. 230.

46. Miller, MS, p. 17; Appleman, *East of Chosin*, pp. 230–31.

47. Stamford, interview with author, 28–29 Oct 1979; Miller, MS, p. 18; Appleman, *East of Chosin*, p. 231.

48. Pfc. James R. Owens, L Co., 31st Inf., Statement, 19 Apr 51; Appleman, *East of Chosin*, p. 236.

49. Lt. Col. Ivan H. Long, letters to author, 21 Mar and 10 July 1979; Appleman, *East of Chosin*, pp. 236–37.

50. Miller, MS, pp. 17–18; Appleman, *East of Chosin*, p. 238.

51. Jordan, letter to author, 5 Jan 1979; Appleman, *East of Chosin*, pp. 253–55.

52. Jones, Report to 7th Div., 4 Dec 50, p. 3; Jones, letter to author, 5 Jan 1970; Stamford, MS, pp. 13–14; Stamford, interview with author, 26 Sept–3 Oct 1979; May undated letter to author, received 22 Aug 1981, p. 6; Appleman, *East of Chosin*, pp. 254–64.

53. May, Report, pp. 9–12; Appleman, *East of Chosin*, pp. 261–63.

54. Stamford, MS, pp. 14–15; Stamford, interview with author, 26 Sept–3 Oct 1979; Appleman, *East of Chosin*, p. 264.

55. Stamford, MS, pp. 14–15; Stamford, interview with author, 26 Sept–3 Oct 1979.

56. Curtis, interview with author, 6 June 1981; Appleman, *East of Chosin*, pp. 266–67.

57. Miller, MS, pp. 19–22; Appleman, *East of Chosin*, pp. 269–70.

58. Campbell, letter to author, 13 Dec 1980; Appleman, *East of Chosin*, pp. 271–72.

59. Ridgway Papers, Box 17, Folder D-L, copy of WO (jg) Edwin S. Anderson's Memorandum on Status of Lt. Col. Don C. Faith, Jr., 9 Jan 51, to Gen. Barr. Gen. Barr provided this copy to Gen. Ridgway because Faith had been Ridgway's aide in the 82nd Abn. Div. and the XVIII Abn. Corps in Europe in World War II, and he knew that Ridgway would want to know its contents. Maj. Edwin S. Anderson, USA, Ret., telephone conversation with author, 3 Nov 1980; Anderson, undated letter to author, postmarked 31 Oct 1980; Appleman, *East of Chosin*, pp. 275–77.

60. See Appleman, *East of Chosin*, p. 277, for more on Lt. Col. Don C. Faith, Jr.

61. 1st Motor Trans. Bn., 1st Marine Div., 14 Jan 1951, Annex Item, to 1st Marine Div., SAR, 8 Oct–15 Dec 1950, p. 10; Lt. Col. Olin L. Beall, USMC, HQ 1st Motor Trans. Bn., 1st Marine Div., Statement (undated, but apparently written in 1951). Copies of both documents in author's possession, courtesy USMC, History Div. See Appleman, *East of Chosin*, pp. 287–92, for more details on this rescue mission.

CHAPTER 6

1. Lt. Gen. Edward M. Almond, USA, Ret., interviews and correspondence with author, 1978–79; Lt. Gen. William J. McCaffrey, USA, Ret., review comments on "Escaping the Trap" MS, 19 May 1979.

2. Montross and Canzona, *The Chosin Campaign*, pp. 197ff.

3. Ibid., and sketch map 17, showing the Hagaru-ri defense perimeter as of 28–29 November. This map has D Co., 10th Eng. Comb. Bn., 3rd Div., wrongly located. It should be placed just east of the Weapons Co. roadblock on the spur ridge coming down from the northeast to the roadblock area. The X Corps Signal Bn. detachment also is located erroneously on this map.

4. Col. Thomas L. Ridge, USMC, Ret., letter to author, 27 Mar 1977.

5. X Corps, WD, 28 Nov 50, PIR No. 63; Geer, *The New Breed*, p. 310; 1st Marine Div., SAR, 8 Oct–15 Dec 50, vol. 2, Annex Charlie, pp. 57–60, 28 Nov 50.

6. Col. Thomas L. Ridge, USMC, Ret., letter to author, 27 Mar 1977; Montross and Canzona, *The Chosin Campaign*, pp. 203–204; Geer, *The New Breed*, pp. 311–12.

7. Montross and Canzona, *The Chosin Campaign*, pp. 206–207 and map 17, Hagaru-ri Defensive Perimeter; Lt. Norman R. Rosen, CO 3rd Plat., 10th Eng. Comb. Bn., 3rd Div., "Combat Comes Suddenly," in Capt. John G. Westover, *Combat Support in Korea* (Washington, D.C.: Association of the Army, Combat Forces Press, 1955), pp. 206–10.

8. Montross and Canzona, *The Chosin Campaign*, pp. 209–11; Geer, *The New Breed*, pp. 313–14; 1st Marine Div., SAR, 8 Oct–15 Dec 50, vol. 2, Annex Charlie, p. 60; Marshall, interview with Col. Bowser and Lt. Col. Winecoff,

1st Marine Div., G-3 Sec., 2 Jan 1951; 1st Marine Div., SAR, G-3 Sec. 2 Jan. 51, p. 6.

9. Montross and Canzona, *The Chosin Campaign*, p. 216; X Corps, WD, 29 Nov 50, PIR No. 64, pp. 3–4.

10. Marshall, interview with Lt. Col. J. L. Winecoff, 1st Marine Div., G-3 Sec., 2 Jan 1951, p. 6, copy in author's possession; Montross and Canzona, *The Chosin Campaign*, pp. 217, 220; 1st Marine Div., SAR, 8 Oct–15 Dec 50, vol. 2, Annex Charlie, p. 60; Geer, *The New Breed*, p. 314.

11. Lt. Gen. William J. McCaffrey, USA, Ret., letter to author, 11 Mar 1978. McCaffrey said the Advance CP location was about 700 yards south of Hagaru-ri. That would place it south of H Co.'s perimeter. Also, this position conforms to the general location given by Lt. Norman R. Rosen, CO, 3rd Plat., D Co., 10 Eng. Comb. Bn., 3rd Div., who was with the Eng. Co. sent to build the Advance CP.

12. Rosen, "Combat Comes Suddenly," in Westover, *Combat Support in Korea*, pp. 206–10.

13. Ibid., pp. 206–208, and sketch map of D Co.'s position, p. 209. This sketch and Rosen's narrative make it clear that Montross and Canzona, *The Chosin Campaign*, Map 17, p. 199, erroneously places a Signal Bn., X Corps detachment, at the lower part of the spur, below D Co., Engineers. The 4th Signal Bn. platoon was not even on the line above D Co., Engineers, according to Rosen's reconnaissance which placed a platoon of South Korean labor troops there. Map 17 of the Hagaru-ri Defense Perimeter for the night of 28–29 Nov in Montross and Canzona, *The Chosin Campaign*, must therefore be considered faulty for this part of the perimeter.

14. Montross and Canzona, *The Chosin Campaign*, pp. 213–14, for the G-3 message. The time given for the opening of the Chinese attack on East Hill, if it referred to the spur-ridge position leading down to the Weapons Co. roadblock, was in error by about 3 or 4 hours, according to Rosen, who was there. It may have been a radio message received from Podolak some hours after the event occurred. The author's account of the action on the spur ridge is based on Rosen, "Combat Comes Suddenly," in Westover, *Combat Support in Korea*, pp. 208–10.

15. Rosen, "Combat Comes Suddenly," p. 210.

16. Lt. Gen. William J. McCaffrey, USA, Ret., letter to author, 30 Mar and 5 May 1978.

17. Rosen, "Combat Comes Suddenly," p. 209; Montross and Canzona, *The Chosin Campaign*, pp. 218–19; Geer, *The New Breed*, pp. 315–16.

18. James A. Field, Jr., *History of United States Naval Operations, Korea* (Washington, D.C.: GPO, 1962), p. 276.

19. Geer, *The New Breed*, pp. 315–16.

20. *Medal of Honor Recipients, 1863–1963*, 88th Cong., 2nd sess., Committee on Labor and Public Welfare (Washington, D.C.: GPO, 1964), pp. 279–80, citation for Maj. Reginald R. Myers, exec. off., 3rd Bn., 1st Marine Div., 29 Nov 50, Hagaru-ri.

21. Montross and Canzona, *The Chosin Campaign*, pp. 217–19, and map 18, East Hill Attacks, 29 Nov 50, p. 212. This map fails to show D Co., 10th

Eng. Bn., positions on the spur ridge above the Weapons Co. roadblock, through which Maj. Myers led his counterattack. For a sketch of D Co.'s position see Rosen, "Combat Comes Suddenly," p. 209.

CHAPTER 7

1. Montross and Canzona, *The Chosin Campaign*, p. 192, testimony of Lt. Comdr. Chester M. Lessenden, regimental surgeon, 5th Marines.

2. Ibid., pp. 200, 205; Brig. Gen. William R. Lynch, USA, Ret., interview with author, 29 June 1978. Lynch was in Smith's CP house once and was stationed near it in the period 28 Nov–4 Dec 50.

3. Montross and Canzona, *The Chosin Campaign*, p. 194; X Corps, WD, 30 Nov 50, PIR No. 65, pp. 3–4, delayed report for 29 Nov; 1st Marine Div., SAR, 8 Oct–15 Dec 50, vol. 2, Annex Charlie, p. 65, 29 Nov 50.

4. The account of the fight at Sachang-ni on the night of 28–29 Nov 50 is based largely on my 1951 interview with Capt. Robert F. Peterson, CO C Co., 7th Inf., 3rd Div., who was in the action. X Corps WD for Nov 1950, p. 38, has a brief reference to the event and records the fight as taking place on 28–29 Nov; Capt. Peterson gave the date as the night of 27–28 and day of 28 Nov. I have not been able to verify the date conclusively from the 3rd Div. records I have seen.

5. X Corps, WD, 29 Nov 50, POR No. 64, p. 2; ibid., 29 Nov 50, Surgeon's Narr.; 1st Marine Div., SAR, 8 Oct–15 Dec 50, vol. 2, Annex Charlie, pp. 65–66, 29 Nov 50.

6. Futrell, *US Air Force in Korea*, pp. 153, 238–39; McCaffrey, undated letter to author, received 19 May 1979, and review comments on "Escaping the Trap" MS.

7. 1st Marine Div., SAR, 8 Oct–15 Dec 50, vol. 2, Annex Charlie, p. 65, 29 Nov 50.

8. Ibid., pp. 65–66, 29 Nov 50.

CHAPTER 8

1. Montross and Canzona, *The Chosin Campaign*, pp. 222–25, and map 19, showing the Koto-ri perimeter; Montross, "Breakout from the Reservoir," pp. 28–30; X Corps, WD, 29 Nov 50, PIR No. 64, pp. 3–4.

2. Eric Linklater, *Our Men in Korea* (London: Her Majesty's Stationery Office, 1952), pp. 36–39; Geer, *The New Breed*, pp. 316ff.; Montross and Canzona, *The Chosin Campaign*, p. 225.

3. Lt. Alfred J. Catania, "Truck Platoon in Korea," in Capt. John G. Westover, *Combat Support in Korea* (Washington, D.C.: Association of the Army, Combat Forces Press, 1955), pp. 49–57.

4. These figures are based on Montross and Canzona, *The Chosin Campaign*, p. 228 (table). This work has the most detailed analysis available, based on official documents and numerous interviews with participants, of the task force and its composition and its actions on 29 November. Some of the gen-

eralized data are uncertain and controversial in the chaotic events that unfolded, as the authors admit.

5. Montross and Canzona, *The Chosin Campaign*, pp. 227–28; Geer, *The New Breed*, pp. 317–18.

6. Montross and Canzona, *The Chosin Campaign*, p. 228; Geer, *The New Breed*, p. 318; 1st Marine Div., SAR, 8 Oct–15 Dec 50, vol. 1, Annex Baker, p. 25.

7. Geer, *The New Breed*, p. 318; Catania, "Truck Platoon in Korea," p. 54. In *The Chosin Campaign*, Montross and Canzona do not include this aspect of the renewed drive northward at 2 P.M.

8. Geer, *The New Breed*, pp. 318–19; Montross and Canzona, *The Chosin Campaign*, pp. 228–29; Catania, "Truck Platoon in Korea," p. 54. Montross and Canzona give the time as about 1:50; Catania says it was 4 P.M. before he was ordered to load B Co. the first time, when it was immediately behind the tanks. It would have to have been later when the column resumed advance. The two platoons of 12 tanks of B Co., 1st Tank Bn., did not arrive at Koto-ri until 3 P.M., and it was some time later when they and 15 trucks started north to join Task Force Drysdale, which they were never able to do. This period of time between noon and 4–5 P.M. cannot be sorted out as to events and times. Montross and Canzona had the most evidence available when they wrote, but they admit it was so confusing and contradictory that it was impossible to reconstruct the scene with certainty.

9. Montross and Canzona, *The Chosin Campaign*, pp. 228–29; Geer, *The New Breed*, pp. 318–19; 1st Marine Div., SAR, 8 Oct–15 Dec 50, vol. 2, Annex Charlie, pp. 63–64, 29 Nov 50; Brig. Gen. C. N. Barclay, *The First Commonwealth Division: The Story of British Commonwealth Land Forces in Korea, 1950–1953* (Aldershot: Gale and Polden, 1954), pp. 37–38; Linklater, *Our Men in Korea*, p. 37.

10. Montross and Canzona, *The Chosin Campaign*, p. 229 and n. 8; Geer, *The New Breed*, p. 319.

11. *Medal of Honor Recipients, 1863–1963*, pp. 231–32.

12. Catania, "Truck Platoon in Korea," p. 54; Geer, *The New Breed*, p. 319; Montross and Canzona, *The Chosin Campaign*, p. 230.

13. Montross and Canzona, *The Chosin Campaign*, pp. 229–35; Geer, *The New Breed*, pp. 319–20; 1st Marine Div., SAR, 8 Oct–15 Dec 50, vol. 2, Annex Charlie, pp. 63–64, 29 Nov 50; Barclay, *First Commonwealth Division*, pp. 37–38; Linklater, *Our Men in Korea*, p. 37; Catania, "Truck Platoon in Korea," pp. 54–55.

14. Col. Thomas L. Ridge, USMC, Ret., letter to author, 27 Mar 1977; Futrell, *US Air Force in Korea*, pp. 299–303, discusses the development of night intruder forces and their use in the Korean War.

15. Catania, "Truck Platoon in Korea," pp. 55–56.

16. Montross and Canzona, *The Chosin Campaign*, pp. 229–33; and maps 20 and 21; Geer, *The New Breed*, pp. 220–22; X Corps, WD, 30 Nov 50, PIR No. 65, pp. 3–4.

17. Montross and Canzona, *The Chosin Campaign*, pp. 232–33; Geer, *The New Breed*, pp. 322–25; 1st Marine Div., SAR, 8 Oct–15 Dec 50, vol. 2, An-

nex Charlie, p. 68, 30 Nov 50. Geer has considerable detail on the surrender negotiations, based on interviews with participants.

18. Catania, "Truck Platoon in Korea," pp. 56–57.

19. Perhaps the most careful tabulation of Task Force Drysdale's casualties is found in a table in Montross and Canzona, *The Chosin Campaign,* p. 234. It is called an estimate, for an accurate breakdown could not be made.

20. Montross and Canzona, *The Chosin Campaign,* p. 235, quoting Gen. Smith.

21. 1st Marine Div., SAR, 8 Oct–15 Dec 50, vol. 2, Annex Charlie, p. 68, 30 Nov 50.

22. Montross and Canzona, *The Chosin Campaign,* pp. 225–26.

CHAPTER 9

1. Montross and Canzona, *The Chosin Campaign,* pp. 236–38, and map 22; Field, *US Naval Operations in Korean War,* pp. 277–78.

2. Col. Robert E. Drake, USA, Ret., letters to author, 10 Jan 1977 and 8 May 1978.

3. Montross and Canzona, *The Chosin Campaign,* p. 240; Geer, *The New Breed,* pp. 325–26. Geer's statistics and data are often exaggerated and unreliable, compiled before all reports had been assembled. But he often presents dramatic and colorful incidents of action, obtained from interviews with participants and not described elsewhere.

4. Col. Drake, letters to author, 10 Jan 1977 and 8 May 1978. *The Chosin Campaign,* the official history of Marine operations in the Chosin Reservoir campaign, does not mention the presence of Drake's tanks on the perimeter defense line and the important combat role they played in this night battle. See pp. 240–43 for the Marine account of the East Hill battle. See also Geer, *The New Breed,* pp. 325–26.

5. *Medal of Honor Recipients, 1863–1963,* pp. 294–95, citation for Capt. Carl L. Sitter, USMC, G Co., 3rd Bn., 1st Marine Regt., 1st Marine Div., Hagaru-ri, 29–30 Nov 50.

6. Montross and Canzona, *The Chosin Campaign,* pp. 240–43; 1st Marine Div., SAR, 8 Oct–15 Dec 50, vol. 1, Annex Baker, p. 42; Geer, *The New Breed,* pp. 325–26; Barclay, *First Commonwealth Division,* pp. 37–38; X Corps, WD, 30 Nov 50, PIR No. 65, pp. 3–4; Drake, letters to author, 10 Jan 1977 and 8 May 1978, with sketch map. Barclay gives the 41st Commando, Royal Marines, casualties during the Chosin Reservoir campaign as 13 killed, 66 wounded, and 20 nonbattle casualties from frostbite and exposure.

7. Col. Thomas L. Ridge, USMC, Ret., letter to author, 27 Mar 1977.

8. Geer, *The New Breed,* p. 342; Montross and Canzona, *The Chosin Campaign,* pp. 245–47; Maj. Gen. Clark L. Ruffner, interview with author, 27 Aug 1951.

9. Montross and Canzona, *The Chosin Campaign,* p. 279. The X Corps figure for casualties evacuated from the Chosin Reservoir area by air differs slightly from the Marine figure given here.

10. Ibid., pp. 246–47.

11. Ibid., pp. 282–83; Montross, "Breakout from the Reservoir," p. 33.

CHAPTER 10

1. Montross and Canzona, *The Chosin Campaign*, pp. 249–51; 1st Marine Div., SAR, 8 Oct–15 Dec 50, vol. 2, Annex Charlie, pp. 69–70, 30 Nov 50; X Corps, WD, 30 Nov 50, G-4 Sec. Narrative, and X Corps, POR No. 65, p. 2, 30 Nov 50.

2. Montross and Canzona, *The Chosin Campaign*, pp. 254–55; Geer, *The New Breed*, p. 334.

3. Montross and Canzona, *The Chosin Campaign*, pp. 253–55; Field, *US Naval Operations in Korean War*, p. 300. On 1 Dec, three Marine fighter squadrons at Wonsan moved to Yonpo to be nearer the scene of combat.

4. Almond, Diary, 30 Nov 50; X Corps, WD, 30 Nov 50, POR No. 65, p. 2; X Corps, WD, Monthly Summary, 1–30 Nov 50, pp. 55–56; Col. Alpha L. Bowser, Jr., G-3, 1st Marine Div., interview with Col. S. L. A. Marshall, 2 Jan 51.

5. Montross and Canzona, *The Chosin Campaign*, pp. 255–59, and maps 23 and 24, p. 256; 1st Marine Div., SAR, 8 Oct–15 Dec 50, vol. 1, Annex Baker, pp. 25–26.

6. Montross and Canzona, *The Chosin Campaign*, pp. 258–59, and map 24, p. 256; Geer, *The New Breed*, p. 346.

7. *Medal of Honor Recipients, 1863–1963*, pp. 259–60, gives the citation for Sgt. James E. Johnson, 3rd Bn., 7th Marines, 1st Marine Div. Geer, *The New Breed*, mentions Johnson's role in the action during the night of 30 Nov–1 Dec 1950 at Yudam-ni.

8. Ibid., pp. 304–305, gives the citation for S. Sgt. William G. Windrich, I Co., 3rd Bn., 5th Marines, 1st Marine Div., 1 Dec 1950, near Yudam-ni. Geer, *The New Breed*, pp. 336–37, gives tribute to Windrich and others in this fierce night battle with the Chinese.

9. Montross and Canzona, *The Chosin Campaign*, pp. 262–63.

10. Ibid., pp. 265–66.

11. Ibid., pp. 266–67.

12. Ibid., p. 268, and map 25, p. 269.

13. Information about the positions of F Co. and the form of the perimeter is based on ibid., p. 180, and map 25, p. 269.

14. *Medal of Honor Recipients, 1863–1963*, pp. 236–37. Cafferata retired from the USMC as a private first class.

15. Montross and Canzona, *The Chosin Campaign*, pp. 180–82; Geer, *The New Breed*, pp. 296–99.

16. Montross and Canzona, *The Chosin Campaign*, p. 191; Geer, *The New Breed*, pp. 301–302; Montross, "Breakout from the Reservoir," pp. 28–30.

17. Geer, *The New Breed*, pp. 296, 303–304.

18. Ibid., pp. 305–306; 1st Marine Div., SAR, 8 Oct–15 Dec 50, vol. 2, Annex Charlie, p. 69, 30 Nov 50.

19. Montross and Canzona, *The Chosin Campaign*, pp. 263–65; Geer, *The New Breed*, pp. 327–32, 307.

20. Montross and Canzona, *The Chosin Campaign*, pp. 269–71; Geer, *The New Breed*, pp. 339–40.

21. *Washington Post*, 20 Aug 1952, has an article on awarding the Medal of Honor, with a photograph of Barber and his family. His citation is given in *Medal of Honor Recipients, 1863–1963*, pp. 230–31.

22. *Washington Post*, 25 Nov 1952, has an article on presentation of the Medal of Honor to Davis, together with a picture of President Truman with Davis and his wife and three children. Davis's citation is given in *Medal of Honor Recipients, 1863–1963*, pp. 243–44.

23. Drake, letters to author, 10 Apr and 8 May 1978, with map Drake used at the time, on which he had marked the farthest point of the Drysdale-Drake advance and the location of enemy positions on Toktong Mountain, north of the road, and one position south of the road. There were no Marine tanks in this sortie. Theirs were the M-46 tanks, which were wider than the Army tanks. They had no difficulty operating on the narrow Korean mountain roads.

24. Montross and Canzona, *The Chosin Campaign*, pp. 272–73; Geer, *The New Breed*, pp. 340–41.

25. Montross and Canzona, *The Chosin Campaign*, pp. 274–75.

26. The experience of Cpl. Michael Houston on 4 Dec is based on a full-page newspaper account written by him and published in the *Richmond* (Virginia) *Times Dispatch* Sunday magazine section, 4 Feb 1951.

27. Montross and Canzona, *The Chosin Campaign*, p. 275. Geer (*The New Breed*, p. 341), says that, from the beginning of the CCF attack on 27 Nov 50 to 3 Dec 50, when Litzenberg and Murray gained the Hagaru-ri perimeter, the Marines had 2,260 battle casualties: 358 KIA, 153 MIA, and 1,749 WIA. In addition, there were 1,072 nonbattle casualties.

28. Montross and Canzona, *The Chosin Campaign*, pp. 271–72.

29. Field, *US Naval Operations in Korean War*, pp. 278–79.

30. Ibid., pp. 279–80.

31. *Medal of Honor Recipients, 1863–1963*. Hudner's citation is on pp. 257–58. According to Geer, the text of the Medal of Honor citation is erroneous in giving the impression that Brown's plane crashed in mountainous terrain and that enemy surrounded it (*The New Breed*, p. 346).

32. Field, *US Naval Operations in Korean War*, pp. 300–301.

33. Montross, "Breakout from the Reservoir," p. 35.

34. Montross and Canzona, *The Chosin Campaign*, pp. 281, 283.

CHAPTER 11

1. 1st Marine Div., Special Action Report, 8 Oct–15 Dec 50, vol. 1, Annex Baker, pp. 13–14; Montross and Canzona, *The Chosin Campaign*, pp. 283–88; Geer, *The New Breed*, pp. 347–49; X Corps, WD, 5 Dec 50; 3rd Inf. Div. Comd. Rpt., 5 Dec 50.

2. Maj. Robert E. Jones, "Hagaru-ri to Hamhung, Period of 6 December–

13 December 1950," HQ, RCT 32, 29 Dec 1950 (hereafter cited as Jones, Statement); Col. Carl G. Witte, letter to author, 5 Nov 1978, with attached statement.

3. Jones, Statement; Witte, letter to author, 5 Nov 1978; Col. George A. Rasula, letter to author, 12 Aug 1981, with copy of his letter to Col. Lester K. Olsen, S-3, 31st Inf. (wounded at Inchon, Sept 1950), 4 Feb 1951 (hereafter cited as Rasula, Letters). Capt. Rasula's letter to Olsen gives a four-and-half-page, single-spaced narrative of the Army breakout action with the 7th Marine Regt. from Hagaru-ri to Funchilin Pass as he knew and experienced it.

4. HQ, X Corps, Special Report on Chosin Reservoir, 27 Nov–10 Dec 50, p. 52.

5. Field, *US Naval Operations in Korean War*, pp. 280–81; Montross and Canzona, *The Chosin Campaign*, pp. 348–50; CG X Corps, Diary, 4–6 Dec 50.

6. Montross and Canzona, *The Chosin Campaign*, p. 313, app. G., pp. 392–98; FEC DIS No. 3233, 17 July 1951, Box 491. This is a monograph of the CCF Third Field Army.

7. Montross and Canzona, *The Chosin Campaign*, pp. 285–87; Geer, *The New Breed*, pp. 348–50; X Corps, Special Report on Chosin Campaign; CG X Corps, Diary, 4–6 Dec 50.

8. Montross and Canzona, *The Chosin Campaign*, p. 294; Geer, *The New Breed*, p. 350, erroneously states that all the CCF here were killed.

9. Rasula, Letters.

10. Jones, Statement; GHQ, FEC, General Order No. 118, 12 May 1951, awarding the Distinguished Service Cross to 2nd Lt. James C. Barnes, Jr. (artillery), Hagaru-ri to Koto-ri, 7 Dec 50. The action on which this award was based apparently took place on the evening of 6 Dec 50.

11. Col. Carl G. Witte, letters to author, 5 Nov 1978 and 24 Jan 1980, together with enclosure of copy of his letter to Eric M. Hammel, 23 Feb 1980.

12. Rasula, Letters; Jones, Statement.

13. Montross and Canzona, *The Chosin Campaign*, pp. 293–98; Geer, *The New Breed*, pp. 351–52; 1st Marine Div., SAR, 8 Oct–15 Dec 50, vol. 1, Annex Baker, pp. 13–14; Rasula, Letters; Jones, Statement; Maj. Robert E. Jones, Amy 32nd Inf. Bn., said the road column reached Koto-ri at 5:45 A.M., 7 Dec 50.

14. Montross and Canzona, *The Chosin Campaign*, p. 297; Geer, *The New Breed*, p. 353.

15. Montross and Canzona, *The Chosin Campaign*, p. 298; Geer, *The New Breed*, p. 353.

16. Montross and Canzona, *The Chosin Campaign*, pp. 298–99.

17. Ibid., pp. 299–300.

18. *New York Times*, 7 Dec 1950, p. 1, col. 6, dispatch from Yonpo airfield, Korea, 6 Dec 50.

19. Montross and Canzona, *The Chosin Campaign*, pp. 289–90; Geer, without having all the facts available to Montross and Canzona, gives a different figure for the Chinese prisoners (*The New Breed*, p. 355).

20. Montross and Canzona, *The Chosin Campaign*, pp. 290–91, and map 26, p. 289.

21. Geer, *The New Breed*, p. 356.

22. Montross and Canzona, *The Chosin Campaign*, pp. 291–93, and map 27, p. 292; Geer, *The New Breed*, pp. 357–58.

23. Field, *US Naval Operations in Korean War*, pp. 283–84.

24. Jones, Statement.

25. Col. Robert E. Drake, USA, Ret., letter to author, 8 May 1978. In an earlier letter to the author, 10 Jan 1977, Col. Drake had commented in a similar vein on the departure of his 31st Tank Co. from its rear-guard station just south of Hagaru-ri on the night of 7 Dec 1950.

26. Montross and Canzona, *The Chosin Campaign*, pp. 300–303; Geer, *The New Breed*, pp. 358–59; 1st Marine Div., SAR, 8 Oct–15 Dec 50, vol. 1, Annex Baker, pp. 13–14.

CHAPTER 12

1. Maj. Gen. Robert Soule, interview with author, 8 Sept 1951; Lt. Gen. William J. McCaffrey, USA, Ret., correspondence with author, 1976–82.

2. Lt. Gen. Edward M. Almond, USA, Ret., "Reflections on the Hungnam Evacuation, Korea, December 1950," 1 Aug 1973, mimeographed copy in author's possession; Almond letter to author, 15 Nov 1976.

3. 1st Lt. Martin Blumenson, "Task Force Kingston, 22–29 Nov 1950," mimeographed MS in files, USA Military History Center, DA; X Corps, WD, 30 Nov 50, PIR No. 65.

4. 7th Inf. Div., WD, 30 Nov 50, POR; 7th Div., Comd. Rpt., Dec 1950, supplementary documents, Box 3176; Maj. Stanley Turk, CO 7th Div. Arty., Dec 1950, in Debriefing Report No. 81, Artillery School, 14 Mar 52; *Infantry School Quarterly*, October 1951, p. 62; Maj. Gen. David G. Barr, testimony in MacArthur hearings, 22 June 51, pp. 2950–55. (There are many errors of detail in Barr's testimony.)

5. Lt. Col. James H. Dill, USAR, Ret., letter to author, 27 Feb 1985, together with copy of his MS, "The Yalu." This 25-page MS is based on contemporary notes Dill made for the unit journal (a diary of sorts) and his recollections and includes a marked map of the area.

6. Dill, "The Yalu," p. 11.

7. Ibid., p. 12.

8. Ibid., p. 13.

9. Ibid., p. 15.

10. Ibid., p. 21.

11. Maj. Jacob W. Kurtz, Graves Registration officer, 7th Inf. Div., "Pukchon Cemetery," in Capt. John G. Westover, *Combat Support in Korea*, pp. 180–82.

12. Almond, Diary, 7 Dec 50, pp. 112–13.

13. Ibid., 7–8 Dec 50; Almond, "Reflections on the Hungnam Evacuation"; Field, *US Naval Operations in Korean War*, pp. 285–86.

14. 3rd Inf. Div., Comd. Rpt., Nov 1950, Sec. 3, Narrative of Operations; Appleman, *South to the Naktong*, pp. 684, 724–48.

15. X Corps, WD, 29 Nov 50, PIR No. 64, p. 4; Capt. Paul J. Kay, Bty. exec.

off., A Bty., 10th FA Bn., Debriefing Report No. 65, Artillery School, 23 Jan 1952, "3rd Inf. Div. in Korea, 15 Nov–30 Nov 51," p. 2; HQ, X Corps, Special Report on Chosin Reservoir Campaign, p. 38.

16. 3rd Inf. Div., Comd. Rpt., Dec 1950, General Order No. 100, HQ, 3rd Inf. Div., 12 Dec 50, Box 2881.

17. Almond, Diary, 2–5 Dec 50; Montross and Canzona, *The Chosin Campaign*, pp. 308–309; 3rd Inf. Div., Comd. Rpt., Dec 1950.

18. Lt. Gen. William J. McCaffrey, USA, Ret., deputy chief of staff for X Corps at the time and well informed on nearly everything concerning the corps, has stressed to me, in conversations in 1976 and 1978 and in a letter to me, 11 Dec 1976, the role of Forney and his views on the deployment of the 1st Marine Div. in the Chosin campaign.

19. Field, *US Naval Operations in Korean War*, pp. 286–87.

20. Maj. Gen. Robert H. Soule, interview with author, 8 Sept 1951.

21. Lt. Gen. William J. McCaffrey, USA, Ret., letter to author, 5 Dec 1975, and interview with author, 4 Feb 1976.

22. Lt. Gen. Edward M. Almond, conversations with author in 1951, 1952, and 1977. Also, see HQ, X Corps, Army Tactical Air Support Requirements, Inf. Bn. TACT, p. 68.

23. X Corps, Comd. Rpt., 5 Dec 50; 3rd Inf. Div., Comd. Rpt., Dec 1950, pp. 8–9, Box 2881; Almond, Diary, 5 Dec 50; and X Corps Special Report on Chosin Reservoir Campaign, Catalogue of Plans and Orders, Operation Instruction 26, 5 Dec 1950.

24. 3rd Inf. Div., Comd. Rpt., 6–7 Dec 50; Lt. Col. Alvin L. Newberry, exec. off., Task Force Dog, "Springing the Chosin Reservoir Trap" 9 pp. (undated typescript MS written in early 1951), copy in author's possession, pp. 3–4. A copy of the 3rd Div. Comd. Rpt. for Dec 1950 is in the Military History Research Center, Carlisle Barracks, Pa., Box 4, as well as in the National Archives (Box 2881).

25. Almond, Diary, 6 Dec 50. This account of the conversation with Collins was a handwritten addition by Almond to his typed diary and was dated 9 Nov 1954.

26. HQ, X Corps, Special Report on Chosin Reservoir Campaign, 27 Nov–10 Dec 50. Information in the narrative is scattered through this 113-page report, with its numerous maps and tables, much of it in the engineer and transportation sections, pp. 51–52, 59, 86.

CHAPTER 13

1. FEC DIS, 16 Feb 51, Box 401; FEC, "Chinese Communist 3rd Field Army," 1 Mar 51, Box 413; ATIS Interrogation Reports (Enemy Forces), Issue 22, No. 2728, p. 73, 18 Dec 50; ibid., No. 2730, 18 Dec 50, and Issue 24, No. 2831, p. 97, 10 Jan 51; 1st Marine Div., SAR, 8 Oct–15 Dec 50, vol. 1, Annex Baker, p. 23; Montross and Canzona, *The Chosin Campaign*, app. G, Enemy Order of Battle, pp. 897–98.

2. ATIS Interrogation Reports (Enemy Forces), Issue 24, No. 2831, Capt. Sun Chen Kian.

3. Montross and Canzona, *The Chosin Campaign*, p. 307, gives the figure as 4,200 men in the Koto-ri garrison and 10,029 from Hagaru-ri, for a total of 14,229 men at Koto-ri on the morning of 8 Dec 50.

4. HQ, X Corps, Comd. Rpt.; "Special Rpt. on Chosin Reservoir, 27 Nov–10 Dec 50," extracts from CG Diary, 4–5 Dec 50. This diary must not be confused with references to Gen. Almond's personal diary. Most of the material is the same, but Almond's personal diary includes some handwritten comments that are not found in the CG Diary, part of the X Corps Comd. Rpt. I have used both.

5. Geer, *The New Breed*, pp. 364–65; Montross and Canzona, *The Chosin Campaign*, pp. 314–15; 73rd Comb. Eng. Bn., Comd. Rpt., Dec 1950.

6. FEC DIS No. 3053, 18 Jan 51, Box 387; ibid., No. 3082, 16 Feb 51, C/M 1, Box 401; FEC Order of Battle Information, CCF Third Field Army, March 1951, pp. 26–27, Box 413. Montross and Canzona, *The Chosin Campaign*, p. 313.

7. Geer, *The New Breed*, pp. 365–66; Montross and Canzona, *The Chosin Campaign*, pp. 315–16. Geer has many details based on interviews with participants soon after the fight.

8. 1st Lt. William J. Davis, "Lessons Learned Up North," *Marine Corps Gazette*, Apr 1952, pp. 48–49.

9. Rasula, Letters; Jones, Statement.

10. Montross and Canzona, *The Chosin Campaign*, pp. 319 and n. 24; Geer, *The New Breed*, p. 364.

11. The narrative on the Treadway bridge is based on a number of sources. The most important are: Maj. James A. Huston, "Time and Space, Part VI," MS (Office Chief of Military History, DA), pp. 85–86; Lt. Gordon C. Bennett, "They Wrote the Book," *Quartermaster Review* 32, no. 4 (Jan–Feb 1953): 50–53; Lt. Col. E. L. Rowney, "Engineers in the Hungnam Evacuation," *Military Engineer* 43, no. 295 (Sept–Oct 1951): 315ff.; Montross and Canzona, *The Chosin Campaign*, pp. 309–12; Geer, *The New Breed*, p. 361.

12. Rasula, Letters.

13. Montross and Canzona, *The Chosin Campaign*, pp. 320–21; Geer, *The New Breed*, pp. 367–68.

14. The order of the exodus from Koto-ri was officially stated in 1st Marine Div., Operation Order 26–50, issued on 7 Dec at Koto-ri.

15. Quoted in Montross and Canzona, *The Chosin Campaign*, p. 321 and n. 27, citing Sawyer's comments.

16. Geer, *The New Breed*, pp. 368–69. There is a large body of contemporary enemy interrogation reports to confirm the difficulty the Chinese had with the cold weather. Some of them will be mentioned.

17. Montross and Canzona, *The Chosin Campaign*, pp. 321–23; Geer, *The New Breed*, pp. 368–70; Montross, "Breakout from the Chosin Reservoir," p. 37.

18. Lt. Col. Alvin L. Newberry, exec. off., Task Force Dog, "Springing the Trap"; 3rd Div., Comd. Rpt., Dec 1950, p. 9; Montross and Canzona, *The Chosin Campaign*, p. 324.

19. Rasula, Letters.

20. Jones, Statement.

21. Montross and Canzona, *The Chosin Campaign*, pp. 324–25.

22. Newberry, "Springing the Trap."

23. Geer, *The New Breed*, p. 371; Montross and Canzona, *The Chosin Campaign*, pp. 325–26; Newberry, "Springing the Trap," p. 6.

24. *New York Herald Tribune*, 11 Dec 50, p. 1, col. 8, UPI dispatch of 10 Dec 1950 from Koto-ri.

25. This description of the situation at Sudong is based largely on Newberry, "Springing the Trap," pp. 6–7; also of use is the 3rd Div. Comd. Rpt., 10–11 Dec 50.

26. Montross and Canzona, *The Chosin Campaign*, pp. 327–28, has the best published acount of the Sudong action, based on extensive interviews and comments of participants. For a detailed account of the actions of Lt. Col. Page, see Capt. Nicholas A. Canzona, USMC, and John G. Hubbell, "The Twelve Incredible Days of Col. John Page," *Reader's Digest*, Apr 1956, pp. 84–89. Lt. Col. Page was awarded the Medal of Honor, Posthumously, by General Order 21, 25 Apr 1957, DA. For this order see *Medal of Honor Recipients, 1863–1963*, p. 282.

27. The account of the action at the rear of the tank column is based largely on Montross and Canzona, *The Chosin Campaign*, pp. 328–31, and numerous footnotes citing a large number of interviews with persons involved in the action. Some details are taken from Geer, *The New Breed*, pp. 371–73. Both authorities show certain discrepancies, which may be expected in an episode of this kind.

28. For the march order and the attack formation out of Koto-ri, see 1st Marine Div., Operation Order No. 26-50, 7 Dec 50. Montross and Canzona, *The Chosin Campaign*, pp. 312, 325–26, 328, and n. 43 summarize the sequence of movements and events that occurred on 9–11 Dec but do not offer an explanation of who was responsible for leaving the tanks without infantry acting as rear guard.

29. Montross and Canzona, *The Chosin Campaign*, pp. 331–32; Geer, *The New Breed*, p. 373; Newberry, "Springing the Trap," pp. 5–6.

30. HQ, X Corps, Special Report on Chosin Reservoir Campaign, 27 Nov– 10 Dec 50, pp. 51, 72, Logistics and Transportation Section. This source says that the train moved these men on 9 Dec. But it must be in error, because the withdrawing Marines and Army soldiers did not reach Sontang until 10–11 Dec. The trains must have carried their loads of wounded and weary men from Sontang into Hamhung on 10 Dec, and possibly some on the eleventh.

31. Montross and Canzona, *The Chosin Campaign*, p. 332, citing the Division Adjutant, SAR, app. 2, p. 3.

32. Newberry, "Springing the Trap," p. 6.

33. Ibid., pp. 8–9; Capt. LeRoy B. Mattingly, exec off., A and B batteries, 92nd FA Bn. (155-mm howitzers), Debriefing Report No. 46, Artillery School, Fort Sill, Okla.

34. Newberry, "Springing the Trap," p. 9; 3rd Inf. Div., Comd. Rpt., 11 Dec 50.

CHAPTER 14

1. HQ, X Corps, Special Report on Hungnam Evacuation 9–24 Dec 50, and enclosed overlays of Phase I, II, and III, together with maps 1–4, copy in author's possession. Also in official records of X Corps, 1950; *Pertinent Papers of the Korean War*, II, 382, CX51102, has MacArthur's message.

2. Maj. Gen. Robert H. Soule, interview with author, 8 Sept 1951, for Soule's argument on the nature of the evacuation perimeter.

3. Almond, Diary, 11 Dec 50. In his typed diary Gen. Almond wrote in ink in longhand this account of his private meeting with MacArthur. The official typed version in the X Corps Comd. Rpt. for Dec 1950 does not contain it. Gen. Almond has repeated this version of the private meeting with MacArthur at Yonpo airfield on 11 Dec 50 twice in interview conversations and in correspondence with the author, and he emphasized that he had no hesitation in serving under Gen. Walker.

4. HQ, X Corps, Special Report on Hungnam Evacuation, 9–24 Dec 50, pp. 10–11, and map 2; Annex to Operation Report, 15 Dec 50, p. 80; 3rd Inf. Div., Comd. Rpt., Dec 1950, p. 13, Box 2881.

5. HQ, EUSAK, General Order No. 132, 11 Mar 51, awarding the Distinguished Service Cross to 1st Lt. Charles L. Butler for action near Singhang-ni, Korea, 15 Dec 50.

6. 3rd Inf. Div., Comd. Rpt., 15 Dec 50, Box 2881; HQ, X Corps, Special Report on Hungnam Evacuation, 9–24 Dec 50, p. 12; FEC, General Order No. 135, 26 May 1951, awarding Distinguished Service Cross to Capt. Powers.

7. 3rd Inf. Div., Comd. Rpt., Dec 1950, pp. 13–16, Box 2881.

8. Maj. Gen. William F. Marquat, "Automatic Artillery in Korea," *Antiaircraft Journal*, Jan–Feb 1951, p. 3.

9. Capt. John G. Westover, "End of the Line," in Westover, *Combat Support in Korea*, pp. 17–18, which is a condensed version of Lt. John Mewha's interview with Carrol W. Guth, 185th Eng. Comb. Bn., the complete version of which is in the files of US Army Military History Center in Washington; 3rd Inf. Div., Comd. Rpt., Dec 1950; HQ, X Corps Special Report on Hungnam Evacuation, 9–24 Dec 50, p. 12.

10. 3rd Inf. Div., Comd. Rpt., Dec 1950, 16 Dec; X Corps, Special Report on Hungnam Evacuation, 9–24 Dec 50, p. 12, and map 3, Annex 3 to POR No. 82, 17 Dec 50.

11. X Corps Special Report on Hungnam Evacuation, 9–24 Dec 50, p. 14; 3rd Inf. Div., Comd. Rpt., Dec 1950, p. 17.

12. HQ, X Corps, Special Report on Hungnam Evacuation, 9–24 Dec 50, p. 14; Lt. Edward L. Murphy, Jr., "Night Fighting," *Combat Forces Journal*, Nov 1953, pp. 18–19.

13. 3rd Inf. Div., Comd. Rpt., Dec 1950, p. 19; HQ, X Corps, Special Report on Hungnam Evacuation, Dec 1950, pp. 14–15; X Corps, Weekly Intelligence Report, No. 96, 22 Dec 50, p. 21.

14. FEC, *History of the NK Army*, p. 53, states that the NK 1st Div. was committed at the Hungnam perimeter in mid-Dec 1951.

15. 3rd Inf. Div., Comd. Rpt., Dec 1950, p. 19; HQ, X Corps, Special Report on Hungnam Evacuation, 9–24 Dec 50, p. 15, and map 4, Annex 2 to POR No. 85, 20 Dec 50.

16. 3rd Inf. Div., Comd. Rpt., Dec 1950, Box 2881; HQ, X Corps, Special Report on Hungnam Evacuation, 9–24 Dec 50, p. 15; Montross and Canzona, *The Chosin Campaign*, p. 343.

17. Field, *US Naval Operations in Korean War*, pp. 293–302.

18. Ibid., pp. 302–305; McCaffrey, review comments on "Escaping the Trap," 1 July 1979.

19. 3rd Inf. Div., Comd. Rpt., Dec 1950, pp. 20–21.

20. Montross and Canzona, *The Chosin Campaign*, pp. 338–39; 3rd Inf. Div., Comd. Rpt., Dec 1950, Box 2881.

21. HQ, X Corps, Special Report on Hungnam Evacuation, p. 18; Field, *US Naval Operations in Korean War*, pp. 288–89.

22. Field, *US Naval Operations in Korean War*, p. 295; HQ, X Corps, Special Report on Hungnam Evacuation, p. 20.

23. Montross and Canzona, *The Chosin Campaign*, pp. 336–37.

24. Ibid., pp. 335–40; HQ, X Corps, Special Report on Hungnam Evacuation, p. 19; 1st Marine Div., SAR, 8 Oct–15 Dec 50, vol. 1, Annex Baker, p. 27.

25. Field, *US Naval Operations in Korean War*, pp. 288, 291.

26. Capt. William McCallam, Jr., USA, "The Evacuation of Hungnam," *Combat Forces Journal*, Aug 1951, pp. 32–35. McCallam was assistant operations officer of the 2nd Eng. Special Brigade during the evacuation. Also, see Montross and Canzona, *The Chosin Campaign*, pp. 342–43, and map 30, p. 344.

27. HQ, X Corps, Special Report on Hungnam Evacuation, pp. 2, 5; Montross and Canzona, *The Chosin Campaign*, pp. 337, 339–41.

28. Field, *US Naval Operations in Korean War*, p. 295; 1st Marine Div., Special Action Report, 8 Oct–15 Dec 50, vol. 1, Annex Baker, pp. 18–19; HQ, X Corps, Special Report on Hungnam Evacuation, pp. 18–21; Montross and Canzona, *The Chosin Campaign*, p. 341.

29. Almond, Diary, 15 Dec 50; HQ, X Corps, Special Report on Hungnam Evacuation, p. 21, and app., Demolition Tables; Montross and Canzona, *The Chosin Campaign*, p. 342.

30. Field, *US Naval Operations in Korean War*, p. 296.

31. 1st Lt. John Mewha, "Destruction in Hamhung and Hungnam by B Co., 185th Eng. Comb. Bn., 15–17 Dec 50" (typescript MS, US Army Military History Center); Montross and Canzona, *The Chosin Campaign*, p. 350.

32. 3rd Inf. Div., Comd. Rpt., Dec 1950, journal entries for 23 Dec 50, and entries for 19–24 Dec 50, Box 2881; HQ, X Corps, Special Report on Hungnam Evacuation, pp. 21–22.

33. 3rd Inf. Div., Comd. Rpt., Dec 1950, 24 Dec; Almond, Diary, 24–25 Dec 50; Montross and Canzona, *The Chosin Campaign*, pp. 343–44; HQ, X Corps, Special Report on Hungnam Evacuation, p. 22.

34. HQ, X Corps, Special Report on Hungnam Evacuation, p. 4. This document gives 103 shiploads and 89 LST-loads, for a total of 192 shiploads. Montross and Canzona, *The Chosin Campaign*, p. 345, using Navy sources, give

193 shiploads employed in the evacuation. Another official report gives a total of 114 ships of various kinds used in the Hungnam redeployment (Action Report, Hungnam Redeployment, 9–25 Dec 50, A16-3/31-wj, 21 Jan 1951).

35. Field, *US Naval Operations in Korean War*, p. 304.

36. The story of the Koran refugees is interlaced in a thousand places in the combat records of the UN forces in the Korean War. Some data on refugees during the Hungnam evacuation are found in HQ, X Corps, Special Report on the Hungnam Evacuation, pp. 23–25; also, see Montross and Canzona, *The Chosin Campaign*, chap. 15.

CHAPTER 15

1. Montross and Canzona, *The Chosin Campaign*, app. E, pp. 381–82.

2. HQ, X Corps, Comd. Rpt., 27 Nov–10 Dec 1950, Cumulative Battle Casualties, X Corps, 27 Nov–10 Dec 1950, p. 97; McCaffrey, comments on "Escaping the Trap" MS, 1 July 1979.

3. HQ, X Corps, Comd. Rpt., 27 Nov–10 Dec 50, pp. 98–99.

4. ORO-R-1 (FEC), 8 Apr 51, "Employment of Armor in Korea," I, 64–67. My opinion that the number of tanks destroyed by enemy action or attack is about 15, rather than three, as given in the above report, is based on this narrative and tank losses described therein.

5. ATIS Interrogation Reports (Enemy Forces), Issue 22, No. 2730, p. 28, 18 Dec 50.

6. 3rd Inf. Div., Comd. Rpt., Dec 1950, PIR No. 26, pp. 10–11, Box 2881.

7. ATIS Interrogation Reports (Enemy Forces), Issue 22, No. 2721, p. 59, 18 Dec 50.

8. FEC DIS No. 3053, 18 Jan 51, Box 387.

9. FEC, Weekly Intelligence Report No. 102, 2 Feb 51, pp. 27–28.

10. 1st Marine Div., SAR, 8 Oct–15 Dec 50, vol. 1, Annex Baker, p. 21.

11. FEC DIS, 16 Feb 51, Box 401.

12. DA, General Order No. 72, 9 Aug 51, awarding the Distinguished Unit Citation to the 1st Marine Air Wing, gives 10,313 enemy casualties and destruction of 723 buildings, 144 vehicles, 9 bridges, 47 gun positions, 19 supply dumps, and other items as well. According to the 1st Marine Div. SAR, 8 Oct–15 Dec 50, vol. 1, Annex Baker, pp. 47–48, the 1st Marine Air Wing claimed 10,000 killed and 5,000 wounded.

13. HQ, FEC, USAF *Intelligence Digest* 1, no. 3 (16–31 Jan 53): 32, Box 225.

14. Montross and Canzona, *The Chosin Campaign*, pp. 352–53, concludes (correctly, I believe) that the Chinese divisions were at approximately three-fourths of full strength, or about 7,500 men each.

15. Ibid., p. 352, erroneously gives the 94th Div. of the 32nd Army as being attached to the 26th Army as its fourth division. These errors are corrected, however, in app. G., Enemy Order of Battle, pp. 397–98. All responsible and detailed intelligence studies in December 1950 and in subsequent months, when more data were collected, confirm the statements given above as to the composition of the CCF IX Army Group. The main intelligence studies and documents used in this narrative are the following: FEC DIS,

16 Feb 51; ibid., No. 3233, 17 July 51, Box 491; FEC, Order of Battle Information, Chinese Third Field Army, 1 Mar 51, Box 413; HQ, FEC, USAF, G-2, "Histories of CCF Army Groups Active in Korea, Part II, Ninth Army Group," *Intelligence Digest* 1, no. 3 (16–31 Jan 53): 32–37, Box 225; FEC DIS No. 3207, 21 June 51, Box 473. The last reference contains probably the most important Chinese order-of-battle document captured in the Korean War. It confirms the IX Army Group composition as given in the text, with only a slight question concerning the 90th Div. as being the fourth division attached in the 27th Army.

16. Montross and Canzona, *The Chosin Campaign*, p. 353, quoting from translation of CCF documents in HQ, 500th Military Intelligence Group Doc. No. 204141, "Compilation of Battle Experiences Reported by Various Armies in Their Operations against U.S. Forces in Korea." I could not find this document in the official records of Department of the Army, National Archives, when I tried to obtain use of it in 1975.

17. Montross and Canzona, *The Chosin Campaign*, p. 354, quoting from document cited above in n. 16.

18. HQ, FEC, *Intelligence Digest* 1, no. 3 (16–31 Jan 53): 34, Box 225.

19. X Corps, WD, May 1951, PIR No. 233, Annex 3, 17 May; PIR No. 234, 18 May, PIR No. 238, 22 May, and PIRs 240 and 241, 24 and 25 May 51.

20. Montross and Canzona, *The Chosin Campaign*, app. D, p. 379.

21. For the Marine figures see Montross and Canzona, *The Chosin Campaign*; for Eighth Army figures see HQ, Eighth Army, Combat Information Bulletin No. 11, Chinese Communist Forces Combat Doctrine, Part II, 12 pp., Box 1170; Eighth Army Comd. Rpt., G-3 Sec., Encl. to 13 Mar 1951, G-3 file. This bulletin has tables of organization charts for the Chinese division and its subordinate units down to company and platoon levels.

22. HQ, X Corps, Special Report on the Chosin Reservoir, p. 102.

23. Smith, Comments.

24. Montross and Canzona, *The Chosin Campaign*, p. 359, quoting Smith's memo, 19 Dec 50.

25. Lt. Gen. Edward M. Almond, "Reflections on the Hungnam Evacuation, Korea, December 1950," 12 pp. (mimeographed, with attachments), p. 9, copy in author's possession.

26. Ibid., pp. 9–10.

27. Maj. Gen. Courtney Whitney, Ret., *MacArthur, His Rendezvous with History* (New York: Alfred A. Knopf, 1956), p. 391. Whitney quotes extensively from some of MacArthur's messages to the Joint Chiefs of Staff. He was an intimate advisor to MacArthur in the Far East Command.

28. Lt. Gen. William J. McCaffrey, Ret., letter to author, 11 Dec 1976.

29. Appleman, *South to the Naktong*, pp. 654–55; McCaffrey, undated letter to author, written in Jan 1977.

Bibliographical Note

The bibliography of published works on the operations of the X Corps in northeast Korea, covering a total period of about two months, from the landing of the X Corps at Wonsan on 26 October 1950 to the evacuation of Hungnam on 24 December 1950, is meager but includes important and reliable works. All of them have been used extensively in this volume. They include:

Appleman, Roy E. *East of Chosin: Entrapment and Breakout in Korea, 1950* (College Station: Texas A&M University Press, 1987). This book tells the story of the Army's 31st Regimental Combat Team in its operations on the east side of Chosin Reservoir, on the right flank of the 1st Marine Division in the Chosin operation, 27 November–1 December 1950. The 31st RCT faced the surprise attack of the Chinese 80th Division, which ultimately destroyed it. Chapter 5 in this volume is a condensed version of the *East of Chosin* story.

———. *South to the Naktong, North to the Yalu (June-November 1950): United States Army in the Korean War,* Office of the Chief of Military History, Department of the Army (Washington, D.C.: GPO, 1961). This is the official history of the first five months of the Korean War, from its beginning on 25 June to 24 November 1950. Chapter 38, "The Corps Advances to the Yalu," covers the preliminary operations of the X Corps in northeast Korea to 24 November 1950.

Field, James A. *History of United States Naval Operations, Korea* (Washington, D.C.: GPO, 1962). This work is based on official US Navy documents relating to the Korean War and can be considered as the official US Navy history of the war. It is a reliable work and has been used in this volume in connection with the naval operations along the coast of northeast Korea and the naval evacuation of X Corps from Hungnam.

Futrell, Robert F. *The United States Air Force in Korea, 1950–1953* (New York: Duell, Sloan and Pearce, 1961). This is the official Air Force history of the United States Air Force in the war. It has useful material on the X Corps in northeast Korea, especially in the dropping of supplies to cut-off troops and the evacuation of wounded from Hagaru-ri.

Geer, Andrew. *The New Breed: The Story of the U.S. Marines in Korea* (New

York: Harper and Brothers, 1954). This is a well-written story of the Marines in Korea, based in part on interviews that supply many details not
found elsewhere.

Gugeler, Russell A. *Combat Actions in Korea: Infantry, Artillery, and Armor*
(Washington, D.C.: Association of the US Army, Combat Forces Press, 1954).
This book comprises accounts of a series of small-unit actions and is based
on interviews in 1951 and later, one of which is a partial account of the
role of the 1st Battalion, 32nd Infantry, in the 31st RCT in the action east
of Chosin. It is not wholly reliable.

Montross, Lynn, and Nicholas Canzona, *The Chosin Campaign*, vol. 3 in *The
U.S. Marine Operations in Korea, 1950–1953*, 4 vols. (Washington, D.C.:
GPO, 1957). This is the official Marine Corps history of its operations in
northeast Korea, the most important part of which was the Chosin Reservoir operation and the retreat to the coast. It is an excellent account of
the Marine operations, based on the official records and much additional
use of interviews and affidavits of individual participants. Although I have
used this work extensively, I had previously examined the official Marine
records of the operations and had made extensive notes on them. The Marine volume makes no pretense of covering related Army activities in any
detail, although its records do refer occasionally to them. This work is an
important reference for any attempt to tell the story of the X Corps in northeast Korea.

Throughout my work on this volume I had the wholehearted coop-
eration of Lt. Gen. Edward M. Almond, retired, who commanded the X
Corps in Korea, and his deputy chief of staff, then Lt. Col. William J.
McCaffrey, now a retired lieutenant general.

Index

Escaping the Trap was composed into type on a Compugraphic digital phototypesetter in nine and one-half point Trump Medieval with two and one-half points of spacing between the lines. Permanent Headline was selected for display. The book was designed by Jim Billingsley, typeset by Metricomp, Inc., printed offset by Thomson-Shore, Inc., and bound by John H. Dekker & Sons, Inc. The paper on which the book is printed bears acid-free characteristics for an effective life of at least three hundred years.

TEXAS A&M UNIVERSITY PRESS : COLLEGE STATION